DATE DUE			

POSTCOMMUNISM AND THE BODY POLITIC

GENDERS 22

POSTCOMMUNISM
AND THE BODY
POLITIC

Edited by Ellen E. Berry

NEW YORK UNIVERSITY PRESS
NEW YORK AND LONDON

NEW YORK UNIVERSITY PRESS
New York and London

ISBN 0-8147-1247-9 cloth
ISBN 0-8147-1248-7 paper

New York University Press books are printed on acid-free paper,
and their binding materials are chosen for strength and durability.

Manufactured in the United States of America

10   9   8   7   6   5   4   3   2   1

Contents

Introduction

Ellen E. Berry

As a contemporary global phenomenon, postmodernism has been characterized by such features as: a generalized crisis in the dominant meta-narratives of Western culture, provoked in part by challenges arising from what these narratives have historically repressed; accelerated time-space compressions; vastly novel restructurings generated by global capitalist investments, communication systems, and information networks; violent reassertions of nationalisms and ethnic fundamentalisms as well as crises in the authority of previously dominant systems including the nation-state as a sociopolitical entity; international migrations of intellectuals, ethnic groups, labor resources, religious movements, and political formations that, again, challenge older conventional boundaries of national economies, identities, and cultures; and a global homogenizing of culture co-existing with both newly emerging local traditions and diverse transcultural flows that exceed bilateral exchanges between nation-states.[1] These features suggest that, as a process and set of effects, global postmodernism is contradictory, ambivalent, and heterogeneous, filled with both the perils and the possibilities arising from radical transformations in inherited, established orders. Within a postmodern moment "everything is contestable, nothing is off limits and no outcomes are guaranteed," as Andrew Ross puts it.[2]

The postcommunist moment in the so-called second world — Central and Eastern Europe and the former Soviet Union — would seem to offer dramatic evidence of this postmodern crisis in the authority of previously dominant systems, a social, political, economic, and cultural crisis of de- and re-structuration that holds multiple perils and opens multiple

1

possibilities. This special issue of *Genders* aims to map aspects of these dramatic and ongoing processes of political and sociocultural transformation in the second world. It does so through an exploration of the varied contingencies and interdependencies among national politics, sexual politics, and body politics, the "lived crises endured by national and sexual bodies."[3] This is a highly charged nexus in any historical moment or cultural location. It is especially so among cultures in which rapid, sometimes cataclysmic changes in material realities and national self-conceptions are occurring as previously secure boundaries of all kinds become more permeable and even disappear. Gender roles and relations, expressions of sexuality or attempts to recontain them, representations of the body — especially the female body — and the larger cultural meanings it assumes, are particularly striking sites for witnessing the performance of complex national dramas of crisis and change.

Delineating the complex and varied connections between constructions of national and sexual identity has been an important focus of recent research. Anthologies such as *Nationalisms and Sexualities* and *Scattered Hegemonies*, and journal issues such as *Genders* 10 on "Theorizing Nationality, Sexuality, and Race" and *Gender and History*'s special number on "Gender, Nationalisms and National Identities," have explored the multiple ways in which gender, national affiliation, and sexual attachment "interact with, constitute or otherwise mutually illuminate each other" in specific cultural contexts and historical moments. They examine how, that is, socio-political, economic, and ideological transformations influence previous consolidations of national and sexual identities, in particular how crises in gender and sexual identities are used to "manage" crises in national self-concept.[4] However, for a number of reasons, not least of which has been the relative unavailability of information from and about the Second World, most discussions have tended to focus almost exclusively on postcolonial contexts or a first world–third world nexus. What does incorporation of a second world postcommunist context add to these evolving theories concerning the cultural specificity of gender and national constructions in moments of transition and to theories of transnational flows — including especially feminist movements — in a postmodern moment? Similarly, as a number of the following essays point out, issues of gender and sexuality which have preoccupied Western scholars have, until quite recently, largely been ignored among scholars of state socialist cultures both in this country and in the second world, a de-emphasis that replicates the insistent erasure of the body, sexuality, and gender relations as topics of public discourse in these cultures. How do certain terms and concepts central to Western theories function to illuminate these vastly different cultural contexts? How do the marked differences of these contexts in turn help to refine our theories and the questions we ask?

The importance of assuming a mutually interrogative stance as a means of constructing more complete and nuanced accounts of the effects of location and difference is nowhere more evident than in the encounter between first and second worlds. For if "nations are forever haunted by their various definitional others,"[5] then it is crucial to acknowledge the distinct roles that Soviet and Eastern bloc cultures have played historically in processes of national self-definition in the West and how such symbolic roles may condition and limit the terms of contemporary encounters. In her essay here, Beth Holmgren positions herself as a cultural mediator of sorts in order to reflect upon the multiple impediments to understandings among Western and Eastern women at this historical moment. These include the dangers of applying Western feminist assumptions, agendas, and concepts to explain what are in fact "two very different contexts of experience, expectation and expression." If Western feminists are to escape making negative judgments about such seemingly regressive moves as Russian women returning to the home or, conversely, if we are to see beyond our nostalgia for socialist feminist ideals perceived as fully accomplished in the former USSR, and if slogan-weary Russian women are to hear something other than an alienating political rhetoric in their contacts with Western feminists then, as Holmgren puts it, "we all must commit to more historically informed, contextually sensitive ways of seeing, hearing, and speaking. We may even need to devise a language of paraphrase to defuse those political buzzwords (the legacy of American and Soviet cold war rhetoric, the market speak of Western developmental politics) that continue to polarize us."[6]

Vida Penezic explores the ways in which this cold war legacy, understood broadly as a specific paradigm of comprehension, may continue to limit our categories of analysis as a set of unacknowledged, perhaps unacknowledgeable, assumptions. Her analysis of the difference of the Yugoslavian woman presumed (even demanded) by U.S. speakers underscores Rey Chow's observation that efforts to acknowledge the effects of national differences on gender and sexual identity often have the effect of reifying the very differences in question. As Chow puts it in discussing Chinese women, "The attempt to deconstruct the hegemony of *patriarchal* discourses through feminism is itself foreclosed by the emphasis on 'Chinese' as a mark of absolute difference. . . . It is when the West's 'other women' are prescribed their 'own' national and ethnic identity in this way that they are most excluded from having a claim to the reality of their existence."[7] Penezic argues that the transformations leading to a postcommunist moment on the global stage must necessarily imply changes in *both* the first world and the former second world, changes that too frequently remain unrecognized and untheorized. Such changes are best understood within an as-yet-incomplete shift in the cold war paradigm and the emergence of a new transcultural, transnational moment.

In Katrin Sieg's essay a different site of confrontation between Western assumptions and Eastern women's lives is invoked: the impasse between West German and former GDR feminists in the newly unified Germany. Despite the significant role played by GDR women in the revolution of 1989, a unified feminist movement (and thus a more powerful negotiating position within the post-Wall patriarchy) has failed to materialize. Such an impasse illustrates "the entanglement of feminist critiques with nationalist imperatives and constraints," thereby providing an instructive example to a feminist movement "increasingly self-conscious about the multiple axes of power criss crossing its heterogeneous constituencies." Moreover, Sieg's analysis of GDR women's critiques of socialist patriarchy as they appear in the genre of the protocol uncovers feminist significatory strategies that "differ drastically from those addressed to late capitalism" and which therefore offer insights that might usefully "inflect and inform the theorizing and politicking of Western feminisms."[8]

Kevin Moss's essay on the underground closet provides another example of the ways in which an analysis of non-Western discourses may usefully expand and refine Western theories. Moss employs Eve Sedgwick's model of the epistemology of the closet to analyze the strategies used by East European writers to conceal not only sexual but — primarily — political dissidence. Despite Sedgwick's assertion that understanding virtually any aspect of modern Western culture must be not merely incomplete but damaged in its central substance to the degree that it omits a critical analysis of modern homo/heterosexual definition, Moss demonstrates that in East European culture in the Soviet period, the major axis of definition structuring thought is not sexual but political. That is, the thematics of knowledge and ignorance is not exclusive to homosexuality alone as Sedgwick implies but functions in relation to other topics depending on the context. These essays and others included here suggest the importance of positing a multidirectionality of cultural flows and influences so that our exchanges with the postcommunist world might produce the possibility of change on both sides of the former East/West divide. Such an understanding is one precondition for developing what bell hooks calls "those shared sensibilities which cross the boundaries of class, gender, race [nation, ideological orientation, political heritage] . . . and promote recognition of common commitments . . . as a base for solidarity and coalition."[9]

A second precondition for developing such shared sensibilities involves understanding more accurately the nature and specific effects of the transition to postcommunism as they are manifested in various East European locations. This applies particularly to the differential material effects of the postcommunist moment on men and women, a difference remarked on in nearly all of the essays. These differences serve as forceful reminders of the fact that "nationalisms are from the outset constituted in gender power"[10] and that when national identities are in crisis women often bear the weight. Such a recognition has largely been ignored in Western media discourses about Eastern Europe which have concentrated almost exclusively on the development of the public sphere, in particular on the economics of the drive toward capitalism in the former Eastern bloc. But as Nanette Funk, among others, has pointed out, women's interests are often being sacrificed in transitions to a market economy. Between 60 and 70 percent of the unemployed in many of these societies are women, as returning women to the private sphere becomes a central mechanism for the move from a full-employment economic system to a quasi-capitalist one. So too, new restrictions in many countries on previously unrestricted abortion rights — combined with a lack of other methods of birth control — consign women even more fully to the maternal role as they ease women from the paid work force, thereby reducing competition with men for jobs. These restrictions act to exclude women from participating in processes to rebuild political as well as economic systems leading to what Russian feminist Olga Lipovskaia calls "the emergence of so-called 'male' democracy." As Hana Havelkova puts it in summarizing the current Czech context, "It may be one of the paradoxes of history that reaction to the communist experience brings forth in ideology, political thinking, and economic practice extremely strong conservative elements, more conservative than was the trend in pre-communist Czech society."[11]

These and other efforts to reassert control over women's bodies in material fact also point to the symbolic roles that women are often made to play in attempts to reformulate national identities and in processes of national myth-making. In her analysis of the Russian body politic, for example, Harriet Murav argues that, while a return to the home by large numbers of Russian women should not automatically be viewed as wholly regressive, it nonetheless is serving regressive ends in some cases. Her essay demonstrates the ways in which the image of woman as mother and keeper of domestic space is employed in the work of the conservative "Village Prose" writers as part of their vision of "a new totality of nation, blood, and soil, a strict Russocentrism immune to the incursions of difference." In this way women's actual bodies are usurped for the symbolization of a conservative Russian body politic. Ewa Hauser identifies a similar move in Poland where "Instead of a vague 'return to Europe,' a return to a repressive patriarchal 'gender regime' is in the making," one legitimated at a national level through a combination of traditional patriotism and Catholic piety.

Many of the essays included here — Murav's and Hauser's among them — also identify cultural practices that critique and propose alternatives to these regressive new national scripts or that rework previous formulations and histories. These include efforts to construct alternative signifying practices and representational strategies — such as overt ironic or parodic inversions of the glorified maternal images found among the Village Prose writers — as well as more covert coded critiques such as the strategies used to encode "sexual dissidence" that Moss explores. They include as well attempts to construct new cultural spaces and genres for the performance of counter-narratives of nation and gender, such as the postcommunist cabaret of Olga Lipinska that Hauser explores in her discussion of new political theater in Poland, and the protocol writing of East German women that Sieg analyzes which encodes the struggle to negotiate between a critique of patriarchy and a commitment to socialism.

Gendering the national body politic often renders invisible the material realities of individual women's lives as "woman" becomes the mute symbolic ground upon which transactions of nationalist history are enacted. Efforts to contest and refigure such reductive symbolizations frequently focus on incorporating those voices and experiences that have been distorted, actively silenced, or simply unrepresented. Relaxation of state censorship practices has helped to make this "new realism" possible. In her essay, Teresa Polowy explores changing literary depictions of alcoholism in Russian literature as a focal point for growing concerns about such issues as gender roles and relations and the increase in social and domestic violence in contemporary Russian culture. Since the early 1980s the subject has been treated with greater openness largely due to the emergence of women's writing as "a viable literary voice in Russia." Whereas previous depictions by male writers tended to focus on the culture and rituals of male drinking and to portray women as either meekly submissive or domineering and shrewish in relation to alcoholic spouses, recent women's writing is notable for its attention to women's everyday lived experiences with the effects of alcoholism. In their frank treatment of this and other social themes, including especially the dynamics of interpersonal and familial relations, and in their refusal to offer pat solutions to these complex issues women writers in contemporary Russia contribute substantially to unmasking the violence of everyday life which, as N. Ivanova claims, is contemporary culture's "primary task."[12]

Catherine Portuges analyzes a similar trend in the work of women film directors in postcommunist Hungary who, in their production of films "under the triple signs of autobiography, exile, and marginality," contest previous understandings of Hungarian national cinema. Like many contemporary Russian women, these directors, partly in an effort to recover historical and national memories repressed in the Soviet era, foreground many formerly taboo topics, ranging from the existence of Stalinist labor camps and the persecution of ethnic minorities to accounts of suicide and depictions of homelessness. Yet these efforts to portray the experiences of those most disadvantaged in a postcommunist moment — women, racial and ethnic minorities, the aged among them — often are construed as "tantamount to a betrayal of these fragile new democracies."

Katrin Sieg maps GDR women's development of and contribution to a distinctive new genre, the protocol, from the 1970s to the 1990s, including especially the ways in which this writing develops a subjective narrative history of women's lives in the East, a "feminist historiographical model" that in many ways contests official histories, subject formations, and gender prescriptions. This counter-history helped to expose "those contradictions whose accumulation and intensification precipitated the ideological collapse" of the GDR. Moreover, as a mutable genre based on collective memory, one therefore able to accommodate multiple, sometimes conflicting voices, the protocols developed in the 1990s have proven useful in further assessing the realities of the past and in addressing the turmoils of contemporary postcommunist society. Karen Remmler also analyzes instances of counter-history and resistant remembrance in GDR women's writing, an analysis which suggests that changed representations of women in the social imaginary may be viewed as necessary steps to producing actual social change including, again, changes in official accounts of the past. Focusing in particular on representations of the female body as a site for the production of this critical counter-memory, Remmler argues that the writing practices of GDR women often permitted the imaginative if not the overt development of an oppositional subjectivity, one that allowed some women to "imagine a socialist livelihood imbued with a desire to break out of state dictated modes of emancipation." Remmler stresses that this "oppositional utopian consciousness" was more widely evident in the work of writers from the 1970s and early 1980s; by the late 1980s the worsening economic and political situation in the GDR culminated in expressions of extreme pessimism played out through images of the female body as physically diseased and psychologically disordered.

Both the importance of returning the repressed to history and public discourse, and the complexities arising from attempts to do so, are nowhere more dramatically evident than in expressions of sexuality in contemporary postcommunist cultures. As Russian sexologist Igor Kon notes, the current sexual revolution in Russia is taking place amid a climate of profound economic, social, political, cultural, and moral crisis among a "sexually ignorant and fundamentally sexist population in spite of the thin upper layer of fairly primitive egalitarian ideology that is inclined to ignore sexual difference."[13] The sexual illiteracy of the Russian public and the almost complete lack of a sex culture there are legacies of the longstanding official puritanism of the Soviet regime toward matters of sexuality and the body, its desire to "root out and disparage all that [is] erotic in human beings"[14] as Kon puts it. It is in relation to this history of the erasure of the body's materiality, its calcification into asexual heroic images and ideas, that Mikhail Epstein offers his "sensuous epistemology": a system of knowledge based on the diversity of erotic experiences, on a comingling of all faiths, all disciplines, on rapprochement with another through intimate physical exchange. Epstein's desire to re-eroticize the body, to extricate it from the ideas and images within which it has been confined (in both East *and* West as he explains in "On the Two Revolutions") also involves revaluing the singularity of the individual, a process Epstein enacts in "Helenology." In her mystery and beauty, her ability to inspire the poetic faculty and divine feeling, Helen may be viewed as an example of the eternal feminine stereotype. Yet this tendency is also offset by the loving particularity conveyed on her by the speaker; Helen becomes a singular and individualized woman who frustrates all attempts to categorize her, whether philosophically, scientifically, or ideologically, and to make her serve as a conduit for ideas.

Among the consequences of relaxed state censorship practices, the emergence of new venues for producing and receiving culture, and the development of new market forces such as consumer demand, has been the energetic proliferation of sexual discourses and commercial activities involving the selling of sex. As Helena Goscilo argues in her essay, however, this new freedom has produced mixed results, especially for women. When pornography is promoted uncritically as evidence of the growth of democratic tendencies, "What — after decades of censorship and regimented puritanism — impresses Russians as hard-won delivery from restraints" in fact merely enacts a substitution: "the sexual Stallion replaces Stalin, institutionalizing a kindred mode of ritualized repression. . . . The porn revolution in Moscow has merely ushered in yet another Party with different organs and members but an all-too-familiar agenda of domination." In her survey of the current porn market in Russia, Goscilo interestingly underscores this point by analyzing depictions of Stalin — as a visual incarnation of an ideal, as, in other words, a pinup — through the iconography of sexuality: both images of Stalin as perfect leader and the porn pinup are in fact structured by the same pornographic aesthetic, she argues.

Masha Gessen's fascinating survey of the birth of the "sex industry" in Russia casts a wider net, providing a valuable context within which to situate Goscilo's essay in its case study of the media's general testing of the limits of the openness called for by Mikhail Gorbachev's policy of glasnost. Sex presented the biggest challenge to this policy, Gessen argues, because more than seventy years of Soviet puritanism ensured that no established public discourse existed through which to discuss it. The sex media may also represent glasnost's biggest success story: "The media

[Gorbachev] had said needed reform had indeed been reformed, becoming the liveliest, most diverse ... most read ... most sexual – if not the sexiest – media in the world."

Taken as a whole, the essays that follow suggest the wide variety of symbolic forms and material effects engendered by a shifting body politic. They map a dramatic, still-evolving landscape on which to witness the performance of distinct expressions of global postmodernism's heterogeneity and contradictoriness, its perils and possibilities.

NOTES

1. For further discussion of these features see among others: Mike Featherstone, ed., *Global Culture, Nationalism, Globalization and Modernity* (London: Sage, 1990); David Harvey, *The Condition of Postmodernity: An Enquiry into the Origins of Cultural Change* (Cambridge, Mass.: Basil Blackwell, 1989); Fredric Jameson, *Postmodernism, Or the Cultural Logic of Late Capitalism* (Durham: Duke University Press, 1991); Jean-François Lyotard, *The Postmodern Condition: A Report on Knowledge*, trans. Geoff Bennington and Brian Massumi (Minneapolis: University of Minnesota Press, 1979).
2. Andrew Ross, "Introduction," in *Universal Abandon? The Politics of Postmodernism*, ed. Andrew Ross (Minneapolis: University of Minnesota Press, 1988), xi.
3. Andrew Parker, Mary Russo, Doris Sommer, and Patricia Yaeger, eds., *Nationalisms and Sexualities* (New York: Routledge, 1992), 13–14.
4. Ibid., 2.
5. Ibid., 5.
6. For additional speculation about the possibilities and the difficulties of dialogues between feminists in the East and in the West, see Nanette Funk and Magda Mueller, eds., *Gender Politics and Post-Communism, Reflections from Eastern Europe and the Former Soviet Union* (New York: Routledge, 1993). See especially Funk's "Introduction: Women and Post-Communism," 1–14 and "Feminism East and West," 318–30. See also her "Feminism and Post-Communism," in *Hypatia* 8, no. 4 (Fall 1993): 85–88 and other essays in the "Special Cluster on Eastern European Feminism."
7. Rey Chow, *Women and Chinese Modernity: The Politics of Reading Between West and East* (Minneapolis: University of Minnesota Press, 1991), 163.
8. For further speculation on the importance of combining feminisms developed in the West and East, see Zillah Eisenstein's "Eastern European Male Democracies: A Problem of Unequal Equality," in Funk and Mueller, *Gender Politics*, 303–17.
9. bell hooks, "Postmodern Blackness," in *Yearning: Race, Gender, and Cultural Politics* (Boston: South End Press, 1990), 27.

10. Anne McClintock, "No Longer in a Future Heaven: Women and Nationalism in South Africa," *Transition* 51 (1991): 122.
11. Lipovskaia, cited in Funk's "Feminism and Post-Communism," 86. Hana Havelkova, "'Patriarchy' in Czech Society," *Hypatia* 8, no. 4 (Fall 1993): 95.
12. Cited in Jane T. Costlow, Stephanie Sandler, and Judith Vowles, *Sexuality and the Body in Russian Culture* (Stanford: Stanford University Press, 1993), 30.
13. Igor Kon, "Sexuality and Culture," in Igor Kon and James Riordan, eds., *Sex and Russian Society* (Bloomington: Indiana University Press, 1993), 28.
14. Kon, in Kon and Riordan, *Sex and Russian Society*, 28.

PART ONE

Gendering the Postcommunist Landscape

Bug Inspectors and Beauty Queens: The Problems of Translating Feminism into Russian

Beth Holmgren

A few years ago, when the Russian writer and lecturer-provocateur Tat'iana Tolstaia was endorsing the "truth" of Francine du Plessix Gray's book on Soviet women, she penned this grim portrait of Western feminists rapping on the collective door of Soviet women and grilling them in the "cold, rigid manner" of bug inspectors: "How do your men oppress you? Why don't they wash the dishes? Why don't they prepare the meals? Why don't they allow women into politics? Why don't women rebel against the phallocracy?"[1] As comforting as it might be to dismiss this image as typical Tolstoyan reductionism, a less extreme version of it recurs in the commentary of Ol'ga Lipovskaia, the editor/publisher of the journal *Zhenskoe chtenie (Women's reading)*. Lipovskaia remarks on Western feminists' bewildered, sometimes alienating contacts with Soviet women — the "real confusion of purposes and activities" manifest in various official meetings between the two groups, Western women's one-track insistence on the value of their own agendas, the problem with effectively translating the most basic Western terms like "feminism," "emancipation," and "gender" for a slogan-weary Soviet audience.[2]

Impressions from the other side of the border record similar misconnections and sometimes vent a counter-dismay. Reporting in a January 1993 issue of the *Nation*, Andrew Kopkind notes the lack of a Russian feminist movement and Russian adoption "in the space of a few months" of "some of the West's most reactionary gender roles and sexual stereotypes."[3] As he selectively interviews self-avowed Russian feminists like Lipovskaia and Anastasiia Posadskaia (the director of Moscow's Center for Gender Studies), Kopkind relays stories and statistics sure to upset a Western feminist readership — for example, Russian women's seeming acquiescence to a new, markedly Western brand of sexploitation (55) or the polls showing the rising number of Russian women who yearn to be full-time homemakers or aspire no further than the very often prone position of "secretary to a *biznesman* who earns hard currency" (50). In an article of 11 February 1993 for the *Los Angeles Times*, Elizabeth Shogren simply frames her survey of Russian women in Western terms, stating that these women "[b]y their own choice and because of mounting new social pressures . . . are less liberated, in the feminist sense, than they were when the Communist Party ruled the country."[4] Even Shogren's Russian source, the social anthropologist Irina Popova, seemingly relies on American analogies: "Russian society is going through a phase similar to that in 1950s America, when homemakers and wholesome stars were idealized, . . . but because of a rebellion against the state-decreed sexual puritanism of the Soviet era, the ideal Russian woman is more sex kitten than homecoming queen."

All of these attempted border crossings, with whatever intent or audience in mind, underscore the real difficulties of translating and transposing even a mainstream Western awareness of gender issues into the Russian (or generally Slavic) context. As one observer remarks, such crossings are liable to produce a kind of "mirror inversion" of images: Whereas Russian women sight the bogeywoman of doctrinaire or self-involved Western feminists, Western women lament what is for them the inexplicable "backwardness" of Russian women retreating to the home or readily consenting to play well-paid male sex object.[5] This mutual misunderstanding seems especially pointed today, but it has existed for decades and pervades both popular attitudes and presumably more complex and considered trends in scholarship. I can offer myself as witness and accessory to this phenomenon. As an American woman trained to be a Slavist and beginning my teaching career in the late 1980s (when women's studies programs were being established throughout the American university system), I have experienced these border troubles firsthand and at length. Already minted as a traditional scholar, I only learned about gender studies "on the job" from patient colleagues in other fields, and much to my surprised delight, this exposure revitalized and transformed my own research and teaching. Yet I quickly discovered that the integration of gender studies into Slavic studies involved complicated acts of translation and adaptation — acts that distanced me somewhat from my colleagues in women's studies and for the most part disaffected or bemused my Slavist colleagues. As I have taught and written my way back and forth across this border, I have come to appreciate that the misunderstanding between Western women and Russian women and, by extension, the recurring difficulties of integrating gender studies into Slavic studies, stem from complex differences between first and second worlds, between two very separate contexts of experience, expectation, and expression. This essay attempts only a utilitarian sketch of these border troubles mainly drawn from a first world angle and focused on a limited number of examples, but it provides, hopefully, a somewhat experienced traveler's "tips" for making a friendly border crossing, a mutually informed and transformative exchange with women in postcommunist Russia.

WHOSE FEMINISM?

When Shogren speaks of Russian women "being less liberated, in a feminist sense," when Kopkind records the absence of a feminist movement, or when I glibly introduce the term "gender studies," we cannot presume a common ideology, but we seem to rely on a common heritage — one founded mainly on the experience of certain privileged groups of Western women and especially manifest in Western feminist movements of the late 1960s. This is not to claim that Shogren, Kopkind, and I represent the broad spectrum of extant Western feminisms or to argue that these feminisms can be reduced to a 1960s agenda. But if we are not to generalize our historical experience (especially when we are assaying comparisons with non-Western women), then it is imperative that we acknowledge the long-lasting formative influence (both positive and negative) of that earlier agenda and its regional context. The 1960s movements largely formed in protest against the situation of middle-class white women in advanced capitalist states — specifically, against their socially assigned and enforced roles as wife, mother, and homemaker; the legal and actual inequities in their professional, social, and economic status as compared with that of middle-class white men; and the general exploitation and commodification of women as objects of desire. Predictably enough, when feminist scholarship furthered this protest, it focused first on its own "first" conditions and articulators — on the models, experiences, and works of privileged first world women. This specialized focus prevailed for some time, as did the notion of gender as *the* unifying category of identity, subsuming other categories like race, class, or sexuality.

Over the last quarter of a century, this bias has provoked much protest, factionalism, and metamorphosis among Western women's groups; internal debate has facilitated a dismantling of traditional presumptions about gender and sexual identity, a greater acknowledgment of class and race differences, the generation of a plurality of feminisms. But despite the attempts of Western feminists to theorize and accommodate difference, we face perhaps the greatest challenge in relating to non-Western women, for such relations require the negotiation of the most complex differences and antagonisms and suffer most acutely from tendencies to generalize the local and stereotype the other. To date, this challenge has been most vividly illustrated and amply studied in relations between first world and third world women. It seems particularly telling that, at least in the early stages of their inquiry, critics writing from third world perspectives asserted regional bias rather than plurality in their readings of Western women; they critiqued Western feminists *in general* for "shortsightedness in defining the meaning of gender in terms of middle-class white experiences, and in terms of internal racism, classism, and homophobia."[6] Elaborating this position in her pioneering essay, "Under Western Eyes: Feminist Scholarship and Colonial Discourses," Chandra Talpade Mohanty charges that Western feminists' presumption of gender as the main source of identity, oppression, and therefore solidarity "implies a notion of gender or sexual difference or even patriarchy which can be applied universally and cross-culturally" and establishes middle-class white Western women as a "normative referent" against which women of other races, classes, and especially third world nations seem lacking or "underdeveloped."[7]

However debatable her position, Mohanty's protest and critique should alert us to the possibility of a similar "early" dynamic between first world and second world women.[8] If relations between Western feminists and women in the postcolonial world sometimes recall (or are perceived to recall) the blind opposition of Western imperialism *versus* colonial resistance, Western approaches to Slavic women can be read as similarly myopic, if somewhat less condescending. Certainly conditions were ripe for miscommunication. By the late twentieth century, decades of cold war politics and Stalinist repression had curiously distorted relations between Soviet women and a wide array of Western feminist groups; in both "camps," the propaganda deployed to demonize the "other" superpower often inadvertently fostered a kind of blinkered idealization. From the vantage point of Western women (even liberal feminists), the public gains of Soviet women under socialism seemed undeniable — the Soviet constitution's guarantee of women's equal professional and economic rights, the access of Soviet women to most areas of the work force, the state's at least partial support for working women (paid maternity leave, public day care). In turn, Western focus on these coveted achievements at times obscured or dismissed the special problems of Soviet women (their unrelieved domestic labor, the lack of consumer goods and services that would ease their domestic burden, the political victimization they shared with men). In fact, in her introduction to *Soviet Sisterhood* in 1985, Barbara Holland readily admits Western feminists' self-serving nostalgia for the "new Soviet woman" of the 1920s, that almost-realized socialist feminist:

Feminists in the West may feel nostalgic for the determined pioneers of the past who, their red kerchiefs firmly knotted round their heads, climbed into the driving seat of a tractor or picked up a shovel on a building site. We may be hurt by the ridicule now attached to these images by Soviet women, themselves anxious to buy our fashionable jeans and dresses, and leave their dirty overalls behind.[9]

It seems predictable, then, that this sort of nostalgia would elicit protest, debate, and correspondingly reductive readings from the Russian side. It is interesting to note that a Russian feminist (Anastasiia Posadskaia quoted by Kopkind) redirects Mohanty's complaints about Western "shortsightedness," in this instance generalizing and critiquing the model of Marxist feminists:

When we met with Western feminists we were struck by their social frame. They were Marxists. We argued with them so much I even cried. How could I say that the system that did all this to me was good? No one wants to hear about solidarity in this country anymore, because for years it was imposed: solidarity with South Africa, solidarity with Cuba. For Western women socialism was a question of values. They said, "At least the Communists put liberation down on paper." (55)

At this point in our relations, if Western feminists are to see beyond their nostalgia and Russian women are to hear beyond an alienating political rhetoric, then we all must commit to more historically informed, contextually sensitive ways of seeing, hearing, and speaking. We may even need to devise a language of paraphrase to defuse those political buzz-words (the legacy of American *and* Soviet cold war rhetoric, the marketspeak of Western developmental politics) that continue to polarize us.

THE CAUSES OF RUSSIAN WOMEN

Indeed, once we examine the political traditions and historical experience of Russian women, we can appreciate that they have had ample cause to critique their own "determined pioneers" and to dismiss Western "nostalgia." If the category of gender has been promoted at times at the expense of all other categories of identity by Western feminists, it has been a self-erasing or non-category — indeed, a non-term — in Russian and Soviet societies. To be sure, a "woman's question" was raised in mid-nineteenth-century Russia to protest noblewomen's unequal legal, political, and economic status and a Russian feminist tradition (under a variety of names) could be said to extend from the 1860s until the October revolution.[10] Yet, for the most part, Russian women have eschewed specifically feminist programs for what they believed to be the larger, more urgent causes of populism or socialism or, in the Soviet period, Party loyalty or dissidence. For them the unifying, galvanizing categories of oppression and solidarity were those of class and allegiance or resistance to the state (be it tsarist or Soviet). Although the program (and sometimes even the practice) of women's equal rights was automatically included in many nineteenth-century revolutionary movements, it remains significant that socialist groups (including the Bolshevik party) denounced any explicitly feminist movement as an exclusionary bourgeois by-product, the self-indulgent agenda of privileged middle- or upper-class women.[11] Not unlike women activists in various third world countries, Russian women were historically conditioned to scorn the presumably middle-class bias of feminism and its seemingly extravagant emphasis on individual fulfillment — especially in light of the material hardships and deficits continually plaguing Russian society.

Moreover, while seventy-odd years of Soviet rule certainly legislated the public image of the happy working woman, its less publicized realities shaped very different desires and goals in its female citizens. The "paper rights" issued to Soviet women guaranteed them an equal status and professional access unprecedented (and still unmatched) in the Western world, but, imposed as they were on an uninvolved populace, these laws neither produced nor were the product of a widespread social revolution. The "right to work" was extended more as responsibility than empowerment, and after a rather chaotic period of social experimentation in the 1920s, Soviet women were left with a monstrous double burden: the state tacitly endorsed their traditional assignment of housework and child care but invested minimal resources in supporting and supplying the domestic sphere.[12] For all the official rhetoric of equality between the sexes, essentialist notions of men's and women's capabilities and roles went unchallenged in daily practice and general social and cultural attitudes, with men and the "masculine" valued as the universal and most accomplished norm, and women and the "feminine" regarded as more limited, secondary, and often second-rate.

Yet, contrary to Western expectations, this double burden and practical inequality did not foment any sizable feminist campaign for a domestic revolution. Instead, the eventual binary opposition of Stalinist state *versus* society — that determiner of all value — generated an almost inverted scenario. Due to the perils and political compromises of public life and a successful "career" in the Stalinist system, the domestic sphere and family life came to be cherished, even by the women who labored there, as a site of psychological and moral refuge. Indeed, Tolstaia argues that Soviet women, more than Soviet men, were able to "remain human" precisely on account of their domestic attachments: "They tried to protect their own little space from the influence of the state. They locked themselves in with family and children."[13] In direct contrast to the many Western women who struggled to escape a devalued home into a powerful professional and political world, many Soviet women (and men) sought sanctuary and fulfillment in the less monitored world of family and friends, a domestic space that was far more capacious and stimulating than obligatory work or meaningless politics.[14] And while the political landscape has changed in the post-Soviet era, I would argue that the moral onus on public life has not diminished, but grown more complex — directed now against ineffectual politicians and unscrupulous businessmen. For Russian women today, the "return to the home" will certainly limit their political clout and professional options, but it may also constitute a kind of self-investment, a long-overdue vacation, even a moral act of dissociation.

In much the same way, this powerful opposition conditioned Soviet women's very different approach to another Western target — the objectification and commodification of women. Over the years the state promoted political icons of Soviet womanhood (the good mother, the heroic shockworker) that invoked carefully maternal and/or maidenly chaste constructions of femininity; these icons implicitly defined and critiqued "bourgeois" constructions that cultivated a fashionable beauty or sexual desirability. At the same time, the state's material neglect of the domestic sphere also limited the production of specialized goods and services for women, including fashion and beauty products. These kinds of goods were obtainable mainly through illegal means and Party connections; they were coveted as emblems of unusual status, even subversive display. To a certain extent, therefore, Soviet women construed the image of the commodified woman as a goal rather than a target, an image valorized by both political censure and material lack. Of course, the commodification of Soviet women did reproduce the degradation and exploitation more explicit in its Western forms; Soviet women were as susceptible as any other group to a manipulative "beauty myth." Yet in the absence of a capitalist market their extreme preoccupation with "looking feminine" (read bourgeois feminine) and obtaining hard-to-get makeup and stylish clothes *also* signified a personalized triumph over state-imposed norms and consumer priorities. Among her peers, the Soviet woman who managed a bourgeois feminine image without bourgeois advantages (in her context, Party ties) was admirable and enviable for her pragmatic ingenuity — her savvy and daring in manipulating various "private" and even illegal connections. As Elizabeth Waters remarks in an article on Soviet beauty contests, such attitudes very likely help fuel the current enthusiasm for beauty pageants and the seemingly unruffled public response to the new capitalist exploitation of women.[15] She notes the "political statement encoded" in these contests and ascribes their visibility to "the long-frustrated desire for Western style, the sudden emergence of the market, and the freedom granted by glasnost to break old taboos, to explore femininity and sexuality." At least in this transitional period, the market value recently tagged on women's beauty and sexual desirability still resonates with an unofficial desire, a past quest in which women did not simply consume a prescribed ideal, but exercised their own creativity and constructed their own "unofficial" (if still convention-bound) self-image.

Yet the dominance of this state/society opposition, with its attendant material priorities, has wielded a reductive impact as well. Material shortages may have lent a "subversive" aspect to women's commodification, but the combination of shortages, conservative social attitudes, and an historical tradition of women's self-sacrifice has had a very negative effect on Soviet women's well-being — most particularly, on their access to safe, progressive modes of contraception and maternity care.[16] As Larissa Remennick notes in a recent study, "IA [induced abortion] has been the principal means of birth control" in the Soviet Union for the last forty years and IA-related mortality rates are shockingly high (10.09 deaths per 10,000 abortions in the USSR as opposed to 0.6 deaths in the US).[17] Contraceptives have always been in short supply; perhaps more surprisingly, sex education has tended to encourage abortion over contraception as "a chosen birth control strategy." Maternity care has varied in quality depending on location, but it has been standard Soviet practice to segregate mothers from their partners and families and to deny women a choice of options during labor and childbirth.[18] Even as it assigned women sole responsibility for their newborns, the Soviet medical establishment invariably treated these mothers as patients, "not person[s]." Summarizing their analysis of Soviet maternity care, Barbara Holland and Teresa McKevitt identify the bitter paradox of Soviet motherhood: "Though in theory the state acknowledges that giving birth is a contribution to society and that mothers are owed respect and support, in practice women undergo lonely, unsupported and powerless labours" (173).[19]

Less overtly, the siege mentality resulting from decades of political opposition (either against a hostile outside world or a hostile state) has also censored women's exploration and expression of their sexuality. In certain specifics, official icons have permeated the general Russian mindset: the role of the good mother still seems to dictate most Russian women's ideal. The uniform model of a virtuous heterosexual woman — the chaste and maternal Party worker, the chaste and maternal dissident — has obstructed the emergence and acceptance of more diversified roles, nontraditional life-styles. It is characteristic that lesbians and bisexuals are not even "seen" in Russian society. Historically, they have surfaced in the criminalized margins of prisons and labor camps (although, unlike gay men, their sexuality was not recognized in the penal code), but most have opted to blend in with the heterosexual majority, to avoid attracting official *and* unofficial disapproval of their difference.[20] While this homogeneity may be challenged in present-day Russia, a patriarchal and conservative hierarchy of "causes" is likely to endure, at least over the next decade, as the most powerful force shaping Russian women's self-worth and political engagement.[21]

COMMON MARKET, COMMON CAUSE?

Grass-roots protest *versus* mandated change, insistence on individual rights and fulfillment *versus* self-sacrifice for presumably greater "causes," career prospects *versus* obligatory work, domestic entrapment *versus* domestic refuge, commodification *versus* improvisation, a constantly generative factionalism *versus* an all-determining opposition — these are the sorts of historical differences that have jammed communications between Western and Russian women. In predictable consequence, these differences have also stymied exchange between scholars of Western cultures and Slavists in the West. The latter group has developed very much under the influence of successive generations of Russian emigré scholars, has become accustomed to regarding the Russian experience as singular and (at times) exemplary, and is especially wary about applying theories and premises based on Western contexts. As a result, many Slavists have been altogether reluctant to recognize gender (not to speak of sexuality) as an influential category of identity, experience, and perception. Their resistance (stiffened at times by a complacent isolationism) has complicated and retarded scholarly and curricular attempts to mediate between the worlds of Western and Russian women.

Yet now that the Soviet system has collapsed and Western and Russian politics and economies seem to be converging (academic convergence struggling to keep pace), we might at last entertain hopes for a more informed, mutually intelligible *dialogue*. Certainly the Russians seem more avid right now for Western goods, more alert to helpful voices in the present cacophony of Western advisors and opportunists. And the need for better, more nuanced translation has never seemed so urgent. Even making allowances for any first world bias, it is striking how much the new Russian powers-that-be are *measurably* diminishing or demoting women in their shift from socialist state to capitalist nation and their concomitant selection and adaptation of various Western "imports." Women's "paper rights" are even now being erased. The new Russian government has already "omitted the legal guarantees of equality for women in the workplace" in its draft constitution; women's representation in the new Russian parliament has dropped precipitously from a once mandated 33 percent to 10 percent; and Yeltsin and other male leaders, by word and example, encourage the old patriarchal distribution of men in politics and women in the home.[22] Lipovskaia characterizes these trends as "the emergence of so-called 'male democracy,' in which women, long associated with the home, are simply not seen in this newly emerging society."[23]

The economic situation of Russian women is even grimmer. Not only has the rocky transition to a "free market" exacerbated women's double burden to inconceivable extremes, but it has generated what I would call, embellishing on Lipovskaia's example, a kind of "macho capitalism" dominated by young male entrepreneurs (the so-called "millionaires' club"), ex-members of the old Soviet nomenklatura, and mafia-like networks of extortion and enforcement. Although some women have emerged as entrepreneurs, their businesses, according to one witness, tend to be "small and scarce" and their owners "less successful because they're more law-abiding."[24] This "masculinization" of private enterprise revives one traditional fiction of man as the more competitive, capable, committed (i.e., undistracted by childbirth and children) employee and evokes corresponding fictions and job descriptions of woman as helpmate — as homemaker or whore. After decades of recruitment into the labor force, women workers are being laid off in large numbers, and in many cases, from more prestigious, higher-earning jobs. Posadskaia gives an eyewitness account of this metamorphosis:

The Soviet pattern was that a woman first got an education, then a lifelong job and finally a pension. . . . It was very stable and secure. Now all this pattern is smashed. Women make up 70 percent of the unemployed. And of these unemployed women, 85 percent have higher or specialized educations. Now the placement officers say they should be cleaners or nurses, the lowest-paid, least prestigious jobs. They say women under 18 or over 45 should not be trained or retrained, because there are no jobs for them. The paradigms of women's lives are changing. Why should they get a higher education? Most of those losing their jobs are engineers in construction or chemistry, for example.[25]

Much like current Russian translations of "democracy" and "capitalism," the extant translation and adaptation of "free speech" also conveys the privileging of men's desires and value at women's expense. In the most flamboyant example, the "free speech" of glasnost has led to "freer" representations of sex and sexuality, but, as Helena Goscilo deftly argues in her essay "New Members and Organs: The Politics of Porn," the new erotica is mainly heterosexual and male-oriented in its focus, projecting for male delectation images of naked or scantily clad, provocatively posed women in all sorts of public fora — television, taxicabs, the mainstream press, commercial advertising.[26] Through the media of the new Russian market, sexual freedom is being purveyed as a heterosexist male prerogative, with women enjoined to consume their own commodification as a means of earning value in men's eyes.[27]

Again (as I must remind myself), such new contextual developments may forever elicit responses in Russian women that differ from what Western feminists (and especially socialist feminists) may expect or presume. But what is particularly frustrating about this moment in Russian history is that we may feel we recognize these "new" commercial manipulations and social values, that we know best the strategies and consequences of capitalism, and it therefore behooves us to play Cassandra, warning Russian women of the feminine mystique, yellow wallpaper, and Stepford wives to come. We can cite chapter and verse: scholars working from Western models have outlined certain scripts of women's devaluation and manipulation under capitalism — their designation as consumer and consumable, the commercial exploitation and careful political containment of their images and desires. We seem to anticipate and perhaps even hope that the same sorts of scripts will unfold in a newly capitalist Russia, so that our expertise might be of value and use.

Yet before we presume one kind of oppression and impose solidarity, we might admit the complexity and possible variation of such scripts. Despite the inequities and ravages of capitalism (or, for that matter, the hidden privileges of democracy), women have not only been made its victims and unwitting accomplices, but have managed to work the system to gain political and economic power. Rather than reprise the role of gloomy prophet, we in the West might help Russian women explore this complexity and consider their own potential. Rather than subscribe to the condescending dynamic of developmental politics, we would do best, I think, to serve as collaborators and interlocutors. Our role seems clearest in terms of intellectual collaboration. In the first place, we must pursue more extensive and diverse literal translation, supplying information and texts about the wide *variety* of gender issues and the wide *variety* of women's experiences and accomplishments in different cultures that remain untranslated and largely unavailable to a Russian audience; we must help subsidize those in-country publications, like Lipovskaia's *Zhenskoe chtenie*, that have already undertaken this mammoth task. We must invest more concertedly in that other, trickier sort of translation — the development and sharing of gender-aware scholarly analyses and teaching materials focused on Russian texts and contexts. While it has been somewhat useful to export various feminist classics, the very language and premises of these texts often make them alien or indigestible reading for a Russian audience. It is far more productive, I think, when we can discuss and debate issues and analyses on common con/textual ground. Above all, we must create venues for dialogue with Russian women and men through both academic and popular conferences, exchanges, and publications.

The next steps in this collaboration are infinitely harder because they require big bucks, insider access, and a constant self-monitoring.[28] In our interactions with the second world we need to strike a careful balance between an exclusionary insistence on women's needs and concerns (the historical Achilles heel of liberal Western feminisms) and the rapid, largely unchecked erasure and devaluation of those needs and concerns in the new Russia. The point of our efforts — whether they take place on paper, in institutional fora, or on the street — should be to keep these issues and concerns *visible* and to offer sample scenarios of women's successful involvement and achievement. It is important that we finance more contingents of women professionals, politicians, and activists to be alternative voices among the advising hordes of retired American executives and Jeffrey Sachs clones. It is imperative, too, that we develop and support specific working exchanges between a wide variety of American and Russian women's groups, that together we establish a carefully reciprocal networking and pooling of resources and expertise.[29] Whatever methods we can manage, it is clear that Russian women can learn much from Western women's struggles to participate in and reform different capitalist and democratic systems. In equal turn, Western women can learn much from Russian women's long experience balancing the multiple burdens of family, home, and job and their effective involvement with other social and political causes. In any event, if we wish to keep the border open and friendly, it is high time we bug inspectors exchange our respective clipboards and "rigid manner" for an open mind, a ready ear, and a briefcase stuffed with concrete possibilities, and, whenever possible, hard cash.

NOTES

A first version of this essay was presented at a March 1993 conference entitled "Rethinking the Second World" and sponsored by the University of California at Santa Cruz. My thanks to Stephanie Jed, Nicole Tonkovich, Pasquale Verdicchio, and Winnie Woodhull for their criticism and comments on subsequent versions; the mistakes remain my own.

1. Tat'iana Tolstaia, "Notes from Underground," (a review of Francine du Plessix Gray's *Soviet Women: Walking the Tightrope*), *New York Review of Books*, May 31, 1990: 3.
2. See Barbara Alpern Engel, "An Interview with Olga Lipovskaia," *Frontiers* 10, no. 3 (1989): 6–10; Ol'ga Lipovskaia, "New Women's Organisations," in *Perestroika and Soviet Women*, ed. Mary Buckley (Cambridge: Cambridge University Press, 1992), 73–74.
3. Andrew Kopkind, "What Is to Be Done?: From Russia with Love and Squalor," *Nation*, January 18, 1993, vol. 256, no. 2, 50, 55.
4. Elizabeth Shogren, "Russia's Equality Erosion," *Los Angeles Times*, February 11, 1993, 1.
5. Jo Anna Isaak, "Reflections of Resistance: Women Artists on Both Sides of the *Mir*," *Heresies*, special Russian/English bilingual edition entitled *IdiomA*, no. 26 (1992): 9–10: "Like many letters of the Russian alphabet that seem reversed to us, the ways in which 'woman' is represented is frequently the mirror inversion of the representation of woman in the West. In looking at the image of women on the other side of this mirror, we have an opportunity (almost as we could with computer image programming) to see how our lot would differ if our image was different."
6. Chandra Talpade Mohanty, "Introduction" to *Third World Women and the Politics of Feminism*, ed. Chandra Talpade Mohanty, Ann Russo, and Lourdes Torres (Bloomington: Indiana University Press, 1991), 7.
7. Chandra Talpade Mohanty, "Under Western Eyes: Feminist Scholarship and Colonial Discourses," the most updated and modified version of which is reprinted in *Third World Women and the Politics of Feminism*, 52–80.
8. In *Feminism and Nationalism in the Third World* (London: Zed Books, 1992), Kumari Jayawardena does frame a more textured reading of this interaction, noting that "[t]he concept of feminism has also been the cause of much confusion in Third World countries" — scorned as a foreign or "bourgeois" product by "traditionalists, political conservatives and even certain leftists" and claimed as a solely Western phenomenon by North Americans and Western Europeans (2).
9. Barbara Holland, "Introduction," to *Soviet Sisterhood*, ed. Barbara Holland (Bloomington: Indiana University Press, 1985), 23.
10. Richard Stites, *The Women's Liberation Movement in Russia: Feminism, Nihil-*

ism, and Bolshevism, 1860–1930 (Princeton: Princeton University Press, 1978), 191. For a perceptive analysis of women's participation in the Russian revolutionary underground, see Barbara Alpern Engel's *Mothers and Daughters: Women of the Intelligentsia in Nineteenth-Century Russia* (Cambridge: Cambridge University Press, 1983).

11. See Laura Engelstein's nuanced analysis of the distinction between Russian and Western societies in the late nineteenth century: "But although they [the Russians] adopted the liberal ideal of the autonomous subject, they often rejected the Western bourgeois regard for self-interest and the goal of self-fulfillment." In *The Keys to Happiness: Sex and the Search for Modernity in Fin-de-Siecle Russia* (Ithaca: Cornell University Press, 1992), 4.

12. In *Women and Ideology in the Soviet Union* (New York: Harvester Wheatsheaf, 1989), Mary Buckley provides a very useful overview of women's situation in the various periods of Soviet history.

13. Tat'iana Tolstaia with Irena Martyniak, "The Human Spirit Is Androgynous," *Index on Censorship* 19, no. 9 (October 1990): 29.

14. See Vladimir Shlapentokh's study, *Public and Private Life of the Soviet People: Changing Values in Post-Stalin Russia* (New York: Oxford University Press, 1989). Shlapentokh argues that after Stalin's death there ensued a process of "privatization" or "destatization" (14) in which the state gradually lost authority "over all strata of the population" (153) and the Soviet people shifted their interest "from the state to their primary groups (family, friends, and lovers) and to semilegal and illegal civil society as well as to illegal activity inside the public sector" (13).

15. Elizabeth Waters, "Soviet Beauty Contests," in *Sex and Russian Society*, ed. Igor Kon and James Riordan (Bloomington: Indiana University Press, 1993), 118, 132.

16. Russian commentator Nadia Kakurina identifies this historical tradition of self-sacrifice, dubbing it "the oppressive power of pity"; while she admits that "[t]here is . . . something deeply moving and decent about [women's] tactful lack of emphasis on their own needs," she recognizes the hazards of such self-denial. "The oppressive power of pity: Russian women and self-censorship," *Index on Censorship* 19, no. 9 (October 1990): 28–29.

17. Larissa I. Remennick, "Patterns of Birth Control," in Kon and Riordan, *Sex and Russian Society*, 45–63.

18. Barbara Holland and Teresa McKevitt, "Maternity Care in the Soviet Union," in Holland, *Soviet Sisterhood*, 145–76. Holland and McKevitt base their analysis in part on interviews with Soviet women.

19. Yelena Shafran's 26 January 1994 article in *Izvestiia*, "Why Women in Russia Are Afraid to Give Birth," cites increasingly grim statistics about maternity care, charting the rise of infant mortality rates by 18 percent in 1992 and 18.6 percent in 1993. Quoted from a translated excerpt of this article in *The Current Digest of the Post-Soviet Press*, vol. 46, no. 4, February 23, 1994: 23–24.

20. Cf. Igor Kon's "Sexual Minorities," in Kon and Riordan, *Sex and Russian Society*, esp. 103: "When talking of homosexuality, Russians almost always

mean male homosexuality; the press has only recently started to mention lesbianism. All the same, life for lesbians is no better. It is true that their relationships do not come under any article in the criminal code, and intimacy between women is less remarkable to the surrounding world. On the other hand, a young girl in our society who is aware of her psychosexual difference finds it harder than a man to find a close relationship. And society's attitude is just as obdurate: ridicule, persecution, expulsion from college or work, threats to take her children away. The idea that homosexuals, men or women, can actually be good parents would be absolutely anathema to virtually everyone in the former USSR." See also Cath Jackson's interview with Olga Zhuk, president of the Tchaikovsky Foundation, a lesbian and gay group based in Saint Petersburg; the interview is published in *Trouble & Strife* 24 (Summer 1992): 20–24. Zhuk speaks of the extreme difficulties of growing up lesbian in Russia — the loneliness and sense of isolation, the lack of any public meeting places for gay women, the fact that most gay women marry "because you are expected to and because women don't identify as lesbians." She describes the "sub-culture of lesbianism" that has been preserved in the camps and she notes gay women's reluctance to come out publicly: "In general lesbians don't want to work politically. They say that nobody's bothering them, everything's okay: it's much better that no one should know they are lesbians and they don't want to draw attention to it." I thank Rebecca Wells for bringing this interview to my attention.

21. For one analysis of how service to these various "causes" has shaped Russian women's self-representation, see my article "For the Good of the Cause: Russian Women's Autobiography in the Twentieth Century," in a forthcoming volume of essays, *Russian Women's Literature*, ed. Toby Clyman and Diana Greene (London: Greenwood Press, 1994).

22. Shogren, "Russia's Equality Erosion," 11.

23. Lipovskaia, "New Women's Organisations," 80.

24. Kopkind, "What Is to Be Done?" 49. This quote also may be attributable to Lipovskaia; Kopkind is citing a Petersburg woman named Olga who is "an astute, ex-hippie feminist intellectual of 38" (Lipovskaia's first name, age, location, and ideological self-identification).

25. Cited in ibid., 55. Shogren's sources state that 80 percent of the unemployed are women (11).

26. Helena Goscilo, "New Members and Organs: The Politics of Porn," in *The Carl Beck Papers in Russian and East European Studies* 1007 (1993).

27. See also Lynne Attwood's discussion of women's representation in current Russian films — their preponderant depiction as an "object of the male gaze" or the passive (and often supposedly symbolic) victim of male violence. "Sex and the Cinema," in Kon and Riordan, *Sex and Russian Society*, 64–88.

28. Extending this principle of self-monitoring, we might also conduct a critical review of the kinds of "capitalist" and "democratic" models Western groups are currently exporting to Russia; we need to ascertain if these exported

models bother or dare to specify policies about women's inclusion, promotion, and rights in government and the workplace.

29. For an excellent example of this kind of networking, see the Cooperatives Initiative Program sponsored by the University of Wisconsin-Eau Claire. Their projects include cooperative seminars to develop women's political participation and empowerment; training and support for women's re-employment and entrepreneurship; and programs to provide better women's health care and child care. Contact: Sarah Harder, Office of the Chancellor, Women's Studies, UW-Eau Claire, WI 54702–4004. There are numerous other programs either in place or in process. For more information on such initiatives, see *Women East-West*, the newsletter issued by the Association for Women in Slavic Studies. Contact: Mary Zirin, 1178 Sonoma Drive, Altadena, CA 91001.

Engendering the Russian Body Politic

Harriet Murav

One political myth that has persisted through the greater part of Russian history, regardless of the particular form in which political power was expressed, imagines Russia (both Imperial and Soviet) as consisting of two sometimes opposed entities: the state and the Russian people or nation. The mythologeme of the "Russian people" was well developed by the end of the nineteenth century and exploited most strikingly in the twentieth by Stalin. The opposition between the state and the people or nation is not gender neutral. The state, be it Tsarist or Soviet, is constructed as masculine, and the people or nation as feminine. As Joanna Hubbs shows, the bifurcation between "Father Tsar" and "Mother Russia" can be traced back to the reign of Ivan the Terrible, but a similar division of roles persists throughout the Soviet period.[1] Nina Perlina points out that although the Russian word for "revolution" is grammatically feminine, the historical revolution "was largely a masculine undertaking" and was mythologized as such.[2]

The radical utopias projected by such revolutionary feminists as Aleksandra Kollantai did little to dislodge traditional Russian gender mythologies. Kollantai, writing in 1921, says that the pregnant woman "ceases to belong to herself — she is in service to the collective — she 'produces' out of her own flesh and blood a new unit of work, a new member of the labor republic."[3] According to Kollantai, the needs of the family will be provided by the state in the form of communal housing, communal kitchens, children's homes, and day-care centers, making it possible for women to combine professional work and family life. This revolutionary restructuring of everyday life was never realized. Furthermore, notwith-

standing Kollantai's Marxist definition of motherhood not as reproduction but as production, Soviet ideology revitalized the traditional myth of
Mother Russia.

Maia Turovskaia, a feminist critic writing in post-Soviet Russia, traces
the representation of this mythology in films made during the time of
Stalin. The 1939 film *The Member of the Government* constructs the heroine's genealogy as a creature of the party of Lenin and Stalin — as Turovskaia puts it, as a creature of "an all-encompassing patriarchal Will."
Chosen to become a member of the Supreme Soviet, Aleksandra Sokolova
proclaims: "Here I stand before you, a simple Russian woman [she uses
the somewhat derogatory term "baba"], beaten by my husband, frightened
by the priest, shot at by our enemies. . . . And the party and our Soviet
power elevated us and me as well to this tribune."[4] Turovskaia shows how
in the postwar film *The Oath* the heroine is transformed into a mythologized "Mother Russia." The heroine presents a letter written by her
husband to Lenin to his new incarnation, Stalin, and in so doing embodies, as Turovskaia puts it, "a purely Russian mythology: the Motherland
[*Rodina-mat'*] before the face of the Father of nations."[5]

Far from disappearing with the last vestiges of Soviet power, this
mythology of Mother Russia, together with certain related constructions
of the feminine, have reappeared with particular force during recent
years, against the backdrop of glasnost, perestroika, and the collapse of
the Soviet empire.[6] These political changes have also made possible the
creation and publication of new forms of criticism, both literary and
social. A new generation of writers has appeared, among whom women
writers figure importantly. Collections specifically devoted to "women's
writing" — certainly a vague and problematic term — have been steadily
published at least since the late 1980s.

This chapter seeks to provide an overview of the reconfiguration of
Mother Russia and the responses, both direct and indirect, to her resurrection. I will begin with the writings of politically conservative authors,
some of whom are well known outside Russia. I will show how the
revision of Mother Russia is itself a response to the perception of a
breakdown in the political, social, and natural order. I then turn to a
specific response to these writings in the work of two very different
authors, both of whom can loosely be identified as politically "liberal."
The last section of the essay examines the prose of several new Russian
women authors, tracing how and to what extent their configurations of

woman represent "oppositionalist" writing. What strategies are deployed
in this writing to defamiliarize Mother Russia? Of particular importance
here will be the image of the female body.

I. MOTHER RUSSIA: TAKE ONE

A 1988 essay by the literary critic Irina Sheveleva, entitled "The Feminine
and the Maternal" offers a very clear example of the conservative construction of woman and the nation.[7] For Sheveleva the feminine is identified with the home and the homeland. The essence of the feminine is the
sense of belonging to a place and a people. In her discussion of women's
poetry Sheveleva writes that "the poetess does not only imprint 'nature,'
she conveys the sense of her own native belonging" (166). The "earth,
one's own native tongue, and strong native roots" constitute for Sheveleva
woman's "dowry." The familiar intimate landscape of the home is linked
to the overarching ethnic construct of the national group and the political
construct of the nation. Woman, as keeper of the home, bears, but does
not define, the values of the nation. Sheveleva asks "To be the mistress of
your own home — what could be more natural for a woman?" To be
mistress means to be the home itself, "to bear its habits and customs in
your blood" (166). The link between the home and the nation is enhanced
by the woman's reproductive function, by means of which she has access
to "the most intimate secrets of being" (167). Sheveleva chastises the poet
Bela Akhmadulina for writing that her baby makes it impossible for her
to work, for there is no greater creative work for a woman than caring for
a child. But significantly, this theme of the maternal is subordinate to the
theme of the home and the native soil and speech. "To accuse women
poets of nostalgic patriarchalism, of an attachment to an age-old image of
home, of the hearth, is the same as accusing them of being women" (167).
To paraphrase Sheveleva, the primary social problem facing Russia today
is the need for women to return home, and the primary function of the
woman poet is to preserve her "inherited native word."

For all her concern with the home and the domestic as opposed to the
public sphere, Sheveleva's construction of the feminine places woman
once again at the service of the nation. The domestic, in Sheveleva's
reading, does not mark out the space in which the individual is free from
the state, as in traditional Western liberal ideology. For Western middle-
class women, the domestic sphere became a prison, but for Soviet and

Eastern bloc women and men, the family could be a refuge. In *How We Survived Communism and Even Laughed* Slavenka Drakulic writes: "When there is no space in society to express your individuality the family becomes the only territory in which one can form it, exercise it, prove it, express it." But Drakulic goes on to say that "a family is too limiting, there is not space enough in it for self-expression either."[8] In more extreme conditions of the labor camp, the domestic offered a form of resistance. Evgenia Ginzburg, who spent seventeen years in the gulag for not denouncing someone, describes how the recreation of some smattering of a domestic space within the prison barracks offers the female prisoners a moment of reprieve from the police state of the prison.[9] For some contemporary Russian feminists, the collapse of Soviet ideology with its emphasis on work, service, and its derogation of the private sphere, means the ideological possibility, if not the economic one, of abandoning the work force and returning home.[10] Under the Soviet system, not working at a government-approved position was tantamount to the crime of "parasitism." The poet Joseph Brodskii was charged with this crime. But for Sheveleva, in contrast, the domestic space, far from offering an alternative to the state, and by the same token, woman, the keeper of the domestic space, are both vessels which are to preserve the identity of the larger national entity, and reproduce its values and language. Indeed, there is no distinction between the public and the private, no moment or utterance that is free from the new totality of nation, blood, and soil that Sheveleva and others like her wish to reestablish for Russia. Sheveleva's construction of the feminine and of the "homeland" denies history, sexuality, and rejects difference altogether. The notion of cultural or social intercourse with culturally distinct others as a constituent part of identity is conspicuously absent from her view. The same absence can be noted in other similar conservative writers publishing in *Our Contemporary* ("Nash sovremennik"), most notably Ksenia Mialo, a participant in a 1993 roundtable entitled "The State of the Russian Nation," who advises "a strict Russocentrism in every word about our future" and urges "all Russians to concentrate on what is their own, their own, their own."[11] This emphasis on homogeneity and inwardness, evidenced in Sheveleva's statement that "for the sensation of the limitlessness of that which is one's own one needs attachment to and rootedness in the earth"[12] offers a striking contrast to Bakhtin's emphasis on the concept of exchange as constitutive of identity: "that which takes place on the boundary between one's own and some one else's consciousness, on the threshold."[13] In Sheveleva's scheme, woman, who has no identity of her own, is the ideal receptacle for the language, culture, soil, and blood that she only inherits, but never forms. Modernity and even the process of historical change are rejected in favor of the endless reduplication of the same. A similar but more subtle framing of the question of woman and national identity can be found in Valentin Rasputin's novella *Farewell to Matera*, published in 1976. Widely hailed as a masterpiece of "village prose," the story tells of the imminent flooding of the Siberian island and village, both called "Matera" for the sake of misguided progress: the Angara river is to be altered as part of a reservoir connected to a new hydroelectric dam.[14] The heroine of the tale, very untypically for Soviet literature, is an old woman named Dar'ia, who quietly resists the destruction of her village and way of life. As David Gillespie writes: "In the almost four decades since Stalin's death, Rasputin's Dar'ia still offers Soviet literature's most profound rejection of the materialist dream of a technological utopia."[15] In contrast to her grandson, who proclaims that man is master ("tsar" is the Russian word he uses) of nature, Dar'ia says that Matera was given to people in order that they might live from its resources and then pass it on to the next generation. Dar'ia thinks of herself and her fellow human beings not as "masters," but as pitiful, weak, "little" creatures, who have forgotten "their place under God."[16] As Gillespie puts it, Dar'ia is the "repository of past values and traditions in the island." Gillespie's choice of words is significant: woman as womb is a "repository" and not a creator of culture. Dar'ia's role as "repository" is expressed in her relation to her dead ancestors and to her house. She goes to the cemetery to ask forgiveness and guidance and there seemingly receives the ghostly answer that she must clean and prepare her house before it is destroyed. She comes to the conclusion that "truth lies in memory"; "he who has no memory has no life."[17] Rasputin's Dar'ia can be seen as a fictitious embodiment of Sheveleva's ideal women, for she has no other role than to be mistress of an albeit doomed house, and to "bear its habits and customs," as Sheveleva writes, in her blood.

For Rasputin, as for Sheveleva, identity is given by place. In *Farewell to Matera*, the narrator comments that "you are not only that which you carry within you, but also that which is around you, and to lose it is to sometimes more terrible than losing an arm or a leg . . . perhaps it is only this that is eternally passed on, like the holy spirit, from person to person, from fathers to children and from children to grandchildren, restraining and guarding them, directing and purifying them."[18] Among all the villagers, Dar'ia has best absorbed "what is around" her, what is passed from fathers and not mothers, to children. Dar'ia alone prepares her hut for its immolation. She whitewashes it and places fir branches in its corners, as if for a holiday, all the while sensing the meaningfulness of her actions. Dar'ia is mistress of her house, but not of Matera. That role is given to a mysterious poltergeist-like masculine figure called the "Master," who prowls the island at night. The woman too old for childbearing or sexuality is the vessel for a masculine-given culture.

In her recent essay "Gynoglasnost: writing the feminine," Barbara Heldt offers the following gender analysis of village prose:

Much of village prose is about the squandering of a female ecology, and concomitant male guilt. Although the Soviet system stands accused, it has a gender – a largely male bureaucracy is set against female Nature. In other words the Good Mother is Russia, but she is either dead or threatened with imminent destruction. The Wicked Stepmother is the Soviet Union who has taken her place and is destroying her children. Traces of the Good Mother can be found in very old women or a younger one who dies or is victimized.[19]

Heldt's reading provides a necessary caution to those who might see Rasputin as offering a pro-feminist gyno-ecologism in Farewell to Matera. Only the aged Dar'ia is positively valued by the narrator; her middle-aged daughter-in-law, in contrast, who lives on the mainland, puts on weight, gets her hair cut in a fashionable style, and becomes interested in and knowledgeable about the illnesses from which she suffers. The narrator comments that the inhabitants of Matera have no time to be sick. The daughter-in-law's knitting is fashionably lacy, and therefore full of holes, but Dar'ia's is waterproof. It should be noted that the production of textiles, one of the most ancient womanly crafts, appears in traditional patriarchal societies as means of establishing, maintaining, and evaluating order, civil, domestic, and even cosmological. The woman weaving in the home is a sign that everything and everyone is in her place. The daughter-in-law's flaws — fashion, illness, and fat — are all symptoms of the overdevelopment, excess, forgetfulness, and loss of homogeneity that comes from leaving Matera. In the story foreignness appears in the form of the government official in charge of the flooding, a character with the unattractive name of "Zhuk," which means both "beetle" and "shyster," who has a "dark gypsy face." The gypsy, who has no native home, is the antinomy of Matera. "Matera," with its associations of both "mother" and "mainland," as Gillespie points out,[20] is a self-sufficient island, which has "enough spaciousness and wealth, and beauty, and wildness, and every kind of creature in twos." Leaving the timelessness and geographic isolation of Matera and entering the historical present — at the time of the story's publication, this meant the Soviet present — inevitably means evil and decay, which Rasputin expresses in specifically and traditionally anti-feminine terms. Both Plato and Tolstoy construe fashion as a sign of the excess of decadent urban culture.[21]

Rasputin's "Cherchez la Femme," published in 1990, returns to the gendered thematics of *Farewell to Matera*, but in a more explicit and direct way. Rasputin begins by quoting from the work of a little-known late nineteenth-century woman writer named N. A. Lukhmanova, whose work was praised, Rasputin adds, by the philosopher Vasilii Rozanov. Rasputin emphasizes that what he is about to quote was written by a woman. The Truth about Woman is uttered by a woman, but only one legitimized by a male. Lukhmanova describes a decline in female beauty, and an increase in women's "nervousness to the point of hysteria . . . bordering on psychopathology."[22] Rasputin finds Lukhmanova's observations to be true of Russian women today. Much has been written about the construction of the hysterical woman in fin-de-siècle Europe, both from the point of view of the hysteric and the doctor, but what is relevant here is the argument that the construction of hysteria was a way of reasserting patriarchal control over women at a time when feminism threatened that control.[23] A similar argument may be made about Rasputin, namely, that his assertion of a resurgence of hysteria is a means of reasserting control over women in post-totalitarian Russia, at a time when the possibility exists for the emergence of a non-Soviet feminism.

Rasputin's cure for the new outbreak of the old pathology is not medical, as it was at the turn of the century, but moral. The age-old cure for hysteria, "wandering womb," is marriage and pregnancy, or, in Rasputin's terms, a return to the "essence" of womanhood, defined as "preservation" or "protection": Shelter, warmth, tenderness, the satisfaction of needs, faithfulness, softness, flexibility, mercifulness — this is what a woman consists of. Feeding her family, caring for her husband, raising her children, being a good neighbor — this is the circle of her concerns.[24]

Rasputin goes on to say that Russian woman's true role is not "civic," but "familial," and that given Russian woman's "character," that role is "sacrificial." For Rasputin, Dostoevsky's self-sacrificing saintly prostitute Sonia Marmeladova is a prime example of Russian womanhood. That Rasputin chooses Sonia from all the other female characters in *Crime and Punishment* is significant. Raskolnikov's sister, Dunia, who repels the lecherous Svidrigailov's advances with a revolver, and who plans to start a publishing company with her fiancé, Razumikhin, is apparently not a typical Russian woman.[25]

Rasputin's "cure" for the "pathology" of late twentieth-century Russian women is really a cure for the pathology of late twentieth-century Russia. Rasputin links the perceived decline in present-day Russian women to a perceived decline in Russian culture as a whole, the burden for which lies on women. The emphasis on "protection" is significant in this regard. From what is it that women are to protect their families, and by extension, all of Russia? From an unwanted intrusion of otherness and change. Translated into national terms, this means restoring and conserving the Russianness of Russia, protecting Russia from heterogeneity. The anxiety over "otherness" evidenced in Rasputin, Sheveleva, and as we will shortly see, another conservative writer, Belov, emerges full-blown as blatant anti-Semitism in their colleague at *Our Contemporary*, Igor Shafarevich, whose notorious essay "Russophobia" characterizes Jews as a hostile subnation within the greater nation of Russia.[26]

The anxiety over otherness in Rasputin is not limited to questions of ethnic identity, but can be traced to the level of gender. A profound distrust of women's otherness lies at the roots of the ideological construction of Rasputin's *Matera* and "Cherchez la Femme." Woman, let out of the house, is not simply dangerous to herself, but to man. In the myth of autochthony that writers like Rasputin seek to create, the original Russians would, like the sown men of ancient Thebes, spring into being without sexual intercourse, and the Russian nation would arise without communication or contact with the outside world — recall Ksenia Mialo's emphasis on Russocentrism. This myth defines women as the first outsiders, the first nonnatives. They are emblematic of all difference and diversity.

Rasputin's masculinist myth is concealed under an insistence on the proto-feminine origins of Russian culture: "at the foundations of our culture lie feminine principles." He reminds his readers of the role of the cult of Mary as the protector of Russia, whose repeated intercession, it was believed, saved Russia from "enemies and misfortunes." Rasputin writes: "Russia from time immemorial believed in itself as the Home of the Mother of God."[27] According to Rasputin, modern Russian women have forgotten that they carry within them "the stamp of the mother of God." The author's vision of women eliminates actual historical Russian women, especially those who happen not to be Orthodox Christians. Extrapolating from Rasputin's argument, a Russian "her-story" can be traced, in which each stage corresponds to a particular construction of Woman, who either serves, rejects, or betrays Man. Premodern, patriarchal Russia corresponds to Russia as the mother of God. Late nineteenth- and late twentieth-century Russia — each time period representing a collapse of Empire — corresponds to Russia the hysterical woman. A further parallel between these two periods is that in each, feminism begins to emerge. To restate the analysis given earlier, Rasputin's diagnosis for each is the same: when women express desires of their own, they forget and deny their truest selves. In repressing their desire to be mothers and homemakers, women become hysterics. A close relative of the Hysteric is a figure that Rasputin calls the Goddess of Revenge and Destruction. Rasputin uses this label for several late nineteenth-century women revolutionaries — Vera Zasulich, who shot at the Governor General of St. Petersburg in 1878 and was acquitted by the jury, and the women who participated in the assassination of Tsar Alexander II in 1881. Mother Russia's "sick" daughters turn on Father Tsar. The rage and repressed desire formerly expressed in the hysteric's language of symptoms is turned outward, against Russia.

It seems that Rasputin fears a resurgence of female violence in the present, or rather, that this violence has infected society as whole. Late twentieth-century Russian society has become feminized in the sense that it has gone mad. Rasputin speaks of its "inability to provide itself with necessities, unwillingness to give of itself in work" and "violent passion for complete license."[28] In this language of unbridled desire and unwillingness for sacrifice is a portrait of woman undomesticated. In accordance with the particular cast of his gender politics, Rasputin links the breakdown of post-Soviet Russian society as a whole with a perceived "breakdown" — this is Rasputin's word — of Russian women in particular. Rasputin's characterization of society's "madness" follows immediately upon his description of the "tragic breakdown of woman," portrayed in, among other literary works, Vasilii Belov's *Raising Children According to Doctor Spock*.

Belov's story chronicles the collapse of the Zorin family. The setting is an unnamed urban area. Zorin, a low-level construction supervisor with a drinking problem, is in constant conflict with his wife, Tonia, who works in a library and earns more than he. Tonia sees "a threat to her independence in his every action."[29] He only wants closeness, she, only distance. The narrator's and Zorin's point of view are indistinguishable here. Zorin is passionately devoted to his little daughter, Lial'ka — unlike Tonia, who, in his words, wants to turn her into a "walking robot" by raising her in senseless obedience to Dr. Spock's principles. "She has to urinate and move her bowels at a definite time of the day!" thinks the exasperated Zorin. For American readers, this portrait of Dr. Spock is somewhat startling, since Spock is known and even blamed for a lack of discipline in his approach to the upbringing of children. In the episode that marks the beginning of the end, Tonia takes Lial'ka for her regular evening walk even when the child is obviously feverish. The next day Zorin is called from the day-care center to bring her home. Shortly thereafter Lial'ka is hospitalized with pneumonia, and her mother refuses to stay overnight with her. Zorin leaves home. He spends a short time with his boss Fridburg, but feels uncomfortable with the "falsely hospitable atmosphere of the Jewish family." Note the gratuitous anti-Semitism of the narrator's characterization.

Near the end of the story, after having been fired from his job, in part due to the letters of complaint written against him by his wife, Zorin muses on the nature of women in general. There is something "fish-like and cold" in women, especially in their tolerance for abortions. He thinks about the "rusalki," the powerful female figures in Russian folklore associated with water and woods, dangerous to men. Women who drowned were believed to become "rusalki."[30] Zorin imagines his wife as a rusalka, who figuratively "drowned" in her job and in her quest for emancipation and then turned on him in revenge. Zorin thinks: "They put their husbands in prison and write denunciations against them."[31] The story's final scene takes place on the street. Tonia beats Lial'ka for disobedience and walks off, leaving her to her father's comforting embrace. From Rasputin's and Belov's point of view, the "tragic breakdown of modern woman" is not only her betrayal of man, but her violence against her children, born and unborn. Modern woman, in this view, is a threat to the future of Russia. Rasputin's most recent word on Mother Russia can be found in the 1993 roundtable on "The State of the Russian Nation," which I have already touched upon. Here Rasputin's tone shifts to a lament over the collapse of the Russian empire. The passage is worth quoting in full:

Even now we do not know the condition of the Russian nation, whether she can still be found in one national body, or whether because of the most recent shocks, attacks, and hostilities, she has been shaken loose from it and scattered among Russian cities and villages which do not have any spiritual or blood ties among them. We will hope that things have not reached this point and that the national instinct and the national memory have not yet been beaten out of us forever. And if this is so, if the nation for all her tragic losses is alive — towards what should we turn for her ingathering, cure, and mobilization, if not to the national spirit, where shall we seek support, if not in national worth and national conscience? [32]

The word that I have translated as "nation," natsiia, is grammatically feminine. Rasputin avoids the term "narod" (people), which is grammatically masculine, and similarly the grammatically neutral "gosudarstvo," which suggests a politically formed entity, and is usually translated as "government." The passage reveals a certain confusion in its metaphors. It is difficult to say exactly what the difference is between the nation and the "national body." It seems that the nation refers to a spiritual quality or identity, and the national body to the physical territory of the former Soviet Union or of Russia. However, Rasputin goes on to draw a distinction between the nation, on the one hand, and the national memory, the national spirit, and the national conscience, on the other, all of which must be relied upon for the "ingathering, cure, and mobilization" of the nation. It is not clear what is meant by the "national body" out from which the "nation" has been "shaken."

The language of diaspora — the Russian nation is scattered among disparate villages and cities — and ingathering is clearly biblical. Compare, for example, Ezekiel 11:17: "Thus says the Lord God: I will gather you from the peoples, and assemble you out of the countries where you have been scattered" and 11:19: "And I will give them one heart, and put a new spirit within them."

The prophetic subtext signals two themes: first, a messianic association of Russia with the biblical Israel, and secondly, Rasputin's engendering of the Russian nation as feminine. Zion's evil is expressed figuratively in many prophetic texts as harlotry. For example, Zion is an unfaithful wife, who has abandoned her husband, God, to play the harlot (Jeremiah 3:6). The pain which Zion then endures is compared to that of a woman abandoned by her lovers. Jeremiah continues: "and you, O desolate one, what do you mean that you dress in scarlet, that you deck yourself with ornaments of gold. . . . Your lovers despise you" (4:30). Diaspora, God's punishment for the unfaithful nation (recall that Rasputin lists "faithfulness" as a specifically feminine virtue), can be seen as in feminine terms: the violation of the physical integrity of the body politic can be compared to a loss of virginity. The nation's "whoring" and subsequent "rape" are two sides of the same coin. In terms of the conservative construction of Russian national identity, "whoring" means cultural intercourse with the West, from rock and roll to democratic pluralism, the abandonment of what conservatives call "historic Russia," and more viscerally, what is referred to in conservative writing as the "sale of Russia," the ceding of territory to Japan, for example, and the rise in prostitution between Russian women and foreigners for hard currency.[33]

The historical processes that have taken place in the former Soviet Union since the collapse of Empire in 1991 are mythologized in biblical terms. The rhetorical strategy is similar to what we have seen earlier. The metaphor of the feminine nation is the prism through which events are evaluated. Diaspora is the ultimate punishment for the loss of the "good mother," to use Barbara Heldt's phrase, expressed in the valorization of such figures as Rasputin's Dar'ia in *Farewell to Matera*, her replacement by hysterical and ultimately violent daughters, and the corresponding dual collapse of the Russian family and of national identity. The engendering of the Russian body politic as Mother Russia in conservative prose denies the possibility of representing women in anything other than a mythological light. Woman is either the pure Mother of God or the evil rusalka. Demystifying Mother Russia, however, opens up the possibility of alternative representations of women and their experience. Similarly, nonmythological representations of women may serve in turn to demystify Mother Russia. The next part of this essay examines these interrelated strategies in recent Russian writing, some of which are direct responses to Sheveleva, Rasputin, and other conservative writers, and some of which are responses to the broader phenomena of glasnost and the end of the Soviet Empire. A preliminary caveat is necessary. To search for "feminist" constructions of Russia and of the feminine in current Russian writing would be mistaken, for many reasons. Any essentializing construction of national or gender identity that neglects actual individual Russians and actual individual Russian women would simply be the other side of the conservative coin: a different content perhaps, but the same totalizing structure. We would be on more certain ground with writing that, while not necessarily "feminist," is fragmentary, ironical, or critical, writing in which old women are not divinized and young women demonized. While not being able to offer an exhaustive survey of current Russian writing, we will discuss some examples, not all of them authored by women, that take this stance.

II. MOTHER RUSSIA: TAKE TWO

In 1992 the Russian emigré writer Fridrikh Gorenshtein published a short story entitled "Last Summer on the Volga" in the liberal journal *The Banner ("Znamia")*. Gorenshtein, the author of a number of film scripts, including "Solaris" and "A Slave of Love," began to attract critical attention in the former Soviet Union in 1991. "Last Summer on the Volga" provoked controversy because of its unattractive images of Russia.[34] The narrator, who announces himself to be a Jew, and as such, forced into a condition of "rootlessness" by the surrounding Russian society, makes one last trip along the Volga before leaving for Berlin. The narrator finds himself surrounded by "symbols" of Russia in the form of two women whom he encounters. These symbols are quite similar to what we have already seen in Rasputin and Belov, but they are given an ironic twist. It is very likely that Gorenshtein refers to Rasputin and Belov indirectly in a scene in which the narrator goes to a restaurant occupied mostly by drunks, who, while realizing that he is not a "local," do not reject him. The narrator comments "in the company of 'Russian wisemen' you can't sit incognito."[35] In other words, the "Russian wisemen," or Russian nationalists, always keep tabs on who is who, who is Russian, who is Jewish, and so forth. "Last Summer on the Volga" as a whole, as we will see, is a parodic response to the "village prose" and postvillage prose of Rasputin and Belov. While in the restaurant the narrator meets a pale blonde, reduced to begging. She eats food left on other people's plates and lives in a shack along the river with a doll for company and a suitcase full of scraps of bread, which she eats with damp gray salt wrapped in a rag. Because of her pallor, and a "lifeless" sinful quality about her, the narrator compares her to a "rusalka." The woman, Liuba, tells the narrator that she has served time in a prison camp for the murder of her mother-in-law, and that she is stranded in this small town on the Volga because she does not have enough money to return to her village and family. The narrator decides that Liuba, "the beggar rusalka," is a symbol of all of Russia.

The second symbol is an old woman with nondescript features, "the kind you see many of and therefore don't notice." What makes this particular old woman so striking is the "enormous pig's head" she holds against her chest, close to her own head. The pig's head gives the old woman "individuality." The narrator is "amazed" at the correspondence between the physical features and expression of the old woman and the pig. It strikes him that the old woman is the perfect image for Liuba's mother-in-law, the "criminal-victim." Furthermore the old woman with the pig's head is a "second hypostasis of Russia, who tramples on and consumes everything around her . . . and in the first place, herself" (50). The narrator concludes that the traditional image of the Russian maiden meeting the "black limousines" of the government officials with bread and salt should be replaced by his two hypostases of the old woman, "Mother-in-Law Russia" carrying an aspic made of her own head, and Liuba, bringing her bread crusts and "damp gray salt."

The grotesque old woman is at once perpetrator and victim, a Mother Russia, or, as Gorenshtein mockingly puts it, "Mother-in-Law Russia," who feeds not Father Tsar or Father Stalin, but Father Apparatchik with her own flesh. The contrasts between Gorenshtein's "Mother-in-Law Russia" and Rasputin's Dar'ia are striking. Gorenshtein's old woman destroys her home by goading her daughter-in-law to murder; Dar'ia is the conservator of hearth and home. Dar'ia is very nearly fleshless and belongs more to the spirit world of her ancestors than to the here and now. Gorenshtein's Mother-in-Law is emphatically corporeal; her alter ego, the pig's head, has features that "swim in fat." In her self-destroying and self-rejuvenating fleshiness, Gorenshtein's Mother-in-Law carnivalizes the saintly spirituality of the old women of village prose.

The final irony of Gorenshtein's "Last Summer on the Volga" is turned against the narrator himself. The rusalka-beggar Liuba turns out not to be what he first thought. When at the end of the story the narrator unfolds the piece of paper on which "Liuba" has written her address, he finds only the name written over and over, with pictures of the sun, moon, clouds, and crosses. "Liuba" had been playing a part, the part she knew was expected of her: the criminal victim with the heart of gold. The narrator's second "hypostasis of Russia" steps out of her prescribed role, at the same time masking her true identity. Gorenshtein's rusalka remains a cipher, unlike the vicious child abusing rusalka of Belov's *Raising Children According to Dr. Spock*. "Liuba" ultimately rejects the narrator's literary stereotypes.[36]

III. MOTHER RUSSIA DECONSTRUCTED

In a recent article entitled "The Russian Question," the prominent liberal critic Natal'ia Ivanova draws attention to the conservative preoccupation with Russia as a monolithic idea, as opposed to Russia the many-sided historical reality.[37] She argues that hidden underneath the "spirituality" of such writers as Rasputin, who, as we have seen, call for a return to "Mother Russia," to the soil, conceived as the source of identity (Sheveleva is another example), there is a perverse embodiment, in the sense that spiritual qualities are linked to a specific territory and a specific nation. The nation is not defined in terms of coexistence through citizenship, but by the link of blood. The "people" are thought of as a biological entity. According to Ivanova, this concept of the "body politic" minimizes the possibility of heterogeneity. For Ivanova gender politics plays a crucial role in the conservative construction of the so-called "Russian idea." Love for Russia is eroticized in the publicistic writings of the conservative authors, whereas in their fiction romantic love is absent, and young women, and female sexuality in general, are portrayed in extremely negative terms. Ivanova writes "all the emotional content is oriented toward the fecund womb." Sexuality is divorced from maternity. She goes on to say that in the writing of Rasputin and Belov "the more we are called on to love the Motherland, the less sexually mature is the relationship between the heroes to women as women."[38] We have already discussed Rasputin's horror at "modern" Russian women, be they of the late nineteenth or the late twentieth century. In Ivanova's view, this eroticized love for Mother Russia, "insulted and injured by foreign rapists" is tantamount to symbolic incest. According to Ivanova, since the nationalists believe Mother Russia to have perished, their love for her is also equivalent to "necrofilia." Ivanova polemically turns the tables on Rasputin, who sees sexual pathology in modern women. Ivanova "diagnoses" sexual pathology in Rasputin.

IV. FROM MOTHER RUSSIA TO "LIVING IN RUSSIA"[39]

Gorenshtein and Ivanova attack the myth of Mother Russia head on. Both can be said to use the techniques of carnivalization, in the sense that they lend a grotesque embodiment to the exalted spiritual love for Mother Russia touted in nationalist writing. Gorenshtein carnivalizes Mother Russia herself and Ivanova carnivalizes love for Mother Russia. Gorenshtein explicitly links his absurd "hypostases of Russia" with surrealist writing, and Ivanova's claim about conservative incest and necrofilia can be seen in a similar light, as surrealist criticism. The technique of carnivalization figures importantly in the literary works of several prominent Russian women authors, including, for example, Tat'iana Tolstaia and Ludmila Petrushevskaia, both of whom have been translated into English.[40] Helena Goscilo argues that these authors use the female body as a source of "rhetorical devices" that oppose the standard male-authored tropes. According to Goscilo, Petrushevskaia emphasizes "the body as a site of violence" and "hyperbolized ingestion and regurgitation."[41] Goscilo sees Tolstaia's techniques of irony as a way of "descrediting the paradigm of stable home, marriage, motherhood, and domestic cares" — a paradigm that, as we have seen, has taken on a political edge in the works of Russian conservative nationalists.[42]

In contrast to this parodic and surrealist writing, the task of demythologizing Mother Russia is also being accomplished by realist writers who focus on everyday Russian life, and in particular, women writers who foreground aspects of women's experience that previously had been ignored or suppressed in officially sanctioned literature. One aspect of this writing operates on the level of exposé. It is now possible to publish work about the horrendous conditions in Russian hospitals, abortion clinics, prisons, and orphanages. Once forbidden topics are now old hat. In recent women's writing, the theme of the hospital, and of the configuration of the body in illness, both in the hospital and without, is of particular significance.[43]

In the conservative writing that we discussed earlier, women's physicality is either divinized or demonized, depending on whether we are speaking about maternity or sexuality. In Rasputin's "Cherchez la Femme," Russian woman is either likened to Mary, the mother of God, or to an allegorical Goddess of Destruction. It should be observed that the divinization of women's ability to bear children is not unique to conservative or to male writers. As Julia Kristeva has observed, the feminine is consecrated as the maternal in Western culture, and Russian culture, with its emphasis on Mary as the Mother of God, is far from exceptional in this regard.[44] Natal'ia Sukhanova's story "Delos," first published in the liberal journal *The New World (Novyi mir)* in 1988, is a case in point. Sukhanova, it should be noted, made her literary debut with this story. The narrator, a male obstetrician, philosophizes in the following terms about the pregnant woman:

I do not know anything more beautiful than a pregnant woman . . . what ideal — cosmic! — roundness of the belly burdened by new life. There is no miracle that is rounder or more even! The son of God also lay with his head down . . . in the weightlessness of the maternal waters. A world within a world . . . I do not know anything baser than the obligation to help a woman get rid of a baby![45]

The pregnant woman, in this view, has aesthetic, cosmological, and Christian significance. But on the very next page, the same narrator castigates "literature" for its descriptions of maternity as "necessarily sacred." If women are cruel, he reflects, then they are portrayed as "the children of hell." He concludes: "But labor and pregnancy — it's indecent to write about such things — men's passion might be dulled." The narrator's paean to pregnancy is ironically undercut by his own characterization of literary stereotypes.[46]

The difference between Sukhanova and Rasputin is the political agenda. Rasputin links alleged female sexual pathology to female political violence. Furthermore Rasputin metaphorically projects the ills of the Russian nation onto the supposed sexual ills of modern women, who have abandoned their role as mothers and homemakers and therefore suffer from "hysteria." These very same women are made to bear the symbolic blame for the waywardness of the Russian nation, expelled and dispersed from the national body. In Rasputin, woman's body is a site for a contest about national identity. Women's bodies as such and women as individuals are rendered invisible. Women and their bodies are usurped by the Body Politic. Women and their experience are absorbed by this forced symbolic service to the conservative vision of the Russian nation.

In contrast, the women's writing that I am going to discuss thematizes the problem of women as individuals in conflict with the state and the oppressive conditions that it imposes on ordinary life. The hospital is the site where this conflict unfolds. In both stories to be discussed the hospital and the prison are explicitly linked. Iulia Voznesenskaia's *The Female Decameron (Zhenskii dekameron)*, first published in Russian in 1987 in Israel, offers an early example.[47] Voznesenskaia was one of the founders of a feminist religious group, called "Mariia." She spent time in Siberia for her work and was exiled from the former Soviet Union in 1980. Her writing is distinguished from the current generation of women writers in Russia in that it is itself a form of dissident activity. In *The Female Decameron*, ten Soviet women are quarantined in a maternity hospital due to an outbreak of a skin infection. To pass the time, they tell stories — about first love, revenge, jealousy, money, and whether it is better as one of a couple to be left or do the leaving. Among the women characters is a party worker who spouts clichés about the family as the fundamental building block of the state (9). This sort of party slogan is juxtaposed to the list of "forbidden topics" that the other women describe as part of their everyday experience: rape, labor camps ("a camp is a camp, whether it's under the star or the swastika" [34]), crime, drug use, and abortion.

The work of Marina Palei explicitly takes up the connection between the hospital and the prison. Palei, one of the "new" women writers, spent some time as a medical student in Leningrad, but finished her studies at the literary institute instead. She has published in the "liberal" journals, in a 1991 anthology called *The New Amazons*, and has a collection of her own. In the preface to her "Day of the Catkins," Marina Palei writes:

I only wanted to show the exceptional peculiarity of that place of transition called the hospital, where the individual appears in the world and where more often he or she leaves it. The existential nature of this institution, which with terrible simplicity reveals the basis of life and death, corresponds to the nature of the army barracks, the prison cell, the module of a spacecraft, the barracks of a concentration camp. . . . The list could be continued.[48]

The hospital, like the other institutions on Palei's list (with the possible exception of the spaceship), is a place of punitive state control. The Foucauldian overtones of the hospital-prison link have been noted by several authors.[49]

It is significant that in Palei's "The Day of the Catkins" the two patients are women. The first is dying of liver cancer, which has been discovered by the surgery she has just undergone. She is tormented by thirst, but is forbidden to drink for unexplained medical reasons. The orderly, a young woman studying to be a doctor, soaks some cotton in water and places it on the woman's lips. She is embarrassed by the profuse gratitude she receives. When the dying woman asks to be taken out into the fresh air, the surgeon (a man) cruelly replies: "Soon! They'll carry you out!" The woman is not told in any other way of her condition. The supervising nurse rebukes the orderly for wasting time on a dying patient. The second patient, an old woman operated on for a bowel obstruction, now suffers from uncontrollable diarrhea. Ignoring the nurse's growing irritation at her, the orderly tirelessly and kindly cleans her and changes her bedding — in violation of the nurse's order not to "waste linen." Outside, the poplar catkins which covered the street and stuck to everything — the "dry hot sperm of summer" — have been washed away by rain.

In "Day of the Catkins" women's bodies are the place where the state's punitive control reveals itself in starkest terms. In the writing of Rasputin, Sheveleva, and Belov, the intersection between women and the state takes place on a mythological plane. The nation is constructed as feminine, and the supposed moral ills of women correspond to the ills of the nation. The actual conditions of women's lives are ignored. Marina Palei redresses this silence. The Soviet state and the nationalist writers may find it convenient to glorify mythological images of Mother Russia, but those images belie the state's brutality toward individual women's suffering. What makes this brutality more horrifying is that it is an unexamined part of everyday life. To depart from it is a waste of the state's time and resources. Palei restores the physicality of women's bodies in nonmythological, "realist" terms. The women patients' thirst, cold, dizziness, and incontinence all merit simple, humane care. Each of these ills is rendered as part of the physical business of living and dying. Women's bodies are reembodied. In "The Nymph from the Canal" ("Kabiriia s obvodnogo kanala") Palei continues her study of the female body in illness.[50] The issues that she raises in this work go beyond the framework of Mother Russia. The story might be called an anti-bildungsroman of a young woman with the absurd name Raimonda Rybnaia ("Raimonda" was the name of a French revolutionary, "rybnaia" suggests "fish"). Raimonda discovers the pleasures of sex at an early age. Her capacity for pleasure is not diminished even as she suffers one illness after the other and ultimately dies. Using a series of remarkable images and philosophical digressions, Palei interrogates what Laura Mulvey, in her study of the pleasure of narrative cinema, has called the coding of woman as that which is to be looked at.[51] Men are the "controllers of the gaze" and women, the objects on display. I call upon Mulvey's work not only because it helps us understand what Palei is about in this story, but also because Palei explicitly refers to one of America's most reproduced film icons. In one scene, a woman's room is plastered with images from forensic medicine. Different types of bullet holes and strangulations are displayed. In one corner, referred to by the narrator as the "icon corner," there is a prominent photograph of Marilyn Monroe. The representation of woman as an object of beauty and sexual desire is linked to violence. This violence is perpetrated by the "normal" police power of the state, by "Western" commercial culture, and by the now collapsed Soviet order. Palei subversively links the aesthetic gaze with the medical therapeutic gaze.[52] The doctor is likened to a voyeur, and at one point in the story, the presence of the patient at a medical demonstration is compared to a striptease. To cut open the patient, and penetrate into the interior is to render palpable and quantifiable that which ultimately cannot be known. The state's power and the intrusive therapies of medical science are intertwined. The main character is at once a product of this specularization — she cares mainly about her figure and her supply of cosmetics — but at the same time, she escapes from it. Raimonda suffers from a disease in which the body sloughs off its skin and mucous membranes. To render the human individual as only body is to kill, but to deprive the human being of unique embodiment is also to deny the possibility of selfhood.

In "The Sterile Zone" Irina Polianskaia, another recent woman author, also publishing in the collection The New Amazons, takes a different approach to the theme of women and the hospital, emphasizing not the physical, but the existential side of women's experience there. A woman, the first-person narrator of the story, enters the hospital for an operation. She welcomes the chance to escape the constant oppressive presence of others in her daily life, in particular, her neighbor, with whom she must share a kitchen and bathroom, and who appears to the narrator as a tormentor, epitomizing her lack of privacy, and threatening her very existence as an individual. The narrator describes how the hospital stay will provide her with a unique opportunity for "complete solitude, inviolable independence"[53] denied her by the political and economic conditions of life in Russia. The woman's body is to be violated — by the surgeon's knife — but her sense of self is enhanced. In the second part of the story, the narrator imagines another "sterile zone." She pictures her father's life in a labor camp many years earlier, and how the primitive scientific laboratory he might have been able to establish would have provided him with the same sense of well-being that she now experiences in her "sterile zone." Only in the hospital and in the prison can the individual experience him- or herself as an autonomous being.

Polianskaia's story, in one sense, recapitulates a theme familiar to readers of Dostoevsky and Solzhenitsyn. The hospital and the prison provide the opportunity for spiritual renewal. In Dostoevsky's "The Peasant Marei" and in Solzhenitsyn's *Gulag Archipelago*, for example, the first-person narrators describe a quasi-religious conversion and a sense of unity with all of suffering Russia. What distinguishes Polianskaia's story is that the heroine finds a momentary release from the enforced collective existence that she ordinarily leads. Her sense of renewal is not in union with "Russia," but independence from "Russia." Her brief escape into individuality — a value highly criticized by Dostoevsky, Solzhenitsyn, Sheveleva, and Rasputin — comes at the cost of great physical suffering.

Polianskaia's heroine undertakes a heroic quest for solitude and privacy (for which there is no adequate Russian word), and more fundamentally, a sense of autonomous selfhood. Given the distortions of life in Russia, she can only do this from her hospital bed. Polianskaia's heroine wants to be able to define the boundaries of her own "I" without being subject to the unwanted and unpredictable intrusion of others. In contrast, in Belov's *Raising Children According to Doctor Spock*, Tonia is vilified for her desire for independence. The question of autonomy brings us back to problems raised at the beginning of this essay. The revolutionary feminist Aleksandra Kollantai promoted the idea that the pregnant woman "ceases to belong to herself," but belongs instead to the collective. In the Stalinist years, women were represented as the creation of an "all encompassing patriarchal will." Throughout twentieth-century Russian history, the left and the right sought to harness women both physically and symbolically to a mythologized collectivity, whether it be the Socialist Russia or, as in the most recent conservative vision, a newly ingathered Mother Russia. The engendering of the Russian body politic as feminine renders individual women invisible and unrepresentable as such. The reembodying of women's bodies — not in the pornographic images that have drawn so much attention in the press — and the reinvention of the idea of individuality may help to unravel trends that have held sway for so long.

NOTES

I am grateful to Bruce Rosenstock and Anna Kaladiouk for their helpful comments on this chapter.

1. See Joanna Hubbs, "From Saintly Son to Autocratic Father: The Myth of the Ruler" in Hubbs, *Mother Russia: The Femine Myth in Russian Culture* (Bloomington: Indiana University Press, 1988), 167–206.
2. See Nina Perlina, "From the Editors," *Russian Review* 51, no. 2 (April 1992): v and 156 of the same issue, where Perlina discusses the symbolic adoption of the revolutionary heroine Larisa Reisner into a divinized and patriarchal Bolshevik Pantheon.
3. Aleksandra Kollontai, "Revoliutsia byta," reprinted in *Iskusstvo kino* 6 (1991): 108.
4. Cited by Maia Turovskaia, "Zhenshchina i kino," *Iskusstvo kino* 6 (1991): 136.
5. Ibid., 137. For more on gender roles and the culture of Stalinism, see Beth Holmgren, *Women's Works in Stalin's Time: On Lydiia Chukovskaia and Nadezhda Mandelstam* (Bloomington: Indiana University Press, 1993), 5–14.
6. For comparable trends in other parts of the world and other historical time periods, see *Gender and History: Special Issue on Gender, Nationalisms and National Identities* 5, no. 2 (Summer 1993), and in particular Samita Sen's "Motherhood and Mothercraft: Gender and Nationalism in Bengal," 231–43 and Beth Baron, "The Construction of National Honor in Egypt," 244–55. For a comparable discussion of gender and nationalism in the Ukraine, see Solomea Pavlychko, "Between Feminism and Nationalism: New Women's Groups in the Ukraine," in *Perestroika and Soviet Women*, ed. Mary Buckley (Cambridge: Cambridge University Press, 1992), 82–96.
7. Irina Sheveleva, "Zhenskoe i materinskoe . . . ," *Nash sovremennik* 3 (1988): 165–68. Further references to this work will be included parenthetically in the text.
8. Slavenka Drakulic, *How We Survived Communism and Even Laughed* (New York: Harper Perennial, 1991), 107.
9. See Evgenia Semyonovna Ginzburg, *Journey into the Whirlwind* (New York: Harcourt Brace, 1967) and *Within the Whirlwind*, 1979.
10. See for example Larissa Lissyutkina, "Soviet Woman at the Crossroads of Perestroika," in *Gender Politics and PostCommunism: Reflections from Eastern Europe and the Former Soviet Union*, ed. Nanette Funk and Magda Mueller (New York: Routledge, 1993), 274–86.
11. Ksenia Mialo, "V kakom sostoianii nakhoditsia russkaia natsiia," *Nash sovremennik* 3 (1993): 153.
12. Sheveleva, "Zhenskoe i materinskoe," 168.
13. Mikhail Bakhtin, "Appendix II," in Bakthin, *Problems of Dostoevsky's Poetics*,

ed. and trans. Caryl Emerson (Minneapolis: University of Minnesota Press, 1984), 287.

14. For a sympathetic study of village prose, see Kathleen F. Parthe, *Russian Village Prose: The Radiant Past* (Princeton: Princeton University Press, 1992).

15. David Gillespie, "A Paradise Lost? Siberia and Its Writers, 1960 to 1990," in *Between Heaven and Hell: The Myth of Siberia in Russian Culture*, ed. Galya Diment and Yuri Slezkine (New York: St. Martin's, 1993), 253.

16. Valentin Rasputin, "Proshchanie s Materoi," in Poslednii srok, *Proshchanie s Materoi: Povesti i rasskazy* (Moscow: Sovetsii pisatel', 1985), 228.

17. Ibid., 285.

18. Ibid., 237.

19. Barbara Heldt, "Gynoglasnost: writing the feminine," in Buckley, *Perestroika and Soviet Women*, 167.

20. Gillespie, 261.

21. For Plato, see Bruce Rosenstock, "Athena's Cloak: Plato's Critique of the Democratic City in the Republic," forthcoming in *Political Theory*. The triad of fashion, illness, and fat appears in Tolstoy's "Kreutzer Sonata."

22. Cited by Rasputin, "Cherchez la Femme," *Nash sovremennik* 3 (1990): 168.

23. See, for example, Chapter 6, "Feminism and Hysteria: The Daughter's Disease," of Elaine Showalter, *The Female Malady: Women, Madness, and English Culture, 1830–1980* (New York: Penguin Books, 1985), 145–64; and also *In Dora's Case: Freud-Hysteria-Feminism*, ed. Charles Bernheimer and Claire Kahane (New York: Columbia University Press, 1985).

24. Rasputin, "Cherchez la Femme," 169.

25. For more on Dunia, see Nina Pelikan Straus, *Dostoevsky and the Woman Question: Re–Readings at the End of a Century*, forthcoming from St. Martin's Press.

26. "Russofobiia" was first circulated in samizdat' form and was first published in *Nash sovremennik* in 1989.

27. Rasputin, "Cherchez la Femme," 171.

28. Ibid., 171.

29. Vasilii Belov, "Vospitanie po doktoru Spoku" In *Belov, Izbrannye proizvedniia v trekh tomakh*, vol. 2 (Moscow: Sovremennik, 1983), 305.

30. For more on the folklore of the rusalki, see Hubbs, *Mother Russia*, 27–36.

31. Belov, "Vospitanie," 317.

32. "V kakom sostoianii nakhoditsia russkaia natsiia," *Nash sovremennik* 3 (1993): 148.

33. See Natal'ia Ivanova, "Russkii vopros," *Znamia* 1 (1992): 192.

34. For more on Gorenshtein and the controversy surrounding his works, see my "A Curse on Russia: Gorenshtein's Anti–Psalom and the Critics," *Russian Review* 52 (April 1993): 213–27.

35. Fridrikh Gorenshtein, "Poslednee leto na Volge," *Znamia* (January 1992): 35. Further references to this work will be included parenthetically in the text.

36. A literary precedent for some aspects of the narrator's relationship with Liuba

may be found in Dostoevsky, whom the narrator mentions more than once in the story. In *The Idiot* the Swiss peasant girl Marie, seduced and abandoned by her lover, now ill with tuberculosis, is the target of the local children, who throw stones at her. Prince Myshkin becomes her benefactor and teaches the children to love her. In "Last Summer" the local children throw stones at Liuba, but the narrator cannot defend her. She defends him against the oldest one, a teenage bully.

37. One of Ivanova's many essays has recently been translated into English. See Natal'ia Ivanova, "Bakhtin's Concept of the Grotesque and the Art of Petrushevskaia and Tolstaia," in *Fruits of Her Plume: Essays on Contemporary Russian Women's Culture*, ed. Helena Goscilo (Armonk, N.Y.: M. E. Sharpe, 1993), 21–32.

38. Ivanova, "Russkii vopros," 200.

39. I take the phrase from ibid., 204.

40. For translations of Tolstaia, see, for example, *On the Golden Porch*, trans. Antonia W. Bouis (New York: Random House, 1989); for Petrushevkaia, see, for example, "Our Crowd," in Helena Goscilo and Byron Lindsey, eds., *Glasnost: An Anthology of Russian Literature under Gorbachev* (Ann Arbor, Mich.: University of Michigan Press, 1990).

41. Helena Goscilo, "Speaking Bodies: Erotic Zones Rhetorized," in *Fruits of Her Plume*, 140.

42. Helena Goscilo, "Monsters Monomaniacal, Marital, and Medical," in *Sexuality and the Body in Russian Culture*, ed. Jane T. Costlow, Stephanie Sandler, and Judith Vowles (Stanford: Stanford University Press, 1993), 217. For more on the image of the body in recent fiction, see the introduction to this collection.

43. For a study of "hospital prose," see Helena Goscilo, "Women's Wards and Wardens: The Hospital in Contemporary Russian Women's Fiction," *Canadian Woman Studies* 10, no. 4 (Winter 1989): 83–86.

44. Julia Kristeva, "Stabat Mater," in *The Female Body in Western Culture: Contemporary Perspectives*, ed. Susan Robin Suleiman (Cambridge: Harvard University Press, 1986), 99.

45. Natali'ia Sukhanova, "Delos," in *Chistenk'kaia zhizn'* (Moscow: Moladaia gvardiia, 1990), 321.

46. For a discussion that emphasizes Sukhanova's anti-abortion stance, see Heldt, "Gynoglasnost," 468–69.

47. See Iulia Voznesenskaia, *Zhenskii dekameron* (Tel-Aviv: Zerkalo, 1987). All references will be given parenthetically in the text. For a somewhat abridged English translation, see Julia Voznesenskaya, *The Women's Decameron*, trans. W. B. Linton (New York: Quartet Books, 1986).

48. Marina Palei, "Preface" to "Den' topolinogo pukha," in *Novye Amazonki*, ed. S. V. Vasilenko (Moscow: Moskovskii rabochii, 1991), 276. I am grateful to Ol'ga Borovaia for presenting me with this collection.

49. See, for example, Costlow et al., "Introduction" to *Sexuality and the Body*, 32.

50. Marina Palei, "Kabiriia s obvodnogo kanala," *Novyi mir* (March 1991), no. 3: 48–81.

51. See Laura Mulvey, "Visual Pleasure and Narrative Cinema," *Screen* 16, no. 3 (Autumn 1975): 6–18.

52. For more on Palei and the gaze, see Goscilo, "Speaking Bodies," 156–57.

53. Irina Polianskaia, "Chistaia zona," in Vasilenko, *Novye Amazonki*, 32.

Women in Yugoslavia

Vida Penezic

INTRODUCTION

As a woman from the "former Yugoslavia" who now lives in the United States, I am occasionally asked to speak about women in Yugoslavia. The request usually comes in the context of an interest in women of Eastern Europe, and has been, since the fall of the Eastern bloc, asked with an increased frequency. Whenever I am asked to speak about this topic, however, I experience unease which has little to do with the actual situation of women in Yugoslavia, and much more with the context and the assumptions within which this question is posed in American popular discourse. This unease has become so overwhelming that it has effectively blocked all my efforts to address the topic. In this essay, therefore, instead of talking about women in Yugoslavia, I explicate some of the reasons for my uneasiness with the request. This essay does not focus on specific traits and living conditions of women in Yugoslavia, but on some aspects of the context in which questions about specific characteristics of Yugoslavian women (and, more generally, East European women) are asked within American popular discourse. Out of a number of very complex political and scholarly issues that the topic raises I will here focus on three. The first concerns the implied nature of the "new" political and discursive space created out of the former first and second worlds. The second concerns the nature of cultural categories as studiable objects. The third concerns the need to partly rewrite current scholarly (and, perhaps, political) paradigms in order to effectively speak about the world today.

The fall of the Eastern bloc can, among other things, be seen as a potential joining of what used to be two ostensibly different worlds (the first and the second) into a larger and more complex political and discursive space. This opens an interesting question: what is (going to be) the socio-cultural nature of this newly (re)created space? What is this new, "fircond," world going to be like? The answer to this question is at issue whenever I am asked about women in Yugoslavia within the context of the Eastern bloc. And it is the assumptions *about this space* implied in the question that cause my unease. More specifically: (1) Yugoslavia is (re)positioned as an Eastern bloc country; and (2) to Yugoslavia is ascribed the difference and inferiority reserved in American popular discourse for an "other," particularly for an other from the former "evil empire." This indicates a distinctly American definition of the discursive space of the "fircond" world, since this particular positioning of Yugoslavia is an American one: the Eastern bloc frequently saw the country as Western, while by the rest of the world it was sometimes seen as third world, because of its nonaligned politics. In the first part of this essay, I discuss these issues by situating them in the context of two paradigms: cold-war and cultural diversity.

In the second part of the essay, I look at the question about women in Yugoslavia in the context of culturally constructed categories as studiable objects. Contemporary culture scholars tend to see all cultural categories as constructed. Seeing concepts such as Yugoslavian women and the Eastern Bloc as constructed rather than natural or self-evident might mean the "end of [American] innocence" with respect to the cold-war paradigm and the desire for genuine "cross-bloc" communication; it is this loss of belief in the givenness, the clear-cutness, the descriptive accuracy of the East/West Bloc division which might make it possible to realize that negotiating the space of the "fircond" world, theoretically at least, means redefinition of *both* of its constitutive discourses.

In the third part of the essay, I look at the question about women in Yugoslavia in the context of the contemporary multicultural, fractured, and multifaceted — and yet interdependent — world. How do we make sense of this world? It seems that nothing can be said about it, until everything is rewritten. I propose a new kind of cultural and theoretical frame to contemplate it within, the transcultural. I suggest that the transcultural can be conceived of in three ways: (1) as a complex, and/or heterogeneous space in which all other cultural categories are immersed, and out of which they are sometimes molded; (2) as an aspect of everybody's culture, and, potentially, as a culture all its own: a culture of people with complex, transcultural experiences and affiliations; and (3) finally, as a mode of interaction which works well among groups and people aware and accepting of cultural difference but not prepared to let that difference permanently divide them. I conclude by briefly looking at the context in which this essay appears in the American discourse. I see this as an example of the transcultural interaction mode.

I

The Cold War Paradigm and Normal Science. When I first came to Ohio, in 1986, Yugoslavia was not overwhelmingly represented in American popular discourse. Many people I came in contact with had only a vague idea where the country was (some did not even know it was in Europe), and a few thought its capital was Prague (the capital of, then, Czechoslovakia). Some people knew of Tito, Yugoslavia's former "communist" president, and others had heard of Dubrovnik, a tourist city on the Adriatic coast (now in Croatia). As for such well-known people who did, originally, come from Yugoslavia (for example, tennis player Monica Seles or pianist Ivo Pogorelic, as well as some basketball players, film makers and scientists), even when Ohioans had heard of them, they were not, in their minds, always connected with Yugoslavia. An occasional joke about Yugo (the only Yugoslavian car on the American market), most frequently pejorative, was more or less all one could hear on a regular basis (although not even Yugo was always associated with Yugoslavia).

Practically without exception, however, everybody I met in the United States at the time classified Yugoslavia as an East European country (that is, as belonging to the Eastern bloc) and myself as East European. This came as a complete surprise, since this was not how we, in Yugoslavia, saw ourselves. I had expected, rather naively as it turns out, that Yugoslavia would be perceived by others the way it perceived itself. Yugoslavia had not been a member of the Warsaw Pact, and it had been a member of Cominform (an international communist information bureau set up by the USSR) only from 1947 to 1948. In 1948, Yugoslavian ties with the Soviet Union were severed.[1] Since that time, Yugoslavia was precariously balanced between the blocs, and was one of the founding members (with Egypt and India) of the nonaligned movement. The first nonaligned nations' summit conference was held in Belgrade, in 1961.[2] Yugoslavian borders were open to visitors from both blocs, and Yugoslavian citizens easily traveled to both Warsaw Pact and NATO Pact countries. Furthermore, the country was full of Western popular culture and, it seemed to me, more West- than East-bloc-oriented. In fact, when I had traveled to the Soviet Union, many years previously, I had been labeled a "Westerner."

In Bowling Green, Ohio, however, I was considered "East European." With the label went a set of assumptions: closed borders, poverty, political and gender oppression, primitive living conditions, a need for guidance by more developed and more democratic nations. Although, as I said before, many people I met only vaguely knew where the country was located, they took these assumptions for granted. (Since all of the above assumptions were seen to uniformly apply to all "East European" countries, not only was I considered "East European," I was also frequently asked to speak for the whole Eastern bloc.) Although people I met rather hungrily sought information about life in the Eastern bloc, however, they, at the time, rarely expected to hear anything that would contradict the image they had already formed of it. In other words, they never expected to be told that the above assumptions were incorrect, but, rather, they wanted more proof that they were correct. When I did happen to provide information which questioned dominant American views of Eastern Europe, I was, as a rule, disbelieved.

I could list pages of examples, but the following should suffice.

One of my frequent complaints about life in Ohio is that washing machines and/or washing detergents do not do as good a job as the ones "back home." With some extremely rare exceptions, this statement always met with vehement opposition. This opposition ranged from attempts to explain this (to my opponents, obviously wrong) belief by my inability to use the machines correctly, to direct accusations of delusions or lying. In the words of one of my friends: "I find it hard to believe that any domestic appliance in Yugoslavia can be better than an American one."

When, on one occasion, I was trying to impress upon one of my colleagues that Yugoslavia was not a member of the Eastern Bloc, he said: "Are you sure? I heard it on NBC last night." I said that only proved that not everything said on television was true. He gave me an indulgent smile and refused further argument.

On the other hand, my stories about things I disliked in Yugoslavia, such as the absence of satisfactorily clean public bathrooms, or lack of

tolerance in public discourse, were in Ohio met with instant belief. Nobody ever said (yet): "Oh, really? I never thought Yugoslavia would have
dirty bathrooms!"

It might be useful to look at this situation in terms of what Thomas
Kuhn calls "normal science." According to Kuhn, "normal science" means
research within a firmly established paradigm. He defines paradigms as
"some accepted examples of actual scientific practice . . . [which] provide
models from which spring particular traditions of scientific research."[3]
These are taught to us in textbooks, and they "for a time define the
legitimate problems and methods of a research field for succeeding generations of practitioners. . . . The study of paradigms . . . is what mainly
prepares the student for membership in the particular scientific community" (10–11).

According to Kuhn, normal science can be compared to jig-saw puzzle-
solving. The picture is already known, we just have to put the pieces in
the right place. "Perhaps the most striking feature of the normal research
problems [writes Kuhn] . . . is how little they aim to produce major
novelties, conceptual or phenomenal" (35). In other words, normal science does not, by definition, produce radically new knowledge. Rather, it
produces the "steady extension of the scope and precision of scientific
knowledge" (52). When nature violates "the paradigm-induced expectations that govern normal science (52)," when, in other words, a discovery
does not fit the paradigm, it is treated as an anomaly. An anomaly does
not automatically create a paradigm crisis. Scientists are aware that no
paradigm is perfect, that all of them are approximations rather than
accurate descriptions of reality. Anomaly is usually treated as a hint that
the paradigm needs adjustment, not that it should be rejected. In fact,
scientific communities are very resistant to paradigm change. According
to Kuhn, this is good: it ensures that paradigms are not rejected easily, at
the whim of a few impatient scientists.

Let us for the moment assume that, with respect to Eastern Europe,
the cold-war picture of the world can be seen as the dominant American
paradigm. This paradigm saw the Western bloc as the "free world" and
the Eastern bloc as a dark communist world behind the Iron Curtain. It
saw the Western bloc as good and the Eastern as bad, or, more precisely,
it saw the Western bloc as progressive, enlightened, democratic, open to
new ideas and committed to the equality of all people, and the Eastern

bloc as lacking in all these areas. It also saw the Western bloc as affluent, colorful, and full of joy, and the Eastern bloc as gray, oppressive, poor, and joyless. In Kuhnian terms, stories about Eastern Europe can be seen as normal science when they can be easily told within and when they confirm this paradigm; and as anomalies when they cannot be contained or explained within it.

During the cold war this was the paradigm used by American popular culture to present Eastern Europe (particularly the Soviet Union) to American audiences. It was present in popular films, popular books, newspapers, and magazines, as well as in television news shows. This also seems to have been the paradigm used by most people to classify and interpret information from Eastern Europe.

When communism "fell," the Eastern bloc became in America a subject of lively popular and academic interest. Although one might have expected that, with the end of the cold war, the cold-war paradigm would be rejected and supplanted by another one, that is not what happened. The cold-war paradigm persisted well into the "new world order" and still sometimes appears to be considered a valid model for interpretation of and research about Eastern Europe. If we look at the popular media's response to the events in Eastern Europe through a Kuhnian lens, it becomes obvious that reporting and interpreting the events were conducted very much within the cold-war paradigm. No new knowledge was produced, at least not the kind of knowledge that might question the dominant paradigm and prompt a search for another one. Like all normal science, it simply added more pieces to the already existing picture.

The news about the fall of communism was accompanied by feelings of euphoria and triumph. Although, in theory, the fall of communism could have been seen as a creation of an entirely new political and discursive space (more complex, contradictory, and larger), in practice it was seen as confirmation of the cold-war paradigm's validity. Communism lost, and the "Free World" won. The American world and its values were not seen as being in any way threatened or even affected by these changes. If anything, they were even more firmly established. "We" had been right, "they" had been wrong. It seemed to be a common expectation that now "they" would become like "us" and that becoming "like us" is what "they" should naturally desire. Any unwillingness on the part of the former Eastern Bloc to see events in this light was pronounced reactionary or shortsighted. It was often said that Eastern Europeans were not used to democracy since they had no democratic tradition, and that they had to learn how to use their freedom. Any warning that the transition might not go as smoothly as expected was met with impatience, sometimes even anger.

Then came the news of wars, the rise of nationalisms, economic disasters, and so forth. These were again explained within the cold-war paradigm and were blamed on the former communist regimes: the oppression of ethnic and national freedoms was seen to have produced a nationalist overreaction. (Whether or not this was true for the Eastern Bloc, Yugoslavia's situation was not quite that simple. The country had been decentered and federal, with multilingual education, publishing, press, television, and so forth. While this regulated and strictly controlled ethnic tolerance might not have been enough to assuage nationalist hungers, reducing the causes of the war to nationalism only is, in my opinion, overly simplistic.) Communist economies and bad financial politics were seen to have made Eastern European countries unable to compete on the global markets. (Again, while this is probably true, it is also probably true that a full explanation would require looking into who controls the global markets, taking into account that global markets are capitalist, as well as that transition from total state control to a free market economy is hard for and economically detrimental to the people in lower income brackets.) And so on.

Popular fiction followed a similar pattern. Popular characters on television incorporated Bosnia into their past. All those sexy, macho, war correspondents now came from Bosnia, or returned to Bosnia, or had had their lives changed by the war in Bosnia. For example, the American journalist with whom Murphy Brown fell in love in one of the winter 1994 episodes has come from and returns to Bosnia. One made-for-television film in the fall of 1993 featured two journalists (a man and a woman) who had reported from Bosnia — before they met in Paris and fell in love. In these cases, the characters (as well as the war) were simply inserted into the already existing formulaic place: the story followed an older formula and, for most people, the (particular) war mentioned was incidental. Whether the hero or the heroine came from Bosnia or Cambodia was of no consequence; it was the war — or, rather, a war — experience that mattered. In other words, neither popular formulas nor the cold-war picture of the world were questioned.

Because the above is its implied context, the question about women in

Yugoslavia, rather than being a simple question about another place (about which the asker knows very little or nothing, and hence is in a position of a less powerful partner in the exchange), frequently strikes me as already containing a number of assumptions which put the askee in a disadvantaged position and limit the answers in kind. These assumptions usually are — or can be translated into — cold-war assumptions. Yugoslavia is labeled an Eastern Bloc country and as such its women are expected to be oppressed, unaware, unsophisticated, unliberated.

I do not mean to say that people who asked did not want to know "how things really were" but rather that "how things are" is an enormously complicated category, whose appearance and moral inflection are to a large degree determined by the conceptual apparatus used to describe it, or even simply to inquire about it. "[O]ne of the things a scientific community acquires with a paradigm," writes Thomas Kuhn, "is a criterion for choosing problems that, while the paradigm is taken for granted, can be assumed to have solutions. To a great extent these are the only problems that the community will admit as scientific or encourage its members to undertake" (37). In other words, the paradigm within which one inquires will affect both the kind of questions asked and the kind of answers expected and considered scholastically valid and valuable. If one violates these expectations by saying that not only are answers impossible within the paradigm, but the question itself is "wrong," this will, to the believers in the paradigm, appear confusing and unscholarly.

Asked, then, in Bowling Green, Ohio, to speak about women in Yugoslavia, I as a rule had to either position myself as East European, or devote the whole time allotted (usually 20 minutes to an hour) to explaining why this classification should not be taken for granted; that, in other words, Yugoslavia in its own eyes had not been an Eastern Bloc country. When, occasionally, I did exactly this, I most frequently confused rather than enlightened my audience. It is hard to shift an audience's worldview in an hour, so what I had to say appeared incoherent and anomalous. The audience felt they had not quite gotten what they had come for. At other times, I accepted the classification and focused on specific examples of difference between Yugoslavian and American beliefs and life-styles. This, as a rule, went down well because it made the audience feel that their knowledge of the subject had become more precise and better. In short, in the former case they felt they had learned very little, while in the latter they felt they had learned a lot. One could argue, of course, that the situation was exactly the reverse. They had learned nothing in the latter case, and a lot in the former, since increasing the precision of knowledge within an already questionable paradigm is far less useful than questioning the paradigm itself.

Women in Yugoslavia and Cultural Diversity. One might wonder why educated and well-meaning people continue to use an oppressive and politically nonliberal paradigm such as the cold-war one, and I would suggest that, in fact, they do not. Although it appears to be a cold-war question, the question about women in Yugoslavia is also and simultaneously (perhaps primarily) asked within another, politically far more "correct," paradigm, that of cultural diversity.

The cold war and cultural diversity paradigms have very little in common. In fact, they are ideologically opposed to each other. To put it simply: the cultural diversity paradigm is (globally) a reaction to (mostly European) imperialisms which tended to favor homogenization over cultural difference, thus devaluing and erasing cultures which they found in their way. Within the American context, the movement for cultural diversity is a reaction to long-term racist policies which have had a similar effect: non-European (as well as some European) cultures have been devalued and made invisible. Cultural diversity can then be seen as an attempt to restore to these cultures their rightful place in the world and in America, and, by doing that, to reposition the whole imperialist, homogenizing picture of the world which assumed strict hierarchies among cultural and political systems, postulating European, industrial, Christian, science-oriented cultures as an ideal. In short, the cultural diversity paradigm favors a dehomogenized, heterogeneous picture of the world in which all cultures are equally visible and in which they all have equal rights.

The cold-war paradigm's worldview is directly opposite. This paradigm is a result of two imperialisms' (the "First" and the "Second" Blocs') collision in their attempts to control large chunks of the globe. After World War II, the two blocs got locked into a stand-still which lasted for decades. During this time they kept an eye on each other and waged a mass-mediated ideological war. More specifically, this consisted in spying on each other, in competing in everything, from sports over arms invention and production to space research, and in consistently painting the other bloc as an evil, dark other. This process led in America to an image of the other bloc as both alien to "us" and homogeneous within itself. At the same time, "our" bloc was also perceived as homogeneous, precisely because of its striking and constantly emphasized difference from the evil, dark other in opposition to which it was being constructed. In other words, while the cultural diversity paradigm makes difference visible, the cold-war paradigm covers it over — *except* when it comes to the difference between the two blocs.

Although considering a group an other and considering it culturally different are not, theoretically, one and the same thing, they appear to be easily confused, or, at least, easily translated into each other. While the end of the cold war removed in America some of the negative charge from the image of the Eastern Bloc, there remained a residue of (a certain negative) difference. This was an obvious, easy way to make sense of Eastern Europe: while not evil (any more) and not "other" in any negative sense, neither was it the same as "us." At least not yet. After all, it had been communist for quite a long time; it is still in a state of transition. While Eastern Europe might now be acceptable to the American general public, communism most certainly is not; and neither is the Eastern Bloc's communist past. Although there is in America a rising awareness that the former Eastern Bloc countries are culturally very different from one another, these cultural differences are still covered over and/or come second when set in the context of Eastern Europe's communist past. In short, the Eastern Bloc is still considered different from "us" and homogeneous within itself (in a certain vaguely negative way) precisely by virtue of that past.

There is in the cultural diversity paradigm an (implied) element of atonement. The paradigm not only teaches that allowing for cultural differences is good, but also that making these differences visible and considering them valid and valuable is a correction of past injustices. The cold-war paradigm has taught us that Eastern Europe was different in precisely the way which merits this kind of treatment. In other words, Eastern Europe is not (has not been) considered different in a way in which, say, Sweden is different. It was considered different in a way taught to us by the cold-war paradigm. This, in fact, was an othering rather than an acknowledgment of real differences. Consequently, Eastern Europe can now be treated in American discourse as an oppressed and wronged culture. And it is, perhaps, precisely because we still think of it as slightly different (in that vaguely negative sense) that we feel we need to acknowledge it, to give it prominence and visibility.

In the development of any science, the first received paradigm is usually felt to account quite successfully for most of the observations and experiments easily accessible to that science's practitioners. Further development, therefore, ordinarily calls for the construction of elaborate equipment, the development of an esoteric vocabulary and skills, and a refinement of concepts that increasingly lessens their resemblance to their usual common-sense prototypes. That professionalization leads, on the one hand, to an immense restriction of the scientist's vision and to a considerable resistance to paradigm change (Kuhn 64).

It also produces a lot of good, precise information. As it was said before, even the resistance to change is, according to Kuhn, useful. It "guarantees that scientists will not be lightly distracted and that the anomalies that lead to paradigm change will penetrate existing knowledge to the core" (65).

I believe one can easily argue that the cultural diversity paradigm is still at a stage where normal science is quite in order. It is a relatively new paradigm, only entering the stage of professionalization, with a lot of blank spaces yet to be filled. Learning more about, and restoring visibility and legitimacy to, different cultural groups whose difference has been covered over by the previous paradigm is both politically and scholastically useful. Within this paradigm, then, a perfectly justified desire to internationalize and interculturalize the curriculum and campus life has led, at Bowling Green and elsewhere, to an increased inclusion of other cultures/countries into both course syllabi and campus events. As a result (as was said at the beginning of this essay), I had been asked to speak about Yugoslavia even before the country had grabbed the world's attention by disintegrating into the chaos of war. I have been asked to comment on leisure in Yugoslavia, women in Yugoslavia, popular culture in Yugoslavia. In other words, I was given visibility and attention which I most likely would not have enjoyed under other paradigms. Why, then, the unease?

For a number of reasons, most of which have already been noted and analyzed by members of other cultural groups who have gone through similar experiences.

1. At the simplest level, it is a common dilemma: on the one hand, I wanted my difference acknowledged; on the other, however, "difference" often implied an inferiority in the eyes of the asker since to be "non-American" (more particularly, to be East European) was by many taken to automatically mean "worse than American."

2. On a more complex level, speaking "as a Yugoslavian woman" could be seen as feeding a paradigm which my talk was supposed to question. I felt I was not contributing to my audience's better understanding of the world, or, for that matter, to the development of scholarship. Gayatri Spivak (among others) suggests that some representatives of other cultures are token representatives. When an audience wants "to hear an Indian speaking as an Indian, a Third World woman speaking as a Third World woman, [writes Spivak], they cover over the fact of the ignorance that they are allowed to possess, into a kind of homogenization."[4] When I spoke "as a Yugoslavian woman" (particularly when what I said met — or could be interpreted to meet — the audience's expectations) I became a token representative of both my imagined culturally pure and purely different group and an imagined proof of the audience's openness toward difference and toward discourses of the "other."

3. What my encounters with the First and the Second Worlds' ideological spaces also show is Yugoslavia's and my own semiotically unstable place within them. The First World considered me East European, the Second World considered me a Westerner. Although my meaning changed as I entered these ideological spaces, my structural position within them was vaguely similar: I was always identified as being — belonging to — "the other." In both cases, the cultural/discursive spaces entered were more powerful (larger and politically and militarily stronger) than my place of origin (at that time, my country, Yugoslavia), so their reading of me (and by implication of my country) carried, so to speak, far more weight than my own reading of myself (and my country's reading of itself).

The cold war could also, then, be seen as a war for classification of Yugoslavia. If the Eastern Bloc had won, Yugoslavia might have found itself classified as Western, and then, in retaliation (who knows?) been far more firmly united, all difference and decentering erased? Since, however, the West "won," Yugoslavia finds itself in the position assigned to it by that discourse; it finds itself an Eastern European country. In other words, until recently semiotically unstable, Yugoslavia now finds itself fixed as

Eastern Bloc. One could take this to clearly indicate at least one definition of the nature of the "fircond" world: the common space, rather than being negotiated among all participants, is defined in American terms. This indicates the victor's prerogative to impose rules, in this case of discourse: it appears that the victors' definition of the "fircond" world space (which now consists of both, the First *and* the Second Worlds) will apply from now on. Yugoslavia will be fixed as an Eastern Bloc country (which is the way it had been most commonly seen by the American popular discourse, but *not* by other discourses on the global stage).

And I, instead of performing on a common stage — created by the opening up to each other of Western and Eastern Blocs' discourses (perhaps the image of one large room created out of two smaller ones by removal of a wall is a better one?) — am actually appearing on a stage which is controlled by the West. Furthermore, I am expected to assume on that stage an already designated place: to be different (specific to my region and culture, as well as to the political past of that region), but to relate my (different) experiences in the conceptual, linguistic, and stylistic categories offered, understandable, and expected by American audiences. And, by implication, I am also expected to walk through the door opened for me by (and into) the Western discourse, without changing that discourse.

So, when I speak as a Yugoslavian woman within the context of the Eastern Bloc, I also help legitimate the redefinition of Yugoslavia as an Eastern Bloc country. I represent and thereby participate in the American cold-war (re)definition of the "fircond" world, and, by the same token, attest to the international legitimacy, indeed, democratic inflection, of that (re)definition. In other words, by performing normal science within the cultural diversity paradigm I am also performing normal science within the cold-war paradigm.

4. And finally: in all of the above-described situations there is a lack of viable cultural space in which I (and other people like me, people with complex and nonlinear affiliations) can move, act, speak. I find most of the categories offered as vehicles of my visibility and identity to be limiting, oppressive, and stifling. This can partly be explained by historical circumstances: Yugoslavia has been semiotically unstable on the global stage, so any one affiliation or definition of it sounds simplistic and inaccurate; furthermore, since the country does not exist any more, Yugoslavian identity might appear fictional rather than real. In other words,

both in the past and in the present, Yugoslavian identity appears to have been clearly something which is culturally constructed. But this historical explanation does not quite suffice. Today most scholars of culture believe that all cultural identities are constructed in one way or another. We are not dealing here with one constructed, "unauthentic" identity in the world of pure and authentic ones; rather, we are dealing with a world full of complex constructed identities. And it is precisely that world that the above categories do not seem to adequately address.

II

Cultural Categories as Objects of Study. There is an assumption, in the question about women in Yugoslavia, of the difference of Yugoslavian women which precedes any empirical information: it is deduced from the postulated radical difference between the two blocs which, in turn, is a result of the cold war. More specifically, it is assumed: (1) that the two blocs are/were completely ideologically different, and that the acceptance of that difference should be the starting point of any communication; (2) that contacts between the two blocs have been and have to remain external: the blocs can only (or at least primarily) relate to each other as separate entities whose separateness, whose difference, defines/colors every phenomenon within a bloc, as well as every perception of all phenomena from the other bloc; and (3) that, since the two blocs' histories have been very different, there is no common cultural space they can draw on in their attempts to communicate.

Although, on one level, these assumptions appear to be quite obviously true, on another none of them quite holds. (1) The blocs were not as ideologically different as popularly thought: for one, their propaganda techniques against each other were quite similar;[5] then, although there were ideological differences, many of their respective educational canons were similar (great books, great philosophers, great scientific discoveries); finally, they were both part of Euro/Western civilization and subscribed to some of the same cultural and economic goals and ideals: industrialization, urbanization, logocentrism, and so on. (2) The blocs' boundaries (borders) were not impermeable: popular and other cultural products, people, political and financial interests, and such like, constantly seeped through, ensuring the continued presence of the other bloc on each of their soils (for example, rock music and popular movies went East, ballet and Russian literary classics traveled West). (3) This constant seepage, together with other globalizing trends,[6] has worked toward creating (or, rather, maintaining?) a common cultural space which frequently (under the cold-war paradigm) went unrecognized.

In other words, an assumption of across-the-board difference between Eastern and Western blocs may not be accurate; furthermore, this assumed difference may not always be descriptive but rather prescriptive: it postulates a difference between the blocs, and this postulate is then imposed on the actual diversity which exists inside the blocs in such a way that only certain characteristics — those which are different — are considered authentic and scholarly acceptable while others are ignored as unclear, or rather, impure. In short, this process as much produces new differences between blocs as it reflects differences which already do exist. It follows that not only is the identity which I am invited to represent a culturally constructed category (and so is the very position of difference from which I am encouraged to speak), but the label "Yugoslavian women" also implies far more difference from all other, non-Yugoslavian, women and far more internal homogeneity among Yugoslavian women than exists in reality. (Among other things, this might not be good for the project which it seeks to support — namely, openness to cultural difference and a "better," safer, more peaceful world — since it is, in fact, yet another kind of homogenization.)

Cornel West points out that "notions of the 'real Black community' and 'positive' image are value-laden, socially loaded, and ideologically charged."[7] So is the category of women in Yugoslavia. And so are the concepts of the two blocs, American and Soviet, as good and bad, as free and behind the iron curtain. Recognizing this might be comparable to what Stuart Hall calls "the end of [Black] innocence"; the "recognition that 'Black' is essentially a politically and culturally constructed category."[8] Facing the cultural constructedness of categories such as Yugoslavian women and Eastern Bloc, means not only the end of "innocence" which characterized the cold-war paradigm and the desire for cross-bloc communication, but also a realization that the opening up of the "fircond" world, theoretically at least, calls for a redefinition of *both* blocs' discourses; that both labels — "the free world" and the "world behind the iron curtain" — need to be rethought. Only then will all the diverse voices (such as those of different national cultures, various ethnic groups, women, different classes, etc.) during the cold war subsumed under homogenizing bloc labels, fully emerge.

III

The Transcultural. The following question remains: how do we talk to one another and about cultures and identities in the global village of the late twentieth century, after the end of the cold war, and within an awareness of cultural diversity (not only within and across the former blocs, but globally)? Or, in other words: what is the nature of the contemporary cultural world?

While attempting to fully answer this is well beyond the scope of this essay, I would like to tentatively propose some ways of thinking about it.

First, it might be useful to ask this: when we say that we are communicating with one another as groups (or as members of different groups), in what space is that communication occurring? Is there a larger space in which all this is happening? In other words, is there a space which in some ways transcends (by being around them, in-between them, and within them) the individual categories such as Eastern Bloc, Western Bloc, Women in Yugoslavia, and other cultural (identity) labels? If so, what is the nature of this space?

Second, we might problematize the pronoun "we," or, for that matter, the pronoun "I," as loci of clear and separate group identities. While in some extreme situations, such as wars or national and ethnic tensions, a sense that the communicating parties belong to opposing groups may indeed cover over everything else (in other words, national or ethnic identity may be foregrounded), in most cases a splintering of the communication into a number of less focused (and possibly less divisive) fragments will occur. The people involved might be wearing similar clothes, have similar tastes in music and films, or similar family situations and problems. In other words, as an I in a communication process, I am a member of numerous groups (oldest children, nonsmokers, rock fans, scholars, dissidents, liberals, women, etc.) which might intersect with the groups of the person I am communicating with. This both opens potential common space we can use in our relationship and problematizes the clarity and simplicity of our respective affiliations to national or ethnic groups that we come from (as well as, for that matter, to any *one* of the mentioned groups). In other words, our affiliations are more complex, more numerous, and less stable than paradigms such as the cold-war one might suggest.

I believe that this points to a cultural space that we can, for lack of a better word, label "transcultural." This does not mean a transcendence into some kind of a universal and eternal space, beyond history and experience, but, rather, as Mikhail Epstein puts it, "a space in, or among, cultures which is open to all of them .... [which] frees us from any *one* culture."[9]

I will finish this section by proposing three ways to conceive of the transcultural. (1) it can be seen as a complex, and/or heterogeneous space in which all other cultural categories are immersed, and out of which they are sometimes molded; (2) it can be seen as an aspect of everybody's culture, and, potentially, as a culture all its own: a culture of people with across-groups-similar values and beliefs, and/or of people with complex, transcultural experiences and affiliations; (3) and, finally, it can be seen as a mode of interaction which works well among groups and people aware and accepting of cultural difference but not prepared to let that difference permanently divide them.

Transcultural Space. One of the ways of looking at this is to suggest that the cultural mixing, which has characterized our world for centuries, has had the effect of producing an enlarged cultural space above, between, and within all individual categories which participated in its production, and that this space now also precedes all new cultural categories. On one level, this space corresponds to what Mike Featherstone and others call global culture and Marshall McLuhan calls the global village. It can be seen as outlined by, among other things, the Gulf War, the intervention in Somalia, the Salman Rushdie affair, the global expansion of Coca-Cola, McDonald's, and the Japanese car industry, as well as by global feminism, rock music, postcolonial criticism, cultural diversity, international contacts of scholars, and so forth. The transcultural in this sense also consists in transcultural occurrences on the local and micro levels, such as the combinations of cultural signs found in big cities, in individual literary, film, television and other texts, as well as in culturally complex individual subjectivities whose constitutive parts come from a variety of cultures without producing chaos or incoherence.

This results in a complex, multilayered world in which old notions of cultural identity, cultural origin, and cultural authenticity do not apply; in which an agreement on what is true, or good, or real, on what has happened and what needs to happen must inevitably be also a matter of negotiation rather than only the discovery of facts. All "new" cultural developments occur within this space, out of this space they are molded, and it is this space that they must count with.

As a frame for culture scholarship, political action, and (last but not least) everyday life experiences and personal choices, the transcultural opens up space not only for categories such as East European women, Western feminists, African Americans, Greek Americans, men, women, and so on, but for whatever is beyond, between, and around them. Furthermore, it is possible to see that not all (if any) individual cultures today have a separate existence which precedes their appearance on the global stage, but, rather, that they sometimes appear on the stage which is already set and hence must negotiate it in order to affirm their individuality. We should then not only look at how individual cultures differ from each other, but, rather, how they are actually negotiated in the contemporary globalized, multicultural, and diverse world.

In this context, it is interesting to ask: why a "pure" identity seems like a better choice at certain times? For instance: why is it easier today to be heard on the global stage as a person of a "pure" identity than as a person of a complex/mixed one? And why many people today get more pleasure out of constructing/choosing a "pure" identity than a complex one? Why, to some scholars, "pure" identities seem more authentic? I do not mean to suggest that choosing a "pure" identity is an invalid choice, but, rather, that it is as much a construction as any other (that it is neither the natural nor the only possible choice) and that, hence, it should be studied/ perceived as such. (For instance, while reemergence of various nationalisms — seen as the return of the repressed national identities — at first seemed liberating, it soon became oppressive, since they allowed only, or at least favored, pure identities. Where does this leave us in terms of affirmation of difference?)

Transcultural People. In today's world, the transcultural is a part of everybody's experience. Transcultural occurrences and texts are so common that the normal *fin-de-millénium* cultural experience is not culturally and/ or nationally pure, but, rather, transcultural. Most (perhaps all) cultural spaces are transcultural in this sense: they incorporate "foreign" elements (frequently) without perceiving them as foreign. Most of us have been forced to (more or less successfully) negotiate this space. And many of us have, in the process, become transcultural people. We know that our values and tastes do not universally apply; we seek cross-cultural experiences; we are aware of the global space around us. This is in part simply the case because we are humans who today live on Earth. Indeed, it is precisely this awareness (that we are all humans with at least some things in common) that war propagandas attempt to rewrite, or put on hold, during wars.

We can also see the transcultural as a culture of people who share a symbolic/value system even though they do not belong to the same national and/or ethnic group. For example: they make similar fashion choices, listen to similar music, belong to similar social classes, or occupy similar or analogous structural positions within their respective countries. These people share a culture even when they do not always interpret all its products the same way.

And finally, it might also be possible to argue that people with complex, multiple group affiliations who are unable to subsume these under one or two simple identity labels most properly belong in the transcultural space (and share a culture?) even when they have little in common beyond the complexity itself. In other words, what they might have in common is not a specific cultural content but rather a certain kind of awareness of the world because they were forced to (due to their complex affiliations) negotiate the reality in similar ways.

The Transcultural Mode of Interaction. A useful way to think about the transcultural (particularly in relation to what was said above) is to see it as a particular mode of interaction; in other words, not to see it as this or that (permanently fixed?) position or identity, but rather as a way we can best interact in a complex and diverse space such as the transcultural. Let me use this essay as an example.

I have been asked (as an East European woman) to write it. When I suggested to the editor of this volume that I was uncomfortable with that classification and that I would like to focus not on Yugoslavian women but rather on the context of the question, I was allowed, no, *encouraged* to do just that. In other words, even though the initial classification fit the cold-war paradigm, what followed was *not* cold-war normal science. Not only was the discursive space in which this contribution was made more complex than any one of its constitutive parts (Eastern Bloc, Western Bloc, Second World), but the interaction mode used to negotiate it was the transcultural interaction mode. It began as an attempt at cross-bloc communication; this was then identified as not quite satisfactory; we renegotiated, taking the other's position into account; in the process, a space which accommodated both of us was not only identified but further opened up.

Perhaps this was partly possible because the transcultural space already existed around us and because we were transcultural people who could see it.

NOTES

1. *Colliers Encyclopaedia*, Volume 23 (New York: Macmillan Educational Company, 1988), 726.
2. Ibid.
3. Thomas Kuhn, *The Structure of Scientific Revolutions, 2nd ed., Enlarged* (Chicago: The University of Chicago Press, 1970), 10. Further references to the text will be included parenthetically in the text.
4. Cited in Simon During, ed., *The Cultural Studies Reader* (London: Routledge, 1994), 195.
5. For specific examples, please see Michael Real, *Super Media* (Newbury Park: SAGE Publications, 1989), 165–222.
6. Some scholars have proposed that, in order to understand the contemporary cultural condition, one has to accept the complexity of its global nature. Arjun Appadurai, in an essay entitled, "Disjuncture and Difference in the Global Cultural Economy," suggests that "[t]he central problem of today's global interactions is the tension between cultural homogenization and cultural heterogenization." Most media studies, he goes on to say, emphasize homogenization, frequently equating it with either Americanization or "commoditization," or both. However, "[w]hat these arguments fail to consider is that at least as rapidly as forces from various metropolises are brought into new societies they tend to become indigenized in one or other way: this is true of music and housing styles as much as it is true of science and terrorism, spectacles and constitutions." Instead of using the center-periphery model as the framework for studying global disjunctures, Appadurai proposes looking at five dimensions of global cultural flow: (a) "ethnoscapes": the movement of groups and persons (tourism, immigration, refugees, exiles, guest workers, etc.); (b) "mediascapes: . . . distribution of the electronic capabilities to produce and disseminate information . . . and . . . the images of the world created by these media"; (c) "technoscapes": technology that "now moves at high speeds across various

kinds of previously impervious boundaries"; (d) "finanscapes": the movement of global capital; and (e) "ideoscapes: . . . concatenations of images . . . often directly political [which] frequently have to do with the ideologies of states and the counter-ideologies of movements explicitly oriented to capturing state power or a piece of it." In Mike Featherstone, ed., *Global Culture* (London: SAGE Publications, 1991).

7. Cited in During, *The Cultural Studies Reader*, 211.
8. Ibid.
9. Ellen E. Berry, Kent Johnson, Anesa Miller-Pogacar, "Postcommunist Postmodernism: An Interview with Mikhail Epstein," *Common Knowledge* (Winter 1993): 110.

Traditions of Patriotism, Questions of Gender: The Case of Poland

Ewa Hauser

It is impossible without reference to Christ to understand the history of the Polish nation.

— Pope John Paul II

After the unparalleled boldness in political imagination and praxis of the heroic Solidarity era, Poland is now busy re-defining the content of its national identity and restructuring the meaning of gender within it.[1] The postcommunist and post-Solidarity period is marked by competing symbolic politics in which pro-Western liberal forces are opposed by nationalistic factions (divided into Catholic and populist anti-Catholic) and all are confronted by an old communist and a new socialist Left.[2] In political discourse the issue of gender has been continuously in the foreground.

The gains of the Catholic nationalist faction have been considerable. Though by fall 1993 Poland had its first woman prime minister,[3] she had been one of the sponsors of the legislation to ban abortion in parliament.[4] Since September 1990, public schools have been offering religious instruction, and grades for these courses count as much as those for any other subject on the students' transcript. On December 29, 1992, a Law on Radio and Television was passed which provides that public radio and television programs should "serve the development of culture, science and enlightenment with a special emphasis on the Polish intellectual and artistic heritage," demonstrate "respect for the Christian value system taken as the basis for universal principles of ethics," "serve to strengthen the family," and "help to obliterate social pathologies."[5] Polish writers issued an open letter protesting the law as a prelude to and a legal basis for a new institutionalization of censorship. Instead of a vague "return to Europe," a return to a repressive patriarchal "gender regime"[6] is in the making in Poland. Any resistance to this regime is complicated by the very fact of its "native," national legitimation in the form of traditional patriotism heavily infused with Catholic piety and influenced by the Church hierarchy.

To understand the tension between nationalism and gender, one has to bear in mind the traditional ethos of Polish patriotism and particularly its confused relationship to gender as a complex and often internally self-contradictory set of propositions, ideological pronouncements, and beliefs. Analysis of several patriotic texts will bring these into view prefaced with some working definitions of the concepts to be employed. By *gender*, I mean "the way the society organizes people into male and female categories."[7] "Gender regimes," as defined by Connell and elaborated for socialist states by Verdery,[8] are understood as consisting of a gendered division of labor and structure of power (versions of which I will address in this article) and a "structure of cathexis" or the "gender patterning of emotional attachments." The last of these is the subject of my analysis. Sentimental attachment to the nation in the postsocialist state serves as the major (if not the only) legitimation of new patriarchal power relations and the new institutionalization of a gendered division of labor.[9] My analysis will explore the ways gender meanings are produced around the category of national sentiment.

Ernest Gellner defines nationalism as a "political principle which holds that the political and national unit should be congruent."[10] The violation of this political principle is what arouses "nationalist sentiment," a demand for the fulfillment of this principle, the force that compels people to willingly give their lives for the abstract idea of a nation. The nation, in turn, is the objectively existing national culture and the subjective realization of membership in, what Benedict Anderson calls, the "imagined political community" — one that is "imagined as both inherently limited and sovereign" — constituted by that culture.[11]

Typically for writing on nationalism, neither Gellner nor Anderson mentions women within the national culture or imagined community.[12] But Anderson alludes to gender while defining nationalism as closer to "kinship and religion" than to the ideologies of the modern world. He then implicitly equates national and gender identity while discussing the belief that "everyone can, should, will 'have' a nationality, as he or she 'has' a gender," even though the concrete manifestations are irremediably particular, such that, "by definition, 'Greek' nationality is sui generis."[13] It is this unfinished parallel between nationalism and gender that I apply to the particular "patriotic" and antipatriotic Polish texts below. Thus, I perceive gender, like nationalism, not as a fixed or "natural" category but as a subject for negotiation, interpretation, and, in the final analysis, a cultural construction.

Anne McClintock points out that "theories of nationalism have tended to ignore gender as a category constitutive of nationalism itself."[14] A recently published book, *Nationalisms and Sexualities*,[15] pluralizes George Mosse's earlier *Nationalism and Sexuality*,[16] both to acknowledge his pioneering work on these topics and to depart from it in rejecting his underlying assumption that one can speak of a generalized "nationalism" and "sexuality" divorced from their respective relational contexts. The authors propose instead a thesis that there is "no privileged narrative of the nation, no 'nationalism in general.' " If we agree that there is no one abstract meaning to which the essence of nationalism could be reduced, this facilitates examining variant forms of nationalism and asking how one or another of them — whether dominant or resistant — seeks to claim a privileged narrative position. For Poland, we find that the authority of the new power holders' nationalism derives legitimacy from the "natural" order of male domination strengthened by the sacred authority of the religious order. The new power holders are redefining both gender and nationalism, but their definitions are also being challenged; each side is actively engaged in a symbolic struggle of self-redefinition in the aftermath of revolutionary political change.[17]

PADEREWSKI'S BURIAL

The Catholic church[18] in Poland not only influences the writing of laws which enforce "Christian values," it also provides the ritual for state ceremonies such as the May 3 Constitution Day (a national holiday during the Second Republic, forbidden during the communist period, now revived to replace the international communist holiday of May Day). By asserting a symbolic unity between state and Church, the Church takes over all the dominant symbolism. It further enforces an equation between Polish men and Catholic knights and Polish women and the Mother of God. Careful examination of one of these ritual observances, which, on the surface, has nothing to do with women, feminism, or gender, will illustrate the subtle ways in which the ideological program of the Catholic nationalists, which is directed against women's equality, is being implemented and the extent of its (limited) success.

Self-consciously and with all pomp, today's Poland presents itself as a direct continuation of the Second Republic (1918–1939). Thus, at his inauguration, Lech Walesa chose to receive the insignia of presidential power from the Polish President-in-Exile, while General Jaruzelski, the last communist president, was not invited to the ceremony.

The reinterment of Ignacy Jan Paderewski was another ritual performed to enact Poland's reclamation of its national history. Paderewski, a renounced pianist and composer, an international legend who was able to befriend heads of state in the early twentieth century, also represented the most conservative trend within Polish patriotic tradition and has a special significance for many Poles.[19] During the Martial Law, a Solidarity activist in America lamented the fact that there was no contemporary Paderewski — both a celebrity and a charismatic politician-patriot, to succeed in the role of a political exile marshaling support and hope for his country.[20] When Paderewski died in New York in 1941, Poland had been overrun by Hitler, the Polish military was fighting in the Battle of Britain, and America was about to enter the war. Roosevelt, in an unprecedented gesture, decided to have Paderewski's body temporarily interred at Arlington Cemetery until he could be reburied in a free Poland. That time had now come, and President Walesa arranged the second funeral of the great Pole. Held on July 5, 1992, Paderewski's state funeral was broadcast live, nonstop on the national television channel.

In light of popular romantic ideas of patriotic exile, the return to Poland of these remains had the potential to generate much positive patriotic and pro-state sentiment. The close and friendly relationship that Paderewski had enjoyed with the leading politicians of his time created an ideal model for new partnerships between the new Polish state and its representative (President Walesa) and the United States and its leader (President Bush). For this occasion, President Bush stopped in Warsaw (for less than five hours) on his way to Germany and a European summit meeting. The ceremony emphatically equated the two presidencies. The

Catholic Church, which dominated the television coverage, profited from the occasion to narrate the story of Polish nationalism, evoking in words and images all of its dominant traditions. What is remarkable is that the attempt seemed largely ineffectual.

The "crowd" at the ceremony was small and appeared apathetic. The event received little coverage in the Polish press.[21] At no time did any reporter venture to ask a passer-by whether he knew who Paderewski was, or what this meant for him, or what he thought about the funeral. In the absence of any spontaneous response or reaction to the event, the unbelievably boring transmission was reminiscent of the Communist coverage of May Day parades in Warsaw. The Communists, however, used to take great pains to produce some appearance of spontaneous support, and, because of the requirement for spontaneity and live coverage, it was always an opportunity for a certain amount of dissent and subversive humor which kept at least some of the spectators intensely amused and engaged. No such gestures were possible at the funeral because it attracted so little notice.

There can be many explanations as to why such a prominent nationalistic figure was met with so little notice. One is certain that had Paderewski been reburied during the last years of communism, the crowds greeting his coffin would most likely have numbered in the hundreds of thousands — as it would have symbolized an opposition to communism, and pride in national ethos by subjected peoples. Free people seem to be more concerned with their everyday economic pursuits and troubles than engaged in supporting the nationalistic cause.

The new Polish Republic is, in its rituals, more exclusive of women than were the Communists. The only two women shown in the four-hour transmission were Barbara Bush and Danuta Walesa, two wives and mothers. The images of the funeral, the intimate voices of the male narrators, the level and type of discourse employed, and the dominant ex-cathedra voice of the Polish Primate, all created an oppressive atmosphere of rather clumsy masculine grandeur, both patriarchal and unsuccessful in its attempt to impose its authority on the spectators. The current Polish officialdom thus constructs a nationhood identified with Catholicism and determined — like the Party — to efface differences including gender.

As the presidents entered the Cathedral, the regular reporter signed off and two disembodied narrators using a special low voice related — and often read from prepared statements about — the events. "Today's celebration has a special religious and national meaning. These two elements are so intertwined in Polish history that it is not possible to distinguish or separate them. It is remarkable that there are no national symbols that would not also be religious at the same time . . . we are now on the main track of national destiny" the voice says. The orchestra plays Polish and American anthems and the narrator's voice fades. Behind the coffin draped in a Polish flag stand the presidents and a church full of invited guests and national celebrities.

The camera shows the main altar which, for this ceremony, is draped in white and red cloth suspended from the gothic ceiling. The cloth surrounds the female icon of Polish patriotism, the Black Madonna whose maternal presence sanctions these masculine rituals of Polish Catholic nationhood. From the distance one can only see the characteristic Byzantine golden halo over the Madonna and child.

The ceremony begins. The Primate of Poland, Jozef Cardinal Glemp, announces that this is the funeral mass for the peace of the soul of Ignacy Jan Paderewski, and, unlike at ordinary Catholic masses, welcomes President Bush, Walesa, the Papal Envoy and other "guests." The blurring of church and state functions is most obvious to a Catholic spectator. Then, a young priest sings a hymn to Mary which begins, "You are the glory of our nation, blessed most from all women folks . . . and ends "so that God will see that you remain on the highest pedestal, for eternity."

During his homily, Cardinal Glemp finally speaks of the deceased. Significantly, from among the hundreds of Paderewski's ardent patriotic speeches delivered after his concerts in the United States, the Cardinal chooses the one in which he addressed the Polish American Roman Catholic Union convention of physicians in Philadelphia in 1917. He quotes from the speech in which Paderewski remarked that medical doctors are rarely true believers and that they should rely more on faith than on reason alone. He commends those doctors who have not left the Church.[22]

The Cardinal continues with a seemingly unrelated statement defining "freedom" as either the freedom to be with Christ or freedom from Christ and calls on believers to choose the first, as Paderewski did. He states that the choice we make to be with Christ is the choice in and about "our families." In case anyone has still missed the message, the Cardinal spells it out: the "choice" is either to be with Christ and life (against abortion) or against Christ and life (pro-choice). "These are two paths that Europe is taking," and he explicitly cites the Pope who has admonished Poles to take the morally correct path.

Soon after the homily, the voice of the priest-narrator re-iterates the basic message of this ceremony: "One cannot understand the history and destiny of the Polish nation without Christ — this great 1,000 year old community which defines each of us." In these words, which are borrowed almost verbatim from the 1978 definition of Polishness offered by the Pope to his countrymen during a speech in Victory Square in Warsaw, the Church, through the prepared words of its spokesman, is asserting both the privileged position of Polish nationalism, claiming it for the religious political tradition in which religion gives depth to politics and in which the position of women is clearly defined and delimited. One of the clearest "religious" messages of Paderewski's funeral is the denial of "choice" for women. This is, according to the Church, the path "with Christ and life" that Poland must take.

THE POLISH MOTHER ETHOS

To better understand the symbolism of the Church's antifeminist message, inherent in its sponsorship of Christian values within the tradition of conservative Polish nationalism, it is necessary to examine more closely the ethos of the "Polish Mother" and the way it has been recently employed. The ethos of the Polish Mother was a romantic creation.[23] Let us look closer at the actual poem which originated its many artistic and discursive renditions.

The Polish national bard, Adam Mickiewicz (1798–1855), codified not one but two models of womanhood in poetic texts which have since become canonical for Polish patriots. The tradition he originated consists of a Romantic elaboration of the numerous political disasters that have befallen Poland since the end of the eighteenth century, especially the defeat of the 1831 November Insurrection against Russian political domination. Two of his poems — "To a Polish Mother" and "Emilia Plater" — bear specific relevance to gender differences within national identity. Although they present two strikingly different images of women (mother of hero-martyrs or a hero-martyr herself), in both poems Mickiewicz defines women's place in society by contrasting, in a way that seems natural, womanhood and agency.

"To a Polish Mother"[24]

O Polish mother, if the radiant eyes
   of genius kindle in thy darling's face
O Polish mother, ill must be his part!
   Before the Mother of Our Sorrows kneel,
Gaze on the sword that cleaves her living heart —
   Such is the craven blow thy breast shall feel!

Though peoples, powers, and schisms a truce declare,
   And though the whole wide world in peace may bloom,
In battle — without glory — must he share;
   In martyrdom — with an eternal tomb.[25]
. . . .
A child in Nazareth, our Savior mild
   Fondled the cross whereon he saved mankind:
O Polish mother, I would have thy child
   Thus early learn what playthings he will find.

His young arms loaded with chains, his body frail
   Full soon have harnessed to a barrow, so
Before the headsman's axe he shall not pale,
   Nor at the swinging halter crimson grow.

This poem, the most somber that Mickiewicz wrote, concentrates on the nation's tragic fate. Written as "an appeal to an unspecified mother of a Polish freedom fighter,"[26] it depicts her in terms of her passive emotional attachment to her son. Because of *his* fate, her fate is comparable to that of the Heavenly Mother. The son is implicitly compared to Christ. Not only did the Polish Mother not become a part of any patriotic action, she does not even take an active part in her son's life by warning him against the dangers of politics. All she can do is to accustom him to his inevitable fate. Whatever the concept of motherhood means for feminists in the West,[27] this "Polish Mother" serves to support a religio-nationalistic patriarchy. Though this model of motherhood is the laughing stock of Western liberals as well as of the political Left in Poland, it remains a potent political symbol and a model for somber reinterpretations of modern Polish history within the patriotic tradition.

Janusz Zaorski's film *Mother of Kings* was one of the most influential films of the 1980s. The heroine is a simple, illiterate, Polish mother. The movie begins with her husband's death under the wheels of a streetcar as she clutches her pregnant belly. She raises three sons (three "kings") despite great economic and political adversity. She has a platonic male friend (not unlike the Holy Family) who, to add local color, is an alcoholic. During the war, she and her friend kill a German soldier who wanders into her apartment suspecting that one of the guests is a Jew. Her favorite son is a hero of the Polish underground, who is arrested and miraculously survives not only Gestapo tortures but Auschwitz. After the war he returns and becomes a Communist. He then is a victim of the Stalinist purges and is tortured by the Communists as he was by the Germans. He does not survive the Communists who are represented as being more brutal than the Nazis. The mother, basically apolitical, honest, hard-working, and Catholic, especially during the Communists' antireligious campaign, sacrifices her entire joyless life to the service of her sons and, through them, to her nation.

The tradition of the martyred Polish mother and her doomed sons is alive in contemporary Polish cinema. The film, like the poem "To a Polish Mother," is not about her, but rather about her sons. Both Polish mothers, the nineteenth-century one and the twentieth-century film-rendition of the same image, were created by men in times when there was no independent Polish state. Both evoked the defensive, heroic patriotism so characteristic of nationalism under siege. For many Poles this film resonates with popular myths about national martyrdom and resilience, and the special role of women in supporting both.

The dominant image of women on Polish national television continues to evoke the Mother of God, the long-suffering producer of Polish martyrs. It is her image that Lech Walesa carries on his lapel and proudly displays to the cameras. During the particularly nasty presidential campaign of 1990, he ridiculed one of his opponents, an emigré married to a Peruvian "Indian" woman, by challenging him to compare Mrs. Walesa, who has borne six children, to the other woman, and decide which was best to fit the role of "Matka Polka" or the "Polish mother." In so doing, he combined the traditions of Polish patriarchy and xenophobia to deliver a potent political blow.

VIRGIN-HERO EMILIA PLATER

Mickiewicz also wrote a strikingly different gender-defining poem, a part of the Polish school curriculum for the fifth grade even today.

"The Death of a Colonel"

In the depth of an ancient forest, a contingent of soldiers
stopped by the hut of a forest ranger
At the door, the colonel's guard is watching,
Inside in a tiny room, their colonel is dying.
Crowds of peasants came to inquire,
A leader of great power and fame he must have been
To raise so much sympathy from the simple folk,
Tears and well wishes.

He ordered his faithful horse to be saddled,
He wanted to see it before death comes
And ordered it to be led into the room
He asked for his uniform, his sword and belt, a rifle and ammunition.
Old warrior — he wants like Czarnecki
Dying — to bid his armors farewell.
Then they led out the horse,
And a priest came in with the last rights
And the soldiers paled with sorrow
While the peasants kneeled outside the threshold.
Even veterans who served with Kosciuszko,
Having spilled so much of their and other's blood
without a tear, now cried
And repeated the prayers after the priest.
In the morning dawn, the church bells rang;
No soldiers were left about the hut,
For the Muscovite was already in the vicinity —
The folk came in to see the body of the knight

On a shepherd's cot he is laid out —
In his hand a cross, by his head a saddle and belt,
By his side, a sword and a rifle.
But this warrior though in a soldier's attire,
What a beautiful, maiden's face had he?
What breasts? — Ah, this was a maiden,
Lithuanian born, a maiden-hero,
The leader of the uprising — Emilia Plater.

Mickiewicz had been fascinated with "patriotic, heroic women," with
women bearing arms; in several of his early, romantic ballads, and narrative poems he re-tells or perhaps sometimes re-invents an active role for
women in the Polish nationalistic ethos. In this warrior's tale, the woman
who took on male attributes becomes a military hero herself and amazes

the "simple folk" with the postmortem revelation of her sex. Significantly, in this poem, there is no image of Mary: only the priest administering last rights to a warrior and the cross that is placed in the warrior's hand. The woman, taking up arms, is treated here with all military honors and complete disregard for her sex. The only possible exception is that as a charismatic woman-leader of men, the love she inspires may be especially sentimental. A woman impersonating an officer and a woman-hero is depicted as an exception which is treated as a man would have been treated. In order for her to gain recognition as a public figure she had to abandon her gender and become culturally male.

Though the poem was learned by heart by all schoolchildren (it was a part of the core curriculum throughout the Communist period) there are no close artistic renditions of this theme as Mother of Kings is for the "Polish Mother" theme. The story of Emilia Plater has been retold in a fifth grade textbook.[28] The text of the poem is immediately followed by a short prose reading of her "real life."[29] From this story, the 11-year-old pupils learn that Emilia Plater from early childhood had been attracted to boys' play. Her father abandoned her and her mother and she grew up playing with her male cousins. She learned how to fight and did very well in fencing. Her room was adorned with reproductions of portraits of Jeanne d'Arc, Tadeusz Kosciuszko, and Prince Jozef Poniatowski (both recent military heroes) and a copy made by herself of a woman hero, a seventeenth-century defender of the fortress in Trembowla, Anna Dorota Chrzanowska.

Upon learning about an insurrection against the Russian domination, she cut her hair, got an insurgent's uniform, and — together with her friend Maria Proszynska — set off to gather a batallion in her native Lithuanian province to attack the Russian occupants. When during one of their first direct combats her companion was wounded, another woman, Maria Raszanowicz, took her place at Emilia's side. Raszanowicz remained at Plater's side until the latter's death following the defeat of the uprising. The women's comradeship in arms has a suggestion of lesbianism for the Western reader; in Poland it has been read asexually and, if anything, lends more propriety to the anomalous gender situation in which Emilia was found. The fact that her foreign-sounding name is never mentioned is also significant. The controversy over Mickiewicz's own Jewish origins as well as those of the Plater family cannot be developed here. Only the fact that the undisputed heroine's possibly "foreign" origin is not mentioned in "real life" testifies to the inclusiveness of the romantic canon of Polish patriotism.

These two poems have long been memorized by all Polish school-children. The poem "Emilia Plater" was especially propagated in the school curriculum during the Communist period despite the anti-Russian content. Since the collapse of communism and the onset of the family-oriented Catholic nationalist campaign, its imagery is largely absent from public discourse, which has been taken over by the Polish Mother ethos.

Bozena Choluj,[30] who significantly ignores the existence of the other myth of a cross-dressing woman-hero (as it is absent from the post-Communist nationalist discourse), explains instead that, in today's Poland the equation of Heavenly and Polish Mother continues as a model of double service for women to follow. This double service entails service to her family and, through the family, to Poland. Fulfilling this double service guarantees the woman a "double satisfaction" which she can obtain within the "domestic" sphere to which the Heavenly Servant-Mother of God destined her. Only through this service can a Polish woman attain an equivalent, though subordinate rank with the Polish male patriot. The Polish woman becomes the model of female patriotism though her role as a mother and by a systematic denial of her sexuality.

PATRIOTIC EXILE OR ESCAPE

The canon of Polish patriotism created by Mickiewicz not only defined ideal roles for generations of women as Polish Mothers but also elaborated the gendered history of Poland and outlined the meaning of the Polish patriotic diaspora in the "gospel of the Polish emigré," a small booklet called *Books of the Polish Nation and the Polish Pilgrimage.* The Polish nation (*narod*) and personified Poland (*Polska*) were both conceived as holy. Because the nation was a democracy (of the nobles) and somehow free from sin (like the Virgin), it became a threat to the increasingly evil and tyrannical neighboring states. So the evil rulers of the neighboring states decided to murder both Poland and Freedom. The satanic trinity of Russia, Prussia, and Austria, with France playing the role of Pilate, completed its conspiracy: the Polish nation, like Christ, was crucified, but:

The Polish nation did not die: its body lies in the grave, but its soul has descended from the earth, that is, the public life, to the abyss, that is, to the domestic life of nations. . . . But on the third day the soul shall return to the body and the nation shall rise and free all the peoples of Europe from slavery.[31]

Denied a public sphere, the Polish nation retreated to domesticity. It was in the "abyss" of domesticity that Poland appears feminized, and assumed the female body form. Artistic renditions of the imagery of Poland (by Artur Grottger and others) were female throughout the nineteenth century. By implication, it is from this feminine form that Poland must be liberated or resurrected into a full masculine public life.

THE ANTIPATRIOTIC TRADITION

Witold Gombrowicz (1900–1967), a modern Polish emigré writer, outlined with irony in his literary diary the creation of the national ethos:

Because we had lost our independence and were weak, he [Mickiewicz] decorated our weakness with plumes of Romanticism, he turned Poland into the Christ of nations, he opposed our Christian virtue to the lawlessness of the partitioners and sang the praises of our beauteous landscapes.[32]

Elsewhere in his diary he directs his wit against himself as well as the Polish national tradition:

In a way, I feel like Moses. Yes, this is an amusing characteristic of my nature: to exaggerate on my own behalf. . . . Ha, ha, why, you ask, do I feel like Moses? A hundred years ago, a Lithuanian poet forged the shape of the Polish spirit and today I, like Moses, am leading the Poles out of the slavery of that form. I am leading the Pole out of himself.[33]

Gombrowicz, the "New Moses" of Polish literature, has now become a part of the Polish canon mainly because he was an emigré whom the Communist critics hated and the censors banned, though he spoke more against the canons of traditional Catholic morality than of communism. His ridiculing as absurd the patriotic proposition that an individual should feel compelled to sacrifice his life for the idea of the fatherland is now repeated especially within elite circles. It is characteristic that his departure from the compulsions of the nationalistic tradition was also expressed in terms of gender, generational, and sexual difference.

Gombrowicz wrote the ultimate antinationalistic novel, *Trans-Atlantic*, during World War II, while himself choosing an Argentine exile from the European continent. Rebelling against the "bad poetry" by Mickiewicz that styled Poland — for Poles and for the West — as the eternal victim, he felt "somewhat responsible" for this fateful "Polish legend," writing *Trans-Atlantic* as an attempt to rectify the false and tainted relationship that the 'Polish' nation and its legend had with the West.[34] He intended it as the greatest provocation and compared it to "laughter at a funeral," when a Requiem mass was expected. His "program" began with an "unceremonious treatment of the sacrosanct Polish tradition." The novel is a parody of Adam Mickiewicz's national verse epic, *Pan Tadeusz*, written in exile as an assertion of the Polish spirit and inspired by the poet's nostalgia. Gombrowicz too wrote *Trans-Atlantic* in exile, but instead of verse, it is in a grotesque, archaic Baroque prose. Instead of depicting the heroic, sentimentally beautiful and fulfilling past, it presents "sublimation in reverse." There are strikingly similar details: the hunting scene — but without hares; a duel — but with empty pistols; and, there is a polonaise — without Poland.

Gombrowicz summarized the novel's "plot" (adding: "for me plots are not very important, they are only a pretext") in his *A Kind of Testament*:

I, Gombrowicz, make the aquaintance of a *puto* (a Queer) who is in love with a young Pole, and circumstances make me arbiter of the situation: I can throw the young man into the queer's arms or make him stay with his father, a very honorable, dignified and old-fashioned Polish major.

To throw him into the *puto*'s arms is to deliver him up to vice, to set him on roads which lead nowhere, into the troubled waters of the abnormal, of limitless liberty, of an uncontrollable future.

To wrench him away from the queer and make him return to his father is to keep him within the confines of the honest Polish tradition.

What should I choose? Fidelity to the past ... or the freedom to create oneself as one will? Shut him into his atavistic form ... or open the cage, let him fly away and do what he likes! Let him create himself! In the novel the dilemma leads up to a general burst of laughter, which sweeps away the dilemma.[35]

It is the author's most public statement about his attitude toward and understanding of the national traditions of patriotism and the fatherland in which the liberation from this tradition is represented in terms of a struggle between the "atavistic form" of the "honest" (heterosexual) Polish tradition and the "freedom to create oneself" in a different (homosexual) engagement.

It is in this novel that the narrator as well as the young object of desire repeatedly ask the question, "Why should there be a 'fatherland,' why not a 'son-land?' " And as for the "martyred Poland": surely no Polish writer ever dared to bid farewell to his homeland as Gombrowicz did in this Baroque flight:

Drift, drift towards your country! Your holy and accursed country! Drift towards that Obscure Monstrous-Saint who has been dying for centuries but cannot give up! Drift towards this holy crank, cursed by nature, for ever being born, newborn for ever. Drift, drift, so that it will neither let you live nor die, and will keep you suspended for ever between Being and Not-Being! Drift towards your Raving Lunatic . . . so that its lunacy can torture you, your wife and your children, so that it can condemn and assassinate you in its agony, by his agony![36]

When we first saw the book, in a Warsaw dormitory, a copy smuggled in from Paris, we staged a group reading and it was this passage that made the biggest impression on us, members of the postwar generation and all of us locked forever into the "Polish tradition." It was the evocation of a stifling oppression, of neither death nor life, that seemed so realistic in his rendition of the Polish fate. We felt that even if, by some miracle, the whole absurdity of the Communist regime would disappear, we would still be left with this "tradition" which would continue to condemn and assassinate us with and by its own agony. But at the time, I missed the fuller force of Gombrowicz's subversion of this tradition. Though confronted with the text, reading it with great attention, we still did not see that one of the problems of "our" tradition had to do with the "seemingly natural" compulsion of love and sacrifice for Poland, embedded in the language and iconography of an exclusively respectable heterosexual love. We knew that it was this "tradition" and this respectability that was keeping our spirit down but we were still unable to leap from the rejection of patriotic clichés to the acceptance of other possibilities.

POST-COMMUNIST AND POST-SOLIDARITY POLITICAL CABARET

The Communist period introduced a distortion to the patriotic – antipatriotic dialogue in the Polish nationalistic debate. At first, it took an antinationalist stand which was complemented with a proclamation of gender equality. The latter was expressed by the proverbial image of a woman on a tractor as well as a woman-soldier. Imposed from abroad and accompanied with very clear signs of another Russian (Soviet) national oppression of Poles, this image had no chance for acceptance within traditional Polish society. In today's Poland, the interstices of nationalism and the subjugation of women have been explored and staged, rather, through satirical political theatre. This takes several forms — on stage, in spontaneous, amateur street performances,[37] and mediated through the camera and projected on the screen. In these popular performances, multifaceted Polish nationalism, embedded in the gender language and iconography of official culture, is now under attack. It is this dialogue between nationalistic ritual oratory (which, by definition, precludes any spontaneous response) on the one hand, and the staged travesty of it, on the other, that allows for a certain level of acceptance of nationalistic-religious ceremony and for reinforcing popular resistance to the imposed sanctity of national ritual.

It appears that the traditional nationalistic signifiers are becoming meaningless and through their ridicule the nation may finally be leaving them behind. Their meaninglessness originates in the current attempt by the ideologues of the Catholic church and their conservative allies in politics to formulate a new Polish patriotism, reclaiming the heritage of the dominant traditions, through a nationalism that clearly denies the agency of women. But although this reformulated nationalism has free access to cameras and loudspeakers, it seems to lack an audience. Instead, this would-be popular nationalist ideology finds itself engaged in an unwilling tango with the leftist and antinationalistic insurgency, an insurgency that attempts, at last, to complete Gombrowicz's injunction to "take the Pole out of himself" — or herself — the new satirists seem to add.

In Poland, one unquestionable advantage attending the end of Communist rule has been the considerable freedom of expression that now exists. (Let us hope that the Law on Radio and Television, with its provisions on Christian Values, will not be implemented.) Even state-run television, along with broadcasts of official rituals like the one just described, continues broadcasting also marvelous parodies of such ceremonies. The Party, in its search for legitimacy, also permitted certain forms of political satire, but the object of satire today has shifted from the "reds" to the "blacks," from the Communists to the clerics.

Today, Polish satire can finally afford to assume the antinationalistic tradition of Grombrowicz and to target the sacred Polish nationalist tradition itself. In the past, because the Party would have welcomed such attacks, satirists rarely parodied this tradition and never did so in any substantial way. At that time, the preferred targets, of course, were the

Russians, the absurdities of Soviet rule, and the "geo-political situation"[38] of Poland. One of the most watched programs on Polish television today[39] is a monthly prime-time event: the satirical political cabaret of Olga Lipinska's theatre.[40] Her sophisticated one-hour-long uninterrupted performances are based on a shared knowledge of the canon of Polish national literature and theatre. Parts of nationalistic songs (such as "To a Polish Mother"), allusions to recent and historical events, restaging of national dramas (Mickiewicz's, Krasinski's, Wyspianski's, etc.) all create a new antinationalist tradition. Lipinska's theatre targets the Catholic clergy,[41] though not the faith itself; the cabaret combines parody and ridicule with occasional gestures more serious in tone.

Thus, one of her most controversial pieces was a musical new prayer to God — performed by one of the actresses dressed in a black dress. The woman asserts her faith in Him, while complaining about and rejecting the viciousness of the treatment she receives from "His bureaucrats," the Church priests and hierarchy. Lipinska was almost put off the air because of this song. Her staging adapts the Polish tradition that represents a suffering woman's endurance of injustice as a criticism of the state. By doing so, she intertwines and implicates the abuses of the old Communist authorities and bureaucracy with the newly empowered oppressive hierarchy of the Church and its officers, thereby exposing and subverting their attempts to enforce submission to their icons and themselves as the sole legitimate representatives of the nation. Lipinska costumes her actors as the clichéd icons of the tragic Polish past and has them perform absurd and funny parodies of national dramas and national dances (polonaise, mazurkas, etc.). The targets of her satires are the new rulers, who are often represented as new faces in old places; the much-touted liberation of Poland is described as this season's new fashion color, black will be worn instead of red, as the officers of the Church replace Party officials as abusers of authority.

Overall, the political message is leftist: while the actors sing that "Of course capitalism must be," one actor pleads from the wings for "exploitation with a human face," an obvious parody of the 1960s reform Communists who called for "socialism with a human face." The songs often portray unemployment among women (textile workers in Lodz as well as workers in heavy industry factories). It is the voices of women workers who bitterly denounce the injustice of having fought for liberation and now having to pay most of the costs of the change while con-men and former functionaries get rich. In one of her programs, a revolutionary song from the Stalinist era was sung with bitter self-irony as the words call not only for slowing down privatization but also for "taking over the factories."

The women who play leading roles are interchangeably dressed in the national costumes, in the garb of workers, or in the Western cabaret tradition of provocative sexuality with, for example, topless short dresses veiled in red. In all her programs there are direct attacks on the Church's anti-abortion campaign: that it is the main issue before the parliament is ridiculed as is the advanced median age of the almost exclusively male Senate. There are frequent sketches and jokes about poor peasant women wondering where the money will come from to feed all the children that "they" (the clergy) are now "making" them bear. In one sketch, the part of the woman is played by a man dressed as a peasant's wife and the mother of a grown son.

The language of direct and threatening songs, such as the one I translate below, continues to be embedded in the sexual language of nationalistic romance. But this time Poland appears as a beautiful and aristocratic woman who is dangerous, while the "nation" itself figures as masculine and threatened. This song is presented by the actor in the troop who always plays the "boss" costumed in the coat of an eighteenth-century gentry-man and in a wig that makes him look remarkably like well-known pictures of Paderewski, addresses President Walesa, the most prominent nationalist spokesman. Walesa's romance with Poland is portrayed as highly romantic: she was devoted to him and he embodied a symbol of a great cause for her. But that was prior to their holy matrimony, after which the sublime romance becomes tawdry farce. Walesa is depicted as an unfortunate suitor who has married a difficult woman who is above him. The church wedding is to blame for this romance going sour. The whimsical lady, true to her class, humiliates her husband the way she would not dare treat her lover. She will also call upon him to keep the promises he made her and may lead a rebellion of the *narod* (nation), angry and drunk — with wedding booze — against her master. The upper-class bride is easily identified as the intelligentsia or Poland (both of the gentry ethos). The singer's tone menaces Walesa as he describes the anger of the "bride" and the fury that threatens to finish Walesa unless he takes special, traditionally masculine, measures to curtail this rebellion.

To take a bride not from your own sphere
is an act of courage or a foolhardiness . . .
She will remind you of your plebeian origin,
show you her tin ring with her crest of arms . . .

Let's stop the belated complaints —
you brought this upon yourself,
You had her love, respect, devotion,
She was ready to lie at your feet,
You were a symbol of a great cause for her
Before the holy sacrament united you two.

And now, she will blame you for her own failures,
Doubt the existence of any of your virtues,
Hold up to you your pre-nuptial promises,
and, lets face it, you gave her a bunch of those.

The nation, drunk from the wedding booze,
Wakes up hung over and has mad eyes;
You've promised 100 million per capita,
Better deliver it before the nation destroys you.

What has happened cannot be undone,
And, one has to admit, you have two bad choices:
Either to take up your bride on a short leash, or
Receive her punches in humility.
    (my translation of fragments of the song — EH)

The complex overdeterminations and deflations of the codes of gender and state politics in this piece leave little in the romantic traditions of Polish nationalism that has not been evoked or subverted. The first stanza alludes to the cross-class alliance between Walesa, a worker, and the upper-class ethos of the intelligentsia or Poland. She behaves as a whimsical princess-bride of a commoner who will remind him of his humble origin by pointing to her crest of arms (even if it were made out of tin — an allusion to the impoverished economic state of the Polish upper classes). The female Poland is here not a mother of martyrs, a virgin-hero, or any sort of victim. She is a powerful agent who is a menacing (though unequal) partner of her brute but impotent husband. It is the sanctification of their union that had caused the problem in this alliance in the first place. Had they consummated their romance without benefit of the holy sacrament, the union might have been a happy one. The obvious allusion to Walesa's ascendance to the Presidency, which cost him his following among the intelligentsia and the masses, is the downfall of the union.

Such popular cabaret suggests significant progress toward freeing the national form from the national cage. As for the author of *Trans-Atlantic*, the point is not to cease being Polish but to allow for an alteration in the terms by which that identity is conceived. As Gombrowicz wrote:

> Some of my compatriots regard me as an exceptionally Polish author — and I may well be both very anti-Polish and very Polish — or perhaps Polish because anti-Polish; because the Pole comes to life in me spontaneously, freely, to the extent in which he becomes stronger then I. . . .
> I wouldn't be at all surprised if the black humor of *Trans-Atlantic* were an almost involuntary expression of Polish pride and liberty.[42]

The major tradition in Polish nationalism views itself as the nationalism of an oppressed nation, without a political state but with a strong aspiration for one. As such, this tradition developed a space for women in the ranks of the warriors for the national cause. In the heroic phase of the national movement, women, as well as other minorities (such as assimilated Jews) were welcomed into the ranks of the nation and the role of women was not limited to producing warriors but instead included a part in the fight. With the transformation from aspiring and defensive nationalism to the celebration of independence, the structural position of minorities and women changed dramatically. It is this phase of nationalism — with unrestricted freedom and among a cacophony of contending voices — that the patriarchal hierarchy once again is attempting to dominate the stage and to direct the staging of the national drama.

The "political community" is now being defined in a rigid and exclusive manner by the pragmatic nationalists of the Christian National Democratic tradition, mobilizing and manipulating images from all the "patriotic" traditions of Poland's past as long as they do not contradict the necessity to keep women in their rightful place. Against this model a new political community is beginning to imagine itself in opposition to the stifling air around the national icons. In this antinationalistic insurgency, women are both well represented and crucial to its construction. Just as Gombrowicz saw himself as a Moses leading the human (male) Pole out of the confines of Mickiewicz's male patriotic ethos, getting the Pole out of the Pole, so it is the female-centered satire of Olga Lipinska's theatre that is aiming to liberate a sexual Polish woman out of her familial self, the Polish Mother, into which the same poet had cast her.

The age of television is just coming to Poland. The official boredom of the Communist vision of the nation has been supplemented by the tedium of the televised spectacles of the new conservatives. The Polish public is as indifferent to these new rites as they were to the May Day parades of the previous regime. What seems most alive on Polish television are the popular satirical cabarets, like Olga Lipinska, and the avant-garde daring of Gombrowicz's revived plays. Both speak a widely understood language of the absurd and both refuse to engage in the narcissistic adoration of Poland's wounded history. Czeslaw Milosz once stated that martial law had a disastrous effect on Polish literature, not because of the repressions and strict censorship but because it forced Polish writers (again) into untenable positions of holiness. It had a similar effect on the cinema (see *Mother of Kings*) and on general popular culture. In Gombrowicz's words, it forced the Pole back into his rigid form. The advent of international electronic culture, together with and through local political satire and theatre, may finally contribute to a liberation of Poles from themselves and — specifically and separately — Polish women out of and away from the ethos of the Polish Mother.

NOTES

1. The first draft of this essay was presented at the Susan B. Anthony Center for Women's Studies at the University of Rochester. I wish to thank Rosemary Kegl and John Michael as well as all my discussants for their comments. I also thank Katherine Verdery and Mira Marody for their reading and helpful suggestions.
2. This classification follows a scheme presented by a Jagiellonian University sociologist, Jacek Wasilewski, during a lecture delivered at the University of Rochester on April 14, 1993.

   In this essay I primarily discuss the symbolic politics of Catholic nationalists and anti-Catholic nationalists. The New Left combining the post-Communist Social Democrats with a left faction of post-Solidarity such as the Labor Union, are staying away from an exclusive ethno-nationalism, proclaiming instead inclusive ideas of citizenship within a nation state. No party or political orientation in Poland, including the nascent feminism represented by a parliamentarian Barbara Labuda, is either explicitly or implicitly antinationalist.
3. Following the September 19, 1993, parliamentary election which toppled the last post-Solidarity openly pro-Catholic government of Hanna Suchocka, the

post-Communist parties, including the atheistic Social Democrats and post-Communist Peasant Party (which is conciliatory toward the Church), now have the majority in parliament and were able to form a government with a peasant prime minister, Waldemar Pawlak. The new government however maintains a good working relationship with the Church and is willing to submit for ratification vote the new Concordat with the Vatican. A vocal opposition from anti-Church forces claims that the proposed Concordat grants the Catholic religion a privileged position within the state and that it is an international agreement which is binding on the state prior to the passing of a new constitution.

4. I refer here to "Ustawa z dnia 7 stycznia 1993 r. o planowaniu rodziny, ochronie plodu ludzkiego i warunkach dopuszczalnosci przerywania ciazy" (Law of January 7, 1993, on family planning, protection of human fetus and conditions for allowing termination of pregnancy) *Dziennik Ustaw Rzeczyspospolitej Polskiej* 17, no. 78, Warszawa, dnia 1 marca 1993 (*The Journal of Law of the Polish Republic*, 17, no. 78, Warsaw, March 1, 1993).

5. Citations from Chapter 4, Article 21, section 2, points 5, 6, 7, and 8 of the "Ustawa z dnia 29 grudnia 1992 r. o radiofonii i telewizji," *Dziennik Ustaw Rzeczypospolitej Polskiej* 7, no. 33, Warszawa, 29 stycznia 1993 r. (Law of December 29, 1992, on Radio and Television, *The Journal of Law of the Polish Republic* 7, no. 33, Warsaw, December 29, 1992).

6. See R. W. Connell, "The State, Gender, and Sexual Politics," *Theory and Society* 19 (1990): 507–44; a University of Warsaw philosopher, Magda Sroda comments on the meaning of the "return": "[d]e-communization and the return to Christian values appears inevitably to point to the inescapable de-emancipation [of women — EH, also my translation]" in "Kobieta: wychowanie, rola, tozsamosc," an article published recently in a collection *Glos maja Kobiety: Teksty Feministyczne* (Women are Speaking: Feminist Texts), ed. Slawomira Walczewska (Krakow: Fundacja Kobieca "Eska," 1992), 9–17.

7. Faye Ginsburg and Anna Lowenhaupt Tsing, "Introduction" to *Uncertain Terms: Negotiating Gender in American Culture* (Boston: Beacon Press, 1990), 2.

8. Connell, "The State, Gender, and Sexual Politics," and Katherine Verdery, "From Parent-State to Family Patriarchs: Gender and Nation in Contemporary Eastern Europe," forthcoming in *East European Politics and Societies* (1994).

9. The new regime is supporting the "family wage" policy which has gained the endorsement of Solidarity leadership. Only the feminists oppose it, suggesting an equal access to labor opportunities. See Ewa Hauser, Barbara Heyns, and Jane Mansbridge, "Feminism in the Interstices of Politics and Culture: Poland in Transition," in *Gender Politics and Post-Communism*, ed. Nanette Funk and Magda Mueller (New York: Routledge, 1993), 257–73.

10. Ernest Gellner, *Nations and Nationalism* (Ithaca: Cornell University Press, 1993), 1.

11. Benedict Anderson, *Imagined Communities. Reflections on the Origin and Spread of Nationalism* (London: Verso, 1983), 15.
12. Verdery, "From Parent-State to Family Patriarchs."
13. Anderson, *Imagined Communities*, 5.
14. Anne McClintock, "No Longer in a Future Heaven: Women and Nationalism in South Africa," *Transitions* (1991): 51–120.
15. Andrew Parker, Mary Russo, Doris Sommer, and Patricia Yaeger, "Introduction" to *Nationalisms and Sexualities* (New York: Routledge, 1992), 1–21.
16. George L. Mosse, *Nationalism and Sexuality: Middle Class Morality and Sexual Norms in Modern Europe* (Madison, Wis.: University of Wisconsin Press, 1985).
17. It is important to note that even the antinationalists' challengers, such as the political cabaret of Lipinska (see below in this text), still are operating within the nationalist script even while attempting to create a re-inscription of national sentiments and to rework the traditional terms of this script.
18. For an excellent overview of the Church-state dialogue prior to 1989, see Adam Michnik, *The Church and the Left* (Chicago: University of Chicago Press), 1993, and especially David Ost's "Introduction" to this book. Under the Marxist-Leninist regime, the Church provided a safe heaven for the opposition while being satisfied with the role of an "eschatological opposition," without any claims on the political sphere. It is the current shift from the apolitical moral authority into the realms of political authority, represented by the Church's demands for a repeal of the constitutional separation of Church and state, and the representation of resistance to these demands that I am focusing on in this essay.
19. In fact, in his memoirs, Paderewski describes his problems with a boycott of his concerts in the United States by Jewish organizations because of the alleged support (which he does not fully disclaim) of the nationalistic and openly anti-Semitic Polish National Democrats led by Roman Dmowski.
20. Private communication with Pawel Bakowski at the time I interviewed him about the Polish underground. See Ewa Hauser, "Underground Publications: An Interview with Pawel Bakowski," *Poland Watch* 6 (1984): 41–62.
21. The only full page devoted to the event was the advertisement placed and signed by the U.S. Embassy in Warsaw. It featured a picture of Presidents Walesa and Bush in a garden with Polish and American flags and read: "Requiem Mass for Ignacy Paderewski. Meeting of Presidents Lech Walesa and George Bush with the citizens of Warsaw." Under the picture it listed the place and time, and the information that the mass would be transmitted through loudspeakers to the Castle Square (*Gazeta Wyborcza*, July 4–5, 1992). The note about the event was about 500 words. The headlines the following day read: "President Bush in Warsaw: America with Poland." The article mentioned the crowds which came to see the U.S. President, and that they became enthusiastic when the President left the bullet-proof cage and shook some hands after the speeches. The journalist assessed the crowd as "about

20,000" people (*Gazeta Wyborcza*, July 6, 1992, pp. 1–2). The most important issue mentioned by both *Gazeta Wyborcza* and *Zycie Warszawy (The Warsaw Voice)* was the fact that President Bush's promises for economic help were limited. "Bush is 'giving' the Poles only what they have already gotten from the USA, namely these same $200 million, a part of the stabilization fund for Polish currency." (Ryszard Bankowicz, "George Bush: America Is with You," *Zycie Warszawy* [July 1992], 3.)

22. In December 1991, the physicians' association in Poland passed a new code of ethics which prohibited doctors from performing abortions (which were legal until February 1993) under penalty of losing their license to practice medicine. When, soon after its entering into force, this code was challenged as illegal before the Tribunal of State by the Governmental Civil Rights Spokesman, Jozef Cardinal Glemp called for his resignation or removal.

23. I will examine this in terms of the poem's contemporary cultural context and not in terms of its nineteenth-century literary nationalist tradition. My focus here is on gender politics of the 1990s, and ventures to the past are made only when absolutely necessary in order to understand the present. For the same reason I quote only excerpts of the long poem; it is not the full artistic effect of the self-consciously tragic poem that I try to convey to the reader but only the essential ingredients of the living myth it originated.

24. Quoted by Adam Michnik, this translation by Jewell Parish and G. R. Noyes appears in English in his *Letters from Prison and Other Essays* (Berkeley: University of California Press, 1985), 275–77.

25. That is, without the hope of resurrection — E.H.

26. In Wiktor Weintraub, *The Poetry of Adam Mickiewicz* (The Hague: Mouton, 1954).

27. See Ann Snitow, "Feminism and Motherhood: An American Reading," *Feminist Review* 40 (1992): 32–51.

28. Jezyk Polski, *Podrecznik do ksztalcenia literackiego i kulturalnego oraz do cwiczen w mowieniu i pisaniu dla klasy piatej szkoly podstawowej* (Polish language. A textbook for literary and cultural instruction and for exercise in speech and writing for the fifth grade of grammar school) (Warsaw: Wydawnictwo Szkolne i Pedagogiczne, 1990).

29. This story is a shortened version of a book *Dioniza Wawrzykowska-Wiercikowska, Sercem i orezem Ojczyznie sluzyly* (With their hearts and arms they served the Fatherland), about Polish women military heroes.

30. In an article by Bozena Choluj, "Matka Polka i zmysly," *Nowa Respublica* 3 (December 1992): 51, a bold feminist reading of the ethos argues that for Polish women, nationalism has been projected as a substitute for sexuality. The translation of the Polish Matka Boska (an adjectival form of God's or Heavenly Mother) and its equation with Matka Polka (the adjectival form of Polish Mother) is read as a semantic equation of the two and, in fact, functions on the same semantic level in which the Polish Mother appears as a secular-national equivalent of the Heavenly Mother.

31. Adam Mickiewicz, *Poems by Adam Mickiewicz*, ed. George Rapall Noyes (New York: The Polish Institute of Arts and Sciences in America, 1944).
32. Witold Gombrowicz, *Diary* (Evanston, Ill.: Northwestern University Press, 1988), vol. 1, 225.
33. Ibid., 36.
34. See the author's own interpretation of his *Trans-Atlantic*, in Witold Gombrowicz, *A Kind of Testament*, ed. Dominique de Roux, trans. Alastair Hamilton (Philadelphia: Temple University Press, 1973), 102–7, from which all the citations in this paragraph come.
35. Witold Gombrowicz, *A Kind of Testament*, ed. Dominique de Roux, trans. Alastair Hamilton (Philadelphia: Temple University Press, 1973), 106–7.
36. Gombrowicz cites this excerpt from his novel *Trans-Atlantic*, in his *A Kind of Testament*, 105.
37. Examples of the latter appeared periodically during the pro-choice demonstrations in the vicinity of the Polish Parliament. For descriptions of those, see Hauser, Heyns, and Mansbridge, "Feminism in the Interstices," 1993.
38. For example, in 1981, prior to the declaration of Martial Law, during the Gdansk Festival of Forbidden Songs, one of the songs ridiculed the association between Soviet and Polish astronauts who, in space, walked into each other's arms and kissed. This song, aimed against the subservient position of Poland vis-à-vis the Soviet Union, has a clearly homophobic message.
39. When Polish television celebrated its forty years on the air, Olga Lipinska's cabaret was listed as one of the three best programs in the forty years of its history in the national viewers' survey, *Donosy*, October 26, 1992.
40. Olga Lipinska is a veteran satirist, who started in the 1960s in the famous Warsaw Studencki Satyryczny (Student Satirical Satire), a writer, performer, director, and producer of a new media theatre on TV. She had been criticized for her continuous involvment with the TV stage even during the actors' boycott of official TV during the Martial Law following the crushing of Solidarity in 1981.
41. Lipinska's cabaret is under constant attack by the Christian National Party. One of its leaders, a member of Sejm (Parliament) Stefan Niesiolowki, when asked what the defense of Christian values meant regarding national television, stated for *Gazeta Wyborcza:* "For instance, it would mean taking off the air such programs as Olga Lipinska's or Polish ZOO [another satirical cabaret]. If Mrs. Olga Lipinska produced her programs among the Muslims and insulted their religious feelings, they would have long since slit her throat. Here, we Catholics are tolerant and will restrain ourselves from slitting Mrs. Lipinska's throat." Quoted in a Polish-language E-mail daily, *Donosy*, October 19, 1992 (translation mine).
42. Gombrowicz, *A Kind of Testament*, 105.

BIBLIOGRAPHY

Anderson, Benedict. *Imagined Communities. Reflections on the Origin and Spread of Nationalism.* London: Verso, 1983. 15.

Bankowicz, Ryszard. "George Bush: America Is with You." *Zycie Warszawy* (July 1992), 3.

Choluj, Bozena. "Matka Polka i zmysly." *Nowa Respublica* 3 (December 1992): 51.

Connell, R. W. "The State, Gender and Sexual Politics." *Theory and Society* 19 (1990): 507–44.

Donosy, Polish-language E-mail daily. October 19, 1992.

Gazeta Wyborcza, July 4–5, 1992; July 6, 1992.

Gellner, Ernest. *Nations and Nationalism.* Ithaca: Cornell University Press, 1993. 1.

Ginsburg, Faye, and Anna Lowenhaupt Tsing. "Introduction." *Uncertain Terms: Negotiating Gender in American Culture.* Boston: Beacon Press, 1990.

Gombrowicz, Witold. *A Kind of Testament.* Ed. Dominique de Roux, trans. Alastair Hamilton. Philadelphia: Temple University Press, 1973.

———. *Diary.* Evanston, Ill.: Northwestern University Press, 1988, vol. 1.

Hauser, Ewa. "Underground Publications: An Interview with Pawel Bakowski." *Poland Watch* 6 (1984): 41–62.

Hauser, Ewa, Barbara Heyns, and Jane Mansbridge. "Feminism in the Interstices of Politics and Culture: Poland in Transition," in *Gender Politics and Post-Communism.* Ed. Nanette Funk and Magda Mueller. New York: Routledge, 1993. 257–73.

McClintock, Anne. "No longer in a Future Heaven: Women and Nationalism in South Africa." *Transitions* (1991): 51–120.

Michnik, Adam. *The Church and the Left.* Chicago: University of Chicago Press, 1993.

———. *Letters from Prison and Other Essays.* Trans. Jewell Parish and G. R. Noyes. Berkeley: University of California Press, 1985. 275–77.

Mickiewicz, Adam. *Poems by Adam Mickiewicz.* Ed. George Rapall Noyes. New York: The Polish Institute of Arts and Sciences in America, 1944.

Mosse, George L. *Nationalism and Sexuality: Middle Class Morality and Sexual Norms in Modern Europe.* Madison, Wis.: University of Wisconsin Press, 1985.

Ost, David. "Introduction." *The Church and the Left.* Chicago: University of Chicago Press, 1993.

Parker, Andrew, Mary Russo, Doris Sommer, and Patricia Yaeger. "Introduction." *Nationalisms and Sexualities.* New York: Routledge, 1992. 1–21.

Polski, Jezyk. *Podrecznik do ksztalcenia literackiego i kulturalnego oraz do cwiczen w mowieniu i pisaniu dla klasy piatej szkoly podstawowej* (Polish language. A textbook for literary and cultural instruction and for exercise in speech and writing for the fifth grade of grammar school.] Warsaw: Wydawnictwo Szkolne i Pedagogiczne, 1990.

Snitow, Ann. "Feminism and Motherhood: An American Reading." *Feminist Review* 40 (1992): 32–51.

Sroda, Magda. "Kobieta, wychowanie, rola, tozsamosc," in *Glos maja Kobiety: Teksty Feministyczne* (Women are Speaking: Feminist Texts), ed. Slawomira Walczewska. Krakow: Fundacja Kobieca "Eska," 1992. 9–17.

Verdery, Katherine. "From Parent-State to Family Patriarchs: Gender and Nation in Contemporary Eastern Europe." *East European Politics and Societies*, forthcoming in 1994.

Weintraub, Wiktor. *The Poetry of Adam Mickiewicz.* The Hague: Mouton, 1954.

Sex, Subjectivity, and Socialism: Feminist Discourses in East Germany

Katrin Sieg

In the midst of racist pogroms, East German workers striking to combat their exploitation by Western business, and the recently legalized eviction of asylum-seekers accused of draining the welfare state, the passing of a tightened abortion law in 1993, now among the most restrictive in Western Europe, aroused little popular attention or protest in Germany. Three years earlier, the question whether to maintain the liberal East German laws on reproductive rights, or the much more paternalistic legislation in the West, was explosive enough to threaten the unification proceedings.[1] The abortion issue attained tremendous symbolic weight, because it had come to signify the progressive accomplishments of a regime denigrated as totalitarian and inhumane by triumphant West German conservatives.[2] At the same time, the inability of women in both parts of the formerly divided country to avert the dismantling of the last "sociopolitical measure" in the former German Democratic Republic (GDR) signals the rifts within feminist constituencies and critiques. The important role East German feminists had played in the "revolution" of 1989 failed to precipitate a unified and invigorated feminist movement and a more powerful negotiating position in the post-Wall patriarchy. While the threat to reproductive rights is not the central concern of this essay, it illustrates the very real effects the recent and ongoing rewriting of German history has on women, which I propose to trace in the domain of cultural production, through the discourses of feminist theater and performance.

Feminists now confront the questions of how far material equality between men and women had actually been achieved in the GDR; of how the ostensible equality of GDR-women relates to their resistance to large-scale and long-term feminist organizing, borne out by recent years; and of how socialist feminism which first emerged in that state during the mid-1970s and resurged in 1989, negotiated a patriarchal critique with a commitment to socialism. These troublesome questions revolve largely around the paradoxical structuration of socialist femininities in political and personal discourses, which is summarized by the misnomer "double burden." Rather than describing one person working two jobs, it designates the practice of contradictory ideologies in public and in private: while the market and the law recognize no difference between the genders, the home is characterized by a sexual division of labor familiar from other, nonsocialist societies. This contradiction has grave consequences for the articulation of socialist subjectivities in the performance genres discussed here, which include the public discourse of the theater as well as the private but theatrical discourse of the so-called protocol. The protocol-genre arranges mostly anonymous testimonials into collective, oral histories which differ considerably from official accounts. It has predominantly been used by women, and highlights the discrepancies between dominant gender prescriptions and subjective experiences. Since the demise of the socialist state was arguably brought about by vast numbers of people sharing a dissatisfaction with the status quo that had never been publicly acknowledged or redressed, I believe that the personal documents collected in the protocol-volumes illuminate precisely those contradictions whose accumulation and intensification precipitated the ideological collapse. In the first section, a reading of two plays, Doris Paschiller's *One Great Family* and Monika Maron's *Ada and Evald*, shows the ways in which East German women experienced, addressed, or challenged the contradiction of the "double burden," especially in view of the strict ideological control exerted by state agencies over public articulations of a political critique. The second section will examine GDR women's representations of subjectivity in a collection of protocols, for their interpellative and/or critical function vis-à-vis official constructions of a socialist subject. These two sections are situated within the nascent feminist critique in the GDR during the 1970s and early 80s. The third section examines the female/feminist identities which emerged in the protocols published between 1990 and 1991 and which revised the "private" mode of representation and address set up by the earlier texts.

At present, the dialogue between feminists from both sides of the former border is stalled. While GDR-feminists resent the admonitions of their capitalist "sisters," West German feminists accuse their Eastern counterparts of complicity with a paternalistic state, thereby risking to duplicate the hegemonic dynamic of condemnation that has fanned the sociopolitical tensions of the last years. The East-West strife among German women illustrates the entanglement of feminist critiques with nationalist imperatives and constraints, which might prove instructive to a movement increasingly self-conscious about the multiple axes of power crisscrossing its heterogeneous constituencies.

During the 1970s, the contradiction between the promise of equality and the praxis of women's socioeconomic disadvantagement sharpened.[3] The government expected women to shoulder the "double burden" of productive and reproductive labor, granting them economic equality in the marketplace, but failing to challenge domestic role-divisions. A calcifying bureaucratic apparatus continued to dispense an egalitarian rhetoric that was no longer implemented through social policies (contrary to official claims), nor experienced at the subjective level. In the mid-seventies, the burgeoning GDR women's literature interpreted these contradictions as symptoms of patriarchal structures, even though the term "feminism" was used with great reluctance due to its Western baggage. The socialist feminist discourse which emerged in women's writing suggested that gender difference and "female" alternatives might yield remedies to the current crisis when imagined concomitantly and dialectically to the state's gender legislation and the principle of gender equality which were supported by women's organizations.[4] The nascent feminist literature provided not only insights and impulses in regard to the vicissitudes of gender in the GDR; it also yielded a fresh perspective from which to invoke a socialist utopia. That place of "innocence" which some feminists endeavored to carve out, however, was no vacant ideological space. Rather, it was fraught with cold war anxieties and taboos, and configured as adversarial to state socialism. Feminist literature, attempting to speak from a socialist perspective outside of "real existing socialism," was caught in a defensive posture, constantly forced to prove its loyalty to a state that suspected its authors of collaboration with the West German women's movement.

Women writers and literary critics in the GDR were visibly uncomfortable with the task of defining and evaluating a "women's literature" whose Western manifestation opposed its own, patriarchal-socialist society. As late as 1989, GDR-critic Ilse Nagelschmidt insisted on the "integrative" aim of socialist women's literature which advocates socialism rather than opposing it, illustrating feminists' effort at legitimation if not apology.[5] Writers accepted the critique of the patriarchy as a peripheral contradiction and subordinated it to the utopia of communism, a goal shared by both genders. With this maneuver, GDR feminism reproduced some of the dominant culture's exclusions and blind spots.

Moreover, the innovative gesture of socialist feminist literature, namely the articulation of a radical critique of the patriarchy with the goal of fundamental social change, was not accompanied or sustained by any social movement. Women's fiction registered the missing base in the displacement of emancipatory impulses to the level of fantasy, the surreal and the grotesque, which by virtue of their subjective formulations gained access to the state-controlled, public repertoire of images. Women's plays were either censored when executing similar moves (*Ada and Evald*), or caught in the shackles of socialist realism (*One Great Family*). The small number of plays written by women during the 1970s and 80s demonstrate a shift from public discourse toward more personal modes of expression. They attest to women's desires, wishes, and utopian longings, but they also register the policing and suppression of those impulses. GDR women's literature, including the drama, functioned not only as a counter-discourse to the socialist patriarchy, but also as a dominant discourse vis-à-vis those who refused the politics of integration. This mechanism can be most clearly observed in the arena of sexuality, in which female noncompliance threatened the socialist subject's national allegiance. Here, difference from the sexual/socialist order was invoked only to be crossed out: alternatives are either deplored as an absence, marked as fantasy, or negated. Since the relation of the socialist subject to state ideology was cast in terms of compulsory heterosexuality, the exploration of political or sexual alternatives fell off the dramatic horizon.

Doris Paschiller's drama *One Great Family* (1975) retains the realist style, but turns the genre against the ideology it was meant to sustain. With depressing accuracy, the play traces the development of its protagonist, Conny Rosen, who throws off the shackles of her marriage with much enthusiasm, only to settle for relationships which represent no great improvement. The formerly obligatory happy ending of the socialist realist drama, its sense of purpose, and its confidence in achieving utopian goals, are missing completely from Paschiller's play. Instead, it exhibits an unprecedented sobriety in the face of obstacles and timespans looming ahead, and the realization of the sluggish pace of historical processes.

Sexual desire in women's literature of the seventies and eighties measured the gap between individual happiness and social progress. Marriage as a symbol of calcified social structures, and women's desire for self-determination could no longer be forced into harmony. The critique of marriage prompted the search for alternatives. In *One Great Family* Conny, who leaves her husband shortly after her thirteenth wedding anniversary, joins a group of students who spend most of their time in a bar. Her initial illusions about the fun life at the side of Victor are shattered when she becomes pregnant and Victor demands she have an abortion. The "great family," which offers Conny a place but little sympathy, does not fulfill her hopes for a good future, but represents at best a first step away from the bad past. When Victor asks Conny in the final scene why she still comes to the bar, she answers: "Where else should I go? We are *One Great Family*, and we will run into each other wherever we go. And we'll have to learn how to get along."[6] The traditional roles which the nuclear family reproduces are not superseded by a socialist model of gender relations. Instead of providing ready-made utopias, the play offers a rough sketch of the possibility of "Menschwerdung" (becoming human), a frequent term in GDR women's literature.

Conny's journey from the privacy of her living room into the public space of the bar suggests the loose network of friendships and acquaintances as one social alternative to the nuclear family. Among these relations, female friendships, such as the bond between Conny and the singer Batseba, a single, independent woman, occupy a privileged position. Dependency and domination are replaced by the principle of support according to individual need, which requires a greater degree of maturity and sensitivity. In the GDR, where alternative life-styles were not encouraged and rarely practiced, Paschiller's insistence on finding alternatives to marriage challenged patriarchal role divisions in the private sphere.[7] However, the single woman who searches for an autonomous identity is always embedded in the context of the "great family," so as to preempt possible separatist or antisocialist interpretations. Thus, the critique of the patriarchy remains within the bounds of reformist suggestions for improvement, and gender roles continue to be securely locked within the rhetoric of the family.

Monika Maron's drama *Ada and Evald*, which was published in a book of short stories by a West German press in 1981, uses fantastic and surreal elements in a style which aligns it with GDR women's fiction of the time. By leaving the realist register, it not only suggests utopian wishes, as in the "miracle" of the final tableau, but attempts to convey gendered power structures through the means of allegory and metaphor.[8] Its fantastic images of desire explode realist representation and its constraints. The relationship between Ada and Evald appears tormented and frozen in rituals. Only Ada's friend Clara, who falls out of the heterosexual economy due to her size and weight, refuses the perpetual return of the same. She breaks out of the patriarchal model of history which constructs progress as humanity's victory over nature, by uniting herself with a tree. Only a miracle can end the self-destructive dynamic of "techno-scientific socialism" (an SED formula). That ideology has taken the instrumentalization of reason to such extremes that its formerly emancipatory thrust has turned into its opposite.[9] Clara's fantastic wedding signals the necessity for a solidarity of the oppressed; however, it also risks duplicating the dominant equation of femininity with nature which has sustained women's exclusion from political power and historical agency.

Intimacy among women gained importance in female (self-)representations of that decade, but it also marks the limits of the socialist feminist critique, delineating the borders where demands for integration run counter to an emancipatory agenda. Brigitte Reimann's novel *Franziska Linkerhand*, which was adapted as a play in 1978, formulates the appeal for female solidarity as an existential necessity when the protagonist's girlfriend kills herself after Franziska turns to a man for love.[10] Here, the survival of the individual woman is at odds with the heterosexual reproduction of the system that denies her subjecthood. The lesbian's death marks heterosexuality as a choice with fatal consequences, suggesting an alternative to homophobia and designating sexuality as a possible site of social change. The women writers' subscription to an ideology to be realized together with the men is inscribed in their texts' commitment to heterosexuality, even though its social institution, marriage, became the target of criticism. In literary representations, heterosex became the arena of gender contestations where ideological constraints became the most visible.

Paschiller marks heterosexuality as the site of women's exploitation and oppression where patriarchal property relations prevail. With Batseba's dystopic demand for paid sexual intercourse — exempting those "capable of love" — Paschiller takes the idea of socializing reproductive services to the extreme, and thus foregrounds the limits of the egalitarian paradigm for feminist politics.[11] The principle of economic equality as model for interpersonal relations is thrown into question, suggesting instead that the utopia of "love," modeled not on equality but on the "wish for fulfillment and self-determination," provides the ground for change in the socioeconomic realm as well.[12]

Maron characterizes heterosexual frustration as a fundamental law, and sexual desire fosters the eroticization of passivity and stasis:

CLAIRCHEN: You're always babbling about love, sadly enough you don't know what you're talking about. You don't see the logic. Which is this: Ada waits for Evald because he doesn't love her. (To Ada) Why don't you wait for Suicy who loves you.

ADA: Because I don't love him.

CLAIRCHEN: Wrong. Because you'd have to stop waiting. And what would you do then?[13]

This recognition mobilizes the women's sexual and political imagination so that they can break out of the loop of eroticized passivity, traditional femininity, and political stagnation. By marrying a tree, Clara leaves the level of human relationships, which can be read as a sign for unimaginable, unrepresentable sexualities. Her "love" emphatically marks a blank, utopian space in patriarchal discourse. In a dream scene, Ada rehearses liberation through a role-play in which she plays Evald, and Clara plays Ada. In this way, she comprehends and distances herself from ritualized behavior patterns and becomes capable of overcoming them. That step empowers her to reclaim the language which Evald and the patriarchal "word-thieves" have stolen from her. Freedom, longing, hope, happiness — terms that have been appropriated and instrumentalized by a stale political rhetoric, are recuperated from an imaginary position outside of socialist reality. Maron stages that wish, but marks it as unrealistic within extant gender and ideological structures, twice removed through the role-reversal within the dream. The breaking away from oppressive roles is here dramatized in the interaction of two women; Evald's cry for Ada at the end remains unanswered. Ada and Clara exemplify two alternatives to heterosexual constraints: while the former signals the refusal of traditional role expectations, the latter marks the leap into the unknown. Within the androcentric parameters of Maron's drama, the women's sexuality cannot be represented realistically. When Clara and Ada vanish from the dramatic horizon, women's exclusion from cultural production is reinscribed into the text.

The production statistics show that feminist plays by women were rarely seen on the stage of GDR theater.[14] The orchestration of "political" discourses by state agencies into public spectacles of consent, and the rising stakes of engaging in a public, political debate exemplified by the wave of expulsions after 1976, effected a change in sites of political articulation. In the absence of counter-cultural spaces, entire institutions in the GDR — such as the theater — became ideologically charged, and turned into potential sites of dissent. I will return to this point later in the essay. The legitimate theater posed the danger of illegitimate interpretations, and was therefore subjected to a high degree of censorship. The representation of contradictions between Party rhetoric and individual, lived experience could no longer occur in public, but was displaced to the "personal" genre of the testimonial. Protocol-collections such as Maxie Wander's *Guten Morgen, Du Schöne* (*Good Morning, Beautiful*, 1978) became one construction-site for a critical socialist subject.[15] The other locus, of course, was the prison and the insane asylum, where the drama of dissent and dissidence was staged covertly.

The protocol functioned as a particularly East German genre, by carving out a voice situated in and speaking from the realm of subjective experience which challenged official, monolithic formulations of a socialist subject.[16] It lent itself to the articulation of gender contradictions which had been confined to the personal arena, barred from public visibility and political import. Wander's landmark collection of women's testimonials made an important contribution to identity politics in the GDR, carving out a female subject position that challenged the ostensibly gender-neutral concept of the socialist New Man, embodied by the worker-hero. As a document of women's consciousness-raising in the GDR, it called attention to the tensions and discrepancies between public and private acts and experiences of gender, but most importantly, it questioned the egalitarian paradigm as a valid political goal for the future of socialism. Couched in the terms and language of personal experience, Wander's critique of real existing socialism was better equipped to address the shortcomings of dominant gender ideology than the public discourse of the drama, although Christa Wolf's claim that the protocol does not obey the rules of literature, and escapes the trap of self-censorship seems somewhat disingenuous.[17] The book's ostensibly apolitical, often lyrical tone exemplifies the "cunning of slave language, the outsmarting of the censor" which Andreas Huyssen notes in regard to subjective, literary discourses in the GDR.[18] The collection deployed a "private" style and mode of address that endeavored to recover and mobilize precisely those energies and impulses that had been excluded from political discourses and which Wolf, who wrote the introduction, regarded as essential for the improvement, even survival, of a socialist society. Central to this enterprise, as in much socialist women's fiction at the time, are dreams, visions, and fantasies. They mark what has been suppressed, censored, and rendered impossible. "When I am continually prevented to deviate from the prescribed path, at home, at school, at work, in politics, even in love, it makes me angry and drives me back into the dream," says one of them.[19] But the dream also points to the hopes, to the longing for alternatives to a flawed reality which these women imagine, and which suggest a politics of "love." That term, partially evacuated from its patriarchal, romantic meanings, and operating as a utopian notion in socialist-feminist discourse, marks the potential of solidarity and community that was lost in the progress of "techno-scientific socialism," and which Christa Wolf calls "sisterliness" in her Introduction.

Last night, I had one of my Kafka-dreams. I always have those when I'm about to die of thirst. A dream of tender love with someone whose face I do not see. And so, early in the morning I run into the city where it is the most crowded, and I want to find him again. But I have a big belly and old breasts, and it is too late. I have dreamt of this man since I was a child, and I still have this longing for the absolute. (20)

Thus begins Wander's collection of women's voices. The displacement of the longing for absolute fulfillment by the dream calls attention to subjective and objective mechanisms of censorship which jettisons Lena K.'s desire from the realist register and articulates it in the language of irrationalism.[20] Lena's longing for "love" indicates a reorientation from the politics of equality to one of difference, sensuality, and wholeness, as

Wolf suggests in her Introduction. By offering "love" as a remedy, this first paragraph posits a radical challenge to the rationalized, patriarchal system.

The intimate explorations of socialist subjectivity, while purporting to "speak privately," actually created a performative, quasi-dramatic genre built on dialogue, diversity, and collective enunciation. In her preface Wander emphasizes the collection's function of rendering audible what had gone unheard, but also wants to provoke resistance, asking her readership to engage in a productive reception of the texts (7).

The seventeen protocols collected by Wander chart a feminist departure from socialist gender ideology. The volume sets out with the voices of exemplary socialist women whom the GDR's gender policies and programs have turned into successful, self-assured, and unquestioning party members. Lena K.'s biography, the first piece in the anthology, provides a point of departure for Wander's critical project. As an academic, party functionary, and mother of three, Lena epitomizes the successful GDR-woman, yet her report throws the accomplishments of socialist femininity into doubt. Lena describes her life as highly instrumentalized: "All of that [her professional, political, and sexual success] is only possible if I can organize and discipline myself, yes, if I become as functional as a machine" (32). In conforming to patriarchal standards of effectivity, she duplicates the most stereotypically derogatory evaluations of her own gender. While Lena K. never questions her gender identification, the reader is led to ask if male standards guarantee a fulfilled life. Her story marks the limit of the egalitarian ideology, and signals the longing and search for alternatives which run through the following pieces.

The largest group of protocols presents those whose lives deviate from the norm, and who raise criticism of "real existing socialism" as a stagnant set of rules rather than a system inspiring its citizens with the spirit of collectivity. Students protest the all-too-orderly process of socialization in the schools. Women who have achieved all the system has to offer, like the physicist Margot W. who has turned to painting, question and reject it. Rosi S., a secretary, questions the decreed historical optimism and sense of accomplishment touted by the party when she describes socialism as a house with red wallpaper: "When you scratch the red color, all the old crap comes to light, one layer beneath the other, back to the times of the empire" (70). Rosi views the current ideology as a thin veneer that has replaced previous belief systems in name only, not in actual behavior. She contends that socialist society has failed to cope with its fascist past, by encouraging conformism and dogmatism instead of curiosity, risk-taking, and the courage to change. Yet her criticism is founded on a communist sense of solidarity and commitment. Change, she contends, must be motivated by love, whether for oneself, one's partner, or society.

A sizable number of protocols exhibit the damage extant conditions have done to women, in effect turning them into subjects incapable of socialism and precariously close to bourgeois gender ideology. Several of them inhabit the newly constructed sleeper cities of the industrialized Southeast. In critical GDR-literature, these so-called "newtowns" had come to represent techno-scientific socialism at its worst, turning the promise of a new beginning, affordable comfort, and communality into concrete nightmares reflecting the bureaucratic response to economic exigencies.[21] While Ruth B. responds to her alienated existence with despair, others, like Doris L., demonstrate the commodity-oriented mentality fostered by such an environment. Doris associates happiness with a pair of expensive boots, illustrating the loss of utopia on the subjective level of imagination and desire.

Sexuality operates as a differentiating factor between the "true" and the "real existing" socialists: while Rosi and Margot are erotically voracious, Doris is frigid. Overall, the book displays a range of sexual experiences, expressions, and desires, extending from same-sex attraction to promiscuity and open relationships, which challenges the sanctioned, monogamous norm. Wander renders the ideological crisis of the GDR in the mid-seventies in the language of sexuality, offering a specifically socialist manifestation of the feminist tenet that the personal is political. *Good Morning, Beautiful* reveals the sexual hierarchy in socialist Germany, topped by the privileged practice of heterosexual monogamy, as a collective collusion not unlike the petrified dogmas sustaining the political hierarchy and its party functionaries. The protocols suggest that a sexual ideology which insures the division of erotic practices into correct and incorrect, moral and immoral ones through surveillance and self-censorship, prevent rather than facilitate the identification of individuals with the larger social order. The student Susanne T., who is taught in school to repeat party rhetoric but watches Western television at home, parallels Angela N., who lies to her parents about her sexual activity, and feels contempt for them because of the hypocrisy they solicit. The perpetuation of oppressive morals is not ascribed to state repression, but rather to the individual, quotidian reproduction of outdated values and inhibitions. Wander deflects the danger of autonomous, female sexualities or bonds between women, by focusing on the compensatory effects of friendships between women. The girlfriend, albeit the object of erotic desire at times, as Lena K. and Barbara F. report, is often the only source of solidarity, help, and care in a life otherwise devoid of love, as is the case with Doris L. The most noteworthy document in this respect is certainly the piece "The Grandmother," in which the 74-year-old Berta H., who otherwise does not think highly of her fellow females, speaks of her intimate connection with the women of her large family. On the one hand, this protocol highlights the regenerative effects of those bonds which benefit the hard-working women but ultimately sustain the system which oppresses them. On the other hand, Berta H.'s long life exemplifies real changes in women's living conditions, which is probably why the piece was accorded the place of honor at the end of the book. The improvements which socialism brought to women are illustrated by Berta's daughter-in-law Anna who "participated in the progress of the village" and, despite continual pregnancies, worked for the establishment of a school, a kindergarten, and a community laundry. "I raised eight of her children, one died when it was only a few weeks old. Anna started out in the cowbarn, then she worked in the fields. Now she drives the new harvester-threshers. She could only do all of those things because of me, the grandmother" (192). Berta's sacrifices have contributed to the eradication of those circumstances which made them necessary: her grandchildren already have "real jobs and don't understand what hardships we went through" (193).

Finally, the book includes the voices of those whose lives testify to the accomplishments of the GDR. Berta H. and Karoline O. are older women whose biographies cross ideological divides. Their personal knowledge of the past places the socialist state, despite all its flaws and shortcomings, in historical perspective as the most beneficial, egalitarian, and just model of human organization. Overall, however, Wander's collection pays remarkably little attention to the past, focusing instead on the present and the future. References to West Germans are uniformly negative, assuaging the fear that a feminist critique implies an outside perspective and a conspiracy with capitalist women.

Wander turned personal narratives into poetic literature while maintaining the fiction of authenticity. That technique was able to sidestep censorship, since any overtly political references are missing from the text, yet as a whole the collection throws into doubt the patriarchal assumptions underlying socialist gender legislation. It stresses the necessity to break the silence concealing individual differences, doubts, questions, experiments, errors, and variations in the process of becoming socialist. The book issued a call to replace egalitarianism as the foundational paradigm of socialism, with the acknowledgment and celebration of diversity. Wander's collection stresses the necessity to mobilize individual fantasies and efforts for a shared ideological goal, if the socialist state did not want to put that very goal at risk. While criticizing "real existing" structures and practices, feminist literature like Wander's collection took over the task of ideological interpellation which the state and its apparatuses performed with increasing difficulty.

Good Morning, Beautiful applied categories of "private" experiences to public discourse when it suggested a politics proceeding from love and "sisterliness." It also politicized the private as the realm of emotions and energies the state couldn't afford not to tap as a powerful, national resource. Endeavoring to do just that, Wander's book, while expanding the parameters of gender performance, duplicated certain silences and invisibilities within dominant discourse. Only with hindsight do the omissions become apparent. Despite the many erotic moments between women, representations of lesbian sexualities or life-styles are missing from this book, along with those dissident voices who did not share in the unspoken consensus of Wander's interviewees, that socialism, despite its many flaws, was in any case preferable to capitalism.[22] Like the drama, the protocol refrained from depicting nonheterosexual desires or intergenerational bonds among women, which took center stage in Western feminist discourse of the 1970s. Feminist literature in the GDR never contested the homophobic casting of the female subject's commitment to an ideology administered by men in the terms of heterosexuality. Women writers challenged the dominant conflation of criticism with sabotage, yet implicitly agreed that a sexuality not oriented toward men was treason. Ursula Sillge's book *In-Visible Women*, published in 1991, excavates a history of lesbian persecution in the GDR, which is based on that assumption.[23]

Good Morning, Beautiful created a space for the discussion of questions and conflicts concerning gender — a space which the theater denied them.

Twelve years later, GDR women authors responded to Wander with the book *Good Night, Beautiful*, continuing the dialogue among and about women in socialism. Many small and studio theaters recognized the dramatic potential of this "pre-literary" genre. They used it by putting Wander's women on stage, thereby creating further opportunities for a dialogue between women and enabling them to touch across biographies and experiences. In her Introduction, Wolf called attention to the polylogous aspect of the collection. She could not foresee the extent of crosstalk initiated by Wander, which would span the decades. Its subjective and collective mode of communication carved out a cultural space that Wolf described as "more spontaneous[ ], also more sociabl[e] than the structures of the novel or the drama."[24] Wander's protocols created an alternative performance site to the state theater, not only in terms of content, but especially in terms of a communicative structure based on a multiplicity of voices, on contradiction during and across moments of enunciation, and the informal articulation of individual and collective utopias. Collections like Wander's stimulated and participated in the informal, but highly reliable networks of communication located in the private sphere. In 1989, Nagelschmidt noted the difficulties and pleasures involved in buying feminist books and discussing them with friends.[25] They attest to the transformation of the private sphere into a growing site of civic consciousness and responsibilities, which has prompted many East European feminists to recast the public/private split in terms of state and family as more appropriate to political culture in socialist societies.[26] In the following section, my reluctance to adopt these terms will become clear, since the 1980s witnessed the emergence of semi-public, quasi-political spaces and relations. Although feminism, or any of the other oppositional practices that emerged during the 1980s, was not formally recognized for the political alternatives it suggested, since political decision making remained the sole prerogative of the state, women's consciousness-raising was no longer restricted to the family or the home.

In the turbulent years around reunification, the protocol as a genre based on collective memory, and by virtue of its collage-like, fragmentary shape, proved congenial to addressing a society in transition. It accommodated the need to rethink the past and come to terms with it, often in painful processes of confrontation and self-examination. The fragmentation and proliferation of identities that occurred around reunification is signaled by the newly specialized identities of their speakers. In the years 1990 and 1991, there appeared a collection of lesbian protocols, an anthology of theater women's voices, and a book of letters and dialogues by women writers, in addition to the three books of testimonials by what is still simply identified as "GDR women," indicating a sense of liberation from the leveling effects of egalitarianism, even as they testified to the devastating effects the erosion of social equality had on women's biographies.[27] In the following section, I will focus on two of those collections. The anthology *You Can't Make a State Without Us* (1990) matches Wander's book in its range of ages, regions, and social strata, and exceeds it because it includes many voices that had been suppressed.[28] The book *I Am My Own Capital* (1991) traces the impact of the historic changes on the lives and experiences of women in East Berlin theater.[29]

These archeological texts,[30] chronicling a system that has ceased to exist but continues to shape the lives of its former citizens, now make possible an assessment of gender and sexuality in the GDR as acts performed in the interstices of official policies and individual realization.[31] They also track the subjective effects of reunification on a population that was particularly hard hit by processes of rationalization, both in the sense of dropping to the bottom of the economic scale, and in the sense of being cast as a stand-in for socialism at large, as the popular discourses around abortion rights have illustrated once again. The feminization of socialism, which has become particularly pronounced in the 1990 controversy around Christa Wolf, is one important aspect of a larger dynamic that can be observed in present inter-German relations, namely the shift from political debate and controversy to moralizing admonitions, confessions, and absolutions.[32] The interpretation of state socialism as the direct heir of the Third Reich, facilitated by the already existing cold war rhetoric of totalitarianism, was dramatized in the ubiquitous talk-show-trials on television, which recreated the post–World War II tribunals.[33] Such a scenario, in which West German "hosts" played judge and jury, cast its Eastern "guests" in the role of defendants who must prove their innocence. That task became increasingly difficult since the interrogation tended to repeat the self-righteous question "why did you stay?" and implied that the only "good" GDR citizens were the ones who had abdicated their citizenship, or at the very least their party membership.

In the historical context of reunification, the term "protocol" took on the ominous overtones of trial records. Especially in the later volume,

Capital, one can observe the consolidation of the scenario described above and the gradual congealing of a monolithic GDR subject marked "guilty." Insofar as interviewees identified with the role assigned to them, the subjective documents presented in these anthologies merely reflect the power dynamic between East and West which was perpetually reenacted in the mass media. However, in the absence of public media that conveyed the perspective of East Germans and enabled a dialogue among them about their own history, the protocols contributed to the task of "collecting diverse views of GDR history" (108). Together, these anthologies assemble a mosaic of observant, critical, sometimes dissident subjectivities which eschewed the rhetorical ruts illustrated by a joke circulating in East Berlin in 1990, that "at present, 15 million resistance fighters are persecuting 15 million stalinists" (50). The period from February 1990 to November 1991 covered by the two anthologies records the turning of relief and self-confidence into guilt and shame – subjective responses to the larger economic, ideological, and cultural developments in the wake of the GDR state.

You Cannot Make a State Without Us records the voices of GDR women during February and March of 1990, a time when the oppositional citizens' groups were operating in high gear toward the pending elections which would decide the GDR's future. It was also a time of vigorous feminist organizing in the newly founded Unabhängiger Frauenverband (UFV, Independent Women's Union), the umbrella organization for a growing number of women's groups. The anthology, edited by two self-described feminists from either side of the former Iron Curtain, acknowledges its allegiance to the GDR women's movement in its title (which quotes the UFV's manifesto), in its concern with feminist issues (from the GDR's sociopolitical measures to underwear and sexual practices), and in its choice of interviewees, some of whom were longtime feminist activists. The collection captures the brief moment of East-West feminist collaboration despite ideological differences. Lux/Fischer's book attempts a historical retrospective of the GDR; they deploy a feminist critique that is clearly historicized as socialist in order to map a broad terrain of political subjectivities. Their joint venture also foreshadowed the differences between Eastern and Western feminism which led to the present strife and stall. "Whether a woman likes or dislikes her breasts is no longer interesting to [Western] feminists," East German journalist Petra Lux remarks wryly, and begs to differ. Nanette Funk points out that terms like "women's equality" were "associated with contempt and disrespect for women, rather than commitment to women's dignity and equal worth as persons"; after the collapse of state socialism, many Eastern feminists wished to explore women's difference in the context of the newly created women's culture.[34] To West German feminists, that project seemed dated, contributing to the prejudice that East German women were "behind" and had to be taught about feminism. Lux's Austrian collaborator Erica Fischer writes, "My superior technical equipment, my childlessness, my political inactivity secured me advantages which my conscience did not always bear easily." Other Western feminists were less self-critical when they regarded their Eastern sisters as liabilities rather than partners in a shared learning process.

The differences of both volumes from Wander's collection shed some light on the (self-)censorship to which the earlier book had been submitted, but also on the changes in GDR culture since the publication of *Good Morning, Beautiful*. The women who speak to Lux/Fischer and Ullrich neither share a commitment to the defunct socialist state, nor to socialist ideology. Some mourn the end of the SED regime while continuing to believe in the Marxist critique, others question the survival of "the idea" without people to realize it; most express relief at the demise of the regime. In contrast to Wander, the women in *State* bracket neither politics nor sexuality in same-sex relationships. The collection provides a sense of the many ways in which women's feminist (and other critical) practices destabilized the socialist state and, conversely, were hampered by it in myriad ways in addition to being outright persecuted. The collections reveal histories of political repression and dissidence, eschewing the division between private and public in which Wander had largely participated. Avoiding the impression of an "army of resistance fighters," they nevertheless attempt to excavate those biographies that are at risk to be twice suppressed: once as political undesirables under socialism, and again after reunification, when West Germans granted dissident status to a select few while condemning the GDR population at large.

The focus of the collection is on the uncovering of feminist identities and organizations at odds with the hierarchical structures of the SED as well as the male-dominated "revolutionary" citizens' groups. The feminist biographies in *State* are characterized as a series of struggles with institutions as well as internalized gender roles. The critique of patriarchal structures frequently moves across various sites of resistance. In the case of Petra L., that includes opposition to xenophobia, whereas the SED's lip service to "international solidarity" did nothing to end the exclusion of and discrimination against foreigners living in the GDR. The formation of critical identities, however, was continually checked by state control and intimidation. Salomea G., a German Jew who returned to the GDR after years of exile in Australia, testifies to the difficulties of organizing a women's consciousness-raising group in the late 1970s: after a few weeks and great fluctuation among participants, "only four women were left, and two of them, perhaps even three, were sent by the secret police or at least reported back to them. Of course, that is not the right atmosphere for consciousness raising" (137). Salomea's experience calls attention to the changing political topography of the GDR in the 1980s. The state and its security agencies created (or at least condoned) certain pockets of social space that were designated "oppositional," "resistant," or "critical." Officially, they were outside of its purview, but nevertheless remained under its surveillance. The Church played an important role in this scenario, since much of the oppositional activity during the late 1970s and 80s took place under its aegis, including feminist, pacifist, environmentalist, and homosexual organizations. At the same time, the state quelled the spontaneous, uncontrolled expression of dissident subjects and practices. Ursula Sillge, co-founder of the first nonchurch-affiliated gay/lesbian club in the GDR, reports the SED's attempts to sabotage that enterprise, preferring homosexuals to remain within the already existing associations sponsored by the Church.[35] In this way, the state carefully engineered the invisibility of its dissenting citizens, while allowing some measure of disagreement. By tracking the state's attempts at ideological containment, the protocols note its failures.

Lux/Fischer's protocols map a complicated notion of sexual politics, no longer bound by the monogamous, heterosexual mandate to which Wander had subscribed. Neither do they add up to a naive sexual glasnost, in which a range of "liberated," open sexualities supplants the socialist state's instrumentalization of women's reproductive capacities and its tendency to restrict and make taboo erotic expression. The women in State describe the impoverishment and alienation of sexual relations subordinated to the state's agenda of population growth. The most illuminating testimonial in this respect is a text entitled "My life is messed up" by the 45-year-old Silvia, an office worker in East Berlin. She points to the contradiction between the state's liberal sociopolitical measures and the lack of eroticism: "The joy of sex, sex as pleasure, was a taboo topic. It wasn't that the pill and officially sanctioned abortion rights created an openness for such an idea. . . . Day care and the kindergarten, all that worked out well so that these young mothers became something like breeding machines" (38). She concludes, "there was no eroticism, no humor, no drive. The uniformity of our lives has broken the men and made them indifferent" (40). She is excited by sex shops, lingerie, pornos, dildos, and vibrators, all of which have for the first time become readily available to GDR citizens after the opening of the borders. Feeling cheated out of individualized options for erotic pleasure, Silvia constructs a narrative of sexual liberation that peaks in Beate Uhse's sex toy imperium, a chain which rapidly expanded eastward after reunification. Reacting against a lifetime of egalitarian gender ideology which, to her mind, turned women into "worker bees," Silvia's longing for the celebration of difference culminates in the dream of complementary gender roles and codes of behavior, of gentlemen holding open doors and ladies in makeup and fancy clothes.

Others, like the canteen manager Johanna B., are more critical of the "liberation" the West has to offer. At a West German train station, she was asked by three different men to turn a trick, which appalled her, because it illustrates the benefits of "sexual freedom" for men but not necessarily for women. Her own experiences testify to a remarkable degree of sexual autonomy. Johanna reports that one day (before unification), her husband had bought an expensive porno magazine on the black market: "He paid 60 Marks for it in a bar. I said, I'll cut your allowance for next week" (119). This remark highlights the contradiction between female self-confidence bought at the expense of a puritanical, sex-negative egalitarianism on the one hand, and sexual liberation purchased for the price of gender inequality as well as class differences on the other. Textile workers in a plant now manufacturing underwear for the prestigious West German Schiesser brand illustrate the same contradiction: their latest product, named "Slipididu," is more attractively designed than the simple ribbed knickers of previous decades, which only came in two variations: pink and beige. Yet the women can no longer afford the sexy panties they sew, and it is questionable whether their sex lives will improve much, considering their increased anxiety and sheer exhaustion resulting from higher productivity norms. Silvia's interpretation of egalitarianism captures the social implications of instrumentalized sexuality: "If a girl doesn't take the pill and has a child at age 16, well, she has a child. There is no finger-pointing, not even if she's unmarried, not even if she has a black baby. That is indifference, no one cares" (38). In view of the resurgence of sexism, discrimination against single mothers, and racism since then, her assertion points to the limits of sexual liberation under capitalism. The protocols in *State*, by recording subjective damages resulting from a rationalistic ideology and instrumentalized social practice, and by refraining from giving or implying solutions (as Wander had done), called for sexual experimentation during a time of political change. Their open-endedness registers the brief period of much-needed reflection and search for alternatives, which was short-circuited by the March 1990 elections when the East German population voted overwhelmingly for the West German ruling party, the conservative Christian Democrats.

The groups whose histories are loosely sketched in Lux/Fischer's protocols developed a feminist critique of the socialist patriarchy and its contradictions which shaped the most intimate experiences of gender. The women who in 1989 organized in the UFV participated in the project of the opposition movement, namely to formulate an agenda for building democratic socialism. In addition, they recognized the importance of creating alternative forms of political organization, exemplified by the round table, minimal consensus, collective reflection — and quotas.[36] In the course of those months, however, feminist activists and programs were progressively marginalized "through the streamlining of politics towards professionalization and efficiency," resulting in a remasculinization of politics.[37]

In the liminal moment between socialism and capitalism, Lux/Fischer assembled heterogeneous subjectivities and accounts of GDR history. In *State*, the women take stock of a system that imposed difficulties and hardships on most of its citizens, as well as dispensing privileges to some. Many voice resentment at having been cheated out of material comfort, as well as professional or life-style choices. However, even in the deeply disorienting year of 1990, most women in *State* pride themselves on having managed their personal and professional lives in a competent manner. In the face of looming unemployment, loss of financial security, and ideological reorientation, many refuse to be pressured into quick decisions, but take the time to withdraw and recenter themselves. That step indicates a still-intact sense of security which is missing from *Capital*, assembled only a few months later. Despite the fear of an uncertain future which pervades most protocols, the optimistic title of *You Can't Make a State Without Us* is programmatic, exuding a sense of self-assurance and confidence that is shared by some of the women Renate Ullrich began interviewing in October 1990. However, the sense of productive contradiction gradually fades from the later collection. The differentiated reckoning with forty years of GDR history is superseded by examinations of one's own complicity and guilt, which accompanied the daily, horrifying revelations of party mismanagement and abuse of power.

The contradictory evaluations and conclusions offered by the protocols in *State* illuminate a politicized terrain of personal experience, engagement, and activism which defies the impression conveyed by Western media, that the opposition movement in the GDR had suddenly sprung into existence in 1989. However, Lux/Fischer's attention to dissident biographies, a much-needed project, may lead one to romanticize the events of the fall of 1989, or to overestimate the practice of resistance garnered from *State*. In 1991, sociologist Hildegard Maria Nickel, a prominent figure in GDR women's studies, flatly stated that the GDR women's movement had done too little too late.[38] Whether that is correct or not (and Wilke's analysis would suggest a different explanation for the UFV's failure to impact the political apparatus), it appears useful and necessary to investigate those subjects who were predisposed to voicing criticism and who, in the fall of 1989, stood at the forefront of political change, and examine their relation to a feminist critique of the socialist state. Renate Ullrich's book *I Am My Own Capital*, published by the Center for Theater Documentation and Information, illustrates the East German notion of theater work as social work and, at best, as political activism, which also motivated the Center's publication of the collected flyers, public letters, and pamphlets produced by theater artists during the fall of 1989, when artists were instrumental in creating public forums for discussions, both in the theater and in the street, turning the latter into a "tribunal of the people."[39] The protocols collected by Ullrich, a theater scholar from East Berlin, map the arrangement of critical, even oppositional subjects within a paternalistic provider state, elucidating that paradox which, I believe, explains in part the opposition movement's failure to bring about the renewal of socialism, as well as the swift implementation of capitalist principles and structures. My reading of Ullrich's protocols is guided by the assumption that indeed, democratic socialism would not have been possible without a challenge to patriarchal structures, as the UFV (and Lux/Fischer) had asserted. However, just as it is important to resist the tendency to heroicize the dissident speakers in *State*, I would similarly refuse to dismiss Ullrich's partners as accomplices.

Assembled roughly a year after *You Cannot Make a State Without Us*, *I Am My Own Capital* records not only the growing fears and existential uncertainty of its subjects, but also a changed outlook on the past. The sense of an exploding multiplicity of voices and perspectives which characterizes *State* is gradually replaced by the discovery of a shared identity as a GDR woman, a process that parallels the dismantling of the East German state, its institutions, and social programs. Although both Ullrich and her interlocutors have lived in East Germany, the editor stages a series of East-West confrontations by phrasing her questions in the language of West German feminism. Since only one identifies as a feminist, feminism in this collection serves in some ways as a stand-in for the Western system with which the theater artists have to contend, and the women's responses to Western feminist rhetoric frequently reflect the refusal to believe in any system of organized thought. "Another social utopia? Not for me," says the young actress Gabriele Streichhahn who tries to survive with a one-woman show (122). That disillusioned stance in part undergirded East German women's reluctance to mobilize against their disenfranchisement under West German law.

Ullrich's interviewees report the first tangible impact of capitalism on their lives, including unemployment and loss of child care. They record their first confrontations with homeless people and beggars in the streets and on stage, and they report their reactions to the resurgence of anti-Semitism and racism. The women describe their theaters' efforts to cope with lack of funding, changed audiences, and a new role in a society that no longer privileged literature or theater and in which the stage had to compete suddenly with modern technology and mass-produced entertainment and information.

The production hierarchy of the theater provides an apt metaphor for social apparatuses in the GDR, foregrounding the subjective, individual re/production of power relations while maintaining a focus on the material conditions framing them. The women in *Capital* address notions of collectivity, responsibility to an audience, and commitment to continued experimentation, but also questions of privilege and complicity, of arranging oneself with a bureaucracy pursuing a politics of inhibition, intimidation, and prevention. These concerns are similar to the ones dominating the culture-at-large. Whereas the majority of women is critical of the institutionalized curtailment of the "creative, subversive" aspect of art, few are willing or able to articulate power differences in terms of patriarchal oppression (107). Ullrich, borrowing vocabulary from West German theater women, raises issues such as the gendered division between actor and director, women's performance of roles written by male playwrights, the relation between actresses as professional gender role models and spectators, and female/feminist perspectives of history.[40] Only a small number of interviewees recognizes the rivalry between actresses competing for a scarcity of roles, and the dependency on male directors and administrators for patronage and support as instances of patriarchal injustice. Trained in applying materialist categories to social relations, several acknowledge covert financial disadvantagement and deplore the shortage of "good" roles for women. In the course of the book, they also point to the effects of capitalism on women, at the same time that they refuse to be driven into an adversarial position toward men. Unfortunately, it would seem that these women's solidarity with their male comrades is unilateral, as the changing status particularly of women from the erstwhile GDR in the united Germany has shown.

The organization of the theater sheds light on two distinct modes in which power relations and socialist subjects were produced in the GDR. On the one hand, the theater, like other bureaucratic apparatuses run by party functionaries, operated as a technology of repression, meting out privileges to those who demonstrated compliance, and censoring the (political and dramatic) representation of dissident subjects. *Capital* provides numerous examples of biographies shaped by cultural-political repression and continual hindrances. Brigitte Soubeyran concludes that critical intelligence was usually punished and harangued, while mediocre opportunism was consistently rewarded.

On the other hand, the theater was defined as an institution that resisted state ideology, a position which was able to absorb the emotional and political energies of its participants and effectively solicit socialist identifications. Theater artists had worked under a stable system of censorship and oppositional readings, which produced stable, dissident subjects defined by way of their distance from official ideology. While relying on an adversarial relationship toward the state as the common, unspoken referent in the performers' interaction with the audience — a constellation that is now thrown into crisis — the theater institution is based on internal homogeneity, continuing to duplicate within its own walls the male-dominated hierarchy that characterizes the political culture at large. Bonding on the basis of their shared resistance to external pressures, its members resisted any critiques they perceived as divisive. That structure prevented a feminist challenge to the male-dominated theater apparatus, and neutralized critical impulses not directed against the enemy outside. In this way, these oppositional identities themselves served to stabilize a system built on unequal access to authority and power.

The designation of the theater as a critical, even dissident space left other axes of power, such as gender, unquestioned, and purchased stable, "oppositional" identities at the price of a feminist perspective or critique. Unlike the feminists introduced by Lux/Fischer, most of Ullrich's inter-locutors agree with the official doctrine that in the GDR, the secondary contradiction of gender inequality has been resolved. As artists, many of these women belonged to a somewhat privileged class, often enjoying the opportunity to travel even to Western countries and a measure of finan-cial security unknown to most Western actors or directors. Like the sociopolitical measures that secured women's financial independence, these privileges had not been negotiated or fought for, but constituted rewards that were dispensed from above, assuring the acquiescence, even gratitude, of those who benefited from the paternalistic "provider state."[41] That system facilitated these women's arrangement within extant power structures. The "provider economy" fostered an attitude which, according to GDR cultural critic Irene Dölling, was largely responsible for the lack of a sustained feminist critique or movement that could have halted the disappearance of the GDR's social net, of which the latest instance is the recent abortion ruling.[42]

At the same time that Ullrich endeavors to record "diverse views of GDR history," her book charts the shrinking cultural/political ground for such a project. The signposts of politicized biographies, including party or dissident activism, which Lux/Fischer had noted, tend to slip into justifications of party membership and a litany of dates of dissociation. Nevertheless, the protocol offers a feminist historiographical model, not only in its concern with women's issues and organizations, but in focusing on the margins of the dominant melodrama of cold war heroes and villains, and salvaging what has already fallen victim to the rationalization of postwar German history. Finally, these documents allow for a rigorous assessment of the question whether we as materialist feminists discard the notion of women's emancipation based on legal and economic equality, or, in the words of feminist scholar Frigga Haug, "[i]n rejecting the former model of socialism, are we dismissing a model of women's emancipation whose fruits we have yet to harvest."[43] The growth of feminist movements in Eastern European countries, shaped by decades of socialist rule as well as diverse indigenous traditions, has produced feminist strategies which differ drastically from those addressed to late capitalism. Since so many of the central assumptions held by materialist feminists in capitalist countries rest on notions that were part of hegemonic, and often oppressive, practices, women's experiences in socialist systems cannot but inflect and inform the theorizing and politicking of Western feminists as well. I believe that the personal and critical documents charting socialist feminism, a frequently effaced discourse, offer a position of critical intervention in the current creation of a post-Communist world order in the arenas of national, parliamentary politics, East-West leftist debates, and international dialogue among feminists.

NOTES

I wish to thank the Henschelverlag in East Berlin, especially Maria Tragelehn, for generously granting me access to their archive.

1. " 'Das zerreißt die Partei,' " *Der Spiegel* 45, no. 20 (May 13, 1991): 18–27.
2. See also Nanette Funk's discussion of the abortion issue in "Abortion and German Unification," in *Gender Politics and Post-Communism*, ed. Funk and Magda Mueller (New York: Routledge, 1993), 194–200.
3. In 1971, the eighth congress of the ruling Socialist Unity Party (SED) confirmed the return to traditional role divisions by assigning reproductive work to women. The family code of law, which was passed in 1965, had already signaled the reversal of earlier policies designed to integrate women into the labor force and socialize reproductive labor. In contrast, the family code of law reassigned primary responsibility for housework and child-rearing to women. See Susanne Stolt, "Leitbilder – Leidbilder: Zur Frauen- und Familienpolitik der SED," in *Irmtraud Morgner's Hexische Weltfahrt*, ed. Kristine von Soden (Berlin: Elefanten Press, 1991), 92–100.

4. The official, party-affiliated women's organization was the Demokratischer Frauenbund Deutschlands (DFD, Democratic Women's Union of Germany), founded in 1947.

5. Ilse Nagelschmidt, "Sozialistische Frauenliteratur: Überlegungen zu einem Phänomen der DDR-Literatur in den siebziger und achtziger Jahren," *Weimarer Beiträge* 35, no. 3 (1989): 454.

6. Doris Paschiller, *Eine grosse Familie* (Berlin: Henschel, 1975), 68.

7. See Jutta Gysi, "Frauen in Partnerschaft und Familie: Sozialistisches Leitbild oder patriarchales Relikt?" in *Wir wollen mehr als ein "Vaterland": DDR-Frauen im Aufbruch*, ed. Gislinde Schwarz and Christine Zenner (Reinbek: Rowohlt, 1990), 106.

8. Irina Liebmann, another young author who began to write during the mid-eighties, resembles Maron in the use of those techniques. In her plays too, surreal images function allegorically. *Quatschfresser: Theaterstücke* (Frankfurt: Frankfurter Verlagsanstalt, 1990).

9. See Lennox's remarks on Christa Wolf's critique of the enlightenment. Sara Lennox, " 'Nun ja! Das nächste Leben geht aber heute an': Prosa von Frauen und Frauenbefreiung in der DDR," *Literatur in der DDR in den siebziger Jahren*, ed. P. U. Hohendahl and P. Herminghouse (Frankfurt: Suhrkamp, 1983), 231ff.

10. Brigitte Reimann, *Franziska Linkerhand*, adaptation by Bärbel Jaksch and Heiner Maaß, *Theater der Zeit* 6 (1978).

11. Doris Paschiller, *Eine grosse Familie* (Berlin: Henschel Verlag, 1975), 40, my translation.

12. Lennox, "Nun ja!" 233, 234.

13. Monika Maron, *Ada und Evald: Ein Stück. Das Mißverständnis: Vier Erzählungen und ein Stück* (Frankfurt: Fischer, 1981), 107, my translation.

14. Peter Reichel, "Anmerkungen zur DDR-Dramatik seit 1980. Teil 1," *Weimarer Beiträge* 29, no. 8 (1983). In my research at the archives of the drama publisher Henschelverlag, I have found only six plays by GDR women written between 1975 and 1985, four of which address gender issues. Maron's plays were published in West Germany. It should be noted that these figures do not accurately represent women's dramatic production during this timespan, because other publishing houses sometimes published plays. In addition, some theaters staged pieces that had not been approved or published by Henschelverlag, the state drama publisher.

15. Maxie Wander, *"Guten Morgen, Du Schöne": Frauen in der DDR. Protokolle. Mit einem Vorwort von Christa Wolf* (Darmstadt: Luchterhand, 1978). See also Sarah Kirsch, *Die Pantherfrau: Fünf unfrisierte Erzählungen aus dem Kassetten-Recorder* (Berlin, Weimar: Aufbau-Verlag, 1973); Gabriele Eckart, *So sehe ich die Sache: Protokolle aus der DDR* (Cologne: Kiepenheuer & Witsch, 1984), and Christine Müller, *James Dean lernt kochen: Männer in der DDR. Protokolle* (Berlin: Buchverlag Der Morgen, 1986).

16. The genre was not, however, invented by GDR authors. West German leftist and feminist Erika Runge is commonly credited with publishing the first

collection of personal narratives, and using the term "protocol" to highlight the documentary character of these subjective reports. Runge, *Bottroper Protokolle* (Frankfurt: Suhrkamp, 1968).

17. Christa Wolf, "In Touch," in *German Feminism: Readings in Politics and Literature*, ed. Edith Hoshino Altbach et al. (Albany: State University of New York Press, 1984), 163. The essay was published as the foreword to Maxie Wander's collection of protocols.

18. Andreas Huyssen, "After the Wall: The Failure of German Intellectuals," *New German Critique* 52 (Winter 1991): 132.

19. Wander, *"Guten Morgen, Du Schöne,"* 7. Further references to this work will be included parenthetically in the text.

20. Lennox notes: "Lena K. pours all those needs into the vessel of romantic love which remain unfulfilled in the society she lives in. She realizes full well that her longing for love springs from her wish for fulfillment and self-determination and that the unattainability of this love – as the allusion to Kafka suggests – is caused by a social system whose structures not only prevent this love, but makes the longing for it appear irrational" (233, 234).

21. For instance, the title figure of Brigitte Reimann's novel *Franziska Linkerhand* is an architect who designs one of those communities.

22. For protocols of those women who wished to leave the GDR and were incarcerated after their application for an exit visa, see Ulrich Schacht, ed., *Hohenecker Protokolle: Aussagen zur Geschichte der politischen Verfolgung von Frauen in der DDR* (Zurich: Ammann Verlag, 1984). The title promises an examination of gender-specific persecution in the GDR, which the text does not deliver.

23. Ursula Sillge, *Un-Sichtbare Frauen: Lesben und ihre Emanzipation in der DDR* (Berlin: LinksDruck, 1991).

24. Wolf, "In Touch," 164.

25. Nagelschmidt, "Vom Wert des eigenen Erkennens," in *Wider das schlichte Vergessen: Der deutsch-deutsche Einigungsprozeß: Frauen im Dialog*, ed. Christine Kulke et al. (Berlin: Orlanda Frauenverlag, 1992), 171.

26. See Czechoslovakian feminist Hana Havelkova's discussion of civic consciousness in relation to the public/private spheres, in "A Few Prefeminist Thoughts," in Funk and Mueller, *Gender Politics and Post-Communism*, 68f., as well as Hildegard Maria Nickel, "Women in the German Democratic Republic and in the New Federal States: Looking Backward and Forward (Five Theses)," in Funk and Mueller, *Gender Politics and Post-Communism*, 138–50.

27. Anna Mudry, ed., *"Gute Nacht, Du Schöne"*: *Autorinnen blicken zurück* (Frankfurt: Luchterhand, 1991); Kerstin Gutsche, *Ich ahnungsloser Engel: Lesbenprotokolle* (Berlin: Reiher Verlag, 1991); Helga Königsdorf, *Adieu, DDR: Protokolle eines Abschieds* (Reinbek: Rowohlt, 1990); Gabriele M. Grafenhorst, *Abbruch-Tabu: Lebensgeschichten nach Tonbandprotokollen* (Berlin: Neues Leben, 1990).

28. Erica Fischer/Petra Lux, *Ohne uns ist kein Staat zu machen: DDR-Frauen nach der Wende* (Cologne: Kiepenheuer & Witsch, 1990).

29. Renate Ullrich, *Mein Kapital bin ich selber: Gespräche mit Theaterfrauen in*

Berlin-O 1990/91 (Berlin: Zentrum für Theaterdokumentation und -information, 1991). Further references to this work will be included parenthetically in the text.

30. The term is used by gay East German author Jürgen Lemke in Jeffrey M. Peck, "Being Gay in Germany: An Interview with Jürgen Lemke," *New German Critique* 52 (Winter 1991): 145.

31. Social scientist Christine Eifler contends that "women's self-realization and self-perception came up against limits set by themselves and by society, and thus their very individuality is of general significance." Christine Eifler, "Identitätsbruch als Orientierungschance: Zu den Nachwirkungen der (auf)-gelösten Frauenfrage in der DDR," in Kulke et al., *Wider das schlichte Vergessen*, 37.

32. See Huyssen, "After the Wall," and Thomas Anz, ed., *"Es geht nicht um Christa Wolf": Der Literaturstreit im vereinten Deutschland* (Munich: edition spangenberg, 1991). It has been fueled by the recent disclosure of Wolf's three-year collaboration with the GDR secret police from 1959 to 1962.

33. I have discussed the public staging of the East-West encounter in "The Revolution Has Been Televised: Reconfiguring History and Identity in Post-Wall Germany," *Theatre Journal* 45, no. 1 (March 1993).

34. Funk and Mueller, *Gender Politics and Post-Communism*, 6.

35. Sillge, *Un-Sichtbare Frauen*, 102.

36. See also Tatiana Böhm, "The Women's Question as a Democratic Question: In Search of Civil Society," in Funk and Mueller, *Gender Politics and Post-Communism*, 151–59.

37. Sabine Wilke, "Wie die altdeutschen Herren ein Land neu verteilten: Die Geschichte der (Wieder?)-Vereinigung als Herrengeschichte," unpublished manuscript 2.

38. Hildegard Maria Nickel, "Modernisierungsbrüche im Einigungsprozess: (k)ein einig Volk von Schwestern," in Kulke et al., *Wider das schlichte Vergessen*, 41.

39. The Zentrum für Theaterdokumentation und -information, now renamed Haus Drama in (East) Berlin, documented the revolutionary involvement of many GDR theaters during the fall of 1989 as part of their publication *Theaterarbeit in der DDR. Wir treten aus unseren Rollen heraus: Dokumente des Aufbruchs Herbst '89*. The editors list nine demonstrations initiated by theater professionals between November 4 and November 20, 1989.

40. Ullrich, like some of her interview partners, attended the symposium "Die Sprache des Theaters und die Frauen," organized by the West German association of theater women (Frauen im Theater — FiT) in the summer of 1991, which for the first time brought together theater women from both Germanies. She acknowledges her debt to West German feminist discourse, Ullrich, *Mein Kapital bin ich selber*, 54.

41. Political scientist Christine Kulke coined the term "Versorgungsökonomie" (provider economy) in "Ferne Nähe: Zum Dialog unter Frauen im rationalisierten Einigungsprozeß," in *Wider das schlichte Vergessen*, 18.

42. Irene Dölling, "Frauenforschung mit Fragezeichen?: Perspektiven feministischer Wissenschaft," in Schwarz and Zenner, *Wir wollen mehr als ein "Vaterland,"* 43, 44.

43. Frigga Haug, *Beyond Female Masochism: Memory-Work and Politics* (London: Verso, 1992), 259.

Deciphering the Body of Memory: Writing by Former East German Women Writers

Karen Remmler

The aftermath of German unification has not been easy for many women of the former German Democratic Republic (GDR). Ironically, the democratization of their land following unification in 1990 has meant a loss of both economic security and reproductive rights.[1] As many feminists in the East and West have pointed out, the conservative body politics of the German government has placed a heavy psychological and economic strain on many GDR women who had come of age within a system that permitted abortion and the guarantee of equal rights.[2] Although women in the GDR could make choices about their bodies, however, restrictive political and social attitudes toward issues of sexuality and female identity often prevented the overt development of a critical oppositional subjectivity. Instead, writers such as Christa Wolf, Irmtraud Morgner, Helga Schütz, Christine Wolter, and others created spaces for utopian consciousness in their literary work that deviated from the more traditional expectations concerning gender roles in the private realms of GDR society.[3] Tellingly, the worsening economic and political situation in the GDR prior to the fall of the Wall, complicated by upheaval in other Eastern European countries, also culminated in an extreme sense of pessimism, best portrayed in Monika Maron's novel *Die Überläuferin* (*The Defector*), first published in 1986 in West Germany.[4] The oppositional utopian consciousness often found in the work of GDR women writers in the 1970s and early 1980s appeared to have disappeared as the semblance of a viable socialist state crumbled under the growing dissatisfaction and demise of its economy in the years directly preceding the end of the GDR.

As former GDR women cope with the new existential and economic burdens that German unification has produced, the temptation to glorify the actual situation of women in the GDR cannot be separated from an understanding of the mechanisms of a resistant remembering that allowed women to imagine a socialist livelihood imbued with a desire to break out of state-dictated modes of emancipation. In the following pages, I will argue that women writers in the GDR often presented an alternative memory in their work that countered the official history of the GDR state. This countermemory became inscribed and located in the bodies of their female protagonists.

Whereas Wolf's works and those of her contemporary Irmtraud Morgner often displayed a subversive interplay between gendered memory and the presumably ungendered official history of the GDR, the pessimistic tone of Maron's novel *The Defector* points to the deterioration of GDR reality. The lack of a critical public discourse about body politics in the former GDR became a hidden subtext in these literary works that portrayed the bodies of female protagonists as sites and conveyers of resistance against state-controlled means of reproduction and remembrance. Rigid definitions of femininity still prevailed in the public discourse in the GDR, despite the implementation of laws designed to provide all citizens, regardless of gender, with access to nontraditional professions. The intersections between the perceived condition of the female body in the GDR and its mediation as a site of conflict and counterremembering in literary texts provide insight into the perception of the female body within the social realm of the GDR in the 1970s and 1980s. In the two decades preceding the fall of the Wall in 1989, the fabric of the GDR security blanket had already become worn and torn, and was on the verge of being ripped apart altogether.

Wolf's *The Quest for Christa T.* first appeared in a limited edition (about 15,000) in 1968 with the East German press Aufbau.[5] It was re-issued in 1973 in a larger edition, partially as a result of Erich Honecker's liberalized cultural politics beginning in 1972. The West German edition, appearing in 1969, was often smuggled into the East. Maron's novel *The Defector* was published in West Germany in 1986. The construction of the body as a site of remembering in both texts exposes the conditions of women living under the constraints of a double standard and growing self-alienation despite state-sanctioned equal rights. In their writing, the deviant or dis-eased female body becomes the vehicle to express desires for an alternative body of remembrance in the GDR. Their work disrupts the GDR state's control of the body politic (as in reproductive rights, abortion, and doctrines on mothering) by portraying the female body not only as a passive entity inscribed with the forces of state power, but also as an agent that undermines the imaginary border between the private and public spheres.

Looking back, we can better understand the imprint of the social conditions of the GDR upon women's lives and memories by looking at the representation of the female body in media that reflect upon the tensions between the official image of women's lives and their lived experience. GDR national politics emancipated women while simultaneously constructing an image of female citizenship based on sex, not gender equality.[6] Despite the heavy emphasis on women and work, women were equally (if not more) rewarded for performing as mothers and upholders of family values. Despite their strong presence in the labor field per se, women tended to work in gender-specific professions while they were underrepresented in positions of state power and economic control. Although a higher percentage of GDR women were able to make ends meet as single mothers, marriage was encouraged through the incentive of increased subsidies for every child born to married couples and easier access to apartments for them. There was a lack of open opposition to the underrepresentation, because here, as elsewhere, cultural values implicitly relegated women to the domestic realms.

Instead of portraying the body politics of East and West Germany as a clear-cut dichotomy, many feminist scholars have pointed to the patriarchal structures that, despite differences in the number of women in the labor force and an official policy of equal rights in the GDR constitution, pervaded both the public and private spheres. Irene Dölling, herself a GDR sociologist, attributes a lack of feminist consciousness to the "patriarchal-paternalistic" structures of a "father state" that appeared to provide for women's needs while, at the same time, perpetuating gender-specific values in the social realm (Dölling, WIG, 129). GDR women were provided with, given, promised, and ensured equal rights by a state apparatus that was patronizing and rigidly structured along patriarchal lines. As Dölling and other feminist scholars from the East and West have shown, in the GDR, femininity retained its political currency (continuing to sustain gender inequality and sexual difference) despite the state's disavowal of women's exploitation in the public sphere.[7] Dölling's analysis of images of women in GDR magazines, for example, concludes that the higher the professional standing enjoyed by a woman, the more feminine her body was portrayed.[8] Any deviation from a subordinate and private female identity had to be compensated for with increased doses of femininity. Women in manual or repetitive positions were usually shown as nondescript, interchangeable, and competent — that is, satisfied with their position, nondistinguishable as women (129). They were apparently less of a threat to the status quo than women in positions of power, whose portrayal in attire and stances signifying the traditionally feminine in industrialized nations diverted attention from their power to their femininity. They were at once recognizable as women, that is, sexual objects, and, according to Dölling, fulfilled the expectation of both male and female viewers that equality at the workplace did not relieve women from the stereotype of being feminine and thus capable of reproducing and/or being sexually available (131). The representational system stabilized a practical and symbolic gender order that portrayed women as good workers, but nevertheless female and, thus, reproducers. Such images confirm what Dölling surmises — equality on paper does not guarantee a substantial transformation of the image of women per se in the social consciousness.[9] Thus, women were "represented" in the most literal sense of the word. The state represented them, that is, took care of their needs for them, while the social semiotic system represented them in terms of traditional universalistic images of femininity.

The GDR state restricted the movement of bodies at the same time it claimed to emancipate them. The lack of a public forum to protest against the state control of women's bodies led some women in the GDR to protest via the text. Female protagonists in particular attempted to create a space in which to remember differently. Like the worn-out Marxist adage that a state measures its emancipation according to the emancipation of the women, women also bear the brunt of a society's inequality. They are more susceptible to the upheavals in society because they inhabit private and public realms most affected by changes in the regulation of reproduction and, thus, women's bodies. To rely solely on statistics for describing the conditions of women's lives only obscures the experiential and psychological dimensions whereby the body itself is a site from which to see the actual gains or losses of social and political upheaval. It is the body that manifests the memories that are unspoken or repressed in the public realm.

In order to explore the literary response to the social disintegration of the public realm in the final two decades of the GDR, I turn to the conceptualization of remembrance as formulated by Walter Benjamin in his theses on the philosophy of history, and the relationship between bodies and history as mapped out by Leslie Adelson in her recent book, *Making Bodies, Making History*.[10] By combining Benjamin's notion of a contemplative and commemorative remembering as resistance (Eingedenken) with Adelson's conceptualization of the body as both the location and agent of history (and, I would add, of countermemory) I will reflect upon body politics in the two aforementioned novels by Wolf and Maron. The representation of female bodies in both texts exemplifies the clash between the limited official discourse on the body in the GDR and the desire of many women to find alternative means of representing and practicing female subjectivity. Like Adelson, who analyzes the representation of gendered identities through the body in works by women authors publishing in the former West Germany, I believe that history can neither be made nor told without reference to the body. In addition, I find Benjamin's notion of a commemorative remembering (Eingedenken) useful for reading the structures of remembrance in the work of GDR women writers, since the context in which they wrote claimed allegiance to the dogmatic Marxist materialist historiography that Benjamin heavily criticized in his essays on the philosophy of history.

The GDR's ideological identity as a Marxist-Leninist state meant that work and production played an important role in the literary and theoretical texts that attempted to portray the everyday life of its citizens. As Dorothy Rosenberg summarizes in her introduction to *Daughter's of Eve*, many GDR women writers used literature "as a forum to probe the question of whether the emancipated socialist woman was in fact living a fully human life" (13). Their work expressed the search for a female subjectivity grounded to a large extent in a utopian consciousness that relied on a counterremembrance for its substance. Given the reduction of women's rights in eastern Germany after unification, and the added instability of personal relationships as previous forms of community networks fell by the wayside in the midst of increased competition and insecurity, looking back can easily become a nostalgic exercise. Women began to take a closer look at their position in the GDR society even before the GDR collapsed under the pressure of the economic and social upheaval in the former Soviet Union and the Eastern bloc countries in the late 1980s.

The state initiatives of the 50s, 60s, and 70s toward equal rights became more and more suspect in the early 1980s as the economy of the GDR entered a crisis period that would culminate in its demise. The subtle contradictions of a state socialism that regarded the struggle for women's rights as obsolete, given the official assurance of the legal right to an abortion upon demand (1972), free child-care facilities, and generous maternity leave, played themselves out upon the female body in the GDR.[11] According to the state, women had equal rights in the economic sector and thus had no reason to fight for equal rights independently of state-run organizations. Despite internal grumbling and the expulsion of a number of dissidents and the voluntary exile of others, the official GDR state organization for women (DDR-Frauenverband) declared in the late 1970s that "the emancipation of women in the GDR had been realized."[12] Gender equality was constitutionally guaranteed and women had been integrated into the work force (105). The apparent protective gestures of the state covered up the deeper inequalities and discrimination against women and the objectification of their bodies manifested in patriarchal state structures. Even as depictions of professional women in workplaces outside the home were commonplace in much of the GDR popular media, the proportionately lower number of women in positions of power in industry and in government exposed the falsehood of appearances. The contradictions between the official representation of women and their bodies, and their own perception of their situation is a common motif in the work of Christa Wolf, beginning with her novel *Divided Heaven*. Along with the growing emphasis on female subjectivity in her work, Wolf's fundamental support of a utopian consciousness honed out of a recognition of the contradictions structuring women's lives in the GDR and the possibility of overcoming them remains a major feature of her work.[13] In comparison, Monika Maron's pessimistic view of the "real existing socialism" in the GDR, as portrayed in *The Defector*, strongly counters Wolf's insistence on creating a space within socialism for female subjectivity. Whereas Wolf's texts express the desire for an alternative consciousness within socialist ideology, Maron's disillusioned depiction of the decay and hopelessness of GDR society anticipates her decision to leave the GDR in 1988 as well as her lack of commitment to the ideal of socialism.

In Wolf's and Maron's texts, the female body is not wholly subject to the state. Yet the tension between the desire for change in the status quo and the seeming impossibility for transformation is expressed in the representation of memory. Thus, in the last two decades of the GDR, more women writers than ever published works about the contradictions of having equal rights on paper, but having to perform traditionally female tasks at home.[14] Wolf and Maron are worlds apart in their stance toward Western feminism and in their relationship to the memory of the GDR state. Whereas Wolf has been embroiled in a controversy regarding her apparent failure to use her position as an acclaimed writer to protest more vehemently against the injustices of the GDR state, Maron clearly supported the GDR state's downfall long before it actually took place.[15] Despite their ideological and political differences, both writers portray women's bodies as sites of resistance and counterremembrance. The resistance is manifested as the superimposing of subjective fantasy upon reality and the replacing of the chronological time that structures dogmatic Marxist views of history with synchronical space. In their texts, female bodies become sites where synchronous moments of past defeat and glimpses of present resistance are in conflict. The conflict plays itself out in the remembering process, which becomes physically manifest as symptoms of disorientation, hysteria, and cancer. Instead of constructing male and female bodies as monolithic, universalistic beings, these writers questioned the implicit restrictions in the GDR placed upon individuals whose sense of identity differed from the norm.

In order to look more closely at the relationship between the representation of the body in the two texts at hand and the situation of women under the specific material conditions of the GDR, I turn to Adelson's work on the relationship of the body to history. As she has noted, any understanding of the correspondences between the social meaning of the body and its representation must account for the material conditions that shape and are shaped by the presence of real bodies. In addition, given the multiple meanings of memory and remembrance across disciplines, I would like to clarify my particular interpretation of the relationship of the body to resistant remembrance, before applying it to the two novels by Wolf and Maron.

Although Western Marxists and descendants of the Frankfurt School and Critical Theory had incorporated psychoanalytical approaches into the reading of social and economic relations, the notion of the body as a textualized, inscribed surface, open to social and symbolic construction, is a foreign notion in a pragmatic socialist paradigm of social relations. From a Marxist perspective, when the body is seen as a site of conflict at all, it is usually an extension of the proletariat in their struggle against capitalism, a struggle played out in the fields of labor. The conception of the gendered body as a social and symbolic construction embedded in social relations is itself a fairly recent one. Such a notion first became evident in texts informed by Critical Theory that incorporated the psychoanalytical paradigms of libido. One of the most prolific contributions in this area was, of course, Herbert Marcuse's work on Eros and Civilization. More recent theoretical discourses have portrayed the body as a text inscribed with the effects of a postmodern "frenzy" of difference, displacement, and pastiche. The body is perhaps the most written about entity of postmodernist criticism, because the actual disintegration and unreflected simulation of real bodies through technology seems to have transformed flesh and blood into electronic bytes at the very moment that individuals are facing the hard reality of physical displacement, torture, hunger, and violence.

Adelson's book *Making Bodies, Making Histories* is refreshingly critical of theoretical approaches to the meaning of the human body that would obscure the interchange between the semiotic underpinnings of the body in discourse and its material reality in social constructions of identity. Adelson eloquently expresses the need to see bodies as locations and agents of resistance:

A discussion of the mediation between bodies as material realities and bodies as discursive constructs must also acknowledge that the mediation may be further deflected by distinctions, contradictions, or tensions between interior and exterior spaces, neither of which in turn can be justifiably considered wholly private or thoroughly constructed. . . . That is to say, bodies constitute a nonontological, material ground for action at specific moments in time. Such ground is, moreover, subject to diachronic shifts as well as synchronic instability. A critical consideration of the body, especially of the body in literature, will perforce rely on a mingling of semiotics and social theory, for both offer insight into the nature of materiality and the construction of subjective agents of history. (Adelson, 15)

Taking Adelson's model as a point of departure to talk about the necessity of seeing the body not as determined solely by material conditions, but also as a player in the production of the meaning of these conditions, I read the work of Wolf and Maron as subversive texts engaged in the production of a critical counter-memory enacted in the female body. In other words, the body as represented in the work of Wolf and Maron is not only a site of resistance that evokes and conveys the remembrance that refuses to be relegated to the constraints of a nongendered official history, but is also a location in which the degree of "subjective agency" can be measured. Instead of adhering to a Marxist notion of economic determinism and emancipation for reading the body in texts by GDR women writers, the insertion of Adelson's differentiated interpretation of the role of bodies in making and representing history allows me to recall the tension between reality and imagination as it is gendered. That is, the images of female bodies both refer to and counteract the position of actual bodies within the structures of the GDR that declared women emancipated on paper without significantly altering the expectation that female bodies functioned in biologically female roles, that is, as mothers and sexual objects of desire. In the two texts, the placement of the female body in relation to a public history that did not significantly alter the gendered representation of female bodies recalls the protest against the erasure of the body from that history.

Instead of portraying bodies as simple imprints of social and political hegemony and/or of institutionalized discourses, Wolf and Maron recall the ambiguity of bodily agency for women in a state that guaranteed equal rights in the public realm of the workplace, but indirectly promoted the perpetuation of traditional gender roles in the so-called domestic realm. In *The Quest for Christa T.* and *The Defector*, the material base of human bodies is differentiated through gendered experience. Instead of a clear-cut dichotomy by which women in the GDR were either repressed or, in contrast, liberated, the shifting power relationships and the meaning of gender itself was generated by a growing dissatisfaction with the contradictions inherent in the "double burden" borne by women in the GDR state.

Major differences in the economic systems of the former FRG and GDR left their mark on the semiotic construction of the female body and the body image of women. Whereas a capitalist market economy promotes, in part, the commodification of the body, and most blatantly the female body, the nonprivate, socialist economy in the east, though not free of commodification, may not have objectified female bodies to the extent the Western media did and does. In reality, however, GDR women had access to Western television and cannot be said to have had a body image less encumbered by the commodification promoted in objectified images of women in Western media. The actual representation of the female body was not bound by the political borders. Accordingly, theoretical discourses about the representation of the body in the West, though not lending themselves smoothly to the analysis of the representation of the body in the East, can be useful for exploring the relationship between the material experience of embodied identities, including gender, and the representation of these identities in textual renditions that focus on the body and memory. Accordingly, Adelson's plea for reading the representations of bodies in texts by women living and writing in the former West Germany as "heterogeneous sites of contested identities" (127) can serve as a springboard for coupling gender with Benjamin's particular notion of historical remembrance as "Eingedenken."

As the infrastructure in the GDR continued to crumble in the mid- to late 1980s, the literature also took on a more ominous tone. Whereas writers like Irmtraud Morgner and Christa Wolf drew upon myth, fable, and Western feminism to portray their female protagonists in their struggle to gain equality and/or a voice, Maron paints a pessimistic picture of the GDR, in which women are obliged to become outsiders, estranged from their bodies altogether in order to survive.[16] Her female protagonists become bag ladies or invalids. Wolf, though ambivalent toward the GDR state, refused to throw the baby out with the bath water. Her texts make clear that socialism was more humane than capitalism, whereas Maron's vehement protests against the GDR state are reflected in her critical rendering of the GDR in her novel. Of course, a major factor differentiating the two novels is the close to twenty-year time span between their publication — *The Quest for Christa T.* (1968) and *The Defector* (1986). Wolf's *Christa T.* was widely read during a time of a cultural political thaw, while Maron's novel cannot be separated from her role as a conservative critic of the GDR regime in the 1980s. It is perhaps surprising, then, to note the resemblances in the two texts between the relationship of alternative forms of remembering and the location of this remembering in the bodies of female protagonists. Despite Wolf's and Maron's diverging backgrounds, both wrote under the threat of censorship, yet published in the West. Given the different temporal contexts in which the two authors wrote the texts in question, the similar connection between resistant forms of remembering and the female body may be attributed to a lack of substantial changes in the experience of women in the GDR from the early seventies to mid-eighties.

In Wolf's *The Quest for Christa T.*, the narrator recalls the desire of her deceased friend for a place in which she can achieve self-realization in her own terms, not those of the state. The narrator's realization that her friend's body exists in time, yet is capable of occupying differing spaces, interrogates the false chronology of a determinist materialist history that excludes the affective attributes of the body. In recalling her friend, the narrator searches for a way of remembering that would adequately recover her friend's lost identity. "The quest for her: in the thought of her. And of *the attempt to be oneself.* . . . I must forget my memory of Christa T. – that is what these documents [diaries] have taught me. Memory puts a deceptive color on things" (3). The remembered friend, Christa T., struggles throughout her life to function as a model citizen of the GDR state, only to retreat more and more into her writing. Her attempts to create an alternative utopian existence manifest themselves, however, in the very images promoted by the state – a house and family. The retrieval of Christa T.'s repressed memories by the narrator depends on factors that are not always under the conscious control of the rememberer. The affective remembering of her friend takes place on a visceral level. The text manifests the physical sensation of pain, disappointment, or joy that takes place through the portrayal of Christa T.'s dying body. The cancerous blood cells of leukemia are the catalysts for remembering, because they are reminders of the susceptibility of the body to internalize external dis-ease. Nevertheless, the dying body gives birth shortly before death. After Christa T. learns that she suffers from leukemia she bears a child: "The child, a girl, was born in the autumn, and was healthy" (182). Although Christa T. suffers a relapse and then dies in February, she leaves behind a legacy not only of pain, but also of contemplation:

She realizes that the blood transfusions are becoming more frequent and are lasting longer than the first time. She sees the other, healthy blood dripping from the glass container into her arm; and she thinks: now no power in the world can stop her bone marrow from flooding her own red blood with the destructive white cells. Lived too soon, she perhaps thought; but nobody can really wish to be born and to die in any time but his own. (183)

The events of Christa T.'s dying are relocated within the context that conjured them in the first place. The affective residue of Christa T.'s femininity becomes imprinted upon her body, which, in turn, develops the means to express the effects of the residue through symptoms that must be deciphered with meaning. Christa T.'s body has meaning in that it represents the ambiguity of being female in the GDR and, at the same time, produces the text that counters the official story.

In order to interpret the structure of remembrance represented through the body in the texts at hand, Benjamin's memorial concept of "Eingedenken" (contemplative insight) provides a starting point for placing literary depictions of the interrelationship between subjective and collective remembering within the present context of GDR literature and society. The countermemory in Christa T., for example, activated by the juxtaposition between and disentanglement of subjective remembrance and official history, relies on its manifestation not only through the empathy between the narrator and the literary figures, but also in the portrayal of physical ailments that are expressions of repressed difference. This countermemory bears strong resemblances to Benjamin's notion of "Eingedenken" (remembrance as "insightful commemoration"). This type of remembrance is not only a reminder of missed redemption, but also a rebellion against the forgetting of the circumstances that thwarted redemption; not a religious redemption, but one firmly based in the imagination of human agency. "Eingedenken" resists forms of public or state-supported remembrance that criminalize deviant, subjective renderings of the past. Christa T.'s struggle to fit in to a society that has no place for her becomes a struggle to remember her life not as one who deviated from the expected route a GDR woman was to take, but rather as one who interrogated the limited spaces for female subjectivity. The narrator in her quest for Christa T. not only thematizes the dilemma-inducing divergence of official history and subjective remembrance in the GDR. She also constructs a textual form of "Eingedenken."

In *The Quest for Christa T.*, for example, and continuing up to the semi-autobiographical works *Störfall* and *Sommerstück*, Wolf explores the intricate workings of both personal and historical forms of remembering reflected in the ambiguity of technological advances that both destroy and cure the body.[17]

How does this untraditional and provocative method of remembering manifest itself in terms of gender difference? Adelson's call for the incorporation of the "notion of positionality" in interpretations of the role of gender in producing power relations between bodies and in history (125) reminds us that gender is only one identity and that it is differently present with other identities, such as race and class. Adelson convincingly demonstrates that the human body as represented in the literary texts published in the former West Germany cannot be understood without knowledge of how gender and racial identities are imbricated in the power relations both engaging and being engaged by the body. By recognizing that bodies are engendered, racialized, and historcized in different ways in different contexts, one can take a closer look at "socioaesthetic constructs of bodies" as they are positioned in literary texts, but not separate from the historical experience that embodies them. If we understand "woman" to be a construct, then the embodiment of this construct as female body allows one to see gender as only one factor in determining difference. Thus, it is not the femaleness of the bodies in Wolf's and Maron's work that produces countermemories, but the choice of the female gender for conveying countermemory that is significant. It is not to say that having or being female gives women a predilection for remembering differently, but rather that the choice of representing resistant remembrance through the female body is a reflection of the double bind in which women found themselves in the GDR.

The remembering process experienced by the narrator in *Christa T.* allows the reader to measure the gap between the perceived agency and the actual lack of it as recorded through the physical limitation of the female protagonist's body. In Benjamin's theses on the philosophy of history, "Eingedenken" signifies a type of remembrance that demands an active and attentive commemorating on the part of the rememberer.[18] Benjamin's famous rendering of history in his description of Klee's *Angelus Novus* describes the dilemma confronting not only historians, but also writers who engage seemingly private images of subjective remembering in their writing. Such authors reject the subsuming of divergent memory images into stifling, homogeneous views of history. Benjamin allegorizes the angel of history:

A Klee painting named "Angelus Novus" shows an angel looking as though he is about to move away from something he is fixedly contemplating. His eyes are staring, his mouth is open, his wings are spread. This is how one pictures the angel of history. His face is turned toward the past. Where we perceive a chain of events, he sees one single catastrophe which keeps piling wreckage upon wreckage and hurls it in front of his feet. The angel would like to stay, awaken the dead, and make whole what has been smashed. But a storm is blowing from Paradise; it has got caught in his wings with such violence that the angel can no longer close them. This storm irresistibly propels him into the future to which his back is turned, while the pile of debris before him grows skyward. This storm is what we call progress. (Benjamin, *Illuminations*, 260–61)

The angel of history, caught between the desire to wake the dead and the yearning to succumb to the winds of progress, has the power, however, to see the actual accumulation of debris that represents resistance not only against the forces of progress, but also against the betrayed remembering of this resistance.

Benjamin's angel of history has been the subject of numerous interpretations, most indicative of the ideological trappings of the interpreter. The various feminist approaches to Benjamin, though provocative and comprehensive, do not commit the angel of history to a particular gender.[19] Nevertheless, the angel can be seen as a metaphor for a type of history that gathers together those memories that are excluded from the homogenous notion of history as progress, and that are represented as waste and debris. In the present study, the memories and imagination of female subjectivity within the GDR state can be said to be representations of the contradictory status of women in that state and as a resifting of the debris. Christa T.'s death can be read as a cry of protest, not resignation to the pressures of living the contradictions through her body. Furthermore the remembering of alternative ways of remembering and the inclusion of the body as the main conveyor of countermemories has a counterpart in Benjamin's angel. The angel sees the chance for resistance against oppression as it appears in a momentary flash amidst the ruin of a present that stifles a critical remembering process for the sake of progress or for maintaining an illusion of health. The angel desires the fulfillment of the process not just for present sufferers, but also in the memory of those who suffered in the past. Similarly, by recognizing the contradictions of the GDR society, Wolf's texts, like Benjamin's metaphorical angel of a resistant history, represent the consequences of progress based on illusion in their expression of the disappointment with and critique of "real existing socialism."

In Wolf's first book to deal with female subjectivity, *Divided Heaven*, the role of remembrance is portrayed as a redemptive, if thankless task. She wrote in an environment where traditional views of historiography as progress were stubbornly and absurdly upheld by the official party line. Wolf constructs textual constellations where past and present momentarily come together in what Benjamin would call the "Jetztzeit" (now time) of "das dialektische Bild" (the dialectical image): "History is the subject of a structure whose site is not homogeneous, empty time, but time filled by the presence of the now" (Benjamin, 263). For Wolf, remembering the past could not be separated from imagining a better future. Her writing represents a process of breaking down the petrified and static linear chronology of official national or public memory into a composite of subjective perspectives. In the moment this composite image appears it is, however, immediately in danger of being reappropriated, reconstituted, and reinscribed into the conventional "Medaillons," petrified images of a collective history void of subjective intervention. Such an intervention takes place at the site of collision between memory images devoid of subjective input and those counterimages that deviate from conventional, rationalized views of the past.

The painful remembering of the past nevertheless coincides with both the impossibility of retrieving the losses *and* the hope of intervening in the present to prevent the further silencing of suffering. Wolf depicts the attempts of protagonists — predominantly of the female gender — to unravel the tightly knit structure of a rationalized collective history that prohibits the intrusion of subjective correctives into its formations. Frequently, the female voices in her novels represent the attempt to overcome the repression of uncomfortable or painful memories through their struggle to establish their identity in terms of the past. Wolf's novel *The Quest for Christa T.* appeared in the GDR at a time when subjective remembering was just beginning to play a major role in breaking down a petrified collective public memory through the inclusion of different perspectives and views of the past.

In *Christa T.* the female body is the site for both subjective and collective remembering. The two types of remembering are not diametrically opposed to one another. Instead they represent different ways of remembering that intersect with one another. Accordingly, subjective remembering refers to the memories and the process of recalling personal experience, while collective remembering signifies the inclusion of historical, public or group memory in an individual's conception of past experience.

Whereas Benjamin's theory of remembrance is often grounded in the artifacts and spatial constellations of the past, present in the built environment, my approach to memory, while drawing from the construction Benjamin describes, locates remembrance in the gendered body.[20] Benjamin's images provide a sensuous component to the notion of materialist historicism. Without explicitly refering to gender — the notion of gender difference was at the very least underdeveloped in Benjamin's writing — the recognition of recording the history of the marginalized could be aligned with the attempts by Wolf to speak from a female perspective. Her work counteracts the official notion in the GDR that gender discrimination had ceased once laws were put into place to assure the rights of women in the workplace.

Instead of seeing the juxtaposition of Benjamin's form of remembering with a gendered countermemory acted out upon and by the bodies of female protagonists in Wolf's texts as an essentialist association of the female with emotion, I see this as a sign of the material experience of women in the GDR that exposed the pitfalls of official history. Many women were expected to take on feminine roles as defined by motherhood, yet they were provided with the material means to seek other forms of production and self-expression. This contradiction played itself out most tellingly upon the figurative bodies of the female protagonists in Wolf's works.

Perception takes place through the body, through vision, and through insight. It is perhaps the latter element that most aligns Benjamin's notion of "Eingedenken" with a gendered remembrance, that is, one structured by the experience of being male or female.[21] The angel, as a figure of redemption is also one of contemplative empathy. As Niethammer points out:

By making history contemporary he [the angel] seeks to redeem the hopes of those who have been passed over by history: that is, to release them for the freedom of further effectivity, so that their existential tradition-affirming power may be brought to bear in the struggle that must halt the catastrophic storm of history. The storm is already blowing from paradise, and is thus a force moving all history. (116)

An approach to history that incorporates an empathic identification with victims of the past is by no means nostalgic or sentimental. In order to fight back, one needs to give up the search for glorious history and victors and, instead, seek out the memories of the vanquished through a historical awareness that illuminates the hopes of those who fought but were defeated (117). The task of the materialist historian is to glimpse the moments in the past when utopian vision was imbued with a desire for change and empowerment by marginalized groups, but defeated by a status quo, by a dictatorship, or by military force. The historian remembers the struggle through a "tiger's leap into the past," thereby giving a voice to the speechless in the text by refusing to reinscribe the body into an official story, but to liberate it from oblivion.

In *Christa T.*, the struggles of the female protagonist to break out of the pressures of conformity and to speak her own voice are portrayed as a slow death. Christa T. experiences how leukemia invades and is circulated through her body. Without reducing real cancer to a mere metaphor, Wolf retrospectively rearranges the scraps of Christa T.'s life in order to form a more complete picture not just of a troubled woman, but also of the social and cultural constellations that restricted her expression and freedom of movement. Thus, the illness is not just a sign of psychological disorder; it is also a reminder of the price that women pay for their difference in a patriarchal society and of the hopelessness of a cure in a society that does not acknowledge the existence of power relations that utilize or naturalize this difference.

Christa T.'s story is remembered by a female narrator who attempts to piece together her friend's life after her death. The nonchronological narrative, a mixture of reminiscences, diary entries, and monologues, traces the life of a young GDR women from her childhood through her death due to leukemia. As much as the novel is about the somewhat eccentric hopefulness and utopian consciousness displayed by Christa T.'s attempts to write and to accomplish the tasks her society expects of her as teacher and mother, it is also about the mechanisms of remembrance and forgetting, of mourning and rejoicing in the actual process of remembering a life. The narrator's re-membering in her quest for Christa T. provides her subject with a second chance to break out of a petrified notion of biography. By thinking Christa T. back to the present, the narrator creates a community of memory in which Christa T.'s body is not dismantled from her mind, and in which female subjectivity can perform according to desires otherwise repressed during her lifetime in the earlier years of the GDR.

Although Christa T. dies, she leaves behind a legacy that pleads for a recognition of the power of subjective forms of remembering. At the same time, however, the finality of her death indicates the necessity of remembering in community. In fact, it is only in the remembrance of the narrator that Christa T. has perhaps lived at all. Her body is the place where her cogent, but subdued dissatisfaction takes its toll. Christa T.'s death, as symbolically as one might read it, represents the impossibility of detaching female subjectivity from the social constellations of the GDR state that defined sexuality as well as social identity. Like the tragic figure Antigone, Christa T. is bound in an old order that desires to return the body to the word[22] and to rebel against an abstraction of the body into a machine or into a reproductive chamber.[23] Like Benjamin's angel of history, she is bound by her body because it is both in and of history. And this body is a gendered one. As Wolf's novel demonstrates, the pressures of performing as both a mother and a worker in the GDR state led to a conflicted existence, particularly for women. Christa T.'s cancerous body becomes the site in which subjective desire and social expectations are pitted against one another. Through writing, Christa T. attempts to articulate the conflict her body expresses.

It is not just the internal cancer that kills Christa T.; it is also the lack of a communal space, in which she can speak her pain openly. The public consciousness was rarely open to seeing the illnesses of the body as signs of the decay and disintegration of GDR society. The drastic amounts of pollution that corresponded to the high rate of cancer in heavily industrialized areas of the GDR were publicly disconnected from one another. Thus, diseased bodies were not seen or understood to be the expression of social or political ills. Resistance to the obscuring of the connection between the state-sanctioned hazards and personal dissatisfaction took the form of isolated protests, emigration to the West, and finally, in the 1980s, of mass demonstrations. In many literary texts, however, resistance to a particular social expectation was often expressed through disease. Ironically, the same thing that expresses the injustice also kills the body.

The portrayal of the female body is less subtle in Maron's novel, as is her pessimistic political stance.[24] Yet her work similarly portrays the structural violence affecting women's bodies and their resistance to it. In her novel *The Defector*, Maron exposes the painful clash between a state-condoned and ordered assembling of the past and the re-membering of it through an imaginative "Eingedenken" that plays itself out upon and through the body of the female protagonist, Rosalind. After waking up one day unable to walk, Rosalind searches for a form of expression that allows her access to the realm of cultural, not just biological, reproduction. Her body becomes the site that undoes the essentialist images of femininity projected upon it, in order to demonstrate the actual social construction of the body enmeshed in semiotic systems of meaning. Thus, her body is subjected to traditional historical icons of femininity while, at the same time, it breaks down these norms.

Rosalind's debilitated body becomes the site of emancipatory imagination and resistance, even as it remains physically passive. Ironically, Rosalind steps out of her preordained role in history (symbolized by her absence from her job at an Institute for Historical Research), by losing the capability of walking her normal route. Her physical immobility prevents her from forgetting: that is, from following the prescribed everyday routine of her job at the Institute for Historical Research in East Berlin. Her bodily confinement transforms itself into a catalyst for re-membering not only deceased family members and friends, but also the repressed parts of herself buried beneath the surface of everyday acquiescence to the status quo. The memory images conjured up as dream montages, fantasy scenarios, and recollections of actual events depict the tension between external (public) and internal (private) types of remembering. The conventional dimensions of time and space are distorted as are those of narrative sequence and perspective.

In the process of mourning the loss of a more rebellious self, Rosalind's voice dis-integrates into three figures: a third-person narrator, a first-person narrator, and Rosalind's *Doppelgänger* Martha. The three voices repeatedly revive one another from their slumber in the crypt of Rosalind's repressed memory as each carries the immobile Rosalind through synchronic spaces of past and present. Having removed herself from the everyday routine, and thus from conformist ways of perceiving the past, Rosalind contemplates her newfound ability to dissolve the restraints of time. Instead of envisioning her predicament as one allowing her infinite time, she transforms the time of remembrance into space: "It made more sense, she thought, to look at time as a restricted space in which she wanted to collect experiences like books in a library, memories accessible to her all the time. . . . She could also recall times past in this room and fuse desired time to a lasting present" (4). The narrator seeks traces of her identity submerged in the interior of her mind and lost in the process of separation between her imagined potential self and the obedient person she has become. By returning to places harboring memories of the dead, Rosalind liberates the previously buried grief over this separation and gains insight into the forces preventing the excavation of both the grief and the fragments of her imagined identity. In her quest for her other selves, Rosalind encounters resistance. Her imagination is imbued with the strictures and real constraints of physical disability. Whereas Wolf remembers the fragility of bodies through the displacment of external contraints to internal illness, Maron, in keeping with the postmodernist conditions of the 1980s, portrays the female body as a convenient place to imagine a different way of moving though space. While moving though space, the body absorbs the remnants of hope that Rosalind's prior consciousness had given up.

The narrator as Rosalind's "I" counters mechanical reactions to dying within GDR society with subjective renderings of delayed grief. By relocating the close emotional proximity between the irrevocable, diachronic leave-taking through death on the one hand and recurring ritualistic farewells like those at train stations on the other, she exposes the living death not only of frustrated, resigned GDR citizens in particular, but also the decay of GDR society in general. In order to depict the rendering of the past as neither linear, progressive nor as circular, mythical, Maron takes the past out of the framework of time and deposits it in the realm of a space imbued with, but not solely defined by, mythic qualities. These qualities invoke the temptation to revert to myth instead of incorporating it into a critique of a rationalized present.

In her novel, Maron conjures up a number of mythical figures (Orpheus, Antigone), in order to visualize an alternative to the static mourning rituals perpetuated by GDR social codes. The comings and goings at the Ostbahnhof (East Berlin train station) symbolize a vaudeville-like reenactment of the Orpheus myth similar to Benjamin's image of departure in the *Passagenwerk:*

Once again we are audience to the worn-out Greek melodrama: Orpheus, Eurydice and Hermes at the train station. In the mountain of suitcases in which they

stand, the craggy corridor arches, the crypt in which they descend, when the
hermetic conductor, in search of Orpheus' moist glimpse, gives the signal for
departure. . . . Scars of farewell, that quiver like the crack of a Greek vase over the
immortalized bodies of the gods. (Benjamin, *Passagenwerk*, L-I,4, 512)

The mythical rendition of farewell rituals contradictorily reinscribes them
with historical meaning by placing them against the backdrop of a rationalized, mechanical gesture estranged from subjective experience. Eternal-
ized in myth and thus removed from time, the scars of departure are
destined to stop short of entering time and thus affecting history. The
train station in Maron's version of this famous myth of farewell revives
the mythical image as it places the observer surveying the image both
outside the event as voyeur and later, within it as participant. The narrator's other, the persona Martha, passionately experiences the theatrical
catharsis of departure and farewell at the Ostbahnhof:

Embraces, tears, oaths, up to the moment which drew Martha here, when the
train began to move with a slight jolt, inexorably increasing the distance with
every instant between those who traveled and those who stayed behind. . . . The
futile gesture when those departing grasped the void in order to grab one another,
the going and the remaining, finding each other again. The spectacle of uncontrolled joy and the sorrow intoxicated her, Martha said; she exulted and grieved at
the same time, and thought she grasped for a few moments the meaning of human
life. (Maron, 100)

Given the mythic quality, the insurmountable grief and simultaneous joy
expressed by Martha remain trapped in an ineffectual time warp, until
they are placed in the perspective of the present. The departure of passen-
gers coincides with the inability of the official practices of commemoration to mourn the loss of the repressed potential for change.

The tightrope act of defying conventional mourning codes of GDR
society and, at the same time, remaining within the bounds of articulation
occupies Rosalind's remembrance of the different deaths of her aunt Ida.
Ida, first introduced in the story as a presumed corpse buried under the
rubble of a bombed-out building, appears three days later and continues
to live another thirty years: "Ida was alive, Ida was not dead, Ida almost
died. It was a miracle that she was still alive, Ida said. My mother said Ida
was a borderline case between life and death" (9). At Ida's hospital death-
bed, Rosalind coaxes her aunt to let go of life, only to feel guilty as her
corpse is wheeled away to make room for the next patient. Remembering
her actions upon returning to Ida's apartment after her death, Rosalind

recalls how she attempted to dismantle her aunt's lingering presence by disrupting Ida's sense of order, thus giving reign to chaos. Objecting to the reappropriation of Ida's memory and subsequent dissolution of it by the lack of a diversified collective forum for mourning, Rosalind's destruction of Ida's order represents an attempt to view Ida's absence not only in body, but also in the things that embody her memory. The presence of Ida's belongings disturbs Rosalind because it keeps a memory alive that depends on the objectification of the dead and not on real empathy for the deceased. Ida's furniture is sold off to an antique dealer whose contempt for Ida's taste maligns her even after death. Rosalind sees herself as an accomplice in this second eradication of Ida. She moves between the realm of conventional mourning and one that defies the calculation of a person's memory in terms of the value of the belongings they leave behind. The disarrangement of the objects allows Ida to be remembered in relationship to the living, not petrified in the objects.

The spatial depiction of remembering as bio-graphics, relayed in the narrator's constant referral to actual streetnames and places in East Berlin, also suggests an alternative to both a rationalized version of mourning and its circular entrapment in myth:

How could she learn a new way of thinking this quickly? she wondered. Paths of thought are like streets, paved with cobblestones or concrete, one went along them as usual, unawares; at best one sought a turning one hadn't noticed before, or beat a small path to the left or right into the unknown. Her articulated system of main and secondary streets, alleys, and trails, quite adequate for her life up until now, turned out to be a trap for every one of her thoughts. In this way, Rosalind thought, all present and future would produce nothing more than the constant repetition of the past, which would only bore and not assist her. (Maron, 14)

The imaginary walks taken by the immobile Rosalind in search of Martha cut paths along historical passages in East Berlin that metonymically commemorate events appropriated by official GDR history. The most cogent reminder of repressed remembering is the concrete border severing East from West and the imagined walling-in of corpses in the Eberswalderstraße after a mysterious slaughter encountered by the narrator on a jaunt into the city. The site of the Berlin Wall becomes a monument painfully visible despite the measures taken by the official GDR story to imbue it with normalcy.[25] For Rosalind her routine walk to work along such borders depicts her internalization of the normalcy. She only resees, and, thus, re-experiences the painful physical division in her imaginary walk as "I."

In her search for Martha, Rosalind as "I" encounters wounded or dead individuals apparently the victims of a gruesome confrontation involving an illegal border crossing, the direction of which remains unclear. In her attempts to find the site of the battle she runs into a wall of police. Again, engaging her voyeuristic talents, she peers through a brief break in the ring of uniformed men and glimpses a mass of corpses, about to be hidden from view by a hastily built wall.

And now they were walling up the eastern entry. Or exit. In between were people, a thousand, two thousand, who knew how many. The next morning pedestrians rushing by would be amazed or not indifferent that where there had been a street the day before, there was now a wall. In a few weeks the wall will be covered with film posters and the call-up for those born in '68 to register for conscription. There used to be a street here, the people will recall, until that too fades into oblivion. (141)[26]

The process of forgetting is allegorized as a state-sanctioned mass entombment of the dead and dying. (The dead or dying might also signify those who have physically left the GDR or who have succumbed to dissatisfaction and frustration by leaving it psychologically). The misremembrance of the dead, like the ring of police representing the brutal, but vulnerable power of the state, obscures the narrator's subjective vision. The collectivized version of the past represented by the obstructed view shows the effects of a collective memory estranged from the subjective perceptions and experiences of the people it supposedly serves.

Consequently, Rosalind's own memories are affected by the presence of the internalized, ineffectual remnants of a stultified way of remembering and fashioning of the present. She recognizes her own complicity in their existence. The interaction between different kinds of remembering and perceiving (nostalgic, monumental, subjective) reveal at once the sociopolitical side of subjective remembering and the impossibility of estranging oneself totally from social forms of remembering.

The alienating effects of an official and exclusive collective history on the psyche of the narrator implicitly comment on the detrimental effects of this history upon an individual autobiography. The existence of a coherent, stable autobiography separate from the historical context forming and being reformed by it, is placed in question by the countermemory produced by the narrator's fantasy and imagined exodus from everyday forgetting. Such forgetting is forged by her complicity in perpetuating the appearance of continuity and progress in traditional historical narratives written by her in her capacity as dedicated historian. She recovers a sense of herself through a mourning process that creates a concrete resistance to the status quo and to the conventional disregard for mourning. The active fantasy of the narrator re-activates the practice of a narrative "Eingedenken," yet, at the same time, dismisses any hope of a utopian consciousness enacted in earlier GDR novels such as *The Quest for Christa T.* Although Maron's novel upholds the significance of subjective fantasy and remembering for textually challenging the petrified and stagnant view of the past propagated through official GDR channels, its bleak ending represents a loss of faith in the power of counterremembrance to promote actual social change. In ending her novel, Maron depicts the reunion between Rosalind and Martha, her repressed, rebellious, sensual, and artistic persona. "I" (Rosalind) traverses the streets of East Berlin in the direction of the train station, and finally finds Martha in the Bowery in New York City. The futility of an imagined freedom is embodied in Martha's condition: she is an alcoholic street person. Instead of demanding external freedom with simultaneous internal liberation, Martha's ambiguous departure from the constraints of an unimaginative environment in the GDR into an image of self-mutilation and marginal existence questions the possibility of fantasy's power for bringing about self-actualization within a social context solely in opposition to the external reality and not in direct protest against it. In retrospect, the actual political changes in the GDR and the accompanying hopes for subsequent reforms surpass the imaginative depiction of rebellion symbolized in Maron's text. Maron's pessimistic view of GDR society and of the role of the writer foreshadowed not only the end of the GDR, but also of the utopian consciousness that had sustained many women writers in their quest for a socialist and female subjectivity within the GDR state.

Unlike the hope implicitly expressed in the closing phrase of Christa T., "when if not now," Maron's novel leaves us with a sense of emptiness. Rosalind's attempts to remember alternatively by taking on a different body become reinscribed into the oppressive status quo of the GDR. The memories become petrified, as though they did not have an afterlife that takes on a different guise depending on the constellations in which they are found.

As texts by Wolf and Maron attest, GDR women struggled with the regulation of their bodies, though they lived in a society that guaranteed them equal rights. Ironically, as much as the collapse of the GDR brought women democracy, it also brought them the confrontation with a capitalist system and forms of gender discrimination that left them feeling victimized. Were they better off in the former GDR, where the material conditions seemed to favor their freedom of choice? Texts by Wolf and Maron imply that agency is only gained in remembrance, a gathering together of past moments and attempts at resistance for the present. It is a remembrance that depends on presence of mind and insight. Yet the affective components of remembrance come about though the body. Wolf's remembering of Christa T. evokes a dilemma of moving beyond mourning to an active contemplation of the meaning of memory, and Maron imagines the possibility of leaving one's body, in order to obtain a differentiated vantage point from which to observe and name the cultural networks that prevent a body's freedom of expression.

NOTES

I thank Ellen Berry, Ute Brandes, and an anonymous reader for their insightful and candid feedback on earlier versions of this essay.

1. In particular, former GDR women lost the right to unconditional, free, and legal abortion during the first trimester of pregnancy, a right that had been guaranteed to them since 1972. For a detailed analysis of abortion politics in the GDR and following unification, see Katherine von Ankum, "Political Bodies: Women and Re/Production in the GDR," *Women in German Yearbook* 9 (1993): 127–44 and Nanette Funk, "Abortion and German Unification," in *Gender Politics and Post-Communism: Reflections from Eastern Europe and the Former Soviet Union*, ed. Nanette Funk and Magda Mueller (New York: Routledge, 1993), 194–200. References to works cited will be included parenthetically in the text after first full citation in the endnotes.

2. Von Ankum demonstrates how the laws legislating women's rights in the GDR clearly saw "women's reproductive work" as "one of the primary indicators of their ideological commitment to socialism" (129). In 1971, the GDR government recognized that their attempt to regulate family growth had failed and they opted for supporting women's productive capabilities in the workplace, while giving them more reproductive freedom. In 1972 abortion became legal (137). For further analysis of the situation of women prior and subsequent to unification, see Irene Dölling, "Alte und neue Dilemmata: Frauen in der ehemaligen DDR," *Women in German Yearbook* 7 (1991): 121–36; Erica Fischer and Petra Lux, *Ohne uns ist kein Staat zu machen. DDR-*

Frauen nach der Wende (Cologne: Kiepenheuer & Witsch, 1990); Ute Gerhard, "German Women and the Social Costs of Unification," *German Politics and Society* 24 & 25 (Winter 1991–1992): 16–33; Agnes Joester and Insa Schöningh, eds., *So nah beieinander und doch so fern: Frauenleben in Ost und West* (Pfaffenweiler: Centaurus, 1992); Hildegard Maria Nickel, "Women in the German Democratic Republic and in the New Federal States: Looking Backwards and Forwards," *German Politics and Society* 24 and 25 (Winter 1991–1992): 34–52; and Dorothy Rosenberg, "Learning to Say 'I' Instead of 'We': Recent Works on Women in the Former GDR," *Women in German Yearbook* 7, ed. Jeanette Clausen and Sara Friedrichsmeyer (Lincoln: University of Nebraska Press, 1991), 161–68.

3. As von Ankum points out, access to abortion on the one hand, and the continued ideological pressure to bear children on the other, produced a conflict for many women in the GDR that played itself out in literary texts. Given that public forums on the matter were extremely limited, literary texts provided a forum for the expression not only of dissatisfaction, but also possible alternatives (137). This consciousness is also prevalent in the short stories of many women writers whose work has been recently translated and anthologized in Dorothy Rosenberg's and Nancy Luken's collection *Daughters of Eve*. For a discussion of women's literature and examples of literary expressions of oppositional consciousness in the GDR, see Eva Kaufmann, "DDR-Schriftstellerinnen, die Widersprüche und die Utopie," *Women in German Yearbook* 7 (1991): 109–20; and Dorothy Rosenberg and Nancy Lukens, *Daughters of Eve: Women's Writing from the German Democratic Republic,* trans. D. Rosenberg and N. Lukens (Lincoln: University of Nebraska Press, 1993). In fact, the exchange between North American feminists, particularly in the field of "Germanistik," and GDR women writers such as Irmtraud Morgner, Christa Wolf, Helga Schütz and literary critics such as Eva Kaufmann in the mid-70s due, in part, to the feminist organization of German teachers and students, the Coalition of Women in German, is worth noting. Seeking kin outside of their own often male-dominated departments, some of the North American Germanists found kindred spirits among the GDR women. The similar pragmatic approach to everyday life, the insistence upon political activism, and the shared sense of the burdens of a double standard, continues to be a fruitful interchange. The extent to which a feminist consciousness went beyond the circle of writers and their readers is the subject of many of the articles in recent volumes on the situation of women in the former GDR. See *Germany and Gender* or *So nah beieinander und doch so fern,* ed. Guido Goldman, Charles Maier, and Andrei S. Markovits, *German Politics and Society* 24 and 25 (Winter 1991–1992).

4. Monika Maron, *The Defector,* trans. David Newton Marinelli (London: Readers International, 1988).

5. I will be quoting from the English version. Christa Wolf, *The Quest for Christa T.,* trans. Christopher Middleton (New York: Farrar, Straus & Giroux, 1979).

6. See Annette Simon, "Was kann Frauen verrückt machen?" in *So nah beinander*

160   KAREN REMMLER

und doch so fern. Frauenleben in Ost und West, ed. Agnes Joester and Insa
Schöningh (Pfaffenweiler: Centaurus, 1992), 145–46.

7. See *Germany and Gender,* and *So nah beieinander und doch so fern* [So close to
   one another, yet so distant].

8. Irene Dölling, " 'Unsere Muttis arbeiten wie ein Mann': Ein Blick zurück auf
   Frauenbilder in DDR-Zeitschriften der vergangenen Jahre," in Joester and
   Schöningh, *So nah beieinander und doch so fern,* 133.

9. Tellingly, the portrayal of women in magazines after unification places them
   in predominantly domestic realms — an image that corresponds to the growing number of women who have lost their jobs and who are apt to spend
   more time at home.

10. References to Benjamin's work cited from Walter Benjamin, *Gesammelte
    Schriften. Unter Mitwirkung von Theodor W. Adorno und Gerschom Scholem,* ed.
    Rolf Tiedemann and Hermann Schweppenhäuser (Frankfurt am Main: Suhr-
    kamp, 1972–1988). See also Leslie Adelson, *Making Bodies, Making History:
    Feminism and German Identity* (Lincoln: University of Nebraska Press, 1993).

11. For a detailed overview of the differences between the experience of work for
    women in the former GDR and FRG, see Rosenberg, *Daughters,* 2ff. Rosen-
    berg also summarizes the statistical information on the actual percentage of
    women working in the GDR.

12. Angelika Bammer, *Partial Visions. Feminism and Utopianism in the 1970s* (New
    York: Routledge, 1991), 105.

13. For analyses of the turn toward subjectivity and utopian consciousness in
    Wolf's work, see Wolfram Mauser, ed., *Erinnerte Zukunft: 11 Studien zum
    Werk Christa Wolfs* (Würzburg: Königshausen & Neumann, 1985).

14. Compare Eva Kaufmann's overview of GDR women's literature.

15. See Thomas Anz, "Es geht um Christa Wolf": Der Literaturstreit im verein-
    ten Deutschland (München: spangenberg, 1991); and Monika Maron, "Zono-
    phobia," *Granta* 42 (Winter 1992): 117–24.

16. Without ignoring the specific temporal genesis of *The Defector* (it was pub-
    lished in 1986), an inevitable rereading of it in light of the circumstances
    leading to, encompassing, and succeeding the opening of national borders in
    the GDR in November 1989 undermines the radicalness of the social criti-
    cism reflected in Maron's text. Nevertheless, the undeniable interrelationship
    between literature and society in the GDR makes a reading of Maron's novel
    all the more timely. It anticipates the concrete reaction of many GDR citizens
    against reified and outdated methods of recording history that refused to
    consider subjective forms of remembering.

17. A number of articles on *Kindheitsmuster,* for example, analyze the juxtaposi-
    tions of different kinds of remembering and the significance of writing about
    the remembering process for dismantling rationalistic, ordered forms of re-
    calling the past and understanding the present. See, in particular, Wulf
    Köpnik, "Rettung und Destruktion: Erinnerungsverfahren und Geschichtsbe-
    wußtsein in Christa Wolfs *Kindheitsmuster* und Walter Benjamins Spätwerk,"
    Monatshefte 84, no. 1 (1992): 74–90.

18. Benjamin's conceptualization of "Eingedenken" in his implicit and explicit readings of Proust, Baudelaire, Freud, and Judaic texts, is more complex than its limited use in my essay would suggest. The concept is, however, a worthy alternative to designations such as "Erinnerung" (remembrance) or "Gedächtnis" (memory) because of the commemorative and thus, potentially critical social task it assigns to remembering. Citations from Benjamin's work are taken from Walter Benjamin, *Gesammelte Schriften. Unter Mitwirkung von Theodor W. Adorno und Gerschom Scholem*, ed. Rolf Tiedemann and Hermann Schweppenhäuser. (Frankfurt a. M.: Suhrkamp, 1972–1988). English translations are from *Illuminations*, edited and with an Introduction by Hannah Arendt, trans. Harry Zohn (New York: Harcourt, Brace & World, 1968), unless otherwise noted.

19. See Lutz Niethammer, *Posthistoire. Has History Come to an End?* trans. Patrick Camiller (London: Verso, 1992). His chapter on "The Blown-Away Angel" is one of the best critiques I know on the gender ambiguity of Benjamin's motifs.

20. Niethammer nicely sums up the studies on Benjamin that attend to gender, such as studies by Susan Buck-Morss, Jeanne-Marie Gagnebin, Krista Greffrath, Karin-Maria Neuss, Marleen Stoessel, Sigrid Weigel, and Liselotte Wiesenthal. The image of the feminine in Benjamin's work can itself be seen as an allegory of hope and simultaneously as a symbol of dread, both common tropes in modernist aesthetics.

21. Niethammer's reading of Benjamin's remembrance in terms of gender is a good place to start for understanding the ambiguity of the angel figure. He interprets the angel of history as the divine messenger, the representative of a belief in redemption "stored in the religious tradition" (112). The angel cannot return to religion, but can remind one of the "human contact with history — both in reference to the past and for political action in the present" (112).

22. Sigrid Weigel, *Topographien der Geschlechter. Kulturgeschichtliche Studien zur Literatur* (Reinbek bei Hamburg: Rowohlt, 1990), 10.

23. By maintaining the right to see what others refuse to see or cannot see, Kassandra, for example, in Christa Wolf's book of the same name, is condemned to die for rebelling against the military order, where heroism is the order of the day. Much like Wolf herself, who remained within the borders of the GDR system, yet attempted to draw attention to its weaknesses, Kassandra relies on other women for companionship and community. See Wolf, *Cassandra: A Novel and Four Essays*, trans. J. von Heurck (New York: Farrar, Straus & Giroux, 1984).

24. The political role played by Christa Wolf before the fall of the GDR and the attempt by a number of Western journalists to discredit her critical stance is well documented. For a summary of the debate, see Anz, "*Es geht um Christa Wolf.*" Maron's open critique of the GDR state and her move to the West in 1988 is further complicated by her family background — her stepfather was a Minister of the Interior under Ulbricht. Both she and Wolf enjoyed a privi-

leged status in the GDR, although their attitude toward unification could not have been farther apart. Whereas Wolf belonged to the proponents of a separate GDR state, Maron embraced unification.

25. As the events in November 1989 demonstrated, the transformation of the Wall from a location of both real and symbolic division into a marketable (and eventually absent) historical monument has also realigned its mediation as a literary trope in GDR literature.

26. Reading this quotation after the border crossings in November 1989, I cannot help noting the twist Maron's satire has taken. The actual historical events have since inverted her depiction of the painful division embodied by the Wall into a pessimistic parody. One could revise her lines to read "There used to be a *Wall* here, the people will recall, until that too fades into oblivion."

WORKS CITED

Adelson, Leslie. *Making Bodies, Making History: Feminism and German Identity.* Lincoln: University of Nebraska Press, 1993.

Anz, Thomas, *"Es geht um Christa Wolf": Der Literaturstreit im vereinten Deutschland.* München: Spangenberg, 1991.

Bammer, Angelika. *Partial Visions. Feminism and Utopianism in the 1970s.* New York: Routledge, 1991.

Benjamin, Walter. *Illuminations.* Edited and with an Introduction by Hannah Arendt. Trans. Harry Zohn. New York: Harcourt, Brace & World, 1968.

— — —. *Gesammelte Schriften. Unter Mitwirkung von Theodor W. Adorno und Gerschom Scholem.* Ed. Rolf Tiedemann and Hermann Schweppenhäuser. Frankfurt a. M.: Suhrkamp, 1972–1988.

— — —. *Passagenwerk.* Frankfurt am Main: Suhrkamp, 1983.

Dölling, Irene. "Alte und neue Dilemmata: Frauen in der ehemaligen DDR." *Women in German Yearbook* 7 (1991): 121–36.

— — —. " 'Unsere Muttis arbeiten wie ein Mann': Ein Blick zurück auf Frauenbilder in DDR-Zeitschriften der vergangenen Jahre." *So nah beieinander und doch so fern. Frauenleben in Ost und West.* Ed. Agnes Joester and Insa Schöningh. Pfaffenweiler: Centaurus, 1992, 125–38.

Fischer, Erica, and Petra Lux. *Ohne uns ist kein Staat zu machen. DDR-Frauen nach der Wende.* Cologne: Kiepenheuer & Witsch, 1990.

Foucault, Michel. *The History of Sexuality,* vol 1: *An Introduction.* Trans. R. Hurley. New York: Random House, 1980.

Gerhard, Ute. "German Women and the Social Costs of Unification." *German Politics and Society* 24 and 25 (Winter 1991–1992): 16–33.

Germany and Gender: The Effects of Unification on German Women in the East and West. Ed. Guido Goldman, Charles Maier, and Andrei S. Markovits. *German Politics and Society* 24 and 25 (Winter 1991–1992).

Joester, Agnes, and Insa Schöningh, eds. *So nah beieinander und doch so fern: Frauenleben in Ost und West.* Pfaffenweiler: Centaurus, 1992.

Kaufmann, Eva. "DDR-Schriftstellerinnen, die Widersprüche und die Utopie." *Women in German Yearbook* 7 (1991): 109–20.

Köpnik, Wulf. "Rettung und Destruktion: Erinnerungsverfahren und Geschichtsbewußtsein in Christa Wolfs *Kindheitsmuster* und Walter Benjamins Spätwerk." *Monatshefte* 84, no. 1 (1992): 74–90.

Lukens, Nancy. "Gender and the Work Ethic in the Environmental Novels of Monika Maron and Lia Pirskawetz." In *Studies in GDR Culture and Society.* Ed. Margy Gerber. Lanham, Md.: University Press of America, 1988: 65–81.

Maron, Monika. *The Defector.* Trans. David Newton Marinelli. London: Readers International, 1988.

Morgner, Irmtraud. *Leben und Abenteuer der Trobadora Beatriz nach Zeugnissen ihrer Spielfrau Laura. Roman in dreizehn Büchern und sieben Intermezzos.* Darmstadt and Neuweid: Luchterhand, 1977).

Mudry, Anna, ed. *Gute Nacht, du Schöne. Autorinnen blicken zurück.* Frankfurt am Main: Luchterhand, 1991.

Nickel, Hildegard Maria. "Women in the German Democratic Republic and in the New Federal States: Looking Backwards and Forwards," *German Politics and Society* 24 and 25 (Winter 1991–1992): 34–52.

Niethammer, Lutz. *Posthistoire. Has History Come to an End?* Trans. Patrick Camiller. London: Verso, 1992.

Rosenberg, Dorothy. "Learning to Say 'I' Instead of 'We': Recent Works on Women in the Former GDR." *Women in German Yearbook* 7. Ed. Jeanette Clausen and Sara Friedrichsmeyer. Lincoln: University of Nebraska Press, 1991, 161–68.

Rosenberg, Dorothy, and Nancy Lukens. *Daughters of Eve: Women's Writing from the German Democratic Republic.* Trans. D. Rosenberg and N. Lukens. Lincoln: University of Nebraska Press, 1993.

Simon, Annette. "Was kann Frauen verrückt machen?" In *So nah beinander und doch so fern. Frauenleben in Ost und West.* Ed. Agnes Joester and Insa Schöningh. Pfaffenweiler: Centaurus, 1992, 139–50.

Weigel, Sigrid. *Topographien der Geschlechter. Kulturgeschichtliche Studien zur Literatur.* Reinbek bei Hamburg: Rowohlt, 1990.

Wolf, Christa. *Kindheitsmuster. Roman.* Darmstadt und Neuweid: Luchterhand, 1979.

———. *The Quest for Christa T.* Trans. Christopher Middleton. New York: Farrar, Straus & Giroux, 1979.

———. *Störfall: Nachrichten eines Tages.* Darmstadt/Neuweid: Luchterhand, 1987. (Accident/A Day's News, trans. H. Schwarzbauer and R. Takvorian. New York: Farrar, Straus & Giroux, 1989).

———. *Was bleibt?* Hamburg: Luchterhand, 1992.

Zwischenzeiten-Frauenforschung aus der DDR. Ed. Ute Gerhart et al. *Feministische Studien* 8, no. 1 (May 1990).

SEVEN

New Members and Organs: The Politics of Porn

Helena Goscilo

Pornographers are the secret police of male supremacy.

— Andrea Dworkin

The wenches don't do anything for my prong, . . . but when I get ready to really put the screws hard to a man, with all the authority vested in me by the state . . . it looks up at the sky, and sometimes I get so worked up that I spatter my britches all over.

— Viktor Erofeyev

Until perestroika, finding pornography in Moscow was less likely than encountering a singing nun at a bazaar. Yet by 1990 *Moscow News* reported a lively trade in girlie magazines at newsstands, an adolescent complained in print about the pornographic videos inundating the city, and metro stations and dashboards of taxis routinely displayed pictures of women wearing only a pout or a smile.[1] Public reactions to the relentless omnipresence of naked flesh pressured Gorbachev, in fact, on 5 December 1990 to establish a commission charged with elaborating measures to safeguard the country's morality. Anyone curious about the effectiveness of that official body may consult reflections on the topic by one of its members — published in the glossy Playboy clone *Andrei!*[2] By mid-1992 pornography was thriving as a mainstay of the novelties introduced, along with kiwis and deodorants, into Russia's capital. Amidst the all-pervasive renewed Petrine drive to "catch up" with the West, such an influx of ostensibly liberating, uncensored materials might appear as an exercise in freedom according to the modern Western model. As the editors of *Andrei* announced in their second issue: "We're certain that *Andrei* and its battle helped strengthen democratic tendencies in the area of social awareness and rights" (*Andrei* 2: 3).

Their certainty is, I contend, misguided. It originates in the fallacy of phallic "freedom," which merely exchanges one form of political enslavement for another. What purportedly furthers the cause of democracy is a publication that specifically targets only the male half of the population, presumably justifying its abusive exploitation of the other (female) half via body instrumentalization on the following grotesque grounds: "The first Russian journal for men . . . is essential today, for it is precisely men who more than anything need liberation from stressful aggressiveness and lack of satisfaction."[3] As the apostle of a new, true Word, the editor vows to combat the psychology of " 'a slavish sexuality' — rigid, crude, hypocritical, and blind," thus unwittingly delineating the profile of his own journal. What — after decades of censorship and regimented puritanism — impresses Russians as hard-won delivery from restraints merely enacts a substitution: the sexual Stallion replaces Stalin, institutionalizing a kindred mode of ritualized repression.

What potential repercussions does the tidal wave of porn that inundated Moscow from 1990 to 1992 have for women's status in Russian society? On what grounds can one legitimately designate pornography a gendered issue? Russians increasingly speak of the widespread current unemployment as a dilemma predominantly affecting women.[4] May the same be said of pornography? Since the materials energetically hawked in Russia's capital and elsewhere rely on Western models or originate in the West, a brief glance at the Western sociocultural framework of porn production and consumption provides a useful point of reference.

BORN TO PORN IN THE WEST

In England, Canada, and America, pornography automatically raises several interrelated issues that fuel impassioned controversy on a recurrent basis: those of definition (porn vs. erotica), legality (constitutional freedom of expression), and morality (motivation and effects of porn). Feminist scholarship (especially by Andrea Dworkin and Catharine MacKinnon)[5] and concerted political action have decisively shifted the focus of discussion in recent years by radically gendering the debate on pornography. That debate shows little sign of slackening, for the voluminous official reports and scholarly studies intended to curb or comprehend the production, dissemination, and consumption of pornography (as well as extensive press coverage of incidents like the Mapplethorpe case) have unwittingly abetted its publicity.[6] The profits of the current American pornography industry reportedly exceed those of the conventional film and record industries combined.[7] And although Denmark may boast of being the first country to legalize all pornography (1967),[8] the United States now holds pride of place as the modern muck Mecca.

Astute in identifying and exploiting new markets, the porn industry has expanded from a low-yield, covert business to "a highly visible multi-billion dollar industry,"[9] branching out into multiple categories of products and services, including film, videos, books and magazines, mail-order sales, under-the-counter materials, sexually explicit computer communications (e.g., SEXTEX), "Dial-A-Porn" recordings, and "sexual devices" and paraphernalia — such as artificial vaginas and penises, lotions, potions, elixirs, whips, and chains — usually stocked in "adult" bookstores and sex or S/M shops.[10] Analyses of porn that confine themselves to written texts of the *Fanny Hill* and *Story of O* variety smack of an earlier, monolithic era predating the current porn boom. Their purview does not take into account "water sports," rectal inflation, and the administration of enemas, for example, as techniques for sexual arousal. Resorting to esoteric models from High Culture, these earlier studies theorize titillation,[11] whereas the ultimate aphrodisiac in today's porn is, patently, annihilation.[12] Yet even commentators who have waded through the entire range of "soft core" and "hard core" pornographic genres confess defeat in pinpointing the constitutive features of porn.[13]

Definition. As Catharine MacKinnon has remarked, the dilemma of definition disturbs only those who attempt to legislate or combat pornography: "No pornographer has any trouble knowing what to make; no adult bookstore or theatre has any trouble knowing what to stock; no consumer has any trouble knowing what to buy."[14] Clearly, like Justice Potter Stewart, they "know it when they see it." Yet scholars, critics, journalists, and various government commissions appointed to investigate the nature and consequences of pornography have struggled unavailingly to arrive at an uncontested definition. Anthony Burgess's concept of a pornographic work as a substitute sexual partner enabling the attainment of sexual catharsis without an "act of erotic congress" — that is, as a "harmless" onanistic device within an Aristotelian sexual drama[15] — is shared by the majority of self-professed intellectual liberals,[16] but not by the official commissions on pornography and censorship, which have failed to reach a terminological consensus.[17]

For the most part, scholarly works, the press, and everyday usage treat "erotica" and "pornography" as synonymous.[18] Among those who draw a distinction, the criteria for differentiating between the two vary significantly. Informal conversations reveal that for many, the degree of explicitness draws the (inevitably blurred) dividing line between erotica and porn. By contrast, those trained in High Culture studies credit erotica (especially in written form) with artistic skill, often teasing out of a text a philosophy of principled rebellion or tragic "thanatic sexuality" that "redeems" it from the ignominy of the "unartistic" — porn.[19] For feminists making the distinction, egalitarianism and mutuality between sexual partners are the decisive factors. The widespread acceptance of a purely stylistic hierarchy, which equates erotica with sophistication (a "higher-class," less crude presentation of the same materials) may explain the preference in recent Russian porn for subtitling any narrative devoted exclusively to graphic copulation, tireless fellatio, and comparable acts "an erotic story" and to adopt such coy titles as Cupid (*Kupidon*) — the Roman Eros — for its pricier porn magazines. (As a guide to contents, the labeling on both is superfluous, for the naked women on the covers and their porn-coded stance instantly signal the genre.) Alain Robbe-Grillet wittily summed up the psychology governing nomenclature in the aphorism: "La pornographie, c'est l'érotisme des autres."[20]

Legality. Whereas most detractors of pornography base their objections on moral grounds, opponents of censorship advance the civil liberties argument.[21] The latter camp posits an all-or-nothing scenario, whereby limiting a pornographer's freedom of expression sets the society on the slippery slope leading to fascism (Cole, 162). The texts regularly invoked to buttress this apocalyptic prediction are novels by Joyce, Lawrence, and Miller, not *Playboy*, *Hustler*, and *OUI*, or films like *Deep Throat* and *Snuff*.[22] The commonplace that censorship of phenomena offensive to some violates the First Amendment may be countered by the argument that dissemination of material abusive to women constitutes a form of defamation and warrants injunction against "group libel."[23] Whether such a restraint is feasible remains moot, while the nature of materials currently accessible to practically anyone interested in porn suggests the impotence of censorship in overseeing its publication.

Marketing Psychology and Morality. The motivation for pornography, on the one hand, and its effects, on the other, have generated considerable heat in the ongoing debate. Even those who do not share the Marxist view of porn as intrinsic to the commodity culture of capitalism acknowledge that the capitalist system of supply and demand regulates the porn market. A desire for sexual stimulation prompts the purchase of porn, while the reward of financial profit drives its production. For that dynamic to operate, sex must be accorded the primacy it enjoys in the United States. Yet anyone who attributes Americans' obsession with sex and porn to their inherently greater sexuality overlooks the commodification of (1) sexual desire and (2) its promised fulfillment via advertising. Both are mythical products promoted by the very same forces that satisfy the needs they artfully create: big business.

As various studies of subliminal seduction have demonstrated, finely tuned strategies of "consumer engineering"[24] have enabled manufacturers to sell everything from cars and furniture to clothes, cosmetics, and alcohol by projecting flattering, illusory self-images onto the potential buyer — as someone subject to that special sexual hunger which, not coincidentally, will be appeased through the acquisition of whatever product is being featured.[25] All media, with varying degrees of sophistry and sophistication, convey the message that sexual desire and desirability (of a visible, marketable sort) are critical to a full life, to popularity, happiness, and so forth. Cleverly packaged, manipulative ads that play and prey upon "illicit" wish-fulfillment fantasies have sold the public, in fact, on a pseudo-normative sexuality shared by those marked for success. That sexuality has become naturalized, in other words, through techniques of psychological suggestion. To consolidate, verify, and propagate national standards of sexual taste, publications like *People* sponsor surveys that elect, for example, The Sexiest Man of the Year. These processes of collusion between power and pleasure and the institutionalization of the resultant identities instantiate what Michel Foucault has called an "implantation of perversions."[26]

Although psychologists, anthropologists, and sociologists increasingly recognize that sexuality is subject to shifting social constructions (its configuration and dynamics reinforced through interest groups operating behind the scenes), die-hard skeptics continue to lyricize sex as the "spontaneous surge" of "natural impulses" — a perception carefully cultivated by the very ads that belie it.[27] Of all forms of mass culture, advertising most clearly testifies to the mainstreaming of pornographic values (Cole, 41). Given advertising's attested manipulative power, that symbiosis surely complicates (if not undermines) the notion that pornography enhances and flourishes amidst liberty — civil or any other.

While few dispute the incentives for the sale and purchase of porn, opinions diverge dramatically about its effects, both on participants and consumers. Proponents of porn endorse it mainly as innocuous, even culturally enriching ("it extends the boundaries of the permissible") or therapeutic (enabling a healthy release of "tension" that otherwise might erupt in physical violence). The antipornography contingent maintains exactly the reverse, adducing if not causal, then at least correlational links between porn and violent crime. Whereas findings strike some (e.g., Williams) as inconclusive, others (e.g., Dworkin and MacKinnon) firmly believe that porn conduces to violence or, at the very least, desensitizes men, intensifies their callousness to women, increases rape myths, and entrenches misogynistic stereotyping.[28]

This notion has been challenged as prescribing an artless "realist" aesthetic to pornography that posits no disjunction or area of negotiability between screen and text on the one hand and everyday life on the other — essentially the same grounds on which the West traditionally has faulted the aesthetic of Socialist Realism (SR). Yet the genre of porn itself adopts realism as its guiding principle.[29] And, just as countless Russian readers "identified" with SR heroes, so do many Americans extrapolate real-life scenarios from screen and page. To abstract the transaction between viewer/reader and his porn materials is to divorce arousal from everyday reality. Theorists may invoke Kant,[30] but porn users want "cunt."

Feminist Perspectives. Feminists have fundamentally revised the pornography debate by spotlighting what until the advent of feminism seemed to have escaped everyone else's attention: the gendered nature of porn. The fact that film, videos, magazines, "fiction," and other categories of porn typically depict naked women as disposable instruments of male pleasure, ready and eager to perform any kind of sexual service, led feminists to reassess the genre in terms of political power. Accordingly, feminists define porn as a practice and presentation of sexual subordination, whereby female submission to male dominance (and violence) is played out in sexually explicit terms degrading to women, for the purpose of arousing a (preponderantly male) audience.[31] In porn, woman fulfills the depersonalized function of stimulating and gratifying men's desires (both within and outside the form); she endures or performs whatever act will ensure male orgasm, from submitting to anal penetration to being whipped or snuffed out, for pornography mandates that women be whores. The feminist critique of porn, then, not only defines it as sexist in content, but deplores its production as exploitative, its effects as misogyny-fostering, and its consumption as destructive to men.[32] In the last decade, however, feminists who fear "runaway" censorship and the consequences of perceived alignment with the New Right have emphasized the liberating and pleasure-giving aspects of pornography, which they characterize as diversified and amenable to female use.[33]

As an East European raised in England and specializing in Russian culture, I fully appreciate the potential hazards of official censorship. As a long-time resident in America, however, I am also bemused by its patriots' naiveté regarding covert censorship — the coercive impositions and prohibitions exerted by the forces of a "free" market economy. Skepticism distances me, then, from both the repressiveness of the unsexy New Right and the self-delusions of the politically correct Left whose identity is currently in garrulous crisis. Inasmuch as my essay examines the Russian porn market (which presupposes exclusively heterosexual male consumers) from the standpoint of gender, it provisionally embraces the feminist definition of pornography disavowed by those who decry any and all censorship.

THE ETYMOLOGICAL VARIANT AND *INTERGIRL* (A QUASI-EXCURSUS)

The etymology of "pornography" points to the debasement of women that inheres in the genre. Derived from the Greek, the term combines graphos — depiction or writing, with porne — prostitute or whore (normally the lowest of slaves in Greece),[34] with the important proviso that the material of "literary" Greek pornography concentrated on aspects of the prostitute's life other than her professional exertions. Otto Brendel defines these early treatments as "novelistic written biographies of celebrated courtesans."[35] In modern times, in fact, the amateur, unofficial status of women's prostitution is crucial to pornography, which rarely concerns itself with paid professionals.

In this respect Vladimir Kunin's *Intergirl* (Interdevochka, 1988)[36] is a curious case of hybridization, whereby a text that is pornographic only according to the etymological definition (we learn mainly about Tania's nonprofessional activities) relies on the titillation attaching to prostitution and sexually transmitted diseases to preach High Culture myths about Russia while sounding the social alarm about the dangers of AIDS. *Intergirl* is Valentin Rasputin's Fire (Pozhar) transplanted to Leningrad's sexual market during extensive Russian emigration. Its implications fully accord with the Marxist view that pornography represents the commodification of sexuality under capitalism.

Issued by the establishment publishing house of Young Guard (Molodaia Gvardiia) in 100,000 copies, *Intergirl* contains two forewords: a brief endorsement by the influential sexologist Igor' Kon, who correctly singles out for emphasis the work's admonitory function; and an essay by a journalist from the *Literary Gazette (Literaturnaia gazeta)*, which itself fulfills that function, as indicated in his title, "In the Group at Risk" (V gruppe riska), referring to AIDS. Tellingly, the text of the novel proper contains no explicit descriptions of sexual acts (a must for porn) and whenever it incorporates expletives or vulgarisms, it opts for such largely desexed terms as "svoloch'," "mraz'," and "podonok" over sexually derived "obscenities" of the "okhuet'" (verb from "khui" – prick) and "pizdet'" (verb from "pizda" – cunt) type. While asexual, the text nonetheless is vulgar in the manner once ridiculed by Tatyana Tolstaya in an interview: in its preoccupation with various brands and names of commodities, which relentlessly repeat themselves whenever clothes, cars, makeup, perfumes, and so on, are mentioned. Needless to say, these are all Western imports, weapons with which the corrupt materialist West invades innocent Russia to tempt and degrade it.

The dominant lexicon of *Intergirl* is that of economics (not sex), of capital (we learn varieties of slang for money in general, for foreign currency, etc.), which makes sense in light of the work's agenda – to propagate traditional Russian/Soviet (i.e., anti-capitalist) myths: (1) the moral superiority of Russians' vaunted generosity, spirituality, and emotional intensity to Western materialist values (the heroine's, the truckdriver Vitia's, the reformed schoolboy Kozlov's); (2) the sacrosanct nature of motherhood — a mother's love, like love *for* one's mother, transcends all other ties (exemplified in Tania and her mother Alla Sergeevna); (3) the sacrosanct nature of the Motherland, which proselytizes the unique inseparability of Russians from their native land (note the sentimental nationalism of Tania, her mother, and Verka, the Moscow ex-prostitute living in Stockholm); (4) and the apparently deathless stereotypes of "whore with a heart of gold" and "woman as nurse," which converge in the person of Tania, who simultaneously is a "warm-hearted" prostitute and an efficient, compassionate, nurturing nurse. A tender, loving daughter, she will go to any lengths to vouchsafe her mother's comfort and happiness; she cares about her patients, loves animals, quotes Pasternak from memory, and so forth. In short, Kunin revives Nikolai Karamzin's bathetic scenario — "Poor Tania," showing that, "prositutes, too, know how to love!" ("ibo i prostitutki liubit' umeiut!").

Kunin operates both sides of the street, so to speak: he treats such provocative topics as prostitution, rape, AIDS, and suicide, in the process dropping an endless trail of brand names of products calculated to stimulate cupidity (not arousal). Yet he wraps everything in a moralistic tract on the level of comic book simplicity. As a solution to Russia's highly complex dilemmas, the work delivers simplistic homilies, such as "death over dishonor," "happiness cannot be found in wealth/possessions," "home [i.e., mother and Russia] is best." It would be difficult to find a less erotic text than this clutch of recipes for safe and sanctioned conduct founded primarily on a rejection of the reductively perceived values of the West. In fact, the porn and pornographic transactions overrunning Moscow in 1991–92 seemed to instantiate the very dangers that Kunin's premonitory parable tried to avert.

THE FIRST GASP: MEAT COMES IN/TO MOSCOW

By a masterstroke of associated pseudo-coincidences, Russia lacks not only effective condoms, but also a developed national tradition of porn. It imports the bulk of its current pornography from Latvia (Riga) and "borrows" from Western sources for its own (re)products, as well as modeling its "original" creations on foreign paradigms.[37] Probably the most subversive aspect of these semi-pirated publications is their infraction of copyright law. In all other respects they conform faithfully to the stringent rules of the genre.

The suddenness of porn's acceptability in Russia has forced its production and circulation into patterns that are simultaneously centripetal and centrifugal. Owing to the scarcity of available materials, the same shots are reproduced randomly on various covers of translated and original fiction (e.g., the identical picture graces the covers of *Fortune* (Fortuna) No. 2 [1991, pd. in Riga] and of the story "Holidays in California" (Kanikuly v Kalifornii); the same nude women reappear throughout entire issues of a magazine (e.g., Nos. 3 and 6 of *Cupid* [pd. in Riga]); the same item surfaces in several different packages (e.g., the story "Weather Station" [Meteostantsiia], printed separately and also in *Sex-Hit*, No. 2). Concurrent with this frugality is a profligacy that presupposes readers' voraciousness for anything vaguely related to sex or the body: certain publications offer a potpourri of wildly heterogeneous items, some of which acquire a risqué coloration or alteration of status by virtue of arbitrary juxtaposition with radically different pieces. How "neutrally" does a reader absorb "scientific" information about biological processes or dictionary definitions of such basic terms as "deviancy" and "frigidity" in a column printed alongside a bared pudendum or pneumatic breast clutched in a male hand?

Such chaotic inclusiveness especially prevails in papers like *More* (Eshche, pd. in Riga), *Sex-Hit* (pd. in Riga), *Entirely Intimate* (Sovershenno intimno, pd. in Riga) *AIDS-Info* (Spid-info, pd. in Moscow), and sex digests. These throw together a dizzyingly mixed assortment of standard porn shots, reports on sexual diseases, illustrations of possible positions for sexual play, personal ads (incomparably more down-to-earth and practical than in the United States),[38] letters from readers seeking advice or sharing their "sexual" experiences (the naiveté of some is extraterrestrial), purely pedagogical or "how to" items, "scandals" gleaned from the Western press, and much more.[39] Particularly jarring for proponents of High Culture is the lack of differentiation between comic book nudes in suggestive poses and reproductions of famous paintings by Rubens and other representatives of Art. Within Russian porn, then, the Venus de Milo is likely to rub elbows, metaphorically speaking, with a *Playboy* centerfold, their sole common denominator being their gendered nudity. For the purposes of the genre, however, both are merely undressed female bodies, artfully "presented."

Apart from films and videos (which my essay excludes from discussion), the categories of porn that have flooded Moscow[40] may be broken down into (1) "static" visual, that is, pinups of individual women on posters or within magazines and newspapers; (2) "dynamic" visual or narrative visual, that is, "action" shots of a couple or series of such, grouped so as to suggest narrative development within a temporal flow; (3) verbal narrative, that is, texts that elaborate a plot (the covers of these normally designate the genre of the contents, via one or more nude bodies, sometimes accompanied by the tautological classification "erotic story" and the revelatory declaration of caution *cum* exclusion, "for men only"); and (4) anecdotes (anekdoty) about "sex." The first three categories both recycle Western forms and slavishly imitate their conventions, which are strictly coded to suggest a single overdetermined scenario.

Static Visual: The Hole as Whole. Pinups by definition are of woman, offered up according to a number of time-tested formulas calculated to commodify her as a generalized object for male use. Completely undressed or with breasts, bottom, and/or vagina exposed and highlighted, she becomes reduced to parts, in what Alan Soble and other Marxists have called the "dismemberment syndrome" that ensures women's alienation.[41] She invariably assumes a position that emanates passivity, submission, languor, or insatiability, and invites sexual possession or violation (e.g., on her knees; crouching, with buttocks thrust out at the camera; supine, with thighs spread wide). Boots pulled up to her naked thighs may be used to evoke the standard sexualized image of horseback riding (Tolstoy lives!), while the leather/suede conjures up bondage or S/M paraphernalia.

Although static in form, the pinup anticipates narration by imaging woman as a hole waiting to be filled, for porn tells and sells the timeless "story of O." Hence the highlighting of her anus, vagina, and mouth — the last, inevitably pouting and moist, sometimes licking, sucking, or encircling a surrogate penis (fruit, bottle, etc). If her face is visible (not mandatory for a genre that works to erase identity), her eyes are either closed in anticipated ecstasy or fixed directly on the viewer, "soliciting" him.

In accordance with porn's privileging of size, pinups favor generous breasts (with nipples darkened and perky — like Lenin, always "on watch" ["na postu"]) — and lush pubic hair,[42] which intimate comparable proportions in sexual appetite and apertures that promise a pornucopia of orgasmic delights. If healthy and robust, the woman exudes a capacity for insatiability and epic exertions (the Amazonian "sex machines" fantasized as "women robots, inflated savages" ["zhenshchiny roboty, nakachannye dikarki", *Andrei* 2: 89]). If delicate or frail, she is sooner coded for S/M pain, accentuated by smudged, dark eye makeup that connotes a bruised sexuality (Cole, 41).

The genre carefully orchestrates appurtenances and setting: animals — especially dogs, cats, and horses — hint at the woman's animal nature (evident in the synonyms of "pussy" and "beaver" for a woman's pudendum) and have specific cultural associations with sex: Dogs, as is well known, have been (ab)used for intercourse with women in porn films. Cats are ambulatory realized metaphors (or hyperbolized metonyms) for a woman's "pussy" (a visual rhetoric exploited in the first issue of *Andrei*, where the centerfold nestles a cat between her legs, her face rapt with pleasure). The horse, especially the stallion, is a traditional symbol of male potency, hence the shot of Katia Volkova, the centerfold in *Andrei* (2: 42), on horseback, arranged so that the neck of the horse resembles an enormous phallus emerging from between her gripping thighs. The purple prose explicating the sexual narrative, however, is transposed to another, less obvious, visual representation of Katia straddling a chair: "She wants to squeeze the hot racer with her legs, give him the spur, feel the ticklish velvet of his brown coat. She feels that she is both a rider and a strong, flexible mare, and a spoiled woman of the world — the one to whom they race along a dangerous road" (2: 43). "They," of course, encompasses the entire male readership of the magazine.

Settings likewise are carefully selected for their associative qualities, with the showcased "goods" sprawled on luxurious sheets, stretched out on the floor, or lolling in abandonment out in the "natural, untamed" outdoors, often beside water (the promise of other liquids). Their pose and environment advert to the women's readiness for "no holds barred" intercourse.

The meticulous choreography that organizes the components of pornography transforms women's nakedness into highly self-conscious nudity, according to John Berger's by now classic insightful distinction.[43] Pornography's display of woman in the "uniform" of nudity objectifies her so that man may perceive himself as the complementary opposite, the invading conqueror of this coded territory ("woman as land"), equipped "to penetrate the mystery within." Submission implies assertion (or violation); passivity invites activity (or violence); "large holes" can be filled only by large penises, and so forth. These aggrandizing devices generate an ego-stroking, cock-inflating image of the implied (omni)potent man that facilitates the male consumer's projection of himself into the picture, so to speak, as the active participant in the implied scenario.

The alternative of voyeurism is built into the cultural disposition of gender roles. According to Penthouse publisher Bob Guccione, women are natural (sic) exhibitionists, whereas men are natural voyeurs (Cole, 36–37). Berger's formulation echoes Guccone's, but in a context that denaturalizes the role assignment and illuminates the origins of female self-voyeurism: "Men look at women. Women watch themselves being looked at. This determines . . . the relation of women to themselves. The surveyor of woman in herself is male; the surveyed female. Thus she turns herself into an object — and most particularly an object of vision" (47). Hence the profusion of mirrors for women's alienating, voyeuristic self-examination in pornographic art, film, and writing. Although pinups literally feature only women, in a more meaningful sense women are ontologically absent, while the dominant presence is male. The male buyer and his desires determine not only the manufacture of the product, but the "layout" of the "parts" that collectively comprise the object — that is, "woman."

Dynamic Visual: The Metaphysics of Absence. In visual pornographic scenarios with two or more players, the male viewer may exercise essentially the same options — identification with the actual male portrayed, voyeurism, or a combination of the two. While this category may appear more even-handed insofar as it incorporates men alongside women into the representation, that impression of gender parity is quickly dispelled. The balance of power between the heterosexual couple (or group members) engaged for example in intercourse, preliminary fondling, or exchange of meaningful looks, duplicates the gender conventions that regulate pinup aesthetics.

Since women are the user-friendly disposables, multiple-participant groupings constellate several woman around one male, for, as Cole remarks, "the dynamic between pin-up and consumers is that of a gang bang" (36). Shots of couples contrast the woman's nudity or her exposure of one or more "key areas" (breasts, buttocks, vagina) with the man's fully or partly dressed state. Like the Godhead, the male penis in pornography tends to be invisible — underlit, so that its contours remain shrouded in darkness, hidden by the man's careful posture, or strategically shielded by the woman's body, which, of course, is fully revealed.[44] As the symbol of male identity ("manhood"), the penis remains largely "unpresentable." Its mode is action (the active male subject), not contemplation (the passive female object).[45] Just as any shot of an erect penis is prohibited as obscene by Canadian law and discouraged as unsettling by mainstream American custom, so among the publications sold in Russia the ratio of exposed (flaccid) male organs to bared pudenda is approximately 1: 100.[46]

The rigid conventions of porn militate against turning men into objects for display, as Bob Guccione discovered when he experimented with *Viva* magazine (1972). Reversing gender roles, *Viva* featured explicit accounts of women's sexual adventures, punctuated with photos of nude men (penises at rest). To emphasize the men's virility, the magazine placed them in forest settings ("man in control of wide expanses"), on ski slopes ("the intrepid sportsman"), and on horseback ("the Marlboro cowboy"). Readers' objections that the men "looked like homosexuals" (which presumably explained the poor sales) forced the magazine to close down. The lesson in lower mathematics? Boobs + butt = quintessentially a woman; pecs + penis = less than a man (Cole, 37–38). Hence their respective bodies appear in postures and at levels emblematic of their unequal image and power: the woman photographed prone, supine, or in some recognizably supplicating position, whereas the man, as the ringmaster in control, sits or stands.

A photograph published in the second issue of *Andrei* condenses a host of genre topoi that beg for closer analysis along these lines. The carefully arranged tableau shows a white (possibly marble) statue of Napoleon on a red tablecloth (coded to suggest blood and passion), standing, arms folded, between a seated woman's spread thighs. The military figure of Napoleon, instantly recognizable through his uniform, universalizes malehood as arrogant conqueror. A monument (literally and figuratively) to boundless power, Napoleon for Russians is the violent invader who confidently enters unknown terrain and by whatever methods necessary imposes sovereignty over it. An unstoppable force, on the one hand, Napoleon nonetheless exudes an aura of Olympian calm, on the other, because he is immobilized (and desexed) through the cool, "tamed" medium of marble or stone that immortalizes him and his historical role. Strategically stationed at the picture's center, he instantly dominates the viewer's attention as the man of action whose garb and pose suffice to establish his unique identity. The land to be forcibly entered and subdued looms behind him as "the field of his activity," where he can "prove himself."[47] It is the anonymous expectant vagina, bared but blocked off from the viewer, who sees only the pubic hair surrounding Napoleon as background. Thus, while physically reduced by compositional proportions to modest (unaroused) penis-size, Napoleon is symbolically inflated to cosmic proportions as historical referent (a cultural monument celebrated by the Western world).

Fragmented, genre-coded as "every man's land," woman here is nothing more than spread legs. A black lacy garter on her otherwise nude right thigh and her black-gloved left hand, resting "protectively" against the left groin and pubic hair, respectively signal frivolity and helplessness in the face of aggression. Faceless, lacking all identity, woman is generalized into "cunt," the fetishized body part that defines her role in the universe of male activity and values. The "hole" of her vagina (i.e., zero of her being) obstructed by Napoleon's figure is transposed onto the enormous ring decorating the gloved finger of her hand (a convention borrowed from striptease routines), playing on the immemorial association between jewels and women's genitals.[48] The picture, then, erases the live woman photographed and dismembered in it, while installing the presence of the man via inert facsimile. Both function as cultural objects — invested, however, with unequal political power.

Verbal Narrative: Hype, Hyperbole, and Taboo. If, as Linda Williams contends, visual pornography strives to make the invisible (i.e., pleasure) visible, then the goal of its Gutenberg counterpart is to print the unprintable. Critics have emphasized the more visceral appeal of the visual, which tends not only to elicit stronger and more immediate audience reactions, but also can function more economically, as acknowledged by the cliché "A picture's worth a thousand words."[49] This may especially obtain when the nude body and its acts are represented, for verbal mediation tends to dilute the instant impact normally attributed to a directly apprehended visual image. Viktor Erofeyev, in an interview on eroticism, declared:

"The power of bare flesh is such that once you've seen it you can forget about what a person is saying."[50] Yet words may strongly affect our perception of the visible nude (the difference between silent and sound film), just as the ability of the written word to conjure up visual images is crucial to published texts. In fact, printed pornography appropriates a number of authentication techniques from film as well as sharing the gender stereotyping that reinforces unequal distribution of power in visual genres.

Porn fiction sold as a separate item in contemporary Moscow has a specific look: a compilation of twelve to fifty-odd pages folded in half and stapled together to form a slim booklet, it usually has a randomly selected cover sporting a naked or near-naked woman in a suggestive pose or couples positioned in some form of sexual readiness, or beyond. Runs of the computer-typed texts vary from 500 to 50,000 copies, offered most frequently for a negotiable price ("tsena dogovornaia" — a pimp eager to make a deal). Barter and exchangeability rule the packaging, in fact, for the identical cover may appear on several different texts or, conversely, the same story may have several different covers, just as it may bear various titles (e.g., "Family Completion" [Rodovoe okonchanie][51] by S. Khalyi surfaces elsewhere as simply "Completion" [Okonchanie]). The narratives belong to one of three categories, not always easy to distinguish because of hurried, sloppy production:

1. Translations from Western sources that retain authors' names: (e.g., Jeanette Rich-Paterson's "Summer Vacation" [Letnie kanikuly] and Michelle de Clercq's "Southern Romance" [Iuzhnyi roman]).[52] Intentionally marketed by its purveyors as a Western commodity for the status that attaches to foreign goods, this category dominates the porn market.

2. Anonymous texts, where the only clue to the country of origin is the characters' names (e.g., Iolanthe de St. Ives in "Adventures in the 'Bright Moon' Hotel" [Prikliucheniia v otele "Svetlaia luna"]), which may not offer completely reliable evidence, since American and English names often mix with Russian ones, without explanation.

3. Original Russian creations, with author's name attached. The likelihood of a market-oriented adoption of pseudonyms seems strong, however, particularly in such cases as "Three-Way" (Shvedskaia troika). Although an indisputably Russian text, it purports to be the inspiration of O. Konner (American or Irish O'Connor?), which not only has a Western

ring (a significant selling point), but evokes the French "con" (not for its current primary meaning of "dumb bastard," but for its earlier one of "cunt."

Both translated and domestic Russian pornography adheres fairly closely to standard precepts of the genre. Action in pornography is the act of sex (the single indispensable element), presented in such a way as to stimulate readers' arousal. In a sense the genre presupposes an impotent as its most "difficult" or resistant reader, for its choices rest on the premise that "regular" sex alone is "insufficient cause" for excitement. To elicit the necessary frisson, what is prohibited must be *ex*hibited. Now, interdictions depend on a hypothetical norm validated by a social community. Thus porn necessarily violates taboos and breaches boundaries in those areas of sexual activity that, according to communal standards, symptomatize deviation from normalcy: (1) location and frequency of act, and; (2) number, age, and position of participants.[53] In other words, non-stop, non-missionary sex, outside of bed, with adolescents and pensioners, preferably in groups. Hence in "Three-Way," Sasha and Vitia have three-way sex with Liliia, a woman in her sixties devoted to masturbating men to orgasm; Viktor in "Out of Hunger" (S golodu) performs cunnilingus on Lin [Lynn?] during her menstruation, extracts her tampon for intensification of pleasure, and finally climaxes together with her son's girlfriend Kim when she urinates on his testicles as they both straddle a toilet seat. D. Harber's "A Ten-Year Sleep" (Desiat' let vo sne) (elsewhere called "A Young Woman's Recollections" [Vospominaniia molodoi zhenshchiny]) condenses perhaps the greatest number of generic topoi: Mutual onanism (hetero and homo), group sex with the aid of aphrodisiacs, fellatio, voyeurism, sodomy, and incest (between father and daughter).

In the narrative structure of porn, sex is the masterplot, with orgasm as its "natural" culminating point. The importance of quantity in porn's economics of pleasure builds repetition into the genre, which is why those who decry porn on other than moral grounds typically complain of boredom at witnessing one mini-odyssey of ejaculations after another. Yet, while the experience of pleasure is iterated, the means of achieving it must vary, which explains why the principle of escalation structures the genre. If the first orgasm is attained through conventional sex, the second must involve either an increased number of partners or some less orthodox route to climax. How the rule of escalation operates is nicely (and nastily) illustrated by Jeanette Rich-Paterson's "Summer Vacation," a classic text of sexual initiation. The fifteen-year-old virgin Ania enjoys her first sexual discharge in the woods when her 25-year-old distant relative Robert manually brings her to orgasm, her second when he actually deflowers her. She then progresses to intercourse with a thirty-five-year-old monk, "brother" Petr, inside a room on church grounds. If at first blush her next coupling — with twenty-year-old "brother" Klement — seems to contradict the imperative of augmentation, the formidable dimensions of his instrument ("23–25 centimeters," she notes in appreciative awe) and the confessional as his Sadean choice of setting dispel that impression. Size and site compensate for reduction of age. Ania next succumbs to forty-five-year-old "uncle" Jim, before moving on to three-way sex and fellatio with both "uncle" and "brother" (the pseudo-familial mode of reference capitalizing on the incest taboo).

The auditory accompaniment is also subject to escalation: heavy, irregular breathing and gasps expand to moans and groans, and reach a crescendo of shrieks and shouts that would put the Hallelujah Chorus to shame, even as the female voice continues to plea for "harder, faster, more." What this text artlessly exposes, then, is the mathematical organization of unappeasable appetite. Not development but increment extends the narrative, which ends only when the author's imagination (masquerading as the protagonists' sexual energy) runs out of steam.

Of course, the performance principle that informs the construction of male sexuality demands tangible evidence of capacity. Consequently, a mainstay of porn is the mathematical formulas invoked regarding size (where male organs are concerned, biggest is still best), frequency (males seem capable of epically heroic reprisals, which correspond to women's constant voracity), and quantity (people virtually bathe in each other's sexual emissions — in a convention doubtless appropriated from the "money shot" in film [authentication via a close-up of external ejaculation]). In short, hyperbole is porn's privileged trope.

What most eloquently testifies to the formulaic nature of porn, like that of the Harlequin Romance, is the "how to" manuals in the West that catalogue the genre's essential ingredients and the recipes for mixing them. Yet, for all their mechanical predictability, over the last decade both genres have pushed back the limits of acceptability. That is why one reads Stephen Ziplow's *Film Makers Guide to Pornography* (1977) with a certain nostalgia for the "gentler, kinder" brand of porn whose definitive features his checklist inventories. Stressing the supremacy of the "money shot," Ziplow also includes masturbation, conventional sex (heterosexual, penis in vagina), lesbianism, oral sex (cunnilingus and fellatio), orgies, three-way sex (heterosexual), and anal sex (the recipient presumed to be female). Sadomasochistic rituals (affectionately called "sadie-max") and thanatic sex, now a commonplace in all categories of porn, are conspicuously absent from Ziplow's list.[54] The rule of escalation, then, affects not only the internal structure of the genre, but also the evolution of the genre itself, which inevitably responds to changes in social values. Yet one constant persists, whatever the permutations: male supremacy. Texts that showcase the sadistic dominatrix merely invert a formula of contrasts at the male masochist's behest.

Hard Lessons and Softening Devices. Not unlike Socialist Realism and the Bildungsroman, some of the porn fiction sold in Moscow has a pedagogical cast, most pronounced in narratives of initiation, which trace the induction of a naif into the mysteries of "forbidden" sex acts by a seasoned specialist. Curiously, the lesson seems also directed at the reader, for many texts resort to a terminology for bodily equipment and (re)actions more likely to inform the ignorant than inflame the excitable. "Western" words with Greek or Latin roots, instead of a purely Slavic lexicon, preponderate in what I would call a purely functional naming: "fallos," "vagina," "sperma," "klitor," "orgazm." The dearth of a rich Russian vocabulary for body parts and sexual activities partly accounts for this reliance on "dictionary" nomenclature, which effectively distances the reader.

Even more curious is the slippage into euphemism and periphrasis — canonical rhetoric within soft porn. Michelle D'Clercq's "Southern Romance" offers a fascinating instance of periphrasis that, nonetheless, installs the paradigm of visual porn analyzed above. In describing his sexual congress with a woman he meets at the beach, the narrator (a married father and experienced sexual athlete) conjures up the image of sex as warfare by repeatedly referring to his penis as "weapon" (oruzhie) and "instrument" (orudie), while words applied to the woman advert to her animal nature: she is "a rider" (naezdnitsa), her vagina a "secret burrowhole" (zavetnaia iama-norka), her clitoris a "a rather strange little animal" (dovol'no strannyi zverek); when she performs fellatio, he analogizes her licking motions with a cat's. The invocation of two distinct sets of associations (military vs. zoological) underscores the author's inscription of those gendered differences that likewise structure the Napoleon-statue porn piece discussed earlier.

If in "Southern Romance" porn's reputed liberating function is belied by gender stereotyping, in "Weather Station" and elsewhere the conformist aspects of the genre manifest themselves in self-censorship. Although this "erotic" novella brims with such generic commonplaces as three-way sex, lesbianism, rape, fellatio, and implement-aided onanism, it either employs coy euphemisms for sexual parts and acts (e.g., "mound" [kholmik], "introduces the 'friend' into the 'little house'" [vvesti 'druga' v 'domik'] or replaces them with ellipses (e.g., "Alesha came up, spread my buttocks and introduced his member into my . . ."; "I started . . . Natasha anew"; "after this, do with me what you will, only . . . me"). Prudery wreaks havoc on narrative continuity when, for instance, a series of question marks and ellipses substitutes for the description of Liia's rape, occasioning a bewildering shift in point of view that makes the ensuing passage incomprehensible. Such devices signal not license, but suppression in a genre touted as promoting and betokening freedom.

Anecdotes: Loss of Oral Potency. Subversive license, by contrast, inheres in the genre of the anecdote (*anekdot*), which Andrei Siniavskii has conceptualized as a peculiarly Russian form of contemporary folklore.[55] In a remarkable operation that evokes the transsexuality motif in pornography (e.g., "Family Completion"), the logic of the current popular culture market has transplanted the anecdote onto the pages of porn and sex publications. In so doing it has transformed an authentic oral art form whose success depends on the individual "teller's" skill in delivery — on a live performance in which timing, tone, accent, and emphasis play a crucial role — into an inert item, mechanically reproducible and reproduced.[56]

Anecdotes not only appear alongside other materials in magazines and papers devoted to sex (e.g., "No-holds-barred SEX" [SEX-bespredel]), but also comprise the entire contents of slim digests (e.g., "Digest of SEX Anecdotes" [Daidzhest SEX anekdotov]) and more substantial collections (e.g., "SEX Anekdoty"), invariably featuring a nude and/or suggestively posed woman on the cover. If Siniavskii's notion that the genre lives by suppression has any legitimacy, this sudden rash of "anecdotitis" may well prove fatal to its survival. For, as Siniavskii maintains:

What lies at the basis of the genre [of the anecdote] and the conditions in which it works, develops, and exists is a violation of certain conventional norms of behavior and speech. It's as if the anecdote wants to be prohibited, liquidated on the spot, and it lives on just this supposition and expectation. Give it freedom, remove the prohibition, and it will die. (Terts, 78)

It would be myopic to deduce publishers' awareness of the transgressive nature of anecdotes from such titles as "Grin and Sin: 72 Anecdotes" ["Smekh i grekh: 72 anekdota" [pd. in Kiev]), for these compilers patently locate transgression not in the genre per se, but in the theme of sex. This much is evident from such packaging techniques as highlighting the "a" "k" and "t" in "anekdot" to stress the sexual *act* implicitly offered by the nudes scattered throughout the paper's pages.

Most collections group anecdotes according to a familiar situational typology (e.g., a gynecological appointment; a spouse's unexpected return home; a visit to a brothel; a trip abroad) that explores sexually related themes, usually cast in a problematic mode: fears of impotence, anxieties about performance, sexual incompatibility, adultery, and the like. While such topics and their treatment might reveal something about prevailing attitudes and mores in Russian society, the specifics of the genre are hardly conducive to reader arousal. The climax to which the anecdote moves is the *pointe* that brings a release of plot tension through laughter prompted by the witty closure. That is why, as Siniavskii correctly argues, "as an authentically folkloric, oral form of poetry, it fades on paper, losing the live voice, mimicry and gestures that accompany it, and sometimes practically reifies it completely, like pantomime" (91). To present this quintessentially oral genre in written form, then, is to castrate it (the Greek etymology of "anekdotos," in fact, means "unpublished"). Without the performance component that is inseparable from its subversive gesture, the anecdote becomes reaccented, drawing attention to its thematic concerns, its significance as social document. Read (as opposed to heard) from this shifted perspective, anecdotes reveal the ubiquity of adultery, mistrust between the sexes, and the currency of the rape myth — at least among the male population. But anyone seeking "porn pleasure" from these pseudo-literary eunuchs is doomed to disappointment.

THE POLITICS OF PORN: AIRBRUSHING A MYTH

If Western pornography is the political product of the capitalist economic system, in Soviet Russia politics has been the pornographic product of a utopian imagination unrestrained by ethics. Whereas Western billboards typically advertise commodities by implicating them in a sexual mystique, Soviet Russian slogans and signs invariably advertise(d) ideology through promises of a future paradise. According to the wish-fulfillment scripts of the politico-socioeconomic structures that have produced them, the larger-than-life symbolic ideals of both advertising campaigns capture (indeed, master) the public imagination. For these carefully elaborated figures suggest the tangible realization of their societies' dominant dreams. Through their visible example, they validate the possibility of formidable achievements in those arenas which collective fantasy invests with significance. If the pinup (or her "tamed" relative, the model) represents the "ideal" of the Western billboard, her Soviet analogue was, unquestionably, Stalin.

Recent Russian scholarship has begun examining the selling strategies used to fashion the image of Stalin along semi-divine lines (a procedure earlier mapped out by the prototyrant Nero).[57] Under Stalin's own supervision, film, fiction, and the press orchestrated a comprehensive drive that enabled Stalin to emerge (like the pinup) as "all things to all men." Stalin's omnipotence, according to this script, derived not from his readiness to murder when expedient (the reality), but from his omniscience in all spheres: His prophetic vision, military prowess, artistic genius, democratic convictions, compassion, and self-abnegation (the illusion). It is undoubtedly the irreconcilable discrepancy between the claims and the reality of Stalinism that prompted Liudmila Petrushevskaia to adduce the following passage from P. Proskurin's *Your Name* (Imia tvoe) as a sample of Russian pornography:

This evening, to his annoyance, Stalin, who loved this very opera with a . . . morbid passion, . . . didn't feel the satisfaction he always anticipated. . . . Briukhanov privately registered Stalin's barely noticeable movement as he abandoned himself with his whole body to what was happening on stage, and Briukhanov realized that he'd been waiting for precisely that moment. . . . From very close Briukhanov saw Stalin's eyes and he was startled at their youthful brilliance.[58]

The perfect congruence between this account and the voyeuristic strain of porn derives from their common transparent deceit: A prearranged scene, with every detail calculated in advance, is presented as the viewer's chance intrusion upon an individual during a moment of private self-oblivion. In porn, the unwary woman might be undressing, bathing, or masturbating; in Proskurin, Stalin is anticipating a "total" pleasure enabled by his musical sensitivity. Both versions of purportedly unwitting self-exposure rely on illusion (the woman's "innocent" sexuality, Stalin's sublime love of the arts) that may be manipulated through lies. Both exact a high price from their consumers, who seek one thing, pay for another, and receive a third. Both mask brutality of sorts through aestheticizing myths.

The homology emerges most clearly in the iconography of sexuality and political power as regards dress, pose, proportion or perspective, setting, props, and facial expression of the subject (i.e., object "on sale"). Shots of the pinup coordinate all details so as to convey sexuality: Her mandatory nudity and suggestive pose (often supine or prone) of intimate invitation, often accentuated by "frivolous" items like see-through lingerie, lacy garter, even toys, and often photographed from above so as to seem powerless. By inverse contrast, Stalin wears his perennial military uniform (even during peacetime), always buttoned up to the throat, so as to project simultaneously his "eagle eye" for detail and his readiness to defend "Mother Russia" and her/his "children." To emphasize his imperturbable control and inspired leadership, he either stands upright above the "teeming masses"[59] or is seated over a map, both variants implying that he controls all he surveys (people, territory, and nature). In group pictures he holds center stage, his "presence" conveyed by the reactions of those surrounding him, its force augmented by the angle of the camera, which captures him from below. Gerasimov's cult painting of him with Voroshilov shows Stalin towering symbolically over the country's capital; in the Stalin statue at the Paris World Fair (1937) the Napoleonic placement of his right hand and the forward movement of his body project Stalin's "cosmic" power. If the pinup's setting and props evoke "naughty" pleasures, Stalin's emblematize power, duty, and competence; hence he is depicted in a battlefield or beside tanks, sporting military boots and reassuringly puffing on a pipe (the Father of all Russia as phallic authority). The centerfold's bushy mound as a promise of sexual bounty has its desexed equivalent in the luxurious fullness of Stalin's mustache, which connotes a military (controlled) rather than sexual virility. And finally, because both pinup and Stalin, as visual incarnations of an ideal, must transcend their physical reality, photographers obligingly airbrush their portraits so as to erase all imperfections. In short, although the power relations they construct for the beholder are polar opposites, the (desexed) Kul't image and the (sexed) pinup image are structured by the same pornographic aesthetic.

To posit such a convergence between pornography and Stalin may strike skeptics as perverse. Yet Moscow's truckdrivers subliminally recognized and celebrated their commonality during glasnost by displacing the portraits of Stalin on their dashboards with pinups. Those who welcome pornography as a long-delayed access to freedom of expression, then, would benefit from reading J. S. Mill's essay "On Liberty," which cautions against freedoms that impinge upon the liberty and selfhood of others. Readers of Russian pornography might ask themselves why, if pornography sings freedom's song, it does so only in male chorus. Why, if scopophilic pleasures are so natural and liberating, they are limited to only half of the country's population and constructed according to musty formulas from the West. Meanwhile, from the vantage point of a Westerner trained in dismantling self-serving constructs, the porn revolution in Moscow has merely ushered in yet another Party, with different organs and members, but an all too familiar agenda of domination.

POSTSCRIPT

By spring 1993 the porn that had overrun bookstalls (lotki) throughout Moscow had virtually disappeared from the streets. *Andrei* was defunct, and the only porn items readily available in the city were the three issues of the Russian edition of *Penthouse*. Ironically, owing to recent market forces, the fate of "Russian" porn now coincides with that of Russian literature. The dynamics of supply and demand determining the sale of printed matter have relegated both to specialty stores. Volumes of such venerated classics as Dostoevsky, Tolstoy, and Mandelshtam prove as rare finds at streetstalls as "Three-Way" or "Summer Vacation." The future of porn in Russia, then, depends on the pleasures and perils sought by its consumer populace and the patterns of a culture and economy that still await stabilization.

NOTES

I thank (1) my procurers of the Russian porn examined in this essay: Vladimir Padunov, Valeria Sajez, Emily Tall, Ol'ga Lipovskaia, and Peter Scotto, who provided my Last Gasp; and (2) Bozenna Goscilo and Martha Snodgrass, the "gentle readers" who offered astute critiques of earlier drafts.

The essay, which appeared in a somewhat diferent version in the *Carl Beck Papers* (No. 1007), grew out of a talk prepared for the third annual meeting of the Working Group on Contemporary Russian Culture (Moscow, June 1992), sponsored by the Joint Committee on Soviet Studies with funds provided by the American Council of Learned Societies and the Social Science Research Council. I thank these agencies, the members of the group, and above all Vladimir Padunov; our conversations inevitably seep into my thinking and writing in incalculable ways.

1. On the market in pornography, see Dmitry Sidorov and Dmitry Demidov, "Pillow Talk," *Moscow News* (1990): 38. See the letter of complaint by a 15-year-old male student in *Moscow at Night* (Vecherniaia Moskva, 25 April 1990): 2. By 1990 pinups of naked women decorated virtually all taxicabs in Moscow.

2. The article, in the form of a diary, is by Leonid Konovalov, "Narod trebuet reshitel'nykh mer," *Andrei* 2 (1991): 16–18. Hereafter references to this issue of *Andrei* are identified parenthetically in the text, as are all citations from works first documented in the notes.

3. This *profession de foi* launched the inaugural issue of Andrei in 1991. By 1993 *Andrei* was defunct, much of its staff having transferred to the Russian edition of *Penthouse*.

4. According to statistics cited by Moscow's Gender Center, by early 1993, women comprised approximately 80 percent of the unemployed in Moscow and St. Petersburg.

5. The transcript of the public hearings accompanying Dworkin and MacKinnon's work for the City Council in Minneapolis (1983) may be found in *Pornography and Sexual Violence: Evidence of the Links* (London: Everywoman, 1988), hereafter cited parenthetically in the text as PaSV.

6. The brouhaha around Robert Mapplethorpe's photograph exhibition in Cincinnati (1990) revived a host of questions normally triggered by the appearance of works considered pornographic by some segments of society. On this, see Robin Cembalest, "The Obscenity Trial: How They Voted to Acquit," *Art News* (December 1990): 136 and "Body Politics," editorial in *Commonwealth* (Nov. 9, 1990): 627.

7. Andrea Dworkin, *Pornography: Men Possessing Women* (New York: E. P. Dutton, 1989), unnumbered page of Preface, following p. xl. At the Minneapolis hearings, Dworkin cited an article claiming that pornography annually accrues about seven billion dollars, which would place it fortieth in the list of

Fortune 500 largest companies in terms of profit (PaSV, 10–11). She has come under fire from partisans of pornography for making unsubstantiated assertions.

8. Douglas A. Hughes, Introduction to *Perspectives on Pornography* (New York: St. Martin's Press, 1970), xiv.

9. U.S. Department of Justice (1986), Attorney General's Commission on Pornography. Final Report 1353.

10. For a rundown on the various categories, see Gordon Hawkins and Franklin E. Zimring, *Pornography in a Free Society* (Cambridge: Cambridge University Press, 1988), 30–52.

11. See, for instance, the influential essay by Susan Sontag, "The Pornographic Imagination," in Hughes, *Perspectives on Pornography*, 131–69. To viewers of such porn classics as *Deep Throat* and purchasers of "under-the-counter" publications, Sontag's ruminations on aesthetics, philosophical speculation, Henry James, and Bataille must have an inter-galactic ring.

12. As Ed Donnerstein (a psychologist at the Center for Communications Research at the University of Wisconsin) testified, porn material "has changed quite drastically" since 1968 (PaSV, 22). See also Donnerstein's book, *The Question of Pornography: Research Findings and Policy Implications* (New York: Free Press, 1987).

13. "Hard core" originally referred to the actual perpetration of the acts represented in the porn materials as part of their production, whereas "soft core" simulated them. Nowadays "soft core" tends to designate less explicit treatments of sexual acts, often euphemized through a romantic haze. This designation has led to analyses of Harlequin romances, for example, as soft porn. Indeed, that genre polarizes gender along lines of dominance, control, power, and violence for men, and submission, helplessness, disempowerment, and acceptance of brutalization by women.

14. Comment at the Women Law Conference in New York, 1986, quoted in Susan Cole, *Pornography and the Sex Crisis* (Toronto: Amanta, 1989), 170, n. 18.

15. Anthony Burgess, "What Is Pornography?" in Hughes, *Perspectives on Pornography*, 15.

   Susan Cole has validly objected that to accept the so-called cathartic value of pornography is difficult "when murder victims' bodies are strewn with pornographs, or when the dresser drawers of child-killers like Clifford Olson are crammed with pornographic magazines" (Cole, 45).

16. The 1980s' emphasis on pleasure merely plays variations on the older liberalist claim: "The true defense of pornography and obscenity, as they encourage sexuality, is that they are harmless or beneficial." Stanley Edgar Hyman, "In Defense of Pornography," in Hughes, *Perspectives on Pornography*, 40.

17. For an assessment of the Johnson Commission (1970), the Williams Committee (1979), and the Meese Commission, see Hawkins and Zimring, *Pornography in a Free Society*, 20–29. On the Final Report of the Attorney General's Commission on Pornography (1986), see Clive Bloom, "Grinding with the

Bachelors: Pornography in a Machine Age," in *Perspectives on Pornography*, ed. Clive Day and Clive Bloom (New York: St. Martin's Press, 1988), 9–25.

18. That point is made about the Russian public by Leonid Konovalov in his piece on the Russian commission. See *Andrei* 2 (1991): 16.

19. Works by the Marquis de Sade, Henry Miller, John Cleland (*Fanny Hill* [1749]), Pauline Réage (*The Story of O* [1954]), and Erica Jong belong to the conventional corpus of "erotic" texts. Commentators such as Susan Sontag, for example, often with the aid of Georges Bataille (*Death and Sensuality: A Study of Eroticism and the Taboo* [1969]), analyze these texts in terms of "artistic superiority." See Sontag, 131–69.

20. Cited in Maurice Charney, *Sexual Fiction* (London: Methuen, 1981), 1.

21. See their essays in the collection edited by Hughes.

22. At the Minneapolis hearings on pornography, Linda Marciano, the Linda Lovelace of Gerard Damiano's *Deep Throat*, testified that throughout the shooting of the film its agent Charles Traynor imprisoned, physically brutalized, and forced her at gunpoint to have sex with animals. See her autobiography, titled *Ordeal*; see also Anthony Crabbe, "Feature-Length Sex Films," in Day and Bloom, *Perspectives on Pornography*, 44–68.

 The feature-length commercial film by the husband and wife team of Michael and Roberta Findlay titled *Snuff* (1976) popularized evisceration of women and their death (they are "snuffed out") as a "turn on." In her book on porn film, Linda Williams argues, with unpersuasive logic, that the film is not pornographic, but a variant on the slasher film. Yet the capacity of porn to assimilate elements from the slasher genre, which also favors female victims, is self-evident. What Williams calls "the replacement of orgasm's 'little death' by real death" actually elides the two. See Linda Williams, *Hard Core: Power, Pleasure, and the "Frenzy of the Visible"* (Berkeley: University of California Press, 1989), 189–95.

23. That has been proposed by Rosemarie Tong, "Feminism, Pornography, and Censorship," *Social Theory and Practice* 8, no. 1 (Spring 1982): 1–18, especially 10–12.

24. This is the title of the definitive guide by Roy Sheldon and Egmont Arens (1932) to the economic control of a mass audience through psychological manipulation grounded in the insights of Freud, Jung, Adler, and Pavlov. On this and other aspects of subliminal seduction, see Stuart Ewen, *Consuming Images: The Politics of Style in Contemporary Culture* (New York: Harper Collins/Basic Books, 1988).

25. See, for instance, Stuart and Elizabeth Ewen, *Channels of Desire: Mass Images and the Shaping of American Consciousness* (New York: McGraw-Hill, 1982); Robert Sobel, *The Manipulators: America in the Media Age* (Garden City, N.Y.: Anchor Press, 1976). An incisive early study that pioneered both the key term and the socio-psychological approach to media material is Wilson Bryan Key, *Subliminal Seduction: Ad Media's Manipulation of a Not So Innocent America* (New York: Signet, 1973).

26. Michel Foucault, *The History of Sexuality*, vol. 1 (New York: Vintage, 1990), 36–49.

27. See, for example, the unsigned article in *Sex-Hit*, which makes the "naturalist" argument for pornography: "Pornography simply shows people as they're made, including their sexual organs." "What's Good and What's Bad?" *Sex-Hit* 2: 3.

28. See Williams, *Hard Core*, 184–228.

   "[T]o show how the concept of pornography conditions and determines the way in which men actually treat women" is how MacKinnon formulated the agenda at the Minneapolis hearing (PaSV, 9).

29. On this and the formative role of André Bazin in the realist theory of film, see Williams, *Hard Core*, 184–96.

30. Indeed, as Susanne Kappeler justly points out, Kant's theory of aesthetics, which lists women among the "soulless" products of fine art, makes woman an object of aesthetic perception awaiting "animation" by the perceiver's genius. Susanne Kappeler, *The Pornography of Representation* (Minneapolis: University of Minnesota Press, 1986), 45–46.

31. Susan Cole stresses the importance of viewing porn not as a concept or a representation, but as a practice (Cole 7–12, 24–25). For a more extended, particularized definition, see Dworkin, xxxiii.

   One might object that lesbian or gay male porn does not represent women, but such an objection ignores the widely recognized fact that in lesbian and gay male relationships the "passive" or less "macho" partner plays out the female role in a heterosexual relationship. "Woman" functions as sign.

32. Alan Soble, *Pornography: Marxism, Feminism, and the Future of Sexuality* (New Haven: Yale University Press, 1986), 150.

33. Even when feminists agree on the definition of heterosexual pornography they are divided as to the means of combatting its possible repercussions. Whereas radicals like Dworkin and MacKinnon unwaveringly opt for strict censorship with a view to elimination, feminists advocating liberal values hesitate to endorse a solution that would compromise their broader political allegiances through cooptation by Fundamentalists. See Varda Burstyn, ed., *Women Against Censorship* (Vancouver & Toronto: Douglas & McIntyre, 1985). Yet another group of feminists is reluctant to adopt a position that would imperil erotica produced by and for women. In short, the pornography controversy continues to divide feminists. See Lynne Segal and Mary McIntosh, eds., *Sex Exposed. Sexuality and the Pornography Debate* (London: Virago Press, 1992).

34. In the ancient world, "pornographos" reportedly referred to inspiring depictions of varieties of sexual intercourse that decorated the walls of a house of prostitution in Pompeii, for instance (Tong, "Feminism, Pornography, and Censorship," 2).

35. Otto Brendel, "The Scope and Temperament of Erotic Art in the Greco-Roman World," *Studies in Erotic Art* (New York: Basic Books, 1970), 64.

36. The Russian original, simply called *Interdevochka*, is available in English translation, *Intergirl: A Hard Currency Hooker*, trans. Antonina W. Bouis (New York: Bergh, 1991).

37. According to "Red Stripe Books," however, several "erotic" texts have merely been suppressed. The publisher, housed in New Jersey, so far has released two novel-length books in English translation: (1) the purported *Memoirs of a Russian Princess: Gleaned from her Secret Diary*, anonymous and, according to the editor's conjecture, "penned about the year 1796"; and (2) from the mid-eighteenth century, *The Russian Serf Girl: The Story of Grushenka*, based on a 1933 Paris edition.

38. The ads supply information not usually found in their Western counterparts: references to men's excessive drinking, assurances of economic health, frank admissions of having children who will have to be reckoned with in any relationship that might eventuate, and the like. They also imply certain trends, e.g., young men's eagerness to meet older women and, in the case of gays, older men; a concern with physical fitness; men's expressed conviction of their ability to bring any woman full satisfaction.

39. Of course, publications of a serious informational nature have also proliferated in recent years: Igor' Kon's articles, reporting on Western trends and offering data à la Kinsey; Aleksandr Nezhdanov's sexological primer, *Popular Sexology* (Populiarnaia seksologiia, Riga, 1990); a book-length examination by various sexologists of typical sexual-emotional problems between heterosexual couples, based on scores of received letters, *Mysteries of a Twosome* (Tainy dvoikh, M., 1990); translations from the Kamasutra, etc.

The third issue of Cupid has advertised a forthcoming sex encyclopedia by Sergei Mamulov, from which it extracts a rundown of various "authorities'" recommended normative doses of sexual activity (the frequencies stipulated indicate that people prefer to watch and talk about sex to engaging in it!). See *Kupidon* 3: 14.

40. Through lack of information about what kind of porn circulates in other Russian cities, my comments pertain to Moscow, since I do not wish to generalize on the basis of materials sold there (and in some cases Petersburg) but possibly unavailable elsewhere.

41. As Soble justly observes, the images of woman perpetuated through porn subject her to alienation through the "dismemberment syndrome" that manifests itself in physical, linguistic, and photographic modes: through the separation of limbs from the trunk of her body during violent sexual or nonsexual assault (and, in the East, through clitoridectomy); through the practice of depersonalizing women by referring to them via "lower" body parts ("cunt," "twat," "piece of ass"); through advertisements that anatomize women's bodies by picturing only their hands, feet, and especially breasts, hips, and buttocks. Pornography merely carries the last a step further by spotlighting their breasts, legs, rears, and genitals. See Soble, *The Manipulators*, 56–58.

42. Women coded for specialists in "woman as child," however, are apt to have small breasts and shaved mounds. According to Florence Rush, the woman-

child is fast becoming the sexual ideal in the States. See Florence Rush, *The Best Kept Secret: Sexual Abuse of Children* (Englewood Cliffs: Prentice-Hall, 1980). In the second issue of *Andrei*, among the comic book images of women drawn by Svetlana Borisova is that of Zosia, lush of body (if emphatically weak of mind), with hair in girlish pigtails, white socks, and a teddy bear beside her (91).

43. John Berger, *Ways of Seeing* (London: BBC & Penguin Books, 1972/1977), 54.

44. Cole points out that the law (e.g., in Canada) treats the penis as "sacred, scary or profane," to be "hidden at all costs" (32).

45. The grammatical usage of the vulgar Russian equivalent for "to fuck" makes the distinction between the two modes crystal clear. When used transitively (and not reflexively), "ebat'" may only have a female object: men "fuck" women, who may only "be fucked."

46. These figures represent a rough estimate of the number of exposed vaginas, as opposed to the precise count of the five uncovered male penises (four at rest, one at attention).

47. There is an ambivalence, however, in the photograph, which simultaneously expresses the male fear of losing the self in the vastness of the overwhelming mother (in Napoleon's case, Mother Russia), of "falling through the crack." My thanks to Bozenna Goscilo for her insight in this area.

48. On the striptease as a ritual that establishes the woman as an object in disguise and on the role of jewels in this process, see Roland Barthes, "Striptease," *Mythologies* (New York: Hill & Wang, 1972), 84–87.
    On the connection between jewels and female genitals, and Diderot's play with that link in his *Les Bijoux indiscrets*, see Williams, *Hard Core*, 1.

49. For the validity and limitations of this view, see Williams, *Hard Core*.

50. Viktor Erofeyev, "Konsul'tatsiia dlia GF," *Gumanitarnyi fond* 12 (1992): 2.

51. The polysemous title is difficult to render into English, for the adjective "rodovoe" means "birth-related," "ancestral," and "family," while "okoncha- nie" has the meaning of "completion" and "termination" – which, in this context, suggests sexual "coming." The playful text does not help in arriving at a satisfactory word choice that would yield a "natural-sounding" English title.

52. Contained in an issue of the paper *Sex-Hit*, printed in Riga, where, judging by the number of publications, the porn industry must keep the city's entire population employed.

53. Vivian Mercier, "Master Percy and/or Lady Chatterly," in *Perspectives on Pornography*, ed. Douglas A. Hughes (New York: St. Martin's, 1970), 27. None of the Russian materials consulted challenged the interdiction against crossing race boundaries and species, although in Villi Konn's science fiction narrative "The Adventures of a Cosmic Prostitute" (Pokhozhdeniia kos- micheskoi prostitutki) the protagonist falls in love with an insect who assumes female form.

54. These aspects of pornography particularly disturb anti-porn feminists, who

have been reprimanded by "liberals" for generalizing about all porn on their basis. Yet the (largely legitimate, though not unproblematic) point feminists try to make is that sadomasochism and thanatic porn only make explicit and carry to a violent extreme what in implicit and more restrained form makes up "regular" pornography. On this, see Dworkin and Cole.

55. Abram Terts, "Anekdot v anekdote," *Sintaksis* 1 (1978): 77–95.

56. On the effects of such processes, see Walter Benjamin, "The Work of Art in the Age of Mechanical Reproduction," *Illuminations* (New York: Harcourt, Brace and World, 1955/1968), 219–53. Of course, without modern technology Russia's recent pirating of masses of Western materials, in violation of copyright, would be impossible.

57. For an intelligent survey of the methods used and the image cultivated in these efforts, see Evgenii Dobrenko, "Sdelat' by zhizn' s kogo? (Obraz vozhdia v sovetskoi literature)," *Voprosy literatury* 9 (1990): 3–34.

58. Liudmila Petrushevskaia, "Nam — seks?" *Inostrannaia literatura* 5 (1989): 238.

59. For instance, in Toidze's painting of Stalin with the railway workers (1926) or in Finogenov's of Stalin at the front (1941). See Ronald Hingley, *Joseph Stalin* (New York: McGraw-Hill, 1974), pages of illustrations between 106 and 107.

PART TWO

Reforming Culture

EIGHT

Sex in the Media and the Birth of the Sex Media in Russia

Masha Gessen

During the first Communist Party congress after he took office, Mikhail Gorbachev outlined his agenda for change. He said the country was in crisis and needed to be reformed. He said the economic system was stagnant and needed to be reformed. And he said that the media was gray and needed to be reformed.

Six years later, Gorbachev was out of his two offices — as general secretary of the Communist Party and president of the Soviet Union — and the two offices had been eliminated, along with the institutions over which they presided. The country he had said needed reform had been dismantled, replaced with a grouping of newly independent states with many blood-drenched borders. The economic system he had said needed reform had collapsed, plunging the country into hyperinflationary chaos. But the media he had said needed reform had indeed been transformed, becoming the liveliest, most diverse, and most read media on the planet. It's just possible, too, that it became the most sexual — if not the sexiest — media in the world.

SEX AND THE STATE

Gorbachev's use of the word "glasnost" to define the era over which he planned to preside sent a potent signal to the makers of Soviet media: Like Khruschev before him, Gorbachev chose to consolidate authority by forcing — not merely allowing but demanding — a discussion of previously suppressed information. While Western media outlets readily accepted the official Soviet translation of glasnost as innocuous openness, the Gorbachev directive to the so-called "organs of the Party" that shape public opinion was laden with historical and political meaning.

The Soviet Russian-English dictionary translates glasnost not as openness *but* as publicity; the Ozhegov Russian dictionary interprets glasnost as the quality of being "accessible for public knowledge and discussion." To most Soviet media makers, who had studied the history of the revolution and lived through the Khruschev Thaw, the word "glasnost" harked back to its uses by both Lenin and the so-called Shestidesiatniki ("the sixties people") — thinkers and writers who came of age during the Thaw. Lenin, who, as historian Mikhail Heller points out, used the word extensively, had advocated glasnost as a potent revolutionary tool that was an end in itself. Activists of the Thaw era saw glasnost as a weapon of social change, the beginning of an active public discussion of Soviet society's problems. When Gorbachev gave the word its third life, he was articulating a government policy of dragging into the public sphere what had been common knowledge yet closed to discussion. When he extolled the virtues of glasnost and criticized the "grayness," "inertia," and "deaf ear to new things" characteristic of Soviet media in his remarks at the twenty-seventh party congress in 1986, he was not giving Soviet media makers license; he was giving them a job to do.

The job was one of identifying and detailing the ills of Soviet society — things that were a part of everyday Soviet life and everyday Soviet conversations but had not been depicted in the media because they could not be allowed to enter the official portrait of the *homo sovieticus*. Gorbachev's speech and related statements constituted a call to a massive, nationwide confession. The population was to confess — in excruciating detail — to such fact-of-life sins as the black market, faulty manufacturing, crime, drug use, and sex. As media makers went about implementing glasnost, articles on these topics found their way onto the pages of publications such as *Ogoniok (The Little Flame)*, a biweekly magazine, and *Moskovsky Komsomolets (Moscow Comsomol Member)*, the daily newspaper of the Communist Youth League — two publications that rose from relative obscurity to become, along with the *Moscow News*, the media flagships of the new era. But of all the topics that journalists had to find new ways to approach, sex presented them with their biggest challenge. For while the unseemly underside of Soviet economics, for example, had never been exposed, a language and a culture for discussing economics had been established in the days of the old propaganda; sex, on the other hand, was a newcomer not only to the pages of the Soviet press but to printed (and printable) discourse of any sort: political, literary, scientific.

"Russian literature of the Soviet era is cleanliness itself," wrote Vladimir Nabokov of the sterilized mirror officially sanctioned Soviet writers had for years held up to their society. Similarly, the Soviet media were virgins. For decades the media had borne the responsibility for enforcing the myth of the gender-undifferentiated wonder of the brave new world. A joke making the rounds in Moscow in the mid-80s took the enforced silence on all matters sexual to its logical extreme:

A young man graduating medical school is taking a final oral exam. Two human skeletons — one female and one male — are placed in front of him, and he is asked to describe them. The man stands dumbfounded. Finally, one of the exam administrators prompts him: "Young man, you have been studying this for six years!" The future doctor exclaims in disbelief: "*These* are Marx and Lenin?"

If doctors couldn't tell female from male from communist, then surely journalists, editors, and filmmakers couldn't either. Rather, they wouldn't want to. "Soviet literary authorities desperately want to forget that a person comes into this world already endowed with sexual organs," wrote Yelena Gessen, an exile literary critic, in an article on the Soviet system of censorship. Noting the gender of literary characters may suggest sex, indicating an awareness and an interest unbefitting anyone entrusted with a role in maintaining public opinion.

The myth of genderless-ness managed to cohabit with conservative dominant views of the proper role of women and the family. While media and literary workers churned out the textual equivalents of *The Laborer and the Collective Farmer*, the famously heroic sculpture, social policies developed along an increasingly conservative trajectory starting in 1934. As the state went about reconstituting the family, re-regulating abortion, and rewarding childbirth, the gap between policy and propaganda widened; the banishment of any discussion of gender from the public stage ensured that the gap would not be bridged.

Even the classics were subjected to censorious scrutiny. Maya Dukarevich, a Moscow psychiatrist, describes encountering the limits of permissible references to sex while she was working as a schoolteacher in Moscow in the mid-1950s. Dukarevich directed a student stage production of nineteenth-century poet Aleksandr Pushkin's epic poem "Poltava," which includes the following verse, spoken by the female lead:

Do you remember in the frightening silence
Of the night when I became yours
You swore you would love me forever?

Dukarevich was summoned to the pedagogical committee – the school's staff governing body, responsible primarily for monitoring ideological purity – and was asked how she had explained to her 14-year-old students the meaning of the phrase "of the night when I became yours." Dukarevich's response – that her students were in no need of an explanation – was deemed improper, and she soon found herself forced out of the school (and, later, the teaching profession).

Sexual content in materials intended for adults was looked upon no more kindly. Yelena Gessen recalled a foreign-fiction anthology that lost a short story in its second go-round with the censor (having been initially approved and typeset) because, as the anthology editor explained, "it contained too much sex – and totally unjustified sex. One would be hard-pressed to explain why it was necessary."

Even specialized journals maintained a virginal facade. Igor Kon, a historian and anthropologist who has become Russia's preeminent scholar of sexuality, remembers a struggle he faced in 1974, when he attempted to place an article on ancient Greek concepts of friendship in the tiny scholarly publication *Vestnik Drevney Istorii (The Newsletter of Ancient History)*. "I was really writing about friendship," recalls Kon. "I wasn't using it as a euphemism for pederasty. But how can you talk about friendship in ancient Greece without addressing homosexuality? Nonetheless, the ladies on the editorial board said that any mention of it would have to go over their dead bodies." Kon finally hammered out a compromise euphemism with the editor in chief: "those idiosyncratic relationships."

SEX AND GLASNOST

Gorbachev's call to glasnost did not in itself spell the end of the multi-tiered system of censorship and self-censorship constructed over seven decades of Soviet rule. Decrees and directives that incrementally decreased the power of the state censorship bureau and ultimately abolished it began as early as 1987, but the process of testing the limits of controls enforced by minor bureaucrats and by media makers themselves would be long and tortuous. Wrote author and critic Yuly Smelkov in a 1989 issue of the journal *Literaturnoye Obozreniye (Literary Review)*: "On the one hand, we are all saying, with growing confidence, that 'everything is allowed that is not forbidden,' but on the other hand, we are still waiting to be told what precisely is permitted." In the absence of regular directives from above, everyone faced with decisions about media content had to set her own parameters within which old limits could be pushed.

These decisions created the first signs of diversity in Soviet media. Though in the early years of glasnost all print and electronic media and publishing houses were state-owned and all films were state-funded, editorial decisions for the first time determined the content of the media. While *Pravda* and *Izvestiya* continued to toe the party line, publications like *Moscow News*, *Moskovsky Komsomolets*, and *Ogoniok* emerged as media outlets that were willing to take risks. The Soviet reading public and Western scholars of Soviet media marveled at their ability to get away with it. Still, some media makers tried to get away with more than their peers were prepared to tolerate.

In early 1988, the Moscow media elite seemed to be in agreement that a young Ukrainian director-screenwriter team, Vasily Pichul and Maria Khmelik, had pushed the envelope too far with their film *Little Vera*. Print-media discussion of the movie began before its painful birth of a national release and continued for over a year after. In the first three months of its release, the film broke all records, selling 50 million tickets. And not only did it manage to grab national attention, but it succeeded in holding it for a staggeringly long time in a period of turbulent social change. What was so compelling about the film? Sex.

Little Vera was made on a shoestring by an unknown director with an obscure cast befitting its subject: family drama in the provincial Russian-Ukrainian working class. If the Russian cinema-going audiences wanted a no-holds-barred reflection of themselves — a full-on confession — the movie gave them that: It was grainy and gritty, and it showed alcoholism and domestic violence in all the rich Soviet shades of gray. It showed gang violence. It showed prescription-drug abuse. It showed an attempted rape. It showed police brutality. It was saturated with references to Communist ideology that simply dripped sarcasm. But all anyone seemed to notice was 80 seconds of positively un-erotic premarital humping in the middle of the two-hour film. Almost every review of and article about *Little Vera* began with a reference to what became the film's defining moment, the scene in which the movie's 18-year-old heroine and her fiancé converse while having what the viewer assumes to be intercourse — though Little Vera's dress stays on, leaving the exact nature of the encounter to the imagination. It became known as "the love scene." Debate centered largely on the movie's "erotic" content. Even in the West the film was presented as erotic, and when *Little Vera* was released in the United States (where it rated a tame "R"), Natalia Negoda, the young actress in the title role, became the subject of a *Playboy* magazine pictorial.

In the Soviet press, controversy centered on the proper place of sex in the movie's — and the country's — confessional litany. The question was of the hierarchy of social ills, and at stake, it appeared, were the country's morals. Wrote Zara Abdullayeva, a literary and film critic, in 1989: "The love scene . . . which has led to various talk about the film, threatens to blind virtuous Soviet viewers and critics to *Little Vera*'s other collisions." Stating this in the first paragraph of her article, she immediately accused other critics of being obsessed with the scene to the detriment of discussing the other "collisions."

Other writers defended the film, defending the scene — on the basis that it was justified (unlike the sex in that ill-fated foreign-fiction anthology). "Now that the picture is being shown in different cities in our country," wrote Smelkov, "it has become absolutely clear that it has not shaken the foundation of our society or even the moral standards of our cinema. . . . [The scene] serves a significant creative goal."

The sex scene was indeed an integral part of their mercilessly realistic portrait close-up of a Soviet family. And that, in addition to being what the viewing public apparently wanted, was what glasnost demanded: the bleak everyday. "This is what happens when art shows us ourselves as we are not used to seeing ourselves," wrote Smelkov. "It's time to get used to it."

Little Vera was the way of the future.

THE WAY THERE

Little Vera appeared a full two years after Gorbachev announced the dawn of glasnost. Pichul and Khmelik weren't the first media makers to broach the subject, but they caused the loudest in a series of explosions. Before

Pichul and Khmelik could show it, dozens of media makers tried to justify it, explain it, and even expose it.

The first media to tackle sex as a subject matter were, naturally, periodicals — newspapers and magazines, the media that reflect societal changes first. Journalists brought to their writing about sex the tools of the trade developed over decades of Soviet press making: bogus statistics; pontificating "scientific experts"; and heavily ideologized interpretation. Sex was presented under the rubric of the social ills Soviet media were now covering with newfound zeal. As early as 1986, the trailblazing *Moskovsky Komsomolets* started devoting page 2 of its four pages to investigative, critical, and controversial content. There, articles about drug use and dishonest workers took turns, incongruously, with profiles of wholesome Soviet families and endless decrees, resolutions, and other incomprehensibly worded pronouncements of the Central Committee. The paper's coverage of matters of sex began in early 1987, with the publication of a letter from an unidentified reader who advocated what she called "test marriages" to allow young potential partners to gauge their compatibility in all areas, including — and especially — the bedroom. "*Glasnost* means giving publicity to something that is already well known," writes Mikhail Heller. But its lack of news value detracts nothing from the shock of a subject broached publicly for the first time. The odd defense of unregistered marriages, appearing in the occasional page 2 category "You and I: A Club for Young Families," started a controversy that, just two weeks later, provided the paper with an opportunity to publish what amounted to a defense of the purity of its morals and its motives:

It's been a long time since the young families club last saw such an overactive response to a letter. . . .

Why did we print the letter? Don't young people face other issues? Young people face plenty of issues . . . and we write about theater and about heroism in the workplace (as one of our readers insistently recommends). But the trouble is, those pesky young people still want more; they want to know everything and speak frankly of everything — including the issue of relations between the sexes. We believe that no subject can be off limits to the newspaper and that everyone has his own point of view. . . .

We do not advocate "free love" or "sexual permissiveness." We advocate thought.

The assertion that a newspaper acts in accordance with the desires of its readers and not the beliefs of its editors may sound like a tired old excuse to Americans, but to Soviet media makers and consumers it was an unfamiliar concept: In the past, the media — "organs of the party" — served not to satisfy demand but to shape it in the Communist mold. In 1987, the concept of a newspaper as a consumer product was still so new that the editors of *Moskovsky Komsomolets* felt compelled to employ the old tool of the self-styled scientific expert to bolster the paper's speech-not-action position. M. I. Leingold, a consultant on questions of sexology to the Moscow City Consultation on Issues of Family and Marriage (a short-lived city-government-sponsored institution that *Moskovsky Komsomolets* itself had exposed as mismanaged and unworthy of its grand name not two months earlier), was called upon to say:

[The letter writer] overestimates the role of sex in family relations. Certainly, sex plays a huge role — but far from a decisive role. The most important thing in a marriage is personalities. . . .

Now, on the subject of premarital sexual relations. Whether we like it or not, statistics confirm that some young people have them. It's a fact that often has negative consequences. But the thing is that the old strategy of teaching ignorance and prohibition has proved fruitless.

. . . We oppose early sexual activity, but we must create a culture of sex that is based on scientific knowledge.

In a society where few things are as privileged as scientific knowledge, this sort of statement placed the paper beyond reproach in its talk of sex — in which it proceeded to engage with the air of authority peculiar to the government press.

A typical example of the sort of article that resulted was a *Moskovsky Komsomolets* interview with Victor M. Zhdanov, director of the D. I. Ivanovsky Institute of Virology in Moscow, which appeared in February 1987 under the headline "AIDS: The Need for a Sober Look. Scientific Data Dissolve the Mysterious Aura of a Little-Known Illness." Zhdanov spoke out forcefully against what he described as Western media attempts to sow panic about AIDS and explained why AIDS would not spread to epidemic proportions in the Soviet Union:

The illness strikes primarily people who lead a chaotic sex life with certain perversions. That is why in the United States and Western Europe nine out of every 10 people infected with AIDS are male homosexuals and women of a certain ilk as well as drug addicts who use drugs by injecting with syringes passed from person to person.

. . . It is clear that the broad and speedy spread of AIDS in the U.S. and the countries of Western Europe is a direct consequence of the much-advertised, in its time, much-celebrated "sexual revolution." It was this revolution that practically legalized chaotic sex life and sexual perversions of various sorts. Consider just this one fact: In the United States, where the rate of AIDS is highest, there are about 2.5 million homosexuals who are officially registered with "clubs." And that's just the official figure.

... One of the achievements of our social system is the very reality that the sphere of intimate relations, the family and its everyday life are, both legally and intuitively, as it were, protected from various sorts of "sex-revolutionary" — and, as we can see from the example of the West, catastrophic — cataclysms.

The bulk of Zhdanov's emphatically presented "facts" appeared to have originated on the spot — one of many indications of a near-total lack of sex-related scholarship. While it is true, for example, that at the time of the interview no one in the Soviet Union had been diagnosed with AIDS (the first diagnosis would be made three weeks after the article appeared, and 25 more would follow before the year was out), earlier that year the health ministry acknowledged the risk of a domestic epidemic by unveiling 45 HIV-testing sites. The places with the highest incidence of AIDS in the world in 1987 were countries of sub-Saharan Africa, where the epidemic affected primarily heterosexuals. And U.S. gay activists would surely have been surprised to find out that they had 2.5 million "registered" members at their disposal.

But by the late 80s disinformation was no longer a conscious goal of mainstream Soviet media. The purpose of the just-the-scientific-facts-comrade approach to the discussion of sexuality was the establishment of a shared set of assumptions about sex — something that had never existed in the public sphere. Convention dictated that this could be accomplished only with the appearance of objective distance, which had a distinct dehumanizing edge. The more Soviet journalists talked about sex, the sharper they drew the distinction between those who did it and those who talked about it. Combined with the continued treatment of sex as a social ill and a source of social ills, this brand of journalism filled even human-interest stories that touched on sex with the kind of voyeuristic compassion that inevitably renders the subject as less-than-human. A May 1987 *Ogoniok* story on the first Soviet diagnosed with AIDS (a gay man whose recorded symptoms dated back to 1982) provided a harrowing example of such pseudo-compassionate intolerant detachment. The article began as follows:

I have seen him — our first, the one who brought us that frightening disease. Emaciated, with protruding shoulder blades, with red splotches on his face, he looks more like an infantile adolescent than a 36-year-old man. He willingly showed himself to the many doctors, from this clinic and others, who had come to look – and in his very readiness to expose himself there was also something unnatural. . . . But the most amazing thing was, he seemed not to comprehend what he had wrought, what kind of loss to this society he was responsible for.

The word "unnatural" is a clear reference to the man's homosexuality – apparently only the second major reference to homosexuality in glasnost-era press (the first had appeared barely two months earlier in *Moskovsky Komsomolets*). It stands to reason that the author placed it in a hospital context. Guided by the belief that sex was not only one of the social ills – or had to be framed as one to make acceptable journalism – but also the province of scientific experts, Soviet journalists looked for many of their early sex stories in hospital rooms. *Moskovsky Komsomolets*'s first major sex-related piece was a nearly page-long article on the young female patients of a sexually transmitted disease ward. Although the author, Aleksandr Borodinkov, acknowledged that "the hospital room has brought the children of incomplete or dysfunctional families together with daughters of diplomats or highly placed scientists and students of some of the most prestigious colleges," he went on to make the following moralistic prediction, wholly unsupported by any of the data he had gathered:

Today's homeless . . . prostitutes, chronic alcoholics, drug addicts – the sediment, the scum, the weight around society's neck – were once patients here. They return periodically, but now they are kept on the closed wards, where treatment is forced, because they present a known danger to society. . . .

The percentage of girls 16–25 among the residents has seen a significant increase recently. . . . So, as it turns out, Svetlana and Alla [two of the article's 17-year-old subjects] are even slow in their development: Some, at their age, have already dropped even lower.

Like the author of the *Ogoniok* piece, Borodinkov blamed his subjects – rendered as nearly speechless – not only for their illness but for the public health problem of which it is a symptom. The order of the day may have been exposing social ills, but these had to be shown to be of a personal, not systemic nature. Not a word in the story concerned the then near-total unavailability of condoms or safer-sex information. Indeed, by stressing that young girls of all economic strata are susceptible to sexually transmitted diseases, Borodinkov asserted that these illnesses are the result of moral decay. To those readers who realized that condoms – which were rapidly becoming black-market currency and were accessible to the privileged — could greatly reduce the risk of sexually transmitted diseases, the accent on the presence of diplomats' and scientists' children communicated that the heart of the problem was moral, not material. And the reference to diplomats' children — ethereal and tainted by the West — gave the article the edge of an old-fashioned exposé of amorality. While the patients themselves were barely quoted, the story's first quote belonged to the head of the department of epidemiology, Olga T. Tesalova: "The only way to eliminate venereal diseases lies through the cultivation of high moral standards beginning in childhood." According to the author, it was the fostering of morals in young people that his piece was about.

A month later, Borodinkov claimed to be tackling the same topic when he penned what may be the most notorious article of the early years of the sexual revolution in the media. Entitled "Gentlemen Dance with Gentlemen" and picked up widely in the West as evidence of a new era in Soviet media, the story was introduced as "another installment in the conversation about the moral education of adolescents begun in the article 'Suffering Without Tears,' " the story on the young patients. With all the authority assumed by the media over the preceding 70 years, the article declared:

For a long time information about homosexuality has been the object of an enormous taboo for everyone but medical experts. In place of objective information, there were gossip, rumors and distortions that led to equally distorted conclusions. Some, relying primarily on their personal views of various kinds of deviations from the norm, believe that homosexuality is either a form of insanity or the embodiment of everything loathsome, despicable, sexually permissive and perverted. . . . Others, who confuse the concepts of democracy and anarchy, take their cue from the West in passionately speaking out in favor of legalizing this form of relations between the sexes.

Clearly, the issue cannot be resolved without the help of doctors who specialize in this very area of sexual disturbance. But when we seek the experts' opinions, we can address an even broader array of questions: Why do these people exist among us? Why do they not become extinct after a time? Why, even in our country, where not only the promotion of, but the very fact of homosexual contact is punishable by law, the number of homosexuals is rising? What is it — an illness, lack of discipline, a criminal act? What is to be done: Do we treat them, educate them, persecute them without mercy, or learn to live with them as with an unavoidable evil? In what ways do they harm society? And, probably, the most important thing: Can we protect our children from this disaster?

If only because Borodinkov used the phrase "relations between the sexes" to refer to homosexuality, the introduction hardly seems well thought-out. This was pure rhetoric, building, with a classic Soviet media rhythm, from the unobtrusive foreplay that established the writer's authority: If he says, in perfect glasnost style, that objective information has until now been inaccessible, then he must be about to present it. But by the end of the paragraph, Borodinkov had doled out the familiar dose of anti-Western sentiment and fiction. People who "take their cue from the West" in calling for the legalization of homosexuality were a product of Borodinkov's imagination. A full two years would pass before the formation of Russia's first gay rights organization was made official at a press conference announced only to Western press representatives. Of the 12 people present that day, only two would disclose their identities. Certainly in 1987 no one dared "speak out passionately" for gay rights in any but the most clandestine setting.

Nor was any information presented to support the premise on which the story was based — that "the number of homosexuals is rising." That was not the point. The point was to establish the outer limits of the conversation about sex that was beginning: to continuously seek out a greater sin and a worse sickness to find out within what borders this new set of assumptions about sexuality would fall. So how grave a sickness was homosexuality? The answer came from the featured "expert," one Viacheslav Maslov, a researcher at the All Union Research and Treatment Center for Sexopathology. Maslov offered the following view of homosexuality:

From the physiological point of view, these people are quite normal. But their behavior . . .
    Those who have encountered members of this tribe at least once in their lives will probably understand what I mean. In observing the behavior of a male homosexual, one is frequently shocked by the femininity with which they move, carry themselves, and dress. . . . Even cosmetics are used here, in their full complement. These signs are so distinct and vivid that they force one to consider, willy-nilly, the possibility of some inborn disturbances in these people's nature. But in reality that is not the case, although the roots of this phenomenon reach into one of the earlier periods of the development of the human being: childhood.

Maslov described the case of a 20-year-old homosexual man raised by an overly affectionate mother-grandmother team who taught him musical instruments instead of sports, precipitating, Maslov said, "what psychologists call a sex-role disturbance." Maslov's sexist analysis wound its way, again, to children's education: He blamed the imaginary spread of homosexuality on women's monopoly on the teaching profession. The author and the "expert" went on to make a number of other outrageous pronouncements: that all aging homosexuals seduce young boys; that homosexuality is a disorder for which there is a medical cure; that homosexuals believe themselves to be the chosen people. But in the end Borodinkov, suddenly and improbably, again asserted that the information he had presented was an argument for educating the public — and children in particular — about sex.

While the article sent better-read readers into fits of rage or laughter, it was, in March 1987, a groundbreaking piece of Soviet journalism, a forerunner of much of the sex-related content in Soviet media. First, Borodinkov addressed homosexuality head-on as a phenomenon that existed in Russia — something that had never been done in the media outside exposés of specific West-tainted figures like the film director Sergei Paradzhanov and the poet Gennady Trifonov. That paved the way for other efforts that were based on the assumption that people in the Soviet Union had sex: If Borodinkov could *say* that homosexual sex existed in the country (and was on the rise, no less), then, perhaps, Pichul and Khmelik could *show* that something less controversial — heterosexual sex, albeit premarital — also existed. Second, Borodinkov's story demonstrated how *Moskovsky Komsomolets*'s original excuse — that it was attempting to advance sex education — could be used to the media's best advantage: You could get away with broaching the most taboo of topics if you only framed them in terms of educating the public. The demand was certainly there. The supply would soon follow.

THE CROWNING OF A SEX EXPERT

Starting in 1989, dozens of educational books on sexuality and related subjects came out from both major state-owned publishing houses and the new small private and semiprivate publishers. Many of their authors — primarily medical professionals — attempted to establish themselves as authority figures in the field of sexuality. Some names began to be recognized in some circles — especially among young people. But one man became a nationwide celebrity. The country's best-known academic since Andrei Sakharov, Igor Kon became the undisputed authority on all matters related to sexuality. "You can't even imagine the level of my popularity," said 64-year-old Kon in 1992. "This sort of thing doesn't happen in America. I am recognized by customs officers at the airport."

Before glasnost, Kon's name was known and respected in academic circles. A historian by education, he was a founder of sociology as a field in the Soviet Union in the 1960s. In the 1970s, he did groundbreaking work in child anthropology and psychology — and this led him to the study of sex. As he began doing research into young-adult sexuality, he started asking foreign colleagues for gifts of books and periodicals on sexuality. By the time the sex taboo began to lift, Kon — who, alone among Soviet students of sexuality, identified as a *sexologist* and not a *sexopathologist* — had accumulated what was almost certainly the country's most impressive library of sex-related material.

This put Kon far ahead of other Soviet scholars, whose first and most important handicap was the total lack of access to relevant scholarship. Kon started writing about sex in the late 1970s, including a chapter on sexuality in his 1979 book *The Psychology of Young Adults*. "It was extremely careful, of course — even more than careful," explains Kon. "For example, I didn't manage to insert a few pages on young-adult homosexuality until the 1989 edition." In the mid-1970s, Kon gave a course called "Introduction to Sexology" at Leningrad's Bechter Institute for the Advanced Study of Medicine, the first course on sexuality offered at any Soviet institution of higher learning. Like many popular lecture courses, the course was transcribed by a stenographer — and the transcript became a samizdat commodity, circulating among Moscow and Leningrad intelligentsia.

The transcript even made its way abroad, resulting in book offers from Poland and Hungary, two Eastern bloc countries with somewhat less puritanical censorship standards. Kon reworked his lecture course into a book, and Soviet censors cleared the book for publication abroad. But this didn't mean that Soviet publishing houses were ready for it. After a colleague convinced Kon to submit the work to Nauka (Science), the publishing house of the Soviet Academy of Sciences, Kon found himself in a decade-long battle to see the book published. Nauka requires that manuscripts be reviewed and recommended by members of the Academy, and Kon's book met and exceeded the requirement by coming equipped with recommendations from 40 individual and two institutional Academy members. Still, says Kon, "they were afraid to publish it even though there was nothing risky about it — the only really risqué thing in the book was homosexuality — and I was ready to make *any* compromise on that."

What was the holdup? "Sex," responds Kon. "Remember — we had no sex." The phrase, a conversational symbol of the virginal gender-undifferentiated myth imposed on Soviet society for so long, originated during a U.S.-Soviet telebridge Phil Donahue hosted in 1986. Uttered by one of the matrons chosen by Central Television to represent the Soviet side, it represented one of the more poignant and embarrassing culture-clash moments of Soviet society's early efforts to join the global village. After an irrepressible giggle swept through the audience on the American side, Central Television called Kon with a request to sit in the audience during the next telebridge. Kon said:

I went with a firm resolve to say nothing and merely watch how we get lied to. The people were very talkative, but when he asked a question about abortions and contraceptives, the room was plunged into absolute silence. Then a woman stood up and said, "Why would you ask such a dirty little question? Let's talk about moral ideals and child rearing." That's when I understood why Soviet television had invited me. So I said what I was there to say: that we are, in reality, an underdeveloped country; that it was cheaper and more profitable for the ministry of health and health professionals to tell the population horror stories about the imagined dangers of hormonal contraceptives than it would have been to manufacture them and re-educate the public; that this is why we are in the situation we are in today.

The message reached almost every Soviet household: In 1986, television was accessible to 93 percent of the population, and the Donahue programs captured almost the entire TV-watching audience.

Kon's 15 minutes of fame turned into years of visibility as an activist expert. As Soviet media opened up the subject of sex, the previously reclusive academic gave interviews, wrote letters and opinion pieces, and appeared on television programs to hammer home his point: that the Soviet government had intentionally kept people in the dark not just about contraception and abortions but about everything that had to do with sex. Kon, a stuttering, froglike small man with a great mane of white hair, became a sort of Soviet Dr. Ruth: an unlikely and unabashed crusader for sex education. By the end of the 1980s, it was difficult to pick up a piece of sex-related material that did not quote Kon extensively or boast an introduction or a cover blurb by him.

In 1988 Kon's *Introduction to Sexology* was finally approved for publication with a press run of 550,000 — but with a caveat: of the first printing of 200,000, no copies would be shipped to bookstores. "In order to avoid corrupting the population, the book was distributed solely through academic and medical institutions," recalls Kon. In addition, apparently as an extra precaution against having the book read by the general public, Nauka removed Kon's glossary of terms. By 1989, however, other publishing houses had shown that sex-education literature was safe and potentially profitable (this was beginning to become a concern as publishers started to lose their state subsidies), and Nauka reinstated the glossary for the second printing and released many of the copies through retail distribution channels.

Kon's book was hardly a radical text. It functioned more as a conversation-starter. Among the things mentioned in it for the first time in Soviet publishing history was the G-spot — which, according to Kon, he is still frequently called upon to educate gynecologists about. Still, it was a book intended for scholars and fairly inaccessible to the lay reader. In 1992, Kon completed and published a more popular book — *The Taste of the Forbidden Fruit* — a sort of everything-you-always-wanted-to-know-about-everything-from-foreplay-to-breast-self-exams. Like Kon's earlier book, it sold out instantly, even in what had become a rather crowded field of sex-education literature.

THE HOW-TO EXPLOSION

Starting in 1988, major publishing houses began green-lighting long-shelved books on sex-related subjects and commissioning new editions of existing titles. Most of these titles were the results of a patchwork editing process that mirrored the way the country was being reformed: the books were sharply de-ideologized and received emergency infusions of what the editors perceived as democratic attitudes, but their basic structure, approach, and, most important, level of information, remained largely unchanged.

These books promised to tell young married couples everything they needed to know or educate women about their health or help parents bring up their children. But all used a familiar greater-good formula — and the greater good here, by contrast with Kon's work or the periodicals, was not the enlightenment of the masses: they approached such topics of sexuality as masturbation, orgasms, and marital sexual happiness by first evaluating their impact on society. This approach was combined with unchallenged assumptions about the proper role and status of women in society and the function of marriage. This is, for example, how sexologist Naum M. Khodakov handled the female orgasm in his manual *For Young Spouses*, a 1979 book he reworked for Meditsina, the publishing house of the Academy of Medical Sciences, in 1988:

A frigid woman who is not satisfied with her sex life may attempt to compensate for her dissatisfaction by striving to take a leading position in society, prove herself as an administrator, a scientist or a politician. Such women are generally power-hungry and strive for positions of visibility. Disappointed by their sex life, some women become irritable, grouchy, unhappy not only with themselves but with others. This is why the elimination of frigidity is significant not only for a happy family life but for public health in general.

The book had a press run of 600,000, with printings in 1988 and 1990. It didn't linger on bookstore shelves; its intended audience — 18- to 23-year-olds — snapped up the copies within months of the printings. The same was true of other books that purported to enlighten the young reader in matters of sex — all of which shared Khodakov's greater-good approach and overriding moralism. This is, for example, how three of the more popular books handled masturbation:

From Khodakov's book:

It would not be entirely correct to think that self-satisfaction is an absolutely normal, physiological act. . . .
    Masturbation is the most common reason for worry, fear and lack of self-confidence. . . .
    It can be said that onanism does as much harm as the masturbator himself imagines. However, there is a form of onanism that is harmful for everyone. This is psychological — or mental — onanism, whereby satisfaction is achieved solely through fantasy, the visualization of seductive, piquant scenes. Psychological onanism must be treated.

From Yefim D. Maryasis and Yury K. Skripkin's *The ABCs of Family Health*:

Masturbation cannot be said to be entirely harmless: Being condemned from a moral standpoint, it creates feelings of guilt and as a result a lack of confidence in one's powers at the commencement of sexual relations. . . .
    In fighting this habit, it is expedient to direct adolescents' attention away from issues of gender toward a greater involvement in physical culture and sports, to teach them to maintain personal hygiene, to cultivate will power and self-control.

From *Your Health, Ladies*, edited by V. I. Kulakov:

If a girl shows a heightened interest in sexual relations or engages in onanism, labor provides an effective distraction.

To be fair, some of the more obvious propaganda had been removed from these books: in the old days, preambles to these discussions of masturbation would have extolled the task of raising future communists and protectors of the socialist state. But most Soviet writers besides Kon still continued to see themselves not as partners in a conversation or even sex educators but as moral arbiters. In the absence of the naked ideology that used to flank their content, these writers felt an even stronger need for moral anchors for their statements. So the component parts of the Moral Image of the Communist — a commitment to physical culture, self-control, and hard work — came out of the old preambles to insert themselves in the substantive text, somewhere between the sexual organs and gratification. Here is how the three books quoted above approached sex education:

Only one thing is important: not to separate sex education [in the family] from the formation of a citizen. *(Spouses)*

The family as well as nursery school and grade and secondary school bear the responsibility for bringing up boys and young men in the spirit of the male virtues. They must be engaged in conversations about their responsibilities to the Motherland and the family. . . .
　He must understand that a real man is noble, firm, stable, somewhat restrained in expressing his emotions as well as in his speech and actions, logical, objective, strong and kind. The primary responsibility for creating a foundation of manliness in boys must rest with fathers and grandfathers, not mothers and grandmothers. Unfortunately, many fathers entrust too much of their sons' upbringing to women! . . .
　Girls, the future keepers of the family hearth, also need life lessons. What we have in mind is the learning of hard work, the cultivation of an ability to love, empathy, sensitivity and the appreciation of such values as chastity. . . .
　When a girl is brought up in a way that does not cultivate femininity, she is unable to appreciate true manliness and imitates pseudo-male "values": rudeness, smoking, drinking and a disregard for the consequences of sexual acts. *(ABCs)*

Assertions that abstinence is harmful, emanating from Western countries engulfed by the smoke cloud of sex, do not correspond to the physiological facts of development.

... Girls who want to achieve the highest level of personal happiness must be taught that they hold one of the keys to it. Its name is chastity. Girlish pride, honor and modesty are a girl's best decoration. *(Your Health)*

Presented as nuts-and-bolts manuals, these books followed the newly hatched truism about the need for sex education with a regurgitation of the few available assumptions regarding sex and gender: advice to keep the girls playing with dolls and refrain from undermining parental authority by telling children that babies were delivered by cranes. They offered nothing that would help bridge the gap between the old virtues and the new expectation placed on the public at large: the expectation of talk about sex. The lack of specifics that crippled these books plagued all efforts to institute this new thing called "sex education." In 1988, when these editions were commissioned, the 1986 curriculum Ethics and Morality of Married Life was officially scrapped because a three-day training course designed to prepare teachers to present the rather circumspect material had proved insufficient. But as long as the myth of the Soviet people — the readers — as virtuous virgins reigned, the authors would be unable to provide the kind of discussion that is usually embraced by the term "sex education" in the West: information on contraceptives or safer sex, for example, or acknowledgment of different kinds of sexual attraction. And if the books' treatment of the topic of sex education was at least beginning to reflect the strain the new era placed on the old morality, then when they came to such topics as premarital sex or homosexuality, previously assumed moral standards emerged entirely unchallenged:

At the present time all civilized societies consider exclusive sexual relations between spouses to be the norm. *(Spouses)*

Sexual perversion is the painful disturbance in either the orientation of sexual attraction or the way it is satisfied. A common kind of sexual perversion is homosexuality, the orientation of sexual attraction toward people of the same sex.
... The work of many scholars has shown that sexual orientation may be influenced by intoxication or trauma during pregnancy. Starting in early childhood, a child with a disturbed psychosexual orientation seeks the company of children of the opposite sex, behaves as they do, and strives to wear the clothing of the opposite sex. . . .
Among both men and women, distinctions between active and passive homosexuals are observed. If such a clear distinction in same-sex love is absent, it is called bisexuality — the presence of attraction to the same and the opposite sex simultaneously. *(Spouses)*

What are the dangers of premarital sex? Premarital sex may lead to venereal disease, inflammatory infections of the vagina, the womb and the ovaries, and consequent infertility, especially if sex partners frequently change. *(Your Health)*

The virginity of young spouses serves as a guarantee of fidelity and increases the depth of feeling. The loss of virginity before marriage frequently leads to disagreements, unpleasant and difficult explanations that can last a lifetime. *(Your Health)*

Some specialists in the area of psychohygiene believe that early sexual relations aid in the development of heterosexual feeling (heterosexuality is sexual attraction to a member of the opposite sex). This can be significant in the prevention of homosexuality (the unnatural sexual attraction to a member of the same sex). . . .

But let's look at some facts that show that the early satisfaction of sexual feeling is harmful. It has a negative impact on physical and mental development; it stands in the way of future adjustment to family life; and it delays a woman's sexual awakening. *(ABCs)*

What the authors of the 1992 *ABCs of Family Health* went on to cite as evidence of the harmful effect of premarital sex was an anonymous survey of 500 young men and women of unspecified age in which 12 percent of the young women said they were satisfied with their premarital relationships while 43.8 percent said they had experienced feelings of guilt and disappointment. That the authors saw these results as proof that premarital sex is harmful — and not as an indication that premarital sex exists against overwhelming odds of societal disapproval — is just one example of their focus on teaching morality instead of the newly printable information that fascinated their journalist counterparts.

Of course, there was a weighty reason (in addition to tradition) that contributed to this choice of focus. After decades of enforced isolation, even the most enterprising of researchers could boast only very spotty knowledge. Original research in the area of sexuality had been actively discouraged; the amount of foreign writing accessible to a researcher depended on her contacts, her knowledge of languages, and the amount of writing that had been published abroad. The less saturated was the Western market on a particular topic, the less likely that publications had penetrated the Iron Curtain. What did get across the border was invariably stripped of its content, and — in a country that had lived with a single truth in every walk of life for decades — was treated as the definitive Western word. For example, the apparently imported idea that the redeeming value of premarital sex lies in its contribution to "preventing" homosexuality appeared in the vast majority of mainstream publications that tackled the topic of premarital sex. (In most of these books, incidentally, this theory cohabited with the assertion that sexual orientation is set by early childhood.)

Still, the books sold. The people who bought these books were schooled in reading between the morally weighted lines to get information they wanted — and what they found in these books was such previously unavailable information as the types and relative efficacy of contraceptives (including the ever-popular rhythm method) and the fact that many women need clitoral stimulation to achieve orgasm. "I used to ask my best friend, 'Tell me — what is an orgasm?' " remembers Olga Lipovskaya, one of Russia's best-known feminist activists, who founded the samizdat journal *Zhenskoye chteniye (Women's Reading)* in 1987, when she was 33. "I didn't know what an orgasm was until I was 30 years old. I had had two children, and I didn't know anything, in theory or practice. In school, I'd had lessons in biology and human anatomy, but no one ever described or explained the genitalia to us." The new books contained glossaries that defined words like "orgasm" and "clitoris."

But terms and techniques addressed only a small part of the hunger that sex literature was expected to fill. The heart of glasnost was in allowing the everyday to be reflected in print. The authors of these books, by refusing to acknowledge, for example, the reality of premarital sex, denied them this reflection. *Little Vera* provided this reflection on film. In 1992, Kon's *Taste of the Forbidden Fruit* provided this reflection implicitly, by addressing all of its readers as sexual beings and abandoning the preachy tone of its predecessors. But two years before *Taste* was published, a tiny, poorly printed book caused a sensation, becoming a sort of *Little Vera* in paperback.

Like *Little Vera*, the book *Love Is Not Part of the Plan: Sex & Perestroika* became notorious before it became available in the Soviet Union. The book was conceived by Moscow journalist Tatiana Suvorova, a veteran of *Moskovsky Komsomolets*, and her West German colleague Adrian Geiges as a cross-cultural close-up of Soviet young people's sexuality, a sort of Phil Donahue meets *Little Vera*. It was slated to be published simultaneously in 1989 in the two authors' respective languages in their respective countries. The book came out as scheduled in Germany, but in Russia, it seemed to be stuck at the bottom of the list at Progress, the publishing house that specializes in translations and foreign-language publications.

Sure, Soviet publishing houses had begun taking risks by putting out sex-related books. But in *Sex & Perestroika* decision makers again felt confronted with something that pushed the limits too far. Geiges and Suvorova chose the most literal, if not the most sophisticated, method of portraying the reality of sex during perestroika: They went to places where they could find young people and then interviewed them at random about their sex lives. They presented the resulting figures and quotes with little analysis.

Geiges and Suvorova found that of 42 married men and women between 18–28, 39 had had sex before marriage. Of 70 unmarried young people, three-quarters said they were sexually active. In addition, 105 of Suvorova and Geiges's respondents believed that premarital sex was an entirely positive experience for both men and women; two people said only men should have the right to engage in premarital sex; and only five said they opposed premarital sex. These raw data contrasted sharply with the sorts of digested results presented in books like *The ABCs of Family Health* to show that premarital sex was bad.

This was just one of the reasons *Sex & Perestroika* was fated to languish on the shelves of a major Soviet publishing house – and to become a favorite topic among young city people, some of whom even translated chunks of the German edition (some of which had originally been written in Russian). Desperate to get the book out in Russian, Geiges, who was 28 and spoke next to no Russian, signed on as an editor at Progress and moved to Moscow, where he hoped he would be able to shepherd the book onto the printing press.

After several months, Geiges realized that the book was hopelessly mired in the Progress bureaucracy and offered some chapters for publication to *Sovremennik*, a magazine that was beginning to test the waters of alternative editing. To no one's great surprise, the issue that carried the chapters sold out quickly, and Geiges proposed that the Sovremennik publishing house bring out the book. The proposal tested the magazine's independent mood. Finally, a compromise was concocted: Sovremennik would bring out a book that contained the original 150 pages of *Sex & Perestroika* accompanied by a glossary and some Western theoretical texts that would place the book in context for Soviet readers. The final table of contents included Shere Hite's "The Best Way to Part," Germaine Greer's "Sex and Destiny," German scholars Sigfried Schnabl and Kurt Shtarke's "Science on Homosexuality," and Gunter Amendt and Shere

Hite's "Sexologists and American Women on Masturbation" (a hybrid article bred by the editors). The final glossary included not only words like "orgasm" and "clitoris," which were beginning to become familiar to consumers of sex-related literature, but entirely new terms like "cunnilingus" ("Today, the once common opinion that cunnilingus is a deviation from the norm has been overcome," the glossary's optimistic authors declared confidently) and defined some tried and true terms in new ways. Thus "frigidity" was defined as "an archaic term . . . no longer used in international scientific literature," designating Soviet literature either unscientific or non-international in a rare — for such books until then — bow to the West. The book's final press run was 5,000 copies, all of which were sold over the course of two hours of Geiges and Suvorova's book party, held in a bookstore housed in the building of Progress, which was beginning to feel the slacking sales of its translations of books about wildlife.

In part because of its small press run and brisk sales, *Sex & Perestroika* became a symbol more than a book: After all, most people who discussed it in endless kitchen-table debates never even saw the work. The strength of this symbolism was even perhaps enhanced by the fact that *Sex & Perestroika* could not be considered a good book by any conventional measure: It was not well written, well researched, or well presented. Kon, who was quoted at length on almost every page, was so upset with the quality of the book's research that he backed out of writing an introduction.

The research may have been primitive, but it painted a picture with unprecedented detail. The book let young people speak for themselves about their sex lives. They said things like:

"I don't need a marriage license to have sex." (A female worker of a metals factory, 23)

"I share a room with my husband and my brother. It's so awful when at night we lie there, listening to sounds from behind the thin room divider." (Repairwoman, 20)

"[In casual sex] I'm concerned only with my own satisfaction." (Radio repairman, 21)

"My only criterion [for casual sexual partners] is that she not give me a venereal disease." (Technical worker, 21)

"It often happens, especially if I've been drinking, that I will coerce a woman into having sex with me, not so much because I want to have sex but because for me it's a question of pride, an opportunity to show my power over her." (Repairman, 25)

"I have a sensitive clitoris, but none of my partners knows that. And I can't admit my desire to them myself: I'm embarrassed." (Engineer, 22)

"I have sexual relations with both men and women. If I like a woman, why shouldn't I be sexual with her? Of course, in our country, it is strictly forbidden. All the women with whom I've had affairs were terrified that someone would find out about it." (Model, 23)

The stories of actual sexually active young Soviets were what made the book a success before it was ever published in the Soviet Union. An entire story from *Sex & Perestroika*, the story of a lesbian couple, was retold in the first issue of *Tema*, the Soviet Union's first gay and lesbian publication, helping create a mystique about this banned-in-Russia volume. What made the book even sexier was the presence of Western voices — both Geiges's participation and the essays included in the Soviet edition.

ALL THE SEX THAT'S FIT TO PRINT

If real-life stories, a pro-Western approach, and a hip tone were sexy, then a newspaper called *SPIDInfo (AIDSInfo)* would be the sexiest newspaper in Russia. The founders got the federal AIDS center in Moscow to act as publisher and four scholars, including Kon, to sign onto the advisory board; this gave the risqué enterprise an instant — and unlikely — air of legitimacy. *SPIDInfo* hit the streets almost as soon as the new press law legalized private-enterprise publishing in 1990--and it was so legitimate that it was one of the few new publications that made it into the kiosks of SoyuzPechat' (UnionPrint), the official all-union media distributor.

With its unusual look — colorful and bold, a sort of 90s Westernized mass-media interpretation of Russian Constructivism — *SPIDInfo* stood out among the mostly gray newspapers in the kiosks. Its layout was challengingly confusing: much of the copy appeared sideways or in fragments. But the most appealing aspect of *SPIDInfo* was that it gave sexual content a respectable package. Though it contained less AIDS information than *Tema*, which ran safer-sex guidelines in every issue, and its provocative covers featured topics like fetishes and prostitution, *SPIDInfo* carried the morally upstanding cachet of being an AIDS information publication. No one had to be embarrassed about reading it. So everyone read it. Not only did it exceed the circulation of such newspapers as *Pravda* and *Komsomolskaya Pravda* (the newspaper for Communist Party youth), but it was one of only two mass-circulation newspapers in Russia to post a gain in subscriptions for 1993.

Several publications attempted to copy the success of *SPIDInfo*. In late 1991 the St. Petersburg AIDS center launched a magazine of its own, *SPID, Sex, Zdorovye (AIDS, Sex and Health)*, whose slogan was "Don't die of ignorance." The magazine failed to hit it big. The biggest difference between *SPID, Sex, Zdorovye* and *SPIDInfo* was that the former published in-depth informational articles written primarily by Soviet scholars and doctors, while the latter printed a lot of translations and interviews with Westerners (though its advisory board, advertised in an oversized staff box in every issue, was full of doctors and scholars). The battle for media audiences had already been won by the West. Over the years of perestroika and post-perestroika, booksellers who had started out carrying Solzhenitsyn, Brodsky, and other suppressed Russian-language literature switched to translations of detective and romance novels, which appealed to a wider consumer public. Movie theaters that in the late 80s screened *Little Vera* and other domestic films that flaunted old taboos had almost entirely switched to U.S. and Western European "B" movies by 1993. And print-media consumers voted Western at every opportunity, as when they chose the hip *SPIDInfo* over the earnest *SPID, Sex, Zdorovye*.

The reasons for this preference extended beyond the residual appeal of all things Western, forbidden for so long. Even the best-intentioned of Soviet medics could not rid themselves of the heavy judgmentality of their past. It came through in their sterilized tone and, often, in their message. This is, for example, how the two publications' writers went about encouraging masturbation as a safer-sex behavior:

SPID, Sex, Zdorovye: Self-stimulation can be pleasurable and can result in orgasm, especially if the woman is playful and willing to provide visual stimulation to her partner.

SPIDInfo (excerpting from a book of selected *Penthouse Forum* letters): I have conducted a wonderful sexual experiment. I made a hole in an orange and inserted my member in it. Believe me, no vagina comes close to the resulting sensation. I added warm water and soap and masturbated like when I was 14. Please do not publish my initials and address as I am a respected person in our town and a member of the local church.

   Dr. Harold Greenwald responds: I will let this piece of correspondence stand without comment. I only want to note that respect should not be dependent on a person's sexual tastes, as long, of course, as they do not do harm to others (and in this case, they certainly don't).

After a few issues, *SPIDInfo* ceased providing specific AIDS-related information. Yet in the most important sense, the editors remained true to the slogan printed on every issue of the newspaper — "SPID [AIDS] is death. *SPIDInfo* is life!" — by providing a forum for continuous public discussion of sex. Every few months, *SPIDInfo* invented a new question-and-answer format. The kind of questions the newspaper was getting in its third year of publication testified to the continued lack of sex education in the country. "I am told that in order to avoid pregnancy I should wash my genitals with my own urine after sex," wrote in a 16-year-old woman. "I know everyone likes using tampons," wrote a 25-year-old woman. "But I think it's so inconvenient to have to take it out every time I go to the bathroom." *SPIDInfo*'s advice columnists — medical doctors all — answered these questions in the nonjudgmentally businesslike manner the name of the question-and-answer department — "Short and Clear" — promised. Their only consistent downfall, ironically, was that they seemed to have no awareness of AIDS and failed to make basic safer-sex recommendations where they would seem logical.

THE INDEPENDENT MEDIA

Like Kon's book, *SPIDInfo* was a winner in a crowded and thriving field. In 1989, at the height of glasnost, it became safe for the most important dissident activity — publishing — to come out of the underground. Samizdat was by then well on its barely legible, carbon-copy way to becoming obsolete. Another year would pass before the press law changed regulations regarding censorship and access to printing and copying technology, but as early as 1989 it was becoming clear that independent publishing would no longer be treated as a crime. The best indicator of this was the number of new publications that suddenly hit the streets, going on sale on the central interchanges of Moscow and St. Petersburg.

   In 1991, the year following the passage of the Press Law, the Russian press ministry registered 1,700 new media outlets. Such statistics are not available for the previous year, when publications were officially required to be "organs" of legally constituted organizations, but it would be fair to say that starting in 1989, thousands of new legal and illegal publications, many of which lasted for only one issue, appeared in Russia. A few of these were legitimized incarnations of samizdat publications. Several were well-financed professional spin-offs of successful glasnost-era experiments of the establishment press. But the vast majority were low-budget realizations of the publishing dreams of individuals or small groups, most of whom had no publishing experience and few resources beyond ambition and a post-office-box address to bring to their publications.

The first two categories of publications rarely, if ever, touched on the subject of sex. Samizdat had seldom concerned itself with sex, and by the late 80s, the only publication that regularly handled the topic was Lipovskaya's *Zhenskoye chteniye*. (Samizdat activists as a group assigned so little importance to topics of gender and sexuality that within the Leningrad underground publishers' Club 81, Lipovskaya was ridiculed for starting the magazine.) The publishers of the new large-circulation newspapers envisioned themselves as creators of the post-Communist newspaper of record and, in reaction to the working-class rhetoric of their predecessors, took an intentionally elitist approach to journalism. This ruled out such low-brow subjects as sex. But many in the third category of publishers, the scrappy new Russian entrepreneurs, thought sex was not only an acceptable subject but their ticket to commercial success.

For some of these publishers, like Roman Kalinin, the 23-year-old founder of *Tema*, sex and sexuality as a subject were a part of a social and political agenda. The newspaper he created was a hodgepodge of material that reflected the varying needs of Soviet gays, just beginning to define an identity and a movement. The first issues of what was theoretically a bimonthly publication but really came out whenever Kalinin could line up a printer — generally every three to four months during the first couple of years of the paper's existence — contained translations of U.S. scholar Simon Karlinsky's writing on homosexuality in Russian literature and culture, translations of safer-sex information, translations of stories such as the one lifted from *Sex & Perestroika*, and translations of Western celebrity-queer gossip. The response to the newspaper, whose printing runs ranged from 5,000 to 15,000 — minuscule by the standards of Soviet publishing gigantism — nearly overwhelmed its volunteer staff of ten:

Letters to *Tema*'s post office box came in at the rate of 250 a week during the first year of its existence. These letters, too, reflected the prevailing lack of sexual awareness in the Soviet Union. A fairly typical query read, "I like to lick my wife's sexual organs. What type of homosexuality do I have?" More often, the letters were from lonely gays, lesbians, and other self-described members of sexual minorities looking for someone to talk to or correspond with. But if the correspondence, which reflected the isolation experienced by people with nonstandard sexualities, threatened to overtax the paper's human resources, *Tema* sales reflected the public's appetite for publications that dealt with topics of sex and sexuality. With additional financial help from Western gay philanthropists, by the time Kalinin graduated college in 1991, he was able to live on the money he made from the paper and even pay contributors.

But the ticket to sales, according to Kalinin, was "pornukha" — a condescending term for anything vaguely erotic or sexual. *Tema* had joined the growing ranks of publications designed to give Soviet men of all sexual tastes erections. These included eight-page newsprint offerings with names like *Seks Daidjest, Erotika Daidjest, After Dark* (a Russian-language publication with an English title) and similarly descriptive titles that carried a definite Western tint. Most of these were indeed digests: haphazard compilations of anything the publishers could get their hands on that contained the word *sex* or one of its derivatives. An issue of *Seks Daidjest*, for example, might contain a selection from *The National Enquirer* on a particularly steamy celebrity love affair; some photocopied photographs from the jackets of Western pornographic videotapes accompanied by fictional copy — or by nothing; statistical "facts" on sexual activity or sexual organs lifted from a Western tabloid or a Soviet sociological survey, or simply the top of the publisher's head; and a tidbit on a particularly interesting transsexual lifted from *Parade* magazine. The entrepreneurs behind most of these publications had no loftier goal in mind than making money and following the powerful impulse that had for years propelled samizdat: the desire to disseminate information that is otherwise unavailable to members of what was still largely a closed society.

Each new publication seemed to spawn five more. The desire to print was so strong and urgent that many budding publishers found quasi-legal ways to circumvent the still-existing press regulations by putting out magazines or newspapers labeled Issue 0 and claiming to have a press run of 999 (a press run of fewer than 1,000, in the absence of ongoing publishing activity, made it possible to bypass the requirements of registration and the censor's stamp of approval). In Moscow, the pedestrian underpass in Pushkin Square, one of the city's busiest interchanges, turned into a sex-media market, with peddlers selling dozens or even hundreds of competing titles. "Have you been to Pushkin Square?" said human rights activist Yelena Bonner in an interview at the time. "People seem to have nothing better to do than describe every possible way of having intercourse, homosexual or heterosexual." The proliferation of sex-related publications changed the face of the city so radically that such American television personalities as Ted Koppel and Geraldo Rivera rushed to film specials on the sexual revolution in the Soviet Union, framed by shots of the publications on sale.

Few of the sex-related publications conceived in the feverish honeymoon of the sexual revolution in print survived the trials that followed. Those that did were the ones that had an identity and an agenda that transcended the mission of pornukha. *SPIDInfo* was among these publications, as was *Tema*. Several other newspapers, such as *Chas Pik (Rush Hour)*, *Chastnaya Zhizn (Personal Life)*, *On i Ona (He and She)*, founded in 1990 and 1991, tried to combine writing about sex with general lifestyle stories — a combination that has served U.S. women's and men's magazines well for years but that seemed to extend the limits of novelty beyond comfortable bounds in the Soviet Union.

But what seemed to push many Soviet bureaucrats, officials, and Mikhail Gorbachev himself out of the comfort zone was the appearance of the sex media itself. By late 1990, Gorbachev seemed to be uncomfortable with the consequences of most of his reforms. After 1989, the Party media began to take an old-style critical look at the changes in the country. In November 1990, *Pravda* declared war on the independent sex media by attacking what was probably its most vulnerable representative: *Tema*. In what was framed as an exposé of the Moscow city council (which had registered *Tema*, as it had registered thousands of organizations and businesses that year), the Communist Party newspaper published an interview that Kalinin and Yevgeniya Debryanskaya, a well-known pro-democracy activist who had written for *Tema* (and was, at the time, the country's only out lesbian) had given to a Moscow small-newspaper reporter when the three got drunk together. The reporter had shelved the interview after he sobered up, but as the mood in the country became increasingly conservative in anticipation of a difficult winter, he apparently decided that an interview in which two homosexuals admit to necrophilia and other perversions was a salable commodity. He was right: *Pravda* published it, and so did scores of local party publications throughout the Soviet Union. A media war ensued. Kalinin and Debryanskaya denied they had ever given the interview. Kon wrote a commentary piece in *Argumenty i Fakty*, a weekly opinion newspaper, defending the gay and lesbian movement. ("It was useless," he said two years later. "The public mood had condemned them.") *Pravda* published a follow-up in which unnamed Moscow city council cleaning ladies said that it was no wonder the city council had connections with perverts: the place was full of depraved politicians whose used condoms had to be swept up every night. (*Pravda* later printed a retraction.) The Moscow city council meekly objected that it knew nothing about *Tema* and had simply granted it routine registration as the private undertaking of Roman Kalinin.

It's unclear what kind of impact this particular media battle had on the credibility of the Moscow city government. And it is entirely possible that its ultimate impact on the gay and lesbian movement was positive. But the controversy articulated the government position on the sex media: It was branded unsavory, an excess rather than a part of glasnost. Yet the publications kept coming out, and the peddlers kept doing a brisk business.

Not for long. In November 1990, Gorbachev was granted the power to rule by decree. He began issuing almost daily decrees on subjects ranging from food prices to morals. The decree on morals, issued in late December, created a commission charged with the betterment of the citizenry's morals. Shortly, reports of the commission's preliminary recommendations appeared in the newspapers; they included proscriptions against a multitude of societal ills, including homosexuality and negative thinking. Combined with the January 1991 announcement that soldiers would begin patrolling Moscow streets alongside city police, this had a truly chilling effect on the sex-media trade. Many street peddlers, unsure of the potential fallout of the morality decree and unwilling to risk a confrontation with the newly ominous police force, decided to get out of the periodicals business and switch to books; others simply dropped anything that could be considered pornographic. Without a reliable retail outlet, most of the sex sheets ceased publication.

The majority of the publications that survived this period were either well financed, like the life-style tabloids, or well connected, like *SPIDInfo*, which had government supporters, and *Tema*, which could by this point be fairly effectively distributed through informal gay community networks. Much of the rest of the market went into hibernation.

Nine months later, following the failed coup of August 1991, a new crop of independent sex publications appeared. The "daidjests" staged a comeback, now joined by some slicker rip-offs of Western porn. Brochures on "sexual secrets" and "sexual potential" proliferated. Compilations of anything sex-related, from labor camp songs to children's jokes, were printed with lightning speed. A dozen gay and lesbian titles were launched.

Book publishers scrambled to catch up again, looking for sex-related titles that would break with the old mold. Starting in 1990, small private publishers put out a number of how-to books that ranged from the in-depth, like Soviet doctor's Larisa I. Remenik's *The Science of Being To-gether: A Short Overview of Sexual Problems*, published by a semiprivate concern in the Caucasus in 1990, to the absurd, like *The French Young Woman's Encyclopedia*, a virtually unreadable book of translated articles on topics from cooking to dressing to lovemaking, and *The Male Sexual Potential*, filled with incomprehensible tables and graphs of unknown origin. These books, not distributed through state channels, went on sale side-by-side in the street, for roughly the same amount of money. In 1992, large publishers brought out two books that broke new ground in sex-related how-tos: Kon's *The Taste of the Forbidden Fruit* and a translation of Alex Comfort's *The Joy of Sex*.

The Joy of Sex, the 1972 British classic, was published by Novosti (News), an establishment house, with all the original artwork and a press run of 300,000, which went nearly as fast as Kon's book, despite taxing prices. Far from a basic how-to manual, the book (which has sold over 8.5 million copies in the United States and Britain) offered gourmet recipes for heterosexual lovemaking. Not all of these were directly applicable to Soviet reality. As Kon wrote in his introduction to the Russian edition,

The Russian translation is complete . . . with no omissions, additions or commentary. This presents certain difficulties for the reader.

We all remember sad jokes about attempts to use the famed prerevolutionary cookbook by Yelena Molokhovets in our conditions. Things are no better where it comes to sexual "cooking." We cannot create "sex rooms" in our homes; we cannot acquire waterbeds, special panties for sex and the like. Soviet people have never even seen many of the sex tools Comfort writes about, which are readily available and widely used in civilized countries.

With the growing emphasis on titillation and translations, there still was no book that addressed sexual issues in the Soviet and post-Soviet context. In the three years since *Sex & Perestroika* was written, no book addressed the problem of having to make love in the room one shares with one's parents, or the problem of being gay in a society that distributes living space on the basis of marital status, or the problem of loving a person who is registered as a resident in a city that's a three-day train ride away. Indeed, with *Forbidden Fruit* and *The Joy of Sex* leaving the shelves as soon as they arrived, there were no books at all — only the booklets and newspapers sold by peddlers. And these were thriving.

Street peddlers, who were granted legal status in Moscow and St. Petersburg in 1992, spread out these publications, offering a daunting selection to people who were now being forced to make the kinds of choices about their money that they had never faced before. As a huge portion of the population slipped below the poverty line, the sex publications were put to the ultimate test: The people of the post-Soviet era would vote on the question of whether publications that informed and titillated sexually were a luxury or an essential item. The result was apparent as Russia's cities adopted the patterns of the new era. Every morning, peddlers would come out to set up on the cities' central interchanges and display their wares, the essentials of life: loaves of bread, sausage, and the sex rags.

The Underground Closet: Political and Sexual Dissidence in East European Culture

Kevin Moss

In *Epistemology of the Closet* Eve Kosofsky Sedgwick argues for the centrality of homo/heterosexual definition in Western culture: "an understanding of virtually any aspect of modern Western culture must be, not merely incomplete, but damaged in its central substance to the degree that it does not incorporate a critical analysis of modern homo/heterosexual definition."[1] While any hermeneutic analysis of literature foregrounds secrets the text may hold, secrets are approached differently by different critics. In *The Genesis of Secrecy* Frank Kermode treats secrecy as a kind of will to be interpreted in all narrative.[2] Feminist critics like Adrienne Rich, Gayle Greene, and Coppélia Kahn, among others, are interested in the silences and gaps in the text that indicate women's experience.[3] Sedgwick claims that secrecy in Western culture invariably points to the homosexual secret, and it was this claim that drew the most flak from critics.[4] In East European culture in the Soviet period the major axis of definition that structures thought is not sexual, but political: dissident/pro-Soviet. While there may be reason to consider how other minority/majority definitions (along racial, ethnic, or gender lines, for example)[5] function similarly or differently or intersect in complex ways, there is at least one similarity between sexual and political dissidence that distinguishes them from the others: in most cases they are not immediately apparent, are not — as race, ethnicity, and gender usually are — publicly and unalterably assigned from birth.[6] This situation foregrounds the issue of knowledge/

ignorance for these categories (sexual orientation, political dissidence) in ways that it does not for the others. Compulsory heterosexism and compulsory political orthodoxy cause sexual and political dissidents to conceal their dissidence. I will argue that the devices used in the West to conceal sexual dissidence, to construct the closet, are often identical to those used in Eastern Europe to conceal political dissidence. To this end I will first look at representations of political dissidence in the Soviet Union and Eastern Europe, then compare Sedgwick's theory of the representation of sexual dissidence in the West; finally I will examine works from Eastern Europe which present both sexual and political dissidence.

Every Russian seems to grow up with two personae, public and private, which are diametrically opposed in many ways. Such double consciousness characterizes minority/majority relations in general. At least one scholar has extended the concept of double consciousness, which presumably originates in discourse on race, to sexual orientation.[7] The minority population must understand the majority consciousness, while the majority does not necessarily understand the minority. In the case of Russia, however, one might wonder whether the pro-Soviet "majority" consciousness could ever be found in isolation. The double consciousness was particularly marked as regards ideology. Before glasnost all but a minuscule percentage of dissidents supported the regime in public; meanwhile the same majority could voice reservations around the kitchen table. Czesław Miłosz describes this role-playing, this passing as ideologically correct, in *The Captive Mind*:

It is hard to define the type of relationship that prevails between people in the East otherwise than as acting, with the exception that one does not perform on a theater stage but in the street, office, factory, meeting hall, or even in the room one lives in. Such acting is a highly developed craft that places a premium on mental alertness. Before it leaves the lips, every word must be evaluated as to its consequences. A smile that appears at the wrong moment, a glance that is not all it should be can occasion dangerous suspicions and accusations. Even one's gestures, tone of voice, or preference for certain kinds of neckties are interpreted as signs of one's political tendencies.[8]

This attention to every potential sign system is one of the things that made Russia such an exciting place: anything and everything was charged with meaning. The "mental alertness" and attention to detail Milosz talks about cut two ways: on the one hand the authorities paid close attention to every word, which led to censorship; but on the other hand this attention may have made literature and art more interesting for the people, who were themselves always trying to decode the underlying meaning. There was thus a kind of symbiotic relationship between censorship and literature. This has become particularly clear since glasnost: with the removal of censorship, many authors are lost — they can no longer figure out what to write or how.

Censorship intersected public and private in a way that produced a kind of public code. Sometimes the difference between public and private coincided with written/spoken. An example from the days before glasnost: one day I went to the Moscow Conservatory to buy tickets for a concert of Russian liturgical music. The posters said "Ancient Russian Music," which was the standard euphemism. The cashier said there were no tickets left, but suggested buying tickets for the next day, because "that's also church music." In other words, a woman in a relatively official public position could call it "church music," but it still couldn't be written on the poster.

Euphemisms surrounding Stalin's purges were particularly charged. For years those executed or who died in the camps were listed with no further explanation as "illegally repressed." One of the first glasnost films, Abuladze's *Repentance* (1984, released in 1986), decodes some of these. Relatives of prisoners who heard the phrase "exiled without the right to correspondence" knew that it meant their loved ones were dead. While the public euphemism itself may have appeared before glasnost, it would never have been translated into the private language of harsh reality, as it is in the film, where the woman responds, "Why don't you just say he's dead?"[9]

But before glasnost exploded this system by decoding it in public, Soviets learned to decode it themselves. Unfortunately, little serious theoretical work has been done on the devices used to circumvent the censors. Lev Loseff's *On the Beneficence of Censorship* defines some of these:[10] devices which function to conceal the referent Loseff calls screens; those which function to draw attention to the referent he calls markers.[11] Screens and markers are really functions which many devices and elements of the text can perform.

In work on Mark Zakharov's film *The Very Same Munchhausen* and on Bulgakov's *Master and Margarita*, I used the term "masking device" to describe what Loseff means by screens.[12] What is fascinating about *Master and Margarita* is how it deals with two different kinds of language taboos:

the religious/superstitious taboo against mentioning the Devil and the political taboo against mentioning the KGB, or the NKVD, as it was called at the time of the novel. Bulgakov takes full advantage of the grammatical, syntactic, and lexical devices at his disposal to mask reference to the secret police, though it is a primary agent in the novel:

Indefinite pronouns and pronominal adjectives:

вошел <u>какой-то</u> гражданин, <u>что-то</u> пошептал
some citizen came in and whispered *something*[13]

Pronouns without established referents:

На вопрос о том <u>откуда</u> спрашивают Аркадия Аполлоновича, голос в телефоне очень коротко ответил <u>откуда</u>.
To the question of *where* they were asking for Arkadii Apollonovich *from*, the voice on the phone briefly answered *where from*. (748)

Надо отдать справедливость <u>тому, кто</u> возглавлял следствие.
You have to be fair to *the one who* was in charge of the case. (750)

Bulgakov uses metonymy to substitute something else for the real agents involved. A *car* came to pick them up, but it never returned (492). Another metonymic reference is used throughout the end of the book: *an entire floor* of a certain Moscow building was lit up; *an entire floor* wasn't sleeping. The *entire floor* was on the case (747).

Bulgakov uses passive, indefinite personal, and subjectless constructions to avoid mentioning the logical subject:

Passive:

Николай Иванович <u>был доставлен</u> в клинику
Nikolai Ivanovich *was taken* to the clinic (577)

<u>Были приняты</u> меры к тому, чтобы их разыскать
Measures *were taken* to find them (757)

<u>Прибавились</u> данные
Evidence *was added* (754)

<u>были обнаружены</u> Никанор Иванович Босой и несчастный конферансье
Nikanor Ivanovich Bosoi and the unfortunate MC *were discovered* (751)

Indefinite personal: [14]

На Садовую <u>съездили</u> и в квартире № 50 <u>побывали</u>
(They) *had dropped by* Sadovaya St. and *visited* apartment 50 (577)

Василия Степановича <u>арестовали</u>
(They) *arrested* Vasilii Stepanovich (611)

за столом уже <u>повысили</u> голос, <u>намекнули</u>
behind the desk (they) *raised* their voice, *dropped hints* (577)

Subjectless: [15]

<u>легко было</u> установить
(It) *was simple* to determine (751)

<u>было известно</u> уже кого и где ловить
(It) *was already known* for whom to look and where (753)

<u>пришлось</u> возиться. . . разъяснять необыкновенный случай
(It) *was necessary* to work, to clear up the unusual incident (751)

The purpose of all of these constructions is to empty the logical subject node either by passivization, which moves the logical object into the grammatical subject node, or some other construction which avoids mentioning the active subject. That these empty agent nodes can be filled by one who knows the code is laid bare when Poplavskii comes to visit from Kiev. All the housing committee officials have been arrested by you know who. When he asks where he can find the president, he gets no answer and only succeeds in upsetting his interlocutor. "Aha!" said the clever Poplavskii and asked about the secretary. Again no response. "Aha!" Poplavskii said to himself. When the man he is talking to is himself led off, Poplavskii draws the right conclusion, but can't even *think* the words to himself: "Ekh, what complications! And wouldn't you know that all of them at once . . ." (614). The ellipsis at the end is telling: not only the subject, but even the operative verb is elided, leaving only an accusative object "all of them." Yet any savvy Soviet reader can fill in the rest: the NKVD took them away.

This process of emptying logical subject nodes is mirrored in the resurrection of dead metaphors involving the word "Devil" in the novel. Such expressions as "the devil take them" and "the devil knows" occur repeatedly. In standard Russian they are merely dead metaphors unmarked for reference to a real Devil. But from the very first scene, when Berlioz's "it's time to throw everything to the Devil and set off for

Kislovodsk" (424) leads to the immediate appearance of what we learn is the Devil himself, the reader is prepared to see the metaphor realized every time the devil is mentioned. Breaking the taboo against calling the Devil by name brings him to life in *Master and Margarita*. The taboo against naming the NKVD, though the NKVD is equally active in the novel, is not broken once by Bulgakov or his characters.

Emptiness or elision in the Soviet system has one meaning: the KGB. This was apparent in everyday discourse as well. At best many Soviets could bring themselves to mention the KGB only in a whisper. This habit remained even among those who had lived in the States for a number of years. Somewhere in a cab or at a restaurant an emigré might say, "Remember Misha? I always suspected he was working [for the KGB]." Since the word for informing also means "to knock," the phrase "for the KGB" was often replaced by a gesture of knocking. "I think he works [knock]" or merely "I think he [knock]."

Some significantly shortened phrases have even made it into the dictionary. Since in Russia one "sits" in prison, "he is sitting" out of context (without mentioning a chair or a room) usually means "he's in prison." Characteristically, this is particularly true of the transitive verb "to seat," which without a location and with the empty "they" (indefinite personal) almost invariably means "to put in prison." Since the same verb is used for planting seeds, there was an early joke about Gorbachev's ideal qualifications for Soviet leader as a former agriculture specialist. He knows why to plant and when = He knows what to put people in jail for and when. Fortunately he didn't live up to the expectations of the humorists.

The map of public and private in this system of coded language differs from that drawn by Western feminists, in which women are relegated to the private (family/domestic/personal) realm, while restricted from the public. For one thing, at the peak of Stalinist power the public for our purposes extended well into the family. Soviet children asked, "Whom do you love more, papa or mama?" could answer, "Stalin!" and Pavlik Morozov, the boy who turned in his parents for hoarding grain, became a Soviet hero. The map of disclosure and trust would be different in different periods and circumstances (like the map of who gay men and lesbians are "out" to). Furthermore, the dichotomy between public and private in Soviet coded language was also not so much between proper spheres of activity as between two linguistic systems or registers in which all native speakers — male and female — were required to become fluent: everyone had to become adept at functioning in both public and private modes.[16] What was at stake was knowledge and information. Knowledge of the code allows one to reinterpret the public message as private information. If one knows that an author is potentially dissident, then one will scrutinize his published works for encoded information. If one knows the code, one can recategorize an author as dissident. It is in part because every text has the potential to contain such information that literature has always been so exciting in Russia. But while the means to encode the information may be rich, the information itself is poor: it can usually be reduced to a binary opposition — Soviet/anti-Soviet.

The open secret in the Soviet Union was the KGB and its role. In European culture, Eve Kosofsky Sedgwick claims, the open secret is homosexuality. Ever since Adam and Eve, knowledge and sexuality have been linked. The birth of the binary opposition was engendered by the first couple eating of the fruit of the tree of knowledge of good and evil. Knowledge of a woman. To know in the biblical sense. Sedgwick remarks that it was obvious to Queen Victoria and Freud that knowledge meant sexual knowledge and secrets sexual secrets, but that by the end of the nineteenth century there had developed one particular sexuality that was distinctively constituted *as* secrecy.[17] Sodomy, as the crime whose name is not to be uttered, can be mentioned only by not mentioning it. This phenomenon is captured in Lord Alfred Douglas's confession, in 1894, "I *am* the Love that dare not speak its name." The thematics of knowledge and ignorance, of secrecy and disclosure, were from then on connected to one topic alone: the homosexual topic. Yet while this information is very poor (homosexual/heterosexual), the devices for encoding it may be rich, and the consequences of disclosure may be as damaging as for the dissident in the Soviet Union (i.e., violence, prison, or death).

Sedgwick cites an example from Beverly Nichols's *Father Figure* in which a father can bring himself to name homosexuality to his son only by leaving him a piece of paper on which he has written, "illum crimen horribile quod non nominandum est."[18] Characteristically the topic is avoided by being mentioned only as unmentionable, and even the language is distanced, as if somehow locking the secret inside the closet of a dead language makes it safer. Such translation was a common Victorian strategy for compartmentalizing sexuality, and homosexuality in particular.[19] In a recent article precisely on the problem of translating sexually explicit passages — especially those referring to homosexuality — from classical Greek and Latin into Russian, M. L. Gasparov curiously resorts to a similar tactic himself. Discussing the inadequacy of published translations of Catullus 16, "Pedicabo ego vos et irrumabo," he presents first the published elliptical and bowdlerized versions, then the best translation ("I will fuck you in the mouth and in the ass") in Russian, but in Latin letters instead of Cyrillic![20] In the Merchant/Ivory adaptation of Forster's *Maurice* the schoolteacher manages to draw a sexually explicit diagram, but he can label it only in Latin: "membrum virile, vulva . . ." Later in the same film, this time following the novel, the translation of Plato's dialogue is censored: "Omit: a reference to the unspeakable vice of the Greeks."[21] Everyone knows what that means.

Sedgwick discusses the textual strategies authors use to mention and at the same time not mention the homosexual topic. Among these she discusses periphrasis and preterition. "Periphrasis," or talking around the topic, comes very close to the kind of metonymic mention found in Bulgakov. "Preterition" is the term Sedgwick uses for mentioning something by not mentioning it, elision with attention called to the elision itself. Again this is the same device Bulgakov uses to point to the unmentionable KGB: passives and indefinite personal forms (they took him away) are used in contexts in which they are strange, in which they call attention to themselves. When the inhabitants of the unlucky apartment vanish one by one, one character says "she knows perfectly well who took away their neighbor and the policeman, but she doesn't want to say it at night" (492). Sedgwick analyzes the strategies Melville uses in *Billy Budd* to mask and at the same time point to Claggart's "hidden nature." The adjectives applied to him include "mysterious, exceptional, peculiar, obscure, notable, phenomenal, and secretive." The phenomenon in question is referred to satisfactorily only as "it."[22]

Sedgwick points out that since homosocial bonds are essential to society and since every man is potentially homosexual, homophobia is a required strategy to regulate relationships between all men. Homophobic violence is terroristic and synecdochic: since it is impractical to do away with all homosexuals, we will isolate them by attacking some. But homosexuals can't tell if they will be the objects of violence; hence they are controlled. And at the same time the larger heterosexual population is regulated, since no man can tell for sure that he is not homosexual. Sedgwick refers to this terrorist potential as the blackmailability of Western maleness through homophobia.[23] On the one hand this blackmailability is literal: the overwhelming majority of actual blackmail cases in the last century have involved homosexuality. This is why, supposedly, the CIA and the Foreign Service banned homosexuals for so long. But because the blackmailability is potentially universal, non-homosexuals may have a paranoid reaction: homophobia and homosexual panic.

The same kind of universal blackmailability applied to anti-Soviet sentiment in the Soviet Union. The worst bogey of the Stalinist era was the "hidden enemy." And paranoid reactions of the majority of the population meant that anyone would be glad to revile an innocent victim just to prove that he himself was loyal. Ignorance of the facts was no obstacle: "I have not read the works of Solzhenitsyn," people wrote, "but he should be deprived of his citizenship for his anti-Soviet views." In *Master and Margarita* Nikanor Ivanovich's wife reacts typically: she presumably knows her husband is innocent, yet she still urges him to come clean so they reduce his sentence (518). This is also another example of how the official public sphere intruded on the private domestic sphere in the Stalinist Soviet Union.

Such devices for concealing and revealing political dissidence are restricted neither to the Soviet Union nor to the novel. In fact it was a trilogy of plays by Václav Havel that first brought home to me the parallels between the devices for concealing political and sexual dissidence.[24] The three plays are linked by the character of Vaněk, a dissident writer, and by his refusal to conform to various groups. This very nonconformity is viewed in the East European context as highly negative and tantamount to dissidence. Vaněk differentiates himself in the first play from the working class, in the second from his petty-bourgeois peers, and in the third from a fellow writer who is officially approved. The circle thus narrows from socio-economic class, to professional values, to political-ideological bent. But there is more involved in Vaněk's nonconformity than politics: sexuality is also an issue in the first two plays.

In the first play, *Audience*, Vaněk works at a brewery loading barrels: as a known dissident writer, he cannot be trusted with any work for which he is qualified. The audience of the title is a meeting with his boss, the working-class brewmaster, who wants to help Vaněk out, but not to get into trouble with the authorities for doing so. The main badge of acceptance for the working class in *Audience* is the Czech national sport, beer drinking. The brewmaster says, "We all drink it here, everybody" (6) and won't even admit the possibility of Vaněk's not liking beer: "Everybody's a beer drinker" (14). At the same time he pressures Vaněk to traffic in women. He keeps insisting he bring the actress Bohdalová to the brewery. This is in fact his last demand, when it seems they can agree on nothing else: "Are you gonna do that much for me? You are gonna do it for me, right? For one damn evening — I'll be okay after that — everything's gonna be different after that — I'm gonna know I didn't waste my life after that — that fucked-up life I got ain't been all the way fucked up — you gonna bring her?" (25).

In the epilogue the audience starts over again, and this time Vaněk chooses a strategy of passing: instead of sipping the beer or pouring it out as he has heretofore, he guzzles it just like the brewmaster. He even takes on the brewmaster's obscene language: "Everything's all fucked up!" (26). Obviously this playwright is also a good actor.

The second play, *Unveiling*, contrasts Vaněk with his friends Michael and Vera. They are perfect representatives of petty-bourgeois materialist values traditionally deplored by the Soviet intelligentsia: *meshchanstvo* [petty-bourgeois ideology] and *veshchizm* [thingism]. But they also criticize Vaněk for his sex life — they think he does it too infrequently — and they offer to demonstrate how they keep their sex life interesting. They also urge him to have children. This is the only one of the plays from which politics in the narrow sense are wholly absent.[25] But then it concerns only the private sphere (the apartment, family relations), and the point is that Michael and Vera care about nothing but things.

The third play, *Protest*, shows Vaněk's meeting with Staněk, an officially sanctioned writer who enjoys the personal and material security his official standing guarantees. Staněk wants to support the dissidents without endangering his comfortable position, that is, without revealing he has done it. Vaněk suggests he join a protest by signing a petition. In Eastern Europe, where the sign, the document, takes priority over physical reality, signing a petition (against the trial of Siniavsky and Daniil, against the invasion of Czechoslovakia) was the quintessential dissident act. *Protest* is maximally political, and here sex plays almost no role (though it is interesting that Staněk considers aiding the dissidents because of his daughter's relationship with the arrested Javurek).

Of course in a play about coming out / being out as a dissident, control over information is most important. Absence, silence, interference with communication are all clues to the significance of the message. Before beginning the important talk, Staněk switches on a tape recorder to play music. This is a characteristic attempt to jam the bugging devices, a trick familiar to anyone who spent time in Eastern Europe in the good old days. It could be replaced, for example, by taking the phone into another room or putting it under a pillow, or by repeatedly flushing the toilet. When Staněk reads Vaněk's play,[26] he complains that "unfortunately we were given a rather bad copy. Very hard to read" (61). The visual equivalent of silence is invisibility, and it has the same meaning: political significance, dissidence. Samizdat manuscripts were produced in many carbon copies (later nth generation xeroxes); the last carbons were necessarily pale — but that made the process of deciphering them all the more rewarding.

The whole play hinges on Staněk's signature: the presence or absence of a name in a series. Staněk first gives Vaněk money, but anonymously, of course. Later, after admitting that his name would acquire value from its previous absence, Staněk decides against signing. Instead he will restrict himself to "backstage diplomacy" (as opposed to coming out on stage, 72) and "private intervention" (as opposed to public disclosure, 63).

The paranoid mechanism kicks in here as well. Staněk criticizes Vaněk for his "moral superiority" (74). He is conscious of these thoughts too: he says people hate dissidents who are a living reproach to them. But in the end he attacks Vaněk in a particularly devastating way: he accuses him of talking in prison. In effect he accuses Vaněk of outing others (which, given that he has outed the brewmaster, seems plausible).

The parallels between strategies for simultaneously concealing and revealing sexual and political secrets are no accident. Loseff, on the one hand, speaks of the reader's cathartic pleasure in decoding Aesopian language and compares it to decoding erotic motifs in literature. He draws an analogy between the function of literary erotica and of Aesopian literature as opposed to the function of their unencoded, more direct correlates, pornography and political journalism. The aesthetic work leads to a psychological effect, while pornography and political journalism lead to a physical effect: an erection or an insurrection.[27] Daniel Rancour-Laferrière points out that this juxtaposition was not, in fact, discovered by Loseff, since Freud consciously borrowed terminology from the political sphere — repression, censorship, distortion — to refer to control of sexual information in the psychology of dreaming.[28] It is perhaps significant that the example of Aesopian erotic language Loseff cites is a homoerotic poem by the gay poet Kuzmin.

What happens when these two kinds of censorship, political and sexual, intersect? What devices are used in the literature of the former Soviet Union and its allies to refer to the homosexual secret? Until very recently there was almost complete silence on anything relating to the subject of homosexuality in Russian literature. There are, however, some recent Russian works in which gay love is a central theme: Evgenii Popov's "Reservoir" (1979),[29] Evgenii Kharitonov's "Oven" (1982),[30] and Nikolai Koliada's "Slingshot" (1990).[31] The first two are short stories and were circulated first in samizdat, then published abroad. The last, a play, was published in the Soviet Union after glasnost. The only word for "gay" or "homosexual" in any of the three texts occurs in Popov's story, where a colonel of working-class origin calls the gay men "pidari" (156), the Russian equivalent of "faggots." Characteristically, the gay men in Popov's story and the more out of the pair in Koliada's play are dead by the end. Kharitonov's narrator lusts after a boy all through the story, but certainly never comes out to him, and by the end he will never see him again. All three depict the extreme negative evaluation (imagined and real) of Russian society. In fact, homophobia is a major plot factor in all three works. The big secret — for the audience, the reader, the narrator, or the other characters — is homosexuality.

Popov's story tells of a scandal in a dacha community in a small Siberian town. The scandal involves two visiting men who are revealed to be lovers (though they are not, of course, explicitly designated as such in the text). Not only did they "obviously avoid our girls," but they "even walked hand in hand" (155). Eventually the girls dress one of the men in drag, the other flies into a rage, and the two fall off a raft and drown, returning as skeletal ghosts to haunt the villagers. It also transpires that the theater director who invited them in the first place has emigrated to America, where such behavior is the norm: "apparently it will be easy for them to indulge there in the vice that here is met by a strict barrier" (157). Anthony Vanchu has pointed out that the primitive view of the narrator, who represents the official moral values of Brezhnevian bourgeois culture, divides the world into "svoi" and "chuzhoi" — "ours" and "the outsiders." In this scheme it is appropriate that homosexuals be lumped together with people who would even think of emigration: all deserve to be sent to some "other world."[32]

There are several patterns here worth pointing out. First, the death of the gay characters. In *The Celluloid Closet* Vito Russo has documented the frequency of death — usually violent death, murder, or suicide — of gay and lesbian characters in American film. In Popov's story homosexuality is conflated both with emigration (a version of dissidence, the connection to which should not now be surprising) and with the supernatural. Again, after Bulgakov, this should be no surprise. Shifting homosexuality into the sphere of the fantastic is nothing new: science fiction / horror characters, particularly vampires, are often portrayed as gay or lesbian to make them even more strange. This is, as Russo points out, the stereotype parodied in *Rocky Horror Picture Show*.[33] Sedgwick discusses the importance of the homosocial in the paranoid Gothic.[34] Popov's ironic twist thus combines two standard plots about gay characters — one in which they are killed off, another in which they are demonized: in Popov's story the gay couple first are drowned, then return as ghosts to scare the good citizens of the dacha settlement away.

Kharitonov's "Oven" is about a 28-year-old who falls in love with a 16–year-old boy, also at a dacha settlement. The story centers on the narrator's attempt to develop a relationship with the handsome Misha without the latter or any of his friends ever suspecting the narrator is gay. Of course he never says he is gay, but the language tells us he's male, and he certainly falls head over heels for Misha. In stream of consciousness / diary form, the narrator reveals his plans and triumphs, always with strategies to interest Misha, to get close to him, without seeming either to be interested in him or to want to get close to him. The stream of consciousness narration does not, however, ever show the narrator contemplating the nature of his dilemma or the possibility of coming out: he seems comfortable in his closet. There is no discussion of why his interest must be hidden or what it means — it's just taken for granted. The age difference, while a factor, is not the major barrier: in fact it only calls attention to the fact that the friendship will be suspect to the observant eye: why should the narrator be so friendly with Misha? What do they have in common? In the end, nothing, and they part when the narrator fails to give Misha his address in a sufficiently casual and offhand way to avoid suspicion of ulterior motives.

While the narrator never comes out, another character does. At a dance in the dacha community the narrator meets Ol'ga, Misha's sister, with a young man who is described as "her husband a handsome Jew" (244).[35] That same day it transpires that his name is Slava and he is not her husband, so he is designated as her "lover." On Saturday the narrator again meets this "lover Slava" in line for beer. Now he is described as "fashionable and unshaven on purpose" (246), and the narrator recognizes that "he looks about my age and from his mannerisms I could see he was from a circle closer to mine than Sergei, relatively" (246). Later he again comments on this "familiar circle of people" (247) and concludes that "maybe he's not even her lover" (248). The attentive reader's suspicion is confirmed that same day, when Slava the Jew and Shurik are escorted to their two-man tent: "And this Shurik, the friend, says lying in Ol'ga's lap – Ol'ga, when did such and such a girl find out I was like that? My god, I get it. And even his voice is like that. But Slava the Jew doesn't look it" (249). The discovery both intrigues the narrator, who returns alone to chat (though they have already gone to sleep), and raises the expectations of the reader for the results of the narrator's quest. The only identification of someone as "gay" substitutes the empty relative/demonstrative adjective "takoi" – "such, like that, that way."[36] Kharitonov has another story entitled "One Boy's Story – 'How I Got Like That.'"[37] Even in the elaboration that "Slava the Jew doesn't look it," the Russian elides the "it": "Slava evrei ne pokhozh."

The thematics of the closet are certainly central to Kharitonov's story, where the narrator is in a double bind: he wants to prevent knowledge of his homosexual intentions while, at the same time, he wants to act them out. Such duality is characteristic of the language of the closet, which often employs ellipsis and preterition to point to the homosexual secret without naming it. In "The Oven," it is not so much the language *per se* that is double-edged, as the narrator's actions: his every move is explicitly designed to conceal his designs on Misha. In our terms the narrator is out to himself and to the reader. He is even out to some friends: when his friend Vanya comes he points out Misha and asks him what he thinks – "Vanya, a man of passions different from my own, confirmed everything about Misha" (240). It is only to Misha and to society at large that the narrator is not out. The reader gets a view from inside the closet while it is being constructed.

For the reader this inside knowledge is more than just knowing what "takoi" means. The narrator compares Misha to Antinous, the emperor Hadrian's beautiful boy lover, knowledge of whom is something of a shibboleth of homosexual identity. The reference is particularly noticeable in a context which contains no other allusions to any person outside the story: Misha's father speaks to him as father to son, "after all for the father there is no Antinous, one boy out of a hundred thousand, but just his sixteen year old son" (251). Earlier, when showing Misha off to Vanya, he makes a similar comment: "I was wondering if he could understand when he had before him a boy who was one in ten thousand" (240).

Koliada's "Slingshot" is the only work of the three in which some kind of sexual interlude actually occurs in the course of the play, but of course it doesn't happen on stage, and it is only referred to as "what happened between us" (24). Upon reading this line the confused reader will flip back through the play to find out what the characters are talking about. It's not there. There is, it's true, a dream interlude in which two unidentified voices say, more or less, "How good . . . how good it is . . . is it good for you?" "It's never, never been so good for me before . . ." (18). This cliché could be staged in a revealing way, though nothing in the stage directions points toward such a solution.

Again there is an age difference between the characters. The handsome Anton is 18, while Ilia, a handicapped beggar in a wheelchair, is 33. At first the two flirt, with Anton apparently more interested in seducing Ilia than vice versa. But in the fifth scene (after the dream episode) Anton comes in drunk to blackmail Ilia: he wants fifty percent of his alms or he'll "go and tell all about him" (22). The apparent cause of Anton's sudden homophobia is that he has been cured of his feared impotence with women. Ilia's verbal gestures of love are met with hysterical cries of "shut up!" Anton has decided to "forget," "tear out," and "erase" what happened between them (24–25). Only in the last scene does a remorseful Anton return to find that Ilia has died.

Anton's ranting homophobic blackmail threats resonate with echoes of Stalinist informers denouncing the "hidden enemy": "I'll go and tell the neighbors, the whole building, the whole street who they've warmed in their midst, who lives here, I'll tell . . ." (22). The phrase for "warmed in their midst" (*kto u nikh pod bokom prigrelsia*) was most often used of political deviants. Anton continues to threaten Ilia with the psychiatric clinic, the place both homosexuals and political dissidents were isolated. In Popov's story, as Vanchu points out, it was the ironic revenge of the dead gay men to threaten the "normal" villagers with the same fate: "the vice of the corpses, gleaming with skeletal lust in the light of the moon, beckons, approaches, frightens, and leads people straight into psychiatric hospitals."[38]

When Roman Viktiuk directed *Slingshot* in San Diego, he turned the internalized homophobia around at the end of the play. When Ilia calls Anton an angel, the latter compares them to rats swimming in shit who see a bat above. The baby rat says, "look mama, an angel" (23). Viktiuk's production was originally to have both actors wear wings, but the wings made did not look right. The director did not want to give up the wings altogether, so they were placed prominently so the audience could see them, then one set flew over the stage at the end.[39] Viktiuk used a similar device in his adaptation of Sologub's *Petty Demon* at the Sovremennik theater in Moscow. The highly idealized boy, Sasha, appeared above the stage at the end of the play winged like an angel. Both versions of this gay *deus ex machina* may in fact be coded references to Kuzmin's 1907 gay-positive novel *Wings*, in which growing wings becomes a metaphor for acknowledging that one is gay — coming out to oneself.

Thus far all of my examples of sexual dissidence in Eastern Europe have centered on prose and drama, on Slavic, and on gay males. Lest the reader assume that the parallels are limited by medium, nationality, or gender, I would like to end with a brief discussion of a Hungarian film about lesbians. *Egymásra nézve*, distributed here as *Another Way*, was released in 1982 by Károly Makk, with a screenplay by Makk and Erszébet Galgóczi based on Galgóczi's 1980 *Törvényen belül*,[40] Within the Law. The film centers on the love between two lesbian journalists in 1958. In his article on Hungarian film in *Post New Wave Cinema in the Soviet Union and Eastern Europe*, David Paul writes that "at first glance the issues of lesbianism and censorship may strike one as unlikely twins."[41] Surely not so unlikely!

Both the film and the story begin with the death of Éva and progress through flashbacks. It is telling both that one lesbian is killed while trying to cross the border (a quasi-suicide) and that the other is shot by her husband, perhaps paralyzed for life. It is Éva, the more out and outspoken of the pair, who is killed. Yet while Éva is politically outspoken, she becomes inarticulate when it comes to explaining her love to Lívia. Confronted by Lívia, whose panties she has stolen earlier, she can only say: "It's very hard and you won't understand . . . you see, there are such feelings . . . now it's hard for me . . . I . . ." The elisions and the visual here say it all: Lívia looks away whenever Éva looks at her and vice versa: they can't look each other in the eye. The absence of communication points to the homosexual secret.

While there is no discussion in the film of the closet *per se*, there are parallels in the world of political censorship. Éva talks about the corridor. In the corridors of the newspaper office people say one thing, but they say another in editorial meetings and in print: "we always speak sincerely only in the corridors." Éva's editor Erdös responds that "when you've tried to speak the truth for 30 years, as he has, you learn to value those corridor conversations." At least there is some space, though it is clearly delimited, where the truth can be spoken. Erdös also refers to "writing for the drawer" — another metaphor familiar from Russian — Bulgakov's *Master and Margarita*, for example, was written for the drawer — put away until such time as it could be taken out and published. Éva says she's tired of "putting things in drawers and sweeping them under rugs," to which Erdös responds that there is a limit to the truths that can be published. Éva, unlike her editor, recognizes no limits. The word used for limit, "határ," also means border. And it is no accident that the title of the novel in Hungarian also points up the inside/outside opposition: "Törvényen *belül*" — "*Within* the Law."

Lesbianism in the film is referred to with the usual empty pronouns and pronominal adjectives: "something like this (ilyesmi)" or just "this (ez)": I've never done "something like this." I don't know anything about "this." You have more experience in "that" than I do, but I don't want any of "this." When the police confront the pair kissing on a park bench they threaten to tell Lívia's husband and her boss if they ever catch her again doing "something like this."

Makk even takes advantage of the absence of grammatical gender in Hungarian to draw attention to the lesbian affair at one point. Just before Dönci shoots Lívia, he asks, "Does he/she have someone? children? a parrot? Tell me about him/her." When he asks, derisively, if the "champion of truth" has anything to do with the affair, Lívia responds that he knows perfectly well who they are talking about. Éva is indeed the "champion of truth," and she struggles to express the truth about her sexuality, as she struggles to express the truth about the 1956 revolution in the newspaper, appropriately named *Truth*.

The curiosity which results from the obligatory suppression of knowledge about lesbianism and about sex between women in particular is played out in an interview between Éva and a detective after Lívia's husband shoots her:

DETECTIVE: hmm . . . what do you feel when you look at me? I can't understand . . . how . . . how do you do it?
EVA: Do what? Tell me what you're curious about.
DETECTIVE: That . . . well, . . . that something . . .

Of course "that something" (a valami) is never named with a noun. Instead, she shows him with her gesture:

We do it with our fingers . . . with one, or two, or three.

Éva breaks a social taboo by describing crossing the border of her partner's body with her fingers. It is immediately after this transgression of her prescribed limits that we see Éva on a train on the way to her attempted political border crossing, which we know results in her death. As in Popov's story, the connection is made between sexual dissidence and defection or emigration. Éva is arrested, and when she protests, the police answer that "we are not in America." The connection is again made when she is killed trying to cross the border, to defect. That defection and dissidence are equivalent is clear in the Hungarian verb "defects": disszidál. Near various physical embodiments of the border — barbed-wire fences, a river — she is told to stop by the guards, who shout at her and fire warning shots. Éva keeps walking in defiance. The film ends as it begins, with a slow-motion sequence of a bird flying over the barbed-wire and watchtowers of the border.

In *Another Way*, then, Makk takes advantage of the similarities between political and sexual dissidence and constructs his film around the intersections of the two. Éva is both politically and sexually dissident, and the film shows just how similar the devices used to conceal and reveal such dissidence are.

The intersection of culture, politics, and sexuality will everywhere and always be a locus of hotly contested power struggles. Now that political and sexual dissent have come out of the closet into the public arena there as well, Russia is no exception. Two cases worthy of comment involve the writers Eduard Limonov and Valentin Rasputin. Limonov, who earned a certain succès de scandale with his semi-autobiographical novel about an emigré disillusioned with America who discovers gay sex, now writes jingoistic articles for Zhirinovsky, the extreme right-wing nationalist, and assiduously avoids the gay activists. At a talk at the Writers' Union in Moscow he was warned by concerned conservative ladies, "Edik, be careful: there are *homosexuals* in the room."[42] Surely the man who wrote in a quasi-autobiographical novel about being raped on the streets of New York was terrified!

Rasputin, the Siberian writer who spearheaded a campaign to oppose the Brezhnev government efforts to divert Siberian Rivers, now wants to exclude homosexuality from Russia: "When it comes to homosexuals, let's keep Russia clean. We have our own traditions. That kind of contact between men is a foreign import. If they feel their rights are infringed they can always go and live in another country."[43] Homosexuality, claims Rasputin, is "chuzhoi" (other/outsiders'/alien), not "svoi" (ours). This is the same gesture we have seen in Popov's "it will be easy for them to indulge [in America] in the vice that here is met by a strict barrier" and in the policeman's comment to Éva, "we are not in America." The same claim was made in 1934, when the Soviet Union criminalized homosexuality (it was decriminalized in 1993).[44] Ironically, the Soviets criminalized homosexuality as proper to Nazism at the same time the Nazis criminalized it as indicative of communism. Simon Karlinsky has demonstrated the absurdity of Rasputin's claim,[45] but it is one more example of the kind of reaction that results from the conflation of political and sexual dissidence.

These observations are only a starting point. In a sense the observation that the thematics of knowledge and ignorance are connected in East European culture to political dissidence argues against Sedgwick's claim that they are connected to one topic alone: homosexuality. On the other hand, she need not be read in such a maximalizing way (though her critics will continue to do so); furthermore, East European culture in the Soviet period is arguably not Western culture, to which Sedgwick restricts her claim. If the experience of Western feminists is any indication, we should be very careful about applying a ready-made queer theory to East European culture. Only in the last decade have significant strides been made by Western feminist critics in addressing Russian literature.[46] The major contemporary Russian women writers, Tatiana Tolstaia and Liudmila Petrushevskaia, are outspoken in their claim that feminism has nothing to do with their projects.[47] Only in the last few years have Russian critics themselves begun to dabble in gender theory.[48] Still many contemporary writers sympathetic to the specificity of Eastern European culture are skeptical of the applicability of Western models.[49] In part this may be because feminism historically addresses gender inequalities specific to Western industrialized capitalism; much feminist theory is also grounded in Marxism, a foundation which has always been problematic for some East European writers. Some of the same problems must be encountered by any effort to apply queer theory as well. The possibilities for cross-fertilization between gay studies and Russian and East European studies hardly end here. Many Western scholars share with Sedgwick a certain theoretical anxiety about our projects. Sedgwick fears she risks "glamorizing the closet itself" and admits that her own discourse "echoes mostly with the pre-Stonewall gay self definition."[50] Western scholars of East European culture similarly risk glamorizing censorship and longing for the pre-glasnost days. We have only begun to map out some of the virgin territory in Slavic which remains to be explored by more adept analysts better trained in gay studies. Still, I hope the comparison of the devices used to conceal political and sexual dissidence, the devices of Aesopian language and the closet, proves fruitful for further study.

NOTES

This chapter was originally presented as part of the Abernethy Series at Middlebury College. I am grateful to the Middlebury Center for Russian and East European Studies for the opportunity to travel to Moscow to continue research on this project. I would also like to acknowledge Anthony Vanchu and Ernest McLeod for their advice and support.

1. Eve Kosofsky Sedgwick, *Epistemology of the Closet* (Berkeley: University of California Press, 1990), 73.
2. Frank Kermode, *The Genesis of Secrecy* (Harvard: Harvard University Press, 1979).
3. Adrienne Rich, "Taking Women Students Seriously," in *On Lies, Secrets, and Silence* (New York: Norton, 1979), 237–46; Gayle Greene and Coppélia Kahn, "Feminist Scholarship and the Social Construction of Woman," in *Making a Difference* (New York: Routledge, 1985), 1–36.
4. Christopher Benfey, "Telling It Slant," *New Republic* (March 18, 1991): 35.
5. Toni Morrison makes a similar universalizing claim for the centrality of race, even in texts by white authors about white characters: see Toni Morrison, *Playing in the Dark* (Cambridge: Harvard University Press, 1992).
6. Sedgwick, *Epistemology*, 34.
7. W. E. B. Du Bois, *The Souls of Black Folk*, in *Three Negro Classics* (New York: Avon Books, 1965), 215; John J. Winkler, "Double Consciousness in Sappho's Lyrics," in *The Lesbian and Gay Studies Reader* (New York: Routledge, 1993), 577–94.

8. Czesław Miłosz, *The Captive Mind,* trans. Jane Zielonko (New York: Vintage, 1981), 54–55.

9. Nancy Condee and Vladimir Padunov provide a wealth of information on such semiotic shifts and the resultant "postmodernization" of Soviet culture in "Perestroika Suicide: Not by Bred Alone," *New Left Review* 189 (Sept.–Oct. 1991): 67–89. The effects of these radical changes in the culture on the aesthetic system are discussed in their "Makulakul'tura: Reprocessing Culture," *October* 57 (Summer 1991): 79–103, and in Michael Epstein "After the Future: On the New Consciousness in Literature," *South Atlantic Quarterly* 90, no. 2 (Spring 1991): 409–44.

10. Lev Loseff, *On the Beneficence of Censorship* (Munich: Verlag Otto Sagner, 1984), 29.

11. Ibid., 51.

12. Kevin Moss, "A Russian Munchausen: Aesopian Translation," *in Inside Soviet Film Satire: Laughter with a Lash,* ed. Andrew Horton (Cambridge: Cambridge University Press, 1993), 20–35, and "Bulgakov's *Master and Margaritia*: Masking the Supernatural and the Secret Police," *Russian Language Journal* 38, nos. 129–30 (1984): 115–31.

13. Mikhail Bulgakov, *Belaia gvardiia, Teatral'nyi roman, Master i Margarita* (Leningrad: Khudozhestvennaia literatura, 1978), 674; further references are to this edition, and all translations are the author's.

14. This form, which consists of the third-person plural of the verb with an elided subject, has the force of our constructions such as "they say . . .": the subject is human, though unidentified.

15. Transformational grammar interprets these constructions, which are very common in Russian, as having the infinitive in the grammatical subject position. The logical subject, which would be in the dative, is optional.

16. Given the gender imbalance of traditional patriarchal Soviet society, it may well be that men have to be more adept at producing the public register than women. Yet since decoding — translation from one code to the other — can occur only in the private sphere (around the kitchen table), both genders must be competent in interpreting the code. Perhaps more men than women master the parole in this system, while women and men equally internalize the langue.

17. Eve Kosofsky Sedgwick, *Epistemology* (Berkeley: University of California Press, 1990), 73.

18. Eve Kosofsky Sedgwick, *Between Men* (New York: Columbia University Press, 1985), 95.

19. John Boswell comments on this practice with some amusing examples. John Boswell, *Christianity, Social Tolerance, and Homosexuality* (Chicago: University of Chicago Press, 1980), 19–20.

20. M. L. Gasparov, "Klassicheskaia filologiia i tsenzura nravov," in *Erotika v russkoi literature, Literaturnoe obozrenie* (Spets: Vypusk, 1992), 4.

21. E. M. Forster, *Maurice* (New York: Norton, 1971), 51.

22. Sedgwick, *Epistemology,* 95.

23. Sedgwick, *Between Men*, 89.
24. Václav Havel, *Audience* and *Unveiling*, trans. Jan Novak; *Protest*, trans. Vera Blackwell; in Marketa Goetz-Stankiewicz, ed., *The Vaněk Plays* (Vancouver: University of British Columbia Press, 1987).
25. Anthony Vanchu has pointed out that, of course, compulsory heterosexuality and reproduction were political inasmuch as they were enforced by the state to varying degrees in Eastern Europe (private conversation).
26. The audience may remember that in the first play the brewmaster had asked Vaněk to promise not to write about his political views. In the third we learn that he has broken that promise: the play Staněk has read is about the brewmaster. The brewmaster has been outed!
27. Loseff, *On the Beneficence*, 227. One is reminded, though Loseff does not comment on it, of Barthes's jouissance.
28. Daniel Rancour-Laferrière, "Review of Loseff, *On the Beneficence of Censorship*," *Russian Language Journal* 41, nos. 138–39 (Winter–Spring 1987): 368.
29. Evgenii Popov, "Chertova diuzhina rasskazov," in *Metropol'* (Ann Arbor: Ardis, 1979).
30. Evgenii Kharitonov, "Dukhovka," in *Katalog* (Ann Arbor: Ardis, 1982), 238–56. A two-volume collection of Kharitonov's works has recently appeared: "Slezy na tsvetakh," *Glagol* 10, nos. 1 & 2 (1993).
31. Nikolai Koliada, "Rogatka," *Sovremennaia dramaturgiia* 6 (1990): 4–28.
32. Anthony Vanchu, "Cross(-Dress)ing One's Way to Crisis: Yevgeny Popov and Lyudmila Petrushevskaya and the Crisis of Category in Contemporary Russian Culture," *World Literature Today* (Winter 1992): 107–18; the "other world" of emigration was in informal Soviet parlance regularly compared with the spiritual "other world," since no one ever returned from either.
33. Vito Russo, *The Celluloid Closet* (New York: Harper & Row, 1987), 52.
34. Sedgwick, *Between Men*, chaps. 5 and 6.
35. Slava's appositive epithet seems less obtrusive to the Russian reader. In Russian culture the definition Jew/non-Jew (i.e., Russian) seems as obligatory and as transparently descriptive (in the view of the majority) as racial and gender designations seem for the majority discourse in English. In Russian the question "Is he Russian?" usually means "Is he Jewish?" and the nationality "Jew" or "Russian" is inscribed as the fifth entry in the Soviet passport. Elsewhere Kharitonov has been accused of antisemitism, yet he also explicitly compares the situation of the homosexual minority in the Soviet Union to that of the Jews. In "The Oven" Slava's nationality does not seem to play a significant role.
36. Forster describes Risley in *Maurice* as "that way" in quotation marks: Forster, *Maurice*, 71.
37. Evgenii Kharitonov, "Rasskaz odnogo mal'chika — 'Kak ia stal takim,' " *Strelets* (1991): 163–67; a translation of this story is forthcoming in the *International Anthology of Gay Fiction*, ed. Mark Mitchell and David Leavitt (New York: Penguin, 1994).
38. Popov, "Chertova," 158.

39. For this information I am grateful to Susan Larsen, who helped Viktiuk in his production.

40. Erzsébet Galgózi, *Törvényen kivül és belül* (Budapest: Szépirodalmi könyvkiadó, 1983), now available in English as *Another Love*, trans. Ines Rieder and Felice Newmann (Pittsburgh: Cleis Press, 1991).

41. David Paul, "The Magyar on the Bridge," in *Post New Wave Cinema in the Soviet Union and Eastern Europe*, ed. Daniel J. Goulding (Bloomington: Indiana University Press, 1989), 192.

42. Related by Zhenia Debrianskaia, one of the activists present.

43. Quoted in Lionel Joyce, letter to the editor of the *New York Review of Books*, April 11, 1991, 61.

44. See Igor Kon, "Sexual Minorities," in *Sex and Russian Society* (Bloomington: Indiana University Press, 1993), 92, and Simon Karlinsky, "Russia's Gay Literature and Culture: The Impact of the October Revolution," in *Hidden from History*, ed. Martin Duberman (New York: NAL, 1989), 347–64.

45. Simon Karlinsky, "Russia's Gay Literature and History (11th–20th Centuries)," *Gay Sunshine* 29–30 (Summer–Fall 1976); " 'Vvezen iz-za granitsy . . .'! Gomoseksualizm v russkoi kul'ture I literature," *Erotika v russkoi literature, Literaturnoe obozrenie* (Spets: Vypusk, 1992), 104–7.

46. Barbara Heldt, *Terrible Perfection: Women in Russian Literature* (Bloomington: Indiana University Press, 1987); *Sexuality and the Body in Russian Culture*, ed. Stephanie Sandler, Jane Costlow, and Judith Vowles (Stanford University Press, 1993); *Fruits of Her Plume*, ed. Helen Goscilo (New York: M. E. Sharpe, 1993).

47. Catherine Portuges notes that the Hungarian director Márta Mészáros also distances herself from feminism; *Screen Memories* (Bloomington: Indiana University Press, 1993), 151 n. 21.

48. Natal'ia Rimashevskaia, "The New Women's Studies," in *Perestroika and Soviet Women*, ed. Mary Buckley (New York: Cambridge University Press, 1992), 118–22; Tatiana Mamonova, *Russian Women's Studies* (New York: Pergamon, 1989) and *Women and Russia* (Boston: Beacon Press, 1984).

49. Francine du Plessix Gray, *Soviet Women: Walking the Tightrope* (New York: Doubleday, 1989); Slavenka Drakulić, *How We Survived Communism and Even Laughed* (New York: Harper, 1993).

50. Sedgwick, *Epistemology*, 68, 63.

Ivan Soloviev's Reflections on Eros

Mikhail Epstein

The majority of readers will be unfamiliar with the name of Ivan Soloviev (1944–1984) unless the former students of one Moscow school, who will recall their prematurely deceased teacher, are among them.[1] Although Ivan Igorevich taught Russian language and literature, his knowledge was encyclopedic, encompassing the most diverse spheres of world culture. He could easily compare the lyrical works of Pushkin, Goethe, and Byron, or the philosophical views of Plato, Nietzsche, and Freud. Quite often his lessons violated the boundaries of traditional scholarly disciplines, thereby provoking keen interest among his students, jealousy among his colleagues, and suspicion and hostility among the higher education officials.

Ivan Soloviev lived alone, spent his leisure time in libraries, thought intensively, and wrote abundantly. It was impossible to dream of publishing any of his works, as they would never have passed the stringent rules of censorship: they did not follow any Marxist precepts, nor were they constructed upon any approved ideological foundations. But his friends were freely given everything that came out of his old rattling typewriter, and they avidly devoured it and discussed it incessantly, as it somehow refreshed the stagnant atmosphere of the late Brezhnev era.

I have preserved some of the finished writings of Ivan Soloviev, as well as the rough drafts of the monumental production the author himself considered to be his definitive work. It was meant to be a kind of compendium of humanity's intellectual inquiries and digressions. One of the sections was tentatively titled "Eroticon, or The Panorama of Desire," from which the following fragments are taken. Their main theme is the diversity of erotic experiences, which, in Soloviev's view, offers a "sensual epistemology," a means to intimate knowledge of the world.

An interesting peculiarity of Soloviev's reflections (especially in his last years) was a tendency to present them as someone else's thoughts; he tried to trace the genealogy of his ideas, to identify their ancestry and possible authorship. Soloviev shared Bakhtin's view of consciousness as a multitude of blending and dispersing voices, and he attempted to reveal the source of every one of them. That is why he signed his texts with various names, ranging from the great philosophers of antiquity to his contemporaries and closest friends. He would say on meeting one of them: "This is what you wrote yesterday," and hand him some freshly typed sheets signed with the interlocutor's name. I have accumulated a number of texts in my archive whose authorship Soloviev conferred upon me. Among the fragments here offered to the attention of the reader, the first is signed Buber — Feuerbach, the second ascribed to me, and only the last bears Ivan Soloviev's own name.[2]

TOWARD A THEORY OF CONTIGUITY

Sometimes I pictured in my dreams a harmonious system of human knowledge based on erotic experience; a theory of contiguity, in which the mystery and dignity of another being consist precisely in the fact that contiguity provides the basis for the comprehension of another world. Under this philosophy, pleasure would become a special, more complete and unusual form of rapprochement with The Other, and it would also become a skill with which we comprehend that which is external to us.

— Marguerite Yourcenar[3]

Who am I? Where do I stand? Who circumcised me? When was I baptized? Uncircumcised and unbaptized, I face the Lord: Thy will be done.

I am baptized in the waters of my mother's womb. I am circumcised at the base of my umbilical cord. I am Thine, Lord, I am baptized and circumcised by You.

The body is a temple: hallowed be Thy name in it. The world is a temple: Thy will be done in it.

Let us touch one another, thus making a weightless temple of Thy name. As a name is composed of letters, a temple is composed of touches. Where one touches another, there is Thy body, Lord.

The Lord reveals Himself in a touch. The beginning of theology is in the flesh. "Then saith he to Thomas, 'Reach hither thy finger, and behold my hands; and reach hither thy hand, and thrust it into my side: and be not faithless, but believing'" (John 20:27). Doubting Thomas confirmed his faith through touching. Belief involves reaching one's finger — a feeling of contiguity.

Nothing is more sacred than touch with the flesh of another human being. The touch of a mother pitying her child. The touch of a husband and wife desiring intimacy. The touch of a doctor healing a patient. Flesh, in the flesh of another, seeks salvation, an exodus into life and immortality. Flesh, in itself, is mortal; immortal is that which emerges between oneself and another.

Let all faiths, all knowledges, touch one another. For it is not fusion or mixture but touch that illuminates and vitalizes life's differences. A touch is desirable and frightening, like everything that is sacred, like the love of God and the fear of God. Nothing is more mystical than another's flesh, containing in itself the mystery of Otherness. One can neither penetrate nor escape this mystery but only touch it. A touch is a sign that I remain outside though contiguous.

Touch operates as a duality: it unites — and separates. It overcomes distance — and constitutes a border. When touching, we simultaneously establish the untouchableness of whatever our fingers approach. With a touch, we sculpt the image of the untouchable. Touch delivers us from both the sin of intrusion and the sin of separation. A touch posits what should be: the boundary. Otherness draws itself with our finger so that we dare not violate it. Holy is the flesh in its boundedness. And contiguity marks the line, the flesh, of this boundary, the site of separation-unity between all creatures. Contiguity keeps them from violence and saves them from loneliness.

Everyone who touches another feels touched. For the first time, she feels her own skin. For the first time, he comes to know the landscape of his surface, its protuberances, grooves, rough spots. Contiguity gives birth to two identities.

Thanks to contiguity, the world becomes more ardent. Two warmths, through touch, become fire. The exterior becomes the interior. What was the surface of one body becomes the heart of two. The boundary proves to be inside, an inner partition of the dual being. In the present state of the world, all things are defined and mediated by their surfaces, but through touch they are interiorized, reappropriated by the core. The whole of existence, cast out by the primordial impulse to the externality of self-separation, stretching out its cold exteriors, then collapses, contracts through contiguity. Everything is inside. Although all physical surfaces remain as they were, they all cling to one another, and palpitate like one enormous heart.

How is a boundary established? How is a person shaped into a personality? Traditional religions' answer: by iron and water. By circumcision and baptism.

Contiguity is baptism for the unbaptized, circumcision for the uncircumcised. The Lord sanctified the flesh of the world when he created us in the flesh and became flesh himself, in order that one's flesh could be sanctified through another's. Contiguity is the fulfillment of commandments, it contains the proscribed purity of water and the depth of the imprint.

ON THE TWO REVOLUTIONS

In the twentieth century, a social revolution took place in Russia, a sexual revolution in the West. But do they not have the same foundation? Any revolution is a reversal, that is, an overthrowing of the upper strata through an elevation of the lower. In the case of the social revolution, these are class extremes: the formerly oppressed strata become the "leading" and "guiding" forces, while the former ruling class is subjugated or exterminated. However, the same process is typical of the sexual revolution, though it is not the social strata that are reversed, but the categories of body and mind. Just as the proletariat comes to dominate the intellectuals, the instincts gain ascendency over the intellect. The oppressed strata of the unconscious ignite the flames of mutiny, break the chains of super-ego, overthrow the tyrant suppressing the libido, and take possession of the whole person, the entire psychic State.

How many echoes there are between these two revolutions, how much resonance! Consider the fact that both of them arose in the wake of World War I, the war that stirred up all that is most ancient and predatory in human nature, that plunged society into the condition of the primordial horde, the primitive commune, which both Freud and Marx considered to be the prototype of a future emancipated humanity. The time of the Bolshevik Revolution and the civil war coincides with an era in which Freudianism rapidly expanded throughout Western culture, an era characterized by literary revolutions ("stream-of-consciousness," dadaism, surrealism, "automatic writing"), political radicalism proceeding from a psychoanalytic basis, and "sexual revolution" itself (the Freudo-Marxist hybrid conceived by W. Reich). All sorts of chaotic, Dionysian forces were fermenting, releasing the dark impulses of a primordial vitality which, until that point, had been restrained by the bonds of civilization. The war proved to be worldwide in its scope precisely because it extended beyond immediate military actions: not only did state frontiers begin to crumble, but also those usually inviolable boundaries which lie inside single states (class struggle, civil war), or inside single persons (psychoanalytic and sexual revolution). This universal war spanned the 1920s and 30s, moving from the military realm to the socio-cultural, and then returning to the battle-fields as the Second World War.

Aristocracy and intelligentsia, artistry and intellect — all was sacrificed to the rebellious masses, the rebellious matter, identified as productive labor in Russia and as the delights of consumption in the West. This difference was prefigured in the very names glorified by the two revolutions: Marx means "hammer," Freud means "joy."[4] The essential difference lies in the fact that the Russian Revolution appropriated society and the settlement of external class antagonism as its sphere, whereas the sphere of the Western revolution was predominantly the individual, the resolution of internal, psychological antagonism. However, victory in both cases belonged to the social and psychological lower strata that had been oppressed for centuries: to the proletariat constituting the physical power of society, and to the libido constituting the energetic potential of the individual. Thus Freud and Marx comprise the "joyful hammer," the "libidinous proletariat" of the new, inverted psycho-social organism-organization.

And yet, there is a flaw in this speculation. Was it really the proletariat who took power in the aftermath of the Bolshevik Revolution? There was barely any proletariat left in a Russia ruined by WW I and civil war. It is only ideology that makes claims to "the dictatorship of the proletariat," "the power of workers and peasants," "the republic of the working people." Actually, the power shifted to ideology itself and to the omnipotent ideologists, that is, it leapt to the heretofore unattained upper level of mind and ideas. Before the Revolution, under the feudal system, the aristocracy had ruled, — "blue blood," or "white bone," as they say in Russia; but blood and bone are still concrete, organic, while an idea is abstract, constructed. Later, under the capitalist system, money, profit, and calculation came to rule, but these are still connected to "base" matter, to the natural cycles of substances and the economic circulation of goods. At the very least, although abstract, money has a tangible referent; one can sell or buy something palpable, material, whose existence is not dependent on any ideology. So feudalism and capitalism are still bound to the material, to actual labor, much more than "the triumph of the laborer," as proclaimed by revolutionary ideology. The idea of labor is far more abstract than the reality of blood and riches. "Idea" constitutes the highest level in the hierarchy of generalizations: it alone claims to see and to subjugate the future, making far-reaching plans for the mastery of humanity. Only theoretically did the material lower strata gain victory in the Revolution; actually, it was theory itself which conquered the material realm. In this way, the rule of the upper "ideal" strata was not overturned, but rather ascended still higher — the Revolution was merely a springboard for this ascent to the kingdom of Ideas.

Is this not the same paradox inherent in the sexual revolution? No doubt manners and morals became more openly permissive, the libido expressed itself more liberally. But even before this happened, those who wished to sinned desperately, though only under cover of night, in brothels, in dens of iniquity, in the underground, in the innermost recesses of the unconscious. The sexual revolution did not cause any substantial changes in the libido itself; rather it brought the libido to the light of day, revealed it to the conscious mind. If, previously, a person had concealed his incestuous impulses from himself, now he permitted himself to indulge them according to the demands of a properly enlightened consciousness. Herein lies the question: was it "natural" instinct that prevailed, or was it consciousness that expanded its authority to include even the formerly inaccessible and innermost parts of body and soul? In essence, Freud, this Marx of sexual revolution, while claiming to relinquish priority to the libido, effectively raised consciousness to the level where it could enlighten the libido, make it transparent to rational self-understanding. The psychoanalytic challenge to consciousness: higher and farther. Think the once unthinkable!

For both Marx and Freud, the attempt to understand the material and the unconscious became the means to their rational control. If, for Marx, the disastrous crises of an anarchic capitalist economy could be solved only by a planned socialist economy, then, for Freud, the diseases of psychic neuroses could be treated only by conscious recognition and the regulation of repressed impulses. What results, therefore, is, superconsciousness, a post-classic consciousness that embraces the once unconscionable and uses it as an instrument for the expansion of consciousness. Therefore, the result of the sexual revolution frequently proved to be not so much the triumph of sex as the triumph of consciousness over sex. If, earlier, sex stubbornly hid itself in the pants, under the skirt, under the blanket, while still being spontaneously excitable and uncontrollably pleasant, now consciousness dragged it into the light in order to use it everywhere, in any position, for any purpose, be it commerce or revolution, be it the maintenance or the destruction of the status quo. . . . The orgasm itself, extracted from the spermatic ducts, became the conduit for political ideas, aesthetic trends, and economic profits. All these rational applications of sex, including its commercial and ideological exploitation and portrayal, can be called pornography.

Thus, social and sexual revolution intersect. "Ideology and pornography are twin-sisters."[5] Both claim the priority of the social and biological lower strata: the working classes, the sexual organs. On the socialist banners, a mighty working hand; in the capitalist ads, a mighty model's body. In both cases, the texture of the body is sensually and sensationally exposed.[6] However, these forms of extreme materiality are nothing but "eidoses": ideas and images. They are instruments of power for the superconsciousness. The classic, pre-revolutionary (both sexually and socially) consciousness still separated itself from material life and eschewed the extremes of spontanaeity, striving for the Spiritual, the Sublime, the Good and the True. Then came the revolution — essentially not social or sexual, but mental: superconsciousness overthrew the immature classic consciousness by means of the material, in order to raise itself above the material, all the while making it a tool of supremacy.[7]

The scenes of ardent labor. The scenes of inspired lechery. Two forms of abstraction: "ideo" and "porno." Labor turned into "logy"; lechery turned into "graphy" — such is the quintessence of material life, extracted for the benefit of thinking and the pleasure of writing.

HELENOLOGY

(An attempt at the construction of a new science)[8]

1. Helenology, unlike most other sciences, is the science of only one person, henceforth designated as Helen.

2. The sciences about one person, such as Shakespearology, Napoleonology, Pushkinology, Marxology, and so forth, study the contribution of the given person to history, literature, social thought, and so forth. Unlike all of these outstanding people, who are interesting for what they have done, Helen is interesting for what she is.

3. As much as Being in itself is higher than its separate accomplishments, so Helenology is higher than Napoleonology, Marxology, and other disciplines devoted to the unique achievements of a single individual, since it is devoted to the very existence of the unique. Helenology studies not what Helen has achieved or how she has expressed herself, but what she is by herself, regardless of any historical or aesthetic manifestations, in the simple depth of her immanence. Helenology is the first independent science about one single being who startles us by the very fact that she *is*, not by what she has become or could have been.

4. In Aristotle's opinion, the source of every cognition is wonder. "For it is owing to their wonder that men both now begin and at first began to philosophize. . . . And a man who is puzzled and wonders thinks himself ignorant . . ."[9] Therefore, the most important sciences emerge from the greatest sensations of wonder. Doubtless, Helen amazes people who meet her much more than molecules or gases or numbers, the wonder of which gave rise to the hard sciences: physics, chemistry, mathematics. One would have to possess very little sensitivity not to be astonished by Helen after seeing her once; and, after seeing her twice, not to elaborate this wonder into an entire system of cognition corresponding to the complexity of the subject.

5. If judged by the strength of its generative impulse, Helenology must gradually outstrip all other sciences and become predominant, integrating their uncoordinated efforts. Physics, mathematics, history, literary criticism — all of these sciences are interesting and instructive, mostly because they help us to understand various aspects of the world in which Helen could appear. For none who ever saw this world was surprised with it to the degree that one is amazed with Helen. Thus, Helenology becomes the avant-garde of all scientific development.

6. Each science begins with certain intuitions and ends by synthesizing them into a system of concepts that holistically renders its subject. In this case, we are to connect the following notions that provide a glimpse of the internal and the external worlds of Helen:

(a) the azure and green tint of her eyes framed by their generally grey color;

(b) an attachment to a dog named Aka;

(c) strange knocks at night in her apartment, especially when the moon is full;

(d) the desire to work as a nurse in a retirement home;

(e) a narrow social circle along with the readiness to make new acquaintances easily;

(f) an aversion to the subway and to wearing hats;

(g) a belief in star signs, and also a strong, but not always compliant sense of destiny;

(h) a need to re-read Salinger's *Catcher in the Rye* periodically, and a love for Tsvetaeva's poems; [10]

(i) an abundance of daily projects to change her way of life: from moving to another apartment to moving to another country;

(j) a wish to be at the seashore when she is only at the river bank;

(k) a special interest in the writer Fyodor Sologub and in the concept of the demonic in his works; [11]

(l) a sense of the absence of her own personality and of the inexplicableness of her own actions;

(m) the mysterious relationship of inner closeness and outer alienation for the subject named *I*. . . . [12]

(z) an uncertainty that, in the world, there could be found even one man who is ready to sacrifice, for her, anything, anything at all, for example, his life.

7. Doubtless, all the above-mentioned features converge only in the singular entity in the world who is called Helen, and only because of her do they acquire general meaning and interconnection. Never, nowhere and in no one else could the dog Aka and the writer Salinger, the wish to find herself on the seashore and the desire to work as a nurse in a retirement home, conjoin and comprise one whole in which these diverse phenomena unite in the most unexpected and wondrous way, inspiring further investigation.

In Helen, a new reality unknown to previous sciences is revealed, where one American writer is closer to a mutt than to any other American writer, and a subway trip is closer to wearing a hat than to taking a trip in any other vehicle. This enigmatic reality, inexplicable through other scientific methods, demands a special philosophical-poetical approach and the creation of a new science satisfying the most rigid criteria of singularity. Zoology and literary criticism, medicine and geography — at the intersection of these disciplines, Helenology arises, which is not reducible to any of them.

8. Helenology is an integral area of scientific knowledge which, in its ascension to the Singular, uses the results of generalizing sciences, but is not limited by them, because Helen is incommensurably superior to any generalization, being exclusive of all rules and the rule for all exclusions. In the development of Helenology, the main contributions are made by her intimates and acquaintances as they deepen their knowledge of her. Gradually, a new social milieu of interprofessional communication is taking shape, a milieu which unites physicists and mathematicians, linguists and art historians, psychologists and sociologists, astrologers and navigators, all those who, through their particular paths, approach the enigma of Helen and find in Helenology the unifying thread of universal knowledge about the world.

9. The goal of Helenology is not only to expand our general knowledge about the universe, but also to introduce methods and criteria, elaborated in the study of Helen, into other disciplines. Since Helen is interesting by herself, other disciplines cannot avoid reflecting this interest as they exemplify and expand upon features of Helen's personality. For example, architects cannot help but be interested in Helen's sharply negative attitude to subways. Futurologists must inevitably pay attention to the multiplicity of shifting scenarios of the future which is especially characteristic of Helen, but also of all humanity. Landscape architects will doubtless be interested in Helen's view on the skyscape of clouds and their influence on the earthly landscape, a view that she allows herself to share, in part, with I . . . Whether Helen's master's thesis contributes significantly to Sologub studies or not, Helenology will make a powerful impact on the development of this minor discipline. Helen's particular interest in the study of Fyodor Sologub is deeply characteristic of his artistic conception of the demonic and opens the possibility of new metaphysical, psychological, mythological, and other approaches to this prob-

lem in accordance with the integral character of Helenology. For further research, the following themes are particularly recommended: "Aka and the Image of the Dog in Works of Sologub"; "The Combination of Green, Blue and Grey in the Symbolism of Sologub"; "Nèdotykomka (nether-creature) and the Moon in Works of Sologub, in Connection with the Night Knocks in Helen's Apartment," and so on.

10. The importance of the above-mentioned points (section 6) is self-evident:

(a) For the development of painting and art criticism;
(b) For new theoretical insights in the study of canines, especially in the exploration of mongrels;
(c) For empirical substantiation of occult knowledge;
(d) For the development of gerontology and medical deontology.

And so forth and so on.

In truth, Helenology is capable of enriching all sciences, because Helen contains an inexplicable enigma that underlies all of them; this enigma does not itself become more decipherable, but aids in deciphering the enigmas of other disciplines.

11. Each phenomenon contains something helenesque, therefore while wandering around a crowded city or an endless forest, in any condition or on various occasions, one is tempted to pronounce Helen's name, relating it . . .

. . . to the cloud, because it is completely helenesque;

. . . to the grass, because it is green like Helen's eyes;

. . . to the lake, because it shimmers like Helen's eyes;

. . . to the ant, because once Helen compared her everyday life with its;

. . . to the tree, because it bows from the wind and branches abundantly like Helen's fate;

. . . to the asphalt, because Helen often peers at it, wandering with head bent;

. . . to the tramway, because on a similar tramway, Helen once went to visit someone;

. . . and to any passerby, because he, as a simple human, might chance to see Helen and wonder at her, but is likely devoid of this capacity.

All helenesque phenomena, like Helen herself, comprise the subject matter of Helenology, which studies, in her person, the entire world in its most profound and mysterious hypostasis. The Helenological aspect of all things implies their possible, though unattainable, perfection: to be close to Helen and necessary for her.

12. One of the fundamental notions of Helenology is the chastity of play or the purity of temptation, which are manifest in such contradictory phenomena as . . .

. . . the greenness of the forest and the blueness of the sky, which are mediated by the transparent grey, dimly glittering air;

. . . heightened egocentrism without egoism: ego in everything, but nothing for the ego;

. . . a firm character with a complacent will, which is fascinated by everything yet subjugated by nothing;

. . . an aspiration to burden herself with useful work and a tendency to easily neglect labor and utility of any kind;

. . . a capricious meandering pattern of conversation in which sentences say less than words, words less than pauses, but still more meaningful are: (1) steps, (2) looks, (3) touches, (4) the state of nature, (5) smells, (6) recollections, (7) seasons, (8) the location of the clouds, (9) surrounding objects, (10) unspoken thoughts, (11) wishes kept secret, (12) wishes uncovered, and so on.

13. The point is that each feature in Helen is revealed to the degree that it contrasts with another, as some specialists believe. Other specialists hold that Helen is a meek, faithful, and loving being who has not yet awakened from the dream of pre-existences, and thus experiences, at the same time, all stages of the organic development of personality: larva, cocoon, and butterfly. It is premature to separate these stages of larva-ingenue, cocoon-coquette, and butterfly-princess, but what is evident is their continuing metamorphosis, leading to the formation of a winged soul. A third group of specialists sees the specificity of the phenomenon in its early charm which leads to a fixation on the infantile stages of development. In spite of this struggle within various schools of Helenology, all specialists coincide in the opinion that knowledge, as the process of confluence between subject and object, is still unattainable for them;

and the same wonder that so excites their minds proves to be the unsurpassable obstacle to knowledge.

14. Recently, among Helenologists, one awful heresy arose, which was condemned and expelled from the mainstream of the science. According to this heterodox dogma, Helen is love, and nothing but love, and since the subject and object of knowledge must eventually coincide, then Helenology is nothing but the growing love for Helen, the highest of all possible acts of knowledge.

15. However, all these heretics do not provide a single convincing argument that Helen is love. The absence of arguments is justified by the hypothesis that the manifestation of this secret quality of Helen can proceed only from her. The greatest duty of those persisting in heresy is to wait patiently for this manifestation, which will confirm the validity of their faith.

16. What is argument in science is sacrifice in faith, and there is nothing to be added to it, since I have reached point Z.[13]

NOTES

1. (Editor) This work of Epstein's, written under the name of Ivan Soloviev, contains many conscious allusions and references to the legacy of the greatest Russian philosopher Vladimir Soloviev (1853–1900). Vladimir Soloviev was the founder of the philosophy of "total-unity," later adopted by many other Russian thinkers. In the twentieth century, one of its outcomes, ecumenism, became an increasingly influential movement for the reunification of all Christian churches and denominations. Vladimir Soloviev was also the founder of Sophiology, the doctrine about Sophia, the feminine hypostasis of Godhead, the divine wisdom, and the "soul of the universe." The poetry of Vladimir Soloviev and his followers, Russian symbolists such as Alexander Blok, describes the mystical encounters of the lyric hero with Sophia, personified in the image of Beautiful Lady. According to Vladimir Soloviev, sexual love is the means to overcome individualism and to unite the masculinism and feminine elements as the prototype of the desired total-unity. Vladimir Soloviev developed many aspects of Platonic philosophy, in particular the theme of ideal love, which ascends from the beloved woman to God; however, Soloviev does not oppose the world of Ideas to the material world, but confesses a "religious materialism" that unites Platonism with the Christian notion of the holiness and divine justification of the flesh. "Ivan Soloviev's Reflections on Eros," in particular the fragments on contiguity and Helenology, offer "serious parodies" of the cherished conceptions of Vladimir Solo-

viev and locate them in the intellectual context of the end of the twentieth century.

2. (Editor) The Russian original of this publication includes ten fragments. See M. N. Epstein, "Razmyshleniia Ivana Solovyova ob Erose," *Chelovek* 1195 (Moscow: Nauka, 1991): 212.

3. (M.E.) Ivan Soloviev took these words from the French writer's novel *Mémoires d'Hadrien* (1951) as an epigraph for his "Theory of Contiguity."

4. (I.S.) Incidentally, "Lenin" means "laziness," but it occurred much later that laziness took possession of the world of Vladimir (which means in Russian "the master of the world").

5. (M.E.) In Russian, both words are feminine. Further, this is a parodic paraphrase from Mayakovsky's poem "Lenin": "Lenin and the Party are twin-brothers." This expression was one of the most famous ideological clichés of the Soviet epoch.

6. (M.E.) The Soviet emblem of the crossed hammer and sickle, symbolizing the union of the worker and the peasant, can also be interpreted as a symbol of male and female sexual union since it frankly presents the phallic hammer entering the half-circle of the sickle.

7. (I.S.) Superconsciousness has followed the instruction given by Niccolo Machiavelli to the Prince: "you assist at the destruction of one by the aid of another who, if he had been wise, would have saved him; and conquering, as it is impossible that he shouldn't with your assistance, he remains at your discretion" (*The Prince*, in *Great Books of the Western World* [New York: Encyclopaedia Britannica, 1952], vol. 23, 32). Superconsciousness destroyed the classic consciousness with the aid of economic and biological materialism, so that material life itself remained a defenseless victim at the discretion of superconsciousness. Since Machiavellianism is considered to be a prototype of totalitarian strategy in the twentieth century, the Prince may also be regarded as a symbol of superconsciousness.

8. (M.E.) This fragment is one of the last ones completed by Ivan Soloviev not long before his death. As to the strict thesis-like form, the explanation can be found in another of Soloviev's papers: "Form must oppose content, and the more passionate the one the more impassive the other" ("Style as failure").

9. (M.E.) Aristotle, *Metaphysics*, Book 1, ch. 2, 892 b, in *A New Aristotle Reader*, ed. J. L. Ackrill (Princeton: Princeton University Press, 1987), 258.

10. (M.E.) Marina Tsvetaeva (1892–1941), Russian poet and essayist, the author of very passionate lyrical verses, where fury and sarcasm are mixed with gentle confessions.

11. (M.E.) Fyodor Sologub (1863–1927), Russian novelist and poet, close to the symbolists and skilled in the presentation of the morbid and perverse aspects of an "evil" reality, the author of the novel *The Petty Demon* (1907).

12. (M.E.) We exclude here those paragraphs — (n) to (y) — that deal with the intimate sides of the lives of I. and Helen. As to the relationship of the unique and the universal in the name of Helen, one can cite here a judgment of Ivan Soloviev about the great Russian philosopher Vladimir Soloviev: "He created

his Sophiology, a doctrine about eternal femininity and God's wisdom, only because all his life he was in love with Sophia Petrovna Khitrovo. Sophiology is the doctrine of this Sophia."

13. (M.E.) In Russian, *ia* is both the personal pronoun *I* and the last letter of the alphabet. See point Z in Section 16.

The following remark from Ivan Soloviev's article "The Semiotics of Silence" may be illuminating: "*I* is the only linguistic sign in which the speaker also becomes the referent. The coincidence of the subject and the object overcomes the duality of sign (signifying/signified) and thus abolishes the very foundations of speech. Therefore, the word "I" is not a sign in the traditional sense, it is rather a border between sign and non-sign, the transition from speech to silence."

ELEVEN

Russian Women Writing Alcoholism: The Sixties to the Present

Teresa Polowy

I simply do not comprehend my existence here on earth . . . you came to the right person with your aching soul: my soul aches too. Only you came looking for a ready answer, while I'm trying to delve into the depths – but it's an ocean. . . . So we drink this loathsome brew.

— V. Shukshin, *I Believe!*

Fyodor wasn't a big drinker. He hardly drank at all in fact . . . and if he did he never acted up. . . . Next morning he'd wake up and say: "Forgive me for yesterday." But what was there to forgive? He was only a man after all.

— I. Grekova, *Ship of Widows*

Alcoholism is one of Russia's oldest and most persistent social problems which over many generations has become a cultural norm and Russian "institution" in the sense that "the popular craving for alcohol has played as equally important [a] role as a set of needs, values, and attitudes related to the most essential determinants of social behavior: needs for food, for sex, for freedom, and for prosperity and success."[1]

Russian alcoholism has been a predominantly male problem – although the incidence of female alcoholism has increased in the late Soviet and post-Soviet period – and its consequences effect the relationships between men and women and those within the family. It is a particularly charged site in contemporary Russian culture because it provides a focal point for burgeoning concerns about such issues as gender roles and

267

relations, and the increase in social and domestic violence. Less than a decade ago, G. Skvortsova identified the "psychological and social position of woman in the man-woman relationship" as being "a touchstone issue of contemporary society," and as the subject of considerable discussion among specialists and the general public.[2] N. Ivanova, writing at the height of Soviet glasnost, claimed that "the unmasking of the violence in everyday life is contemporary culture's primary task."[3] A few examples suffice to illustrate these claims in relation to Russian alcoholism and the interpersonal problems which are engendered: there is a high correlation between drinking and violence (especially violence toward women and within the family);[4] women in families where the husband drinks have an above-average abortion rate (the Russian average is already high at 8);[5] and a full 50 percent of women filing for divorce charge their husbands with alcoholism.[6] The insidious and often devastating effects of alcoholism on familial structure and indications of individual well-being are only now beginning to receive proper attention in post-Soviet Russia.

Since the early 1960s, the dual themes of alcohol abuse and drunkenness have been treated in Russian prose fiction with increasing frequency and directness. Male- and female-authored texts which were published in the Soviet Union between 1960 and 1990 provided models of appropriate behavior vis-à-vis alcohol and gender relations which were officially sanctioned and instrumental in the formation of society's attitudes toward these linked problems. One of the major trends in modern Soviet literature, "village prose" (derevenskaia proza), is predominantly male-authored and male-centered and offers literary treatment of alcoholism more systematically and consistently than any other corpus of recent Russian writing by men which was published in the Soviet Union.[7] The early prose of the "derevenshchiki" (village prose writers) treated themes suggesting that rapid postwar urbanization had created a displaced, frustrated, and lonely population of new city-dwellers and a demoralized and dismal Russian countryside. An increase in alcohol abuse, among other grave social consequences, was the tangible result of this process. Initially the development of the theme of male alcohol abuse was often limited to descriptions of drinking bouts in the village or in a worker's settlement, that is to the culture and rituals of drinking and to the violence that frequently accompanies it. Stories like Solzhenitsyn's "Matriona's Home" ("Matrionin dvor," 1963), Rasputin's "Vasily i Vasilisa" (1968), and Shukshin's "The Bastard" ("Suraz," 1970) and " 'Oh, a Wife Saw Her Husband Off to Paris . . .' " (" 'Zhena muzha v Parizh provozhala . . . ,' " 1971) incorporate drinking into the daily routine but speak to larger issues of the heroes' worldview and of how they live. The connection between quality of life and alcoholism is strongly suggested in these stories, but drinking is simply a common motif which links them. Until recently, Soviet literary censorship tolerated only guarded allusions to the fact that the problem of alcohol abuse was, at least in part, bred and sustained by the system; writers were thus cautious in their treatment of the topic. In pre-glasnost Russia, Vasily Shukshin, whose name is often linked with village prose, was best able to convey the angst, anomie, disillusionment, cynicism, and alienation felt by his protagonists who want to dull their senses and escape from the world around them, perhaps temporarily to an altered reality.

Since the early 1980s, Russian prose fiction has treated the question of alcohol in Russian society even more openly and candidly: it depicts drinkers of both sexes from all social and economic classes – the military, artists, intellectuals, the bureaucracy. To a considerable degree, the expansion in the parameters of the theme was due to the gradual emergence, particularly during the glasnost period, of women's prose as a viable literary voice in Russia.

Russian women's prose published in the Soviet Union has been the most effective corpus of urban-based writing that presents the alcohol problem in literary refraction.[8] Women's writing is noted for its attention to "byt," – that is, to all of the details and activities of daily life that taken together constitute its practical or mundane side – as well as for its themes that reflect the host of problems found in the popular press and in rudimentary sociological surveys, and for its treatment of interpersonal and familial relationships. It is gynocentric writing: drawing on the wellspring of "byt," Russian women give voice (narratively and figuratively) to issues and problems of daily life that profoundly effect them.[9] In greater or lesser detail, these stories depict women living and coping with husbands and fathers and other family members who drink. This prose intuits and anticipates the phenomenon that, along with the alcoholic, the spouses and children, parents and siblings may suffer progressive psychological, emotional, and spiritual deterioration which mirrors that of the drinker. An important element in female-authored prose is its acknowledgment of alcohol abuse and alcoholism among Russian women, a phenomenon which is virtually ignored in male texts. Specific works by women which deal with alcoholism include: I. Grekova's novella *Ship of Widows* (*Vdovyi parakhod*, 1981), Galina Shcherbakova's "The Wall" ("Stena," 1979), Viktoria Tokareva's "Five Figures on a Pedestal" ("Piat' figur na postamente," 1987), "Every Hunter" ("Kazhdyi okhotnik," 1987) by Tat'iana Nabatnikova, "Be Still, Torments of Passion" ("Uimites', volneniia strasti," 1986) by Liudmila Uvarova, "Parade of the Planets" ("Parad planet," 1990) by Larisa Vaneeva, and Liudmila Petrushevskaia's "Ali-Baba" (1988), her novella *Our Crowd* (*Svoi krug*, 1988), and the one-act plays *Cinzano* (1973, premiere 1978) and *Smirnova's Birthday* (*Den' rozhdeniia Smirnovoi*, 1977, premiere 1978). Certainly Petrushevskaia makes alcoholism a prominent theme, while simultaneously portraying the disillusionment and spiritual atrophy which are the consequences of alcoholism at the social level. Shcherbakova examines in great detail the intimate, inner, and destructive workings of a relationship between a typical, well-educated upper-middle-class couple who contend on a daily basis with the husband's alcoholism. In reading these and other stories, it is possible to conceive of the theme of alcoholism in Russian literature as a synecdoche which embraces society at large; subsumed within this larger frame of reference the theme functions as a catalyst which reveals values, attitudes — gender stereotypes and social and cultural myths, for example — as well as perceptions of self and of others. In her 1992 study, *Women with Alcoholic Husbands*, Ramona Asher supports such a conceptualization when she contends that "the social experience and status of women married to alcoholics say something important about the collective experience and status of women in [a given] society."[10]

With these ideas in mind, pertinent questions arise: what are the cultural and social processes which underlie the abuse of alcohol in Russia? Why have women allowed themselves to bear the brunt of it for so long? More specifically, how do Russian women authors manipulate and comment on this phenomenon and its multifaceted effect on womens' lives? Is there a difference in the way in which Russian women and men perceive and represent the problem of alcoholism and its familial consequences in their prose?

Answers to the latter two questions often lie within the literary texts themselves; in order to attempt to answer the first questions, we shall briefly consider both the social function of alcohol in Russia and the general cultural landscape for women and men in that country.

Russian social drinking — that is, nonaddictive, male drinking behavior — incorporates two aspects — the celebratory and the utilitarian. Russians mark virtually every occasion — joyful or sad — and every holiday — religious and secular — with drink. Vodka and brandy are preferred but moonshine ("samogon"), medical spirits, and even technical spirits will suffice.[11] Russians prefer to drink in groups — and as few as three people constitute a serious drinking party — although binge drinking in solitude (zapoi) is the most characteristic behavior of Russian alcoholic males. Drinking to get drunk is a normal behavior favored by much of the male population and drinking in great quantities is regarded as a sign of virility, courage, and character.[12] The "mystique" of vodka in Russian society attributes blame for intoxication to the vodka rather than to the drinker, and drunken antics and even unconsciousness are tolerated because "it can happen to anyone." Even regular sprees do not stigmatize a man as an alcoholic as long as drinking is confined to leisure time and the drinker can continue to provide for his family.[13]

Drinking in Russia also has a crucial utilitarian component for it is used as a means of making contacts, of consolidating business deals, of maintaining good relations with superiors. Alcohol plays a large role in Russia's second economy and is often used as currency. Bottles of vodka go to people who provide a service or who can exert influence; such deals involve anything from connections for receiving good food, fashionable clothing, repairs or renovations, telephone services, apartments, to entrance to private schools and even university.[14] Thus for most interactions between people, alcohol is regarded as a necessity in contemporary Russian society and its role in social and cultural processes is vital. One researcher even suggests a link between the spread and intensification of Russian drinking and the evolution of Soviet society; he interprets these phenomena as being engendered by identical socioeconomic and psychological processes: "widespread drunkenness . . . [is] an essential mechanism of fitting a person to Russian society, a tool for cultural conditioning and for developing national behavioral patterns."[15]

Soviet authorities had sporadically campaigned against alcoholism which affected productivity and involved such legal violations as drunk-driving, disturbing the peace — the so-called "anti-social" activities. However, they were consistently sympathetic to "normal" drinking as an extremely lucrative source of state revenue. While some observers, like economist V. Treml, attribute the permissiveness of the authorities toward drinking to purely cynical financial calculations of the Soviet government (and the Tsarist government before it), others attest to the deliberate "alcoholization" of the Russian people: "National drunkenness is the best way to fog the mind. More than anything else, clear, sober minds are feared by those who are trying to make a nation of 250 million people into a nation of robots."[16]

In order to better understand the historical, political, sociological, psychological, and gender issues that are embedded in literary texts which manipulate the phenomenon of alcoholism, a theoretical model is an appropriate aid. Cultural anthropologist Edwin Ardener's construct of intersecting "dominant" (male) and "muted"[17] (female) circles can incorporate the Russian male alcohol problem within the dominant sphere and the problems of women involved in alcoholic relationships within the "muted" sphere and thus offer some insights into how such women are perceived by the dominant Russian male culture and how they perceive themselves and others.[18] While the "dominant" and "muted" group boundaries of culture and reality largely overlap, there is a crescent of the muted group circle which is not wholly contained by the dominant group. Spatially this zone, which Ardener terms "wild," is forbidden to men and experientially it represents aspects of female life-style which are unlike and outside those of men; in each case there is a corresponding zone of male experience alien to women. However, metaphysically, that is in terms of consciousness, there is no equivalent male space to the female zone. Since all of male consciousness is within the circle of the dominant structure, it is structured by or accessible to language. For men, the female zone is consciously unknowable for the very reason that it lies beyond. For women however, pure male space is knowable because it becomes the subject of legend. This is a crucial point in understanding the persistence of Russian male myths about drinking — the need for "freedom," "release," "time-out" are all the stuff of legend. Russian women know these myths and appear to have internalized them.

Thus, as a recurring theme in Russian literature, alcoholism may be interpreted as a factor which distinguishes the daily life of Russian women from that of men, that is, women's condition from the general condition. Commenting in general terms on women's writing, N. Zekulin suggests that women's lives are fundamentally differentiated from men's by "the domestic aspect of life, with its inequitable distribution of labor, its family pressures, the inadequate social and economic services, and above all *the necessity of living with alcoholism* [italics mine – TP]."[19] Despite the increase in women citing their husbands' alcoholism in divorce cases, coping with a drunken husband (which is reflected as a critical problem in women's prose) is still widely accepted as part of a woman's role in Russian culture, where essentialized roles have long been the norm in gender relations.[20]

Russian men's writing in general, and village prose in particular, paint positive portraits of women as meek, self-sacrificing, forgiving, compassionate, and moral in the tradition of nineteenth-century prose fiction. On the other hand, contemporary, professionally successful women, and those who are self-motivated and striving for personal realization and happiness are portrayed negatively by the "derevenshchiki," for they are perceived as undermining the family as the foundation of society.[21] Vasily Belov, who has been criticized by some Russian women writers for misogyny in his prose, illustrates this view in "Morning Meetings" ("Svidaniia po utram," 1977) through his hero, Zorin: "[M]any modern women had more female vanity than maternal love. Tonja was no exception. Zorin knew that more than once she had sacrificed Lyalka's [their daughter's – TP] well-being to her own idiotic self-assertion. He had been horrified when he made this discovery."[22] When Zorin eavesdrops on the conversation of a group of women talking about their husbands, he indignantly comments that "the woman who felt that men should be fed well to make them drink less was in such a tiny minority that she fell silent instantly. ... In short, it wasn't fashionable to love Slavik – that is, one's own husband – according to this jolly company."[23] Also typical in varying degrees of much of the writing of the conservative and nationalistically oriented "derevenshchiki" is a dichotomy in attitude toward woman-as-mother and woman-as-wife which may be regarded as a variant of the madonna/whore stereotype that is prevalent in much male fiction. The mother, the Heroine and the Savior is Mother Russia – "Rossia-Matushka," while the often shrewish wife is the antithesis of that romantic notion.[24]

In treating the theme of alcoholism, the approach in village prose is quite distinct from that found in women's urban texts. Here the main concern is with male characters and the emotional or physical crises they experience. This male fiction portrays men as frustrated to the point of violence, edgy, and alienated. They seek release in drink, in "a form of national escapism."[25] One critic has succinctly summarized the motif of drinking in the extremely popular short stories of Vasily Shukshin: "Vodka is an obligatory accessory in Shukshin's stories. . . . Vodka as medicine for spiritual pain. And vodka as the single means of going out 'to freedom.' "[26]

Shukshin and Belov almost invariably portray woman-as-wife as a handy scapegoat for the drinking of her husband. She becomes the main obstacle in the male quest for freedom and the soul and the women thus depicted exhibit any number of the negative and stereotypical features outlined above. In the writing of the "derevenshchiki" male self-respect has been eroded and men are made to feel "weak" and "unneeded," confused by and resentful of their wives' demands. Thus, the nagging, sharp-tongued wife is rooted in the real world and is perceived as the ultimate stimulus that pushes the man, who desires so much more spiritually from life, to drink. In Shukshin's stories, alcohol abuse most often acquires an existential mystique: inebriation is an essential part of Shukshin's "holiday for the soul" ("prazdnik dlia dushi") and "spiritual release" ("volia"), which are metaphors for illusory freedom.

A different approach is taken by Valentin Rasputin, whose abusive drinkers embody "the destructive and aggressive male ethos" which threatens the peace and stability created and sustained by the aged Russian women, emblems of Mother Russia, who are his favorite heroines. Younger women, including wives with citified and pretentious manners or with philistine interests, are not sympathetic in Rasputin's writing; however, in contrast to the works of such writers as Shukshin and Belov, a wife is never blamed for her husband's drinking. Indeed in Rasputin's story "Vasily and Vasilisa," a wife evicts her husband after twenty years of married life after he has beaten her and caused her to miscarry. Rasputin attempts no justification of the beating. Vasilisa is a unique heroine within the works of Russian village prose; she is too sympathetic a figure for the paradigm of the hostile Shukshinian wife, yet her rejection of her husband disqualifies her from the male ideal of woman as maternal savior and redeemer. Rasputin depicts Vasilisa as virtually free from the crucial psychological bonds of self-sacrifice, blame, and guilt which dictate a

Russian woman's tolerance of physical and psychological abuse from a drunken husband. At least in this important aspect, Vasilisa's portrayal is nonstereotypical of much women's and men's prose which treats the consequences of alcoholism in relationships. On the other hand, Rasputin's worldview emphasizes the ideologically nationalistic and apocalyptic, and in this story Vasilisa may be conceptualized as Mother Russia. A constant in Rasputin's prose is the often violent, sometimes morose alcoholic who is estranged from his family, and by implication, from his Motherland. Rasputin fiercely condemns alcoholism in Russia as a collective evil, and the relationship between Vasily and Vasilisa has been interpreted symbolically as "a microcosm of the fate of rural Russia in the modern world, where disruption and chaos threaten the order and harmony of centuries."[27]

Village prose reflects the relationship between alcohol abuse and divorce and physical violence against women, but most often the point of view indicates that it is the man who is the victim: all of his vices are glossed over, and women are portrayed as calculating and unfeeling. In "The Anguish of Young Vaganov" ("Stradaniia molodogo Vaganova," 1972), a lawyer reviews a wife's petition against her husband for drunkenness; if found guilty her husband will face a three-year prison sentence. But the lawyer, Vaganov, feels that the husband has been set up by the wife who wants to move in with her lover. In men's writing, portrayal of abuse is usually "motivated" by the nagging of the wife. For example, in another of Shukshin's stories, " 'Oh, A Wife Saw Her Husband Off to Paris . . . ,' " the hero is portrayed as anguished over his unhappy marriage and the prospects of losing his child to divorce. He is driven to distraction by the insults of his wife, who doesn't want to put up any longer with his drinking and neighborhood accordion concerts. When she hits a raw nerve concerning his family, the hero reacts: "That was quite enough from her. It was time to put an end to it! Any more of this self-imposed torment, and he'd become a mental case or an alcoholic. . . . 'One way or another I'm going to kill you today. . . . You've asked for it. And you're going to get it.' "[28]

In the writing of the "derevenshchiki" then, there are two distinct, male-oriented agendas in portrayals of alcoholics. These agendas are formulated at a level which is perceptibly more abstract than the one at which women's prose expresses itself, which is the level of "byt."[29] One formula exalts and romanticizes the existential male striving for "release" and "freedom," while the other, with a nationalistic zeal, abhors that striving for defiling Mother Russia. In contemplating the national character of the Russian, emigré author Andrei Siniavsky, with marked irony, associates the significance of alcohol use with the realization of an essential facet of Russian culture: "The Russian people drink not from need and not from grief, but from an age-old requirement for the miraculous and the extraordinary — drink, if you will, mystically, striving to transport the soul beyond earth's gravity and return it to its sacred noncorporeal state."[30] Predictably, the portrayal of female drinkers by the village prose writers is exceptionally rare; this fact tells us much about the extent to which Russian society tolerates the abuse of alcohol by women, but also, invoking Siniavsky, it suggests that Russia's male-dominant culture is not prepared to share the legend of the miraculous, the extraordinary, the mystical, and ultimately the spiritual, with women.

Much of Russian women's writing is mediated through male-dominated literary structures and, while women's prose is gradually being legitimized in Russia, in general women still lack a suitable code by which to express their views in an acceptable form to men and women brought up in the male idiom. Many Russian women writers, the foremost among them, do not believe that gender is relevant to the creative process: they protest the label "women's writing," refuse to see differences between female and male writing, and adopt male authors as models to emulate. However, this set of beliefs does not hinder the best authors from writing, upon occasion, what Western criticism would call "feminist critiques" of their patriarchal culture.[31]

The basic conservatism of Russian women in terms of their ability to bring to consciousness many womens' issues is rooted in a behavior of accommodation to the patriarchal culture; by examining the theme of alcoholism in women's literature we see graphic proof of this behavior in depictions of women and their reactions to the drinker. Focusing on the manipulation of the phenomenon of alcoholism we can see how the weight of the dominant culture's ordering of the world constrains women; it questions their self-perception and inundates them with literary stereotypes of what a "good wife" should be: meek, self-sacrificing, forgiving, compassionate, and entirely nonthreatening. If a woman does not exhibit these qualities, if she refuses to facilitate or opposes her husband's drinking, then in the writing of men, the wife is typecast as aggressive, overpowering, domineering, treacherous, philistine, selfish, cruel, greedy. Sexual wantonness is often linked with woman's lack of moral scruples and stifling banality. Such stereotypes of women are the surface forms with which men in the Soviet period have articulated their fears about women and sexuality. At base is an ongoing and elemental struggle with the suppressed old Orthodox Christian concept of sex as sin and of woman as its source. With characteristic irony Siniavsky has commented that: "Vodka is the Russian muzhik's [male's — TP] White Magic; he decidedly prefers it to Black Magic — the female."[32] The underlying feelings of insecurity and enmity toward women/sex so widespread in Russia have combined with many other sources of anxiety in a male complex of drunkenness, for alcohol temporarily alleviates hostilities and sexual anxieties.

As an attempt to escape from any type of hardship or trouble, Russian men take to drink.[33] Folk sayings, truisms, and jokes — the mouthpiece of the dominant culture — respond to this phenomenon. For example, consider the maxim "when times get tough, men get drunk and women head for church"; the punchline to a joke "I'm not a ladies man, I'm a decent Russian alcoholic"; a ditty which names an alcoholic spouse as one of the "cornerstones" in the life of the average Russian woman "In her right hand — a string bag/ In her left hand — snot-nosed Tos'ka/ On her back — dead drunk Ivan/ Before her — the Five-Year Plan."

Author and playwright Zoia Boguslavskaia alludes to the extent to which women in Russian society have internalized these myths when she comments upon the traditionally closed nature of Russian society: "any information about women, the family and relations between the sexes was considered washing our dirty linen before strangers."[34] Another commentator corroborates this view and sees ostentation as pronounced in Russian society and responsible for destructive effects in personal and family life, since "much effort is expended on maintaining form and appearances."[35] One of I. Grekova's characters illustrates this attitude in relation to the alcohol problem: "My late husband drank but I stuck it out. If he threw up, I wiped it up so that I wouldn't have to be ashamed in front of the neighbors. I did his laundry, the mending and ironing — spick and span, neat as a pin."[36]

Feminist critic Barbara Heldt has called such literary treatments of women's role in society "the phoney glorification of making do." The occurrence of women's writing which "wears a smile" could, in Soviet Russia, be directly related to its accommodation to the male-dominated literary establishment: "Works on women publishable in the Soviet Union may show women's difficult lives, weak or inadequate men, nasty interactions at work, losses great and small; but always they must contain hope for the future, show male reasonableness at the very top . . . and end on a positive note for the main character."[37]

How *do* Russian women write alcoholism? Their treatment typically conveys a deeply personal concern about the drinker, his problem and its repercussions in the life of a woman and of her family. The heroine is usually the wife, lover, sometimes mother of the drinker; she bears the direct brunt of the drinking and is always aware of the larger context of trying to reconcile his needs with her own and with those of her family, if there is one. This type of all-encompassing, processual approach to problems reflects widely held gender expectations of women in general which relate to self-involvement and tending to the whole.[38] From a woman's perspective, usually conveyed in first-person narration or through quasi-direct discourse,[39] this corpus of fiction, mainly stories and novellas, presents emotions, thoughts, and the psychology of the Russian woman through such stylistic and narrative devices as retrospection, irony, and interior monologue, all of which coalesce to create a personal and confiding narrative tone. There is no generalized moral judgment of the problem in women's writing, rather each story attempts to rationalize and explain the motivations of an individual and particular drinker. There is also a sense of the need to give voice to a certain type of lived experience which is common and shared.

In Viktoria Tokareva's recent story "Five Figures on a Pedestal," we see a reflection of many of these characteristics. The heroine, Tamara, a journalist married to a sculptor who is a hopeless alcoholic, is cognizant of many aspects of her situation. For example, at times she regards the myth of the alcoholic creative artist ironically: "He has a lovely way of putting it: 'the pathology of the gifted.' Similarly pathologically gifted friends, or simply smart bums, will come around — people who are just as degenerate as the husband of old Dusya, the yardkeeper, only they've read more";[40] she has closely analyzed her husband's pattern of drinking — two weeks in an alcoholic stupor, a period of remission in which he works, and then pre-alcoholic ennui which signals the onset of another binge; and she is even aware that "wives of alcoholics" may be considered "a separate social subunit, capable of being studied as an individual group or species" (Tokareva, 155). Tamara is also very concerned about both the environmental and biological effects of the father's drinking on their son. She regards her own position as a typical Soviet woman with an alcoholic husband with heavy irony: "Nowadays, in the 1980s, it was the woman who kept the family afloat. Women toiled like Volga boatmen, giving men the opportunity to be true to themselves, to be creative, and not to bring home any money" (Tokareva, 154). Yet when the opportunity for a more satisfying life presents itself, predictably with a man whom she meets on a business trip, Tamara rejects it. Although Iura possesses only redeeming features (she perceives him as an angel), Tamara ends their affair essentially because he is from a Ukrainian city and she believes that her Muscovite "mentality" would inevitably clash with his "provincial" ways. The story ends as she returns home to a husband who does not even know she has been gone, but who "hid his face in her hair, and clung to her, like a child in the dark. . . . Tamara led her husband out of the studio. He held her hand tightly, as if afraid he might get lost" (Tokareva, 197). Tokareva's use of maternal imagery reflects the same iconization of motherhood that is so prevalent in much Russian men's writing. The literary expectation that fictional women and female narrators should be "good" mothers, not only to their children but to their men, reflects the larger cultural expectation which is realized in domestic relations.

Typically, Tamara prefers to stay on her "treadmill" and use her job as an escape: "In addition to the money it brought in, the editorial department was a social club for Tamara. Here she could breathe a sigh of relief and get away from the storms that were always threatening to break at home. . . . [H]ere, Tamara was in touch with herself, with her standing in society" (Tokareva, 156).

Tokareva's story is fairly representative of the corpus of women's writing which treats the theme of alcoholism; the wives of the drinkers experience a lengthy and trying relationship which rocks the foundation of their self-definition and social worth. They are often portrayed in a variety of self-abnegating modes: pity and overprotectiveness toward the drinker, feelings of responsibility and guilt, and self-sacrifice. While such stances have been labeled as "codependent" in Western studies of substance abuse, the women involved often perceive them as simply protective or caring behavior and a form of marital obligation.[41]

Like Tamara, most of the wives depicted in women's writing are aware of the dynamics of their husband's drinking and its effect on themselves and their families. Nonetheless, they hesitate to take decisive action and are most often portrayed as engaged in some sort of coping behavior. For example, at the beginning of Tokareva's story Tamara reflects that she has not divorced her husband because she believes he will fall apart if she does, yet she knows that if she stays with him, *she* will fall apart. By story's end, however, she has reached the conclusion that "everyone is dependent on everyone else . . . [but] no matter how much life puts you through the meat grinder, no matter what kind of mincemeat it makes of you, other people aren't supposed to be affected, to suffer" (Tokareva, 200). These noble words are applied only to herself; she does not hold her husband accountable to the same standard. Thus for the sake of her child, her mother, her husband, she will continue as before: "she had to go on holding their life together single-handedly . . . a confident May Day-parade smile always on her face" (Tokareva, 156).

Women's feelings of guilt are evident in this particular body of female-authored prose and they frequently underlie plot choices which keep relationships together. For example, Tamara feels guilty toward her son and her mother for "she had wanted to be happy without them, apart from them. But what about them?" (Tokareva, 191). In I. Grekova's *Ship of Widows*, one of the women has had a son by another man but is reunited with her husband after World War II. We read that: "Anfisa, always conscious of the wrong she'd done [her husband], was shy and deferential with him."[42] When her husband takes to drink and periodically threatens her or beats her, Anfisa takes the entire blame onto herself. On one occasion, she effectively nullifies his apology: " 'But it's my fault. . . . It's all right if you hit me, Fedenka. It's better than I deserve.' Fyodor waved her aside disdainfully" (Grekova, 76). Clearly, an element of self-sacrifice (martyrdom) is emotionally related to women's guilt in these excerpts, but self-sacrifice is motivated by other factors as well. For example, a desire to maintain appearances is a mode which is also portrayed. A psychologically revealing internal monologue from Galina Shcherbakova's "The Wall" discloses much about both the wife, V.I., and her alcoholic husband:

For them, the better things are, the worse they get. But nobody knows that, not a single soul! She hates women who moan and complain. Nothing and nobody will force her to speak badly of him. But does he know what that costs her? How badly she wants to yell sometime! But she can't. She can't allow herself that luxury. Let everybody think that everything between them is as it was at the beginning.[43]

In these thoughts are undeniable elements of self-sacrifice and an unhealthy suppression of the speaker's emotions, particularly of her anger, all for the sake of preserving an outward facade of well-being.

A sense of moral superiority provides yet another motivation for a self-sacrificing stance: in Shcherbakova's story, V.I. has a prestigious job and many connections, yet she is powerless to save her husband from his alcoholism. She is aware though, that her position and influence can keep him dependent on her; he knows that she can "pull him out" of any alcoholic predicament. She feels a smug satisfaction as she thinks:

> One day he'd have a heart attack, and she'd have to pull him "out of there." She'd do it with her characteristic conscientiousness and pull him out . . . she was certain of her own abilities and strength. Of how she'd get all the specialists going, secure a private ward and sick-nurse, and obtain any medicines from any country. (Shcherbakova, 106)

Beyond the range of behaviors of wives who choose to stay with their husbands, very occasionally Russian women's prose which writes alcoholism depicts a woman who ends the relationship. For example, in Liudmila Uvarova's "Be Still, Torments of Passion," the heroine decisively terminates her relationship with her common-law alcoholic husband and is compelled to reject him yet again when he returns years later, asking for another chance:

> [Veronika] cried, choking, cursing herself and her misfortune, cursing Arnold, whom she gradually began to despise — not pity; not hate, of course, but despise. . . .
> "That's it," Veronika told Nastia. "We've got to put an end to this whole business." . . . And soon Arnold vanished from the house, vanished as if he had never been there at all. . . . Veronika didn't have a tear in her eye. She silently held out her hand to him. "Take care of yourself," she said rather calmly.[44]

Veronika goes on to develop her career as a successful actress and to live in a supportive family-like grouping of women with no feelings of guilt or remorse about the decision she has made.[45] The author counterposes Veronika's self-assurance and independence to a second female point of view, that of Nastia the housekeeper. Such a duality is a common technique used by Russian women authors and here it serves to implicitly question Veronika's judgment:

> So Ver[onika] didn't miss him after all. That meant she was satisfied with everything that had happened, and that was the main thing. She wasn't suffering

because of anybody. She wasn't heartbroken over anyone. But just the same, Nastia felt sorry, sorry for Arnold, poor fellow. It happens, and often, a man just can't control himself. He'd rather not drink, but he can't help himself; he doesn't have the strength, the will, the discipline. But Nastia didn't say any of this aloud. No point. (Uvarova, 182)

This story ends with Veronika's vindication — on a tape-recorded message Arnold admits that her decision had been the right one: " 'Well, what do you say to that?' Veronika turned to [Nastia]. 'As you can see, he blames himself for everything; not me, but only himself' " (Uvarova, 190). Both Veronika and V.I. are depicted as women whose professional aspirations and subsequent position afford them a good measure of autonomy and social value (and therefore social power), crucial factors in staving off a disruption and alteration of self-identity which, to varying degrees, happens to the wives in some of the stories examined above.

As a corpus, however, Russian women's fiction rather infrequently portrays wives who deal directly and decisively with the drinking of their husbands. Only indirectly does it reflect the statistical incidence of divorce on the grounds of alcohol abuse: it is not unusual in women's writing that the heroine is a single mother who has left her alcoholic and possibly abusive husband. Similarly, when women's writing does acknowledge the violence — physical, psychological, and emotional — inflicted upon wives by drunken husbands, it does so not with a sense of outrage but as a quiet statement of the facts. For example, in Shcherbakova's story, the upper-middle-class couple has substituted the arguments and physical beatings that accompany drinking in working-class homes and amongst the peasantry with subtle and sophisticated variations of those activities; theirs is an ongoing but silent physical and psychological battle. Silence has evolved as a weapon to be used against each other, but even the limited verbal exchange that occurs between them is described in a narration which employs such verbs as "attack," "ambush," "defend," and "barricade." A possible explanation for such omissions and silences in women's writing may have to do with the message, which was pervasive in Soviet Russian male-dominated society, that only as a last resort should families be disrupted by separation or divorce. One Soviet commentator gave the following advice regarding divorce in a newspaper article: "There are simple cases of heavy drunkenness, betrayal, cruelty. . . . But all the same, don't hurry to take the final step."[46] Debates in the popular media, agencies such as family consultation services, and discouragement of divorce through the legal system all conveyed this message which alluded to a deep concern about demography and gender relations in contemporary Russia.[47]

Generally in this particular corpus of women's writing, male drinkers are portrayed as objects of pity — tender creatures whose motivations for drinking are valid and need to be understood by a stoic wife who most often functions as a mother-figure. These men are essentially kind but lack strength and self-esteem. In "Ship of Widows" the husband explains: " 'I don't know why I do it myself. . . . You're sobbing inside with depression sometimes, and there's nothing you can do but drink. And then it doesn't matter any more and everything seems better" (Grekova, 79). The "maternal complex" in Tokareva's story reaches its culmination as Tamara contemplates her husband's latest sculpture — a fallen warrior and five grieving women — which is thematically reminiscent of the Pieta. She instantly fathoms the depths of her husband-child's emotions and implicitly excuses his alcoholism: "he, with an artist's sensibility, had intuited the pain of the times. . . . So everything that hurt people hurt him. That was why he was an artist. And why Tamara was an artist's wife" (Tokareva, 196). In this excerpt Tamara's maternal pity for her husband becomes inseparable from her feelings as a wife and the passage acquires a tone of near-exaltation as Tamara evokes the deep-rooted myth of the artist as alcoholic which has a very rich tradition in Russian culture. This passage is reminiscent of the words of an Esenin poem: "And I, myself dropping my head, fill my eyes with wine so as not to see fate's face, so as to think, at least for a moment, about something else." In the Soviet period alone, this tradition extends from such romanticized and mythologized literary figures as Aleksandr Blok and Sergei Esenin in the 1920s through to Vladimir Vysotsky and Vasily Shukshin in the 1980s. Thus, conveniently linked together are two myths of the male-dominated culture (the image of woman as mother and the image of the sensitive alcoholic artist), which Russian women have internalized and accept as valid.

In contrast to images of drinking men, the comparatively rare portrayals of women drinkers by women are "positive"; the woman drinker is debased (but no more so than others around her), and at times she is openly rebellious or nonconformist. A sense of irony and a rejection of patriarchal society and men as validators are key elements in this portrayal, for these heroines are mostly unmarried women, usually divorcees. Additionally, women writers who portray drinking women do not engage in moral statement, and do not pass judgment on their protagonists; their implied criticism lies elsewhere and is aimed at such targets as the inevitable double (gender) standard in Russian society, normative views of gender roles, and at a degenerate society in general. For example, in Liudmila Petrushevskaia's 1988 novella *Our Crowd*, the first-person narrator, a divorced mother, finds that she is terminally ill. Hero(in)ically, she renounces her son in order to save him but she accomplishes this in a way specific to Russian society, a way which reveals much about gender relations in that country. She deliberately stages a "drunken" scene and beats her child in front of her ex-husband, knowing that a nonprivileged woman with a drinking problem in Russia will have her children taken from her. In a weird psychological twist she reasons that in order to ensure that the father will take responsibility for the child, she must debase herself and prompt the father into righteous action; without the threat that the boy will be placed in an orphanage while she is still alive, the father will never agree to look after him after her death.

I've arranged his [her son's — TP] fate at a very cheap price. Otherwise after my death he'd have gone from one boarding school to another and would have had a hard time being received as a visitor in his father's own home. . . . The whole child-beating scene . . . gave a push to the long, new romantic tradition in my orphan Alyosha's life with his noble new foster parents, who'll forget their own interests, but will watch over his. That's how I calculated it all, and that's the way it will be.[48]

Clearly this mother does not fit the stereotype of most women portrayed in Russian fiction written by men; she is neither submissive nor amorphous, nor is she amoral, materialistic, or egotistical. Motivated solely by concern for her son, her decisive actions and means of achieving her goal fly in the face of Russian cultural perceptions of motherhood. In a wonderful combination of farce and tragedy, she acts the part of the villain, the father becomes the savior, and she directs the entire spectacle with great flair. Ironically she employs the traditionally male vehicle of alcohol to effect a tangible change for the better rather than for the worse. Even more iconoclastic in the Russian cultural context is the heroine's attitude toward her own death: once her son's future has been secured, death becomes inviting and preferable to remaining alive. Petrushevskaia rejects the Russian cultural glorification of motherhood, but she does reclaim it on her own terms: she creates an image "whose authority proceeds from the maternal body and subverts the power and authority of the male-generated abstract icon of the maternal."[49] In this way, *Our Crowd* provides fitting commentary on the tradition of the "mother image" in Russian culture which is "symbolized and valorized as long as it is within non-female discourse."[50]

Heroines who drink in such female texts as Vaneeva's "Parade of the Planets" and Petrushevskaia's "Ali-Baba" are depicted as profoundly lonely, and prostitution, either explicitly or implicitly, accompanies their drinking. Family and friends have abandoned them or cannot be counted on to help. Both Petrushevskaia's and Vaneeva's stories are examples of the "chernukha" (darkening) which has appeared in recent Soviet and post-Soviet writing, although Petrushevskaia has for years been critically berated with this term for her theme of "the fate of woman in a cruel world."[51]

"Ali-Baba" is stylistically typical of Petrushevskaia's "hyperrealism" or her "post-Soviet naturalism."[52] She depicts a homeless young woman, the story's namesake, whose drunken one-night stands inevitably lead to suicide attempts. Only in the story's final sentences do we learn that these episodes provide her with the only truly human contact now available to her:

Ali-Baba ... lay in a clean bed in a ward for mentally-disturbed women. She would be there no less than a month and there would be hot breakfasts, talks with the doctors, the woeful tales of the other patients. She had a lot to tell too, especially about the first time she took the tablets when she went blind for a month, or about the second time when she slept for thirty-six hours solid, and about the sixth time when she woke up at 8 am, absolutely sober.[53]

Larisa Vaneeva's "Parade of the Planets" produces a startling effect through the combination of its subject matter and its disjointed modernist narrative. The narration alternates between a first- and third-person point of view. The protagonist, "I"/Savaleva, observes herself both internally and subjectively through the first-person narration or externally and objectively through narration in the third-person. She is a woman whose body and mind have been ravaged by many years of alcohol and tobacco abuse and by moonlighting as a prostitute. The story takes place during one of her alcoholic highs. We are within her hallucination: we see the four red-headed aliens from a UFO, we hear the sounds of the after-hours subway station where Saveleva has fallen into a drunken sleep, and we are privy to recounted bits of Saveleva's violent and unhappy recent and distant past which mingle with other elements in the hallucination.

As we piece together the deterioration of her life we learn that her daughter has become a prostitute and a drug addict who sneers at her mother's alcoholism: "Saveleva's daughter had always despised her, as all drug addicts despise alcoholics. Alcoholics are crude, uncultivated creatures who don't understand or know how to achieve a pure high, her daughter thought."[54] Until recently, prostitution *per se* was a taboo subject in (Soviet) Russian literature. The loosening of literary censorship in the late 1980s occurred in tandem with a rapid proliferation of pornography and an increase in prostitution with its concomitant substance abuse. It remains to be seen how these phenomena will be further refracted in women's literary texts.

Most of the women's texts that I have discussed which deal with alcoholism were published during Gorbachev's six-year campaign for glasnost; the fact of their appearance can be taken as a sign of the potential impact that social change can have on gender portrayal in Russian literature, particularly in women's writing. One critic has, in fact, already acknowledged the "salutary subversiveness of [Russia's] indiscreet women's writing."[55] Contemporary Russian literature now has a small body of iconoclastic texts by women authors who present their heroines through nonstereotypical points of view and engaged in nontraditional life-styles which give a fuller and more complete picture of women's lives in late-Soviet and post-Soviet Russia.

In general, the images of women in the fiction of Russian women writing alcoholism in many ways still resemble those dominant models found in male prose, which portrays positive images of self-sacrificing, forgiving, compassionate, and supremely moral women. Both feminine and masculine writing is guilty of a normative approach to gender roles and of attributing certain characteristics (irrationality, emotionality) and traits (concern about money, appearance, material possessions) to women. However, the deviations in women's writing on alcoholism from the stereotypical norm — the wives who leave, the female alcoholics — and the problematizing of worn-out formulations, are significant. Coupled with the uniqueness of a "holistic" perception and approach to the problem, they highlight myths that Russian culture, which is still largely created within a male idiom, takes for granted. They also speak to the great need for the empowerment of women in Russia at levels above those of the family.

The prose of a younger generation of women writers has begun to evidence broader thematic and stylistic representations of women; it consciously manipulates language, it is engaged in the exploration of physiology and the concomitant de-mythologizing of the body, and it is spiced with a healthy dose of skepticism. It is one critic's opinion that "the coercive exemplar of 'femininity' has perceptibly weakened its hold over women's self-conceptualization. . . . Nowadays female authors ironize or impugn gender stereotypes, adduce alternatives to sanctioned models, or write as though the latter did not exist."[56] Such changes, supported by the gradual legitimization of women's writing in contemporary Russian culture, indicate the great potential of Russian women's writing to aid in the de-mythologizing of male alcoholism. Such an achievement would, in turn, help to release women from a sense of personal inadequacy and to gain some awareness of the gender politics which transmit the essentialized view of gender still prevalent in today's Russian society.

NOTES

I am indebted to Barbara Heldt and Gerald S. Smith for their helpful comments, suggestions, and references.

1. Boris Segal, *The Drunken Society: Alcohol Abuse and Alcoholism in the Soviet Union: A Comparative Study* (New York: Hippocrene Books, 1990), 527. Apropos of the late Soviet period, economist Vladimir Treml has written that "the magnitude and scope of alcohol abuse and the severity of its impact on Soviet society are unique in terms of international experience." "Alcohol Abuse and the Quality of Life in the USSR," in *Soviet Politics in the 1980s*, ed. Helmut Sonnenfeldt (London: Westview Press, 1985), 56. Some comparative data are useful to gauge the "magnitude and scope" of the Soviet alcohol problem. In total alcohol consumption by litre for persons fifteen years and older, the Soviet Union ranked fourth or fifth in 1980 among thirty countries for which data was available. However, the Soviet Union ranked first in the world in per capita consumption of strong alcoholic beverages (i.e., drinks with an alcohol content of 40 percent and higher). In terms of "severity of impact," strong alcohol is acknowledged as being more detrimental than wine and beer to health (according to the incidence of chronic and acute poisonings, and mental disorders) and the social environment (as gauged by the incidence of violence, accidents, absenteeism). See Treml, "Alcohol Abuse," 56–57.
2. Galina Skvortsova, "Sem'ia i lichnoe shchast'e (Muzhchina i zhenshchina na

poroge XXI veka)" ("The Family and Personal Happiness: Men and Women on the Threshold of the 21st Century"), *Sever* 10 (1987): 106–13.

3. Natal'ia Ivanova, "Zhizn' prekrasna?" ("So Life is Great?"), *Iunost'* 1 (1991): 60–63.

4. Demographic economist Anastasia Posadskaia writes that "in the private sphere [the greatest threat to women today] is violence. We have many institutions in our society where sexual life is barbarous. This is not to speak of the effects of alcoholism . . . on men's behavior in marriages, which leads to a great deal of violence." "Self-Portrait of a Russian Feminist (Interview)," *New Left Review* 195 (Sept.–Oct. 1992): 17. Based on a 1978 study, Boris Segal estimated that of 11.1 million annual incidents of Soviet women beaten by their husbands, 9.4 million of such incidents could be attributed to alcohol. *The Drunken Society*, 267.

5. *Women East-West* (November 1990): 6.

6. Tat'iana Mamonova, "Is There Perestroika for Women," *Women East-West* 23 (May 1990): 5. Anastasia Posadskaia gives the supplementary statistic that every third marriage in Russia breaks up and that women initiate 60 percent of the divorces; Posadskaia, "Self-Portrait," 14.

7. According to Katheleen Parthe, "village prose" ended as a literary movement in the late 1970s, its canonical texts appearing from the mid-1950s to 1980. *Russian Village Prose: The Radiant Past* (Princeton: Princeton University Press, 1992), xii. Other male-authored texts written between 1960 and 1990 which treat the theme of alcoholism were never published in the Soviet Union. These include poems and songs by Vladimir Vysotsky and Aleksandr Galich, and fictional works by Viktor Nekrasov, Venedikt Erofeev, Sergei Kaledin, Sasha Sokolov, Aleksandr Zinov'ev, etc. By 1991, when the Soviet Union ceased to exist, most of these authors had emigrated.

8. I will confine my discussion to women's texts which were written and published in the Soviet Union and post-Soviet Russia since the 1960s. It would be worthwhile to compare these images with those in works which treat the theme of alcoholism by such emigré writers as Julia Voznesenskaia, Ruf' Zernova, and Liudmila Shtern.

9. In its approach, "literatura byta" (the literature of daily reality) treats the individual rather than the universal, does not resolve personal or general problems, and comments neither on philosophy nor ideology. Because women's writing shares these features with the genre, "literatura byta" has increasingly become synonymous with the derogatory critical term "damskaia proza" (ladies' prose) despite the fact that one of its most successful practitioners was Iurii Trifonov. In general, Russian literary criticism has assumed female experience to be too narrow or parabolic as compared to the "universality," logic, and rationality of male experience. For a detailed discussion of this issue, see Barbara Heldt, "Gynoglasnost: writing the feminine," in *Perestroika and Soviet Women*, ed. Mary Buckley (Cambridge: Cambridge University Press, 1992): 160–75; and Helena Goscilo, "Skirted Issues: The Dis-

creteness and Indiscretions of Russian Women's Prose," *Russian Studies in Literature* 28, no. 2 (1992): 3–17.

10. Ramona Asher, *Women with Alcoholic Husbands: Ambivalence and the Trap of Codependency* (Chapel Hill: University of North Carolina Press, 1992), 201.

11. Cocktails and mixed drinks are disdained, while male drinkers categorize wines and champagnes as "ladies' drinks." The typical style of drinking requires that vodka be drunk by the glassful accompanied by a light appetizer; the effect is rapid intoxication. A feature of grain-based drinking is the rapid oscillation between friendly and affectionate feelings and irritability, resentment, and anger.

12. See Segal for a description of the different drinking styles of various social groups in Soviet society; *The Drunken Society*, 108–27.

13. Social female Russian drinking behavior follows a rather different pattern and approximates the norm for American female drinkers. Women tend to drink wines and champagnes, although small amounts of vodka or brandy are acceptable. The degree to which public intoxication of women is tolerated by Russian society is significantly lower than its toleration of the same behavior in males.

14. Moonlighting tradespeople are a particularly notorious group in this respect; without vodka, an electrician, plumber, mover, or repairman is not to be had. It is additionally difficult to engage their services since they are often drunk.

15. Segal, *The Drunken Society*, 525.

16. V. Nekrasov, "Vzgliad i nechto" ("An Opinion and Something Else"), *Kontinent* 13 (1977): 27. For the opposite view, see Treml, "Alcohol Abuse," 60–61.

17. By the term "muted," Ardener refers to problems both of language and of power.

18. For a full explication of Ardener's construct, see Edwin Ardener, "Belief and the Problem of Women" and "The Problem Revisited," in *Perceiving Women*, ed. Shirley Ardener (New York: Halstead Press, 1978), 1–17, 19–27. I have adapted this model so that each circle contains subgroups: in the dominant circle, I posit the subgroups "male alcoholics" and "male writers"; in the muted circle the subgroups are "women + alcoholics," "women writers," and "female alcoholics." Given the magnitude of the Russian alcohol problem it is safe to assume that the subgroups "male alcoholics" and "women + alcoholics" are not much smaller in size than the respective full groups. Thus the discourse about Russian female and male perceptions of alcoholism and about each other is maintained at the broadest societal level. The alcohol factor within both subgroups appears to amplify aspects of gender relations in Russia that are present in the larger groups.

19. N. Zekulin, "Soviet Russian Women's Literature in the Early 1980s," in *Fruits of Her Plume: Essays on Contemporary Russian Women's Culture*, ed. Helena Goscilo (Armonk: M. E. Sharpe, 1993), 43.

20. As Segal states: "Russian women have been expected to take care of their drunken husbands and sons"; *The Drunken Society*, 235.

21. For an excellent discussion of Soviet ideas on sex differences and sex-role socialization, see Lynn Attwood, *The New Soviet Man and Woman: Sex-Role Socialization in the USSR* (London: Macmillan, 1990), especially 183–212.

22. Vasily Belov, "Morning Meetings," in *The Image of Women in Contemporary Soviet Fiction*, ed. and trans. Sigrid McLaughlin (New York: St. Martin's Press, 1989), 145.

23. Belov, "Morning Meetings," 141.

24. Barbara Heldt writes: "The Mother Image remains timelessly static in Russian writing. . . . [M]otherhood has overwhelmingly been used in modern Russian literature to generate images of patriarchal value, or as an icon to symbolize Russia." "Motherhood in a Cold Climate: The Poetry and Career of Maria Shkapskaia," *Russian Review* 51 (April 1992): 160, 161–62.

25. Posadskaia, "Self-Portrait," 16. Segal also links Russian drinking to escapism: "drinking was not only a source of pleasure, it was also the most stable ritual-related custom and the most reliable means of escapism." *Russian Drinking: Use and Abuse of Alcohol in Pre-Revolutionary Russia* (New Jersey: Rutgers Center of Alcohol Studies, 1987), xvii.

26. Michel Heller, "Vasily Shukshin: In Search of Freedom," in *Snowball Berry Red and Other Stories*, ed. Donald M. Fiene (Ann Arbor: Ardis, 1979), 222.

27. David Gillespie, *Valentin Rasputin and Soviet Russian Village Prose* (London: Modern Humanities Research Association, 1986), 17.

28. Vasily Shukshin, " 'Oh, A Wife Saw Her Husband Off to Paris . . . ,' " in *Snowball Berry Red and Other Stories*, ed. Fiene, trans. Geoffrey A. Hosking, 103.

29. Barbara Heldt suggests that contemporary Russian writing be broadly conceived as "feminine" and "masculine," with the gendered dichotomy referring to the text rather than to the sex of the author: "Feminine writing . . . is about how all the little things in life go wrong. . . . '[M]asculine' writing . . . may be politically daring [but] this sort of writing tend to be conservative on gender issues. Masculine writing is about how all the big things go wrong. Big things include history, ecology, and patriarchal values, such as religion and the family. 'Masculine' writing often rings with accusatory rhetoric"; "Gynoglasnost," 169–70. Heldt makes it clear that "masculine" writing may be written by women and "feminine" writing by men.

30. Andrei Siniavsky, *Unguarded Thoughts*, quoted in Deming Brown, *Soviet Russian Literature Since Stalin* (Cambridge: Cambridge University Press, 1979), 348.

31. A reason for this apparent paradox is suggested by Helena Goscilo: "The stumbling block . . . is less feminist theory . . . per se than the label 'feminist.' Discredited by class associations in earlier phases of Soviet history and still rendered suspect by disillusionment with any comprehensive political agenda, the term 'feminism' as entertained by Russians is culturally overmarked and consequently stigmatized." "Monsters Monomaniacal, Marital, and Medical:

Tatiana Tolstaya's Regenerative Use of Gender Stereotypes," in *Sexuality and the Body in Russian Culture*, ed. J. Costlow, S. Sandler, and J. Vowles (Stanford: Stanford University Press, 1993), 219.

32. Siniavsky, *Unguarded Thoughts*, 348. He continues that in Russia "the skirt-chaser, the lover, take on features of the foreigner, the German . . . the Frenchman, the Jew. But we Russians will surrender any beauty for a bottle of pure spirits."

33. A recent wire-service report illustrates this phenomenon. Reporting about families in Russia with children suffering from AIDS, the article tersely states: "As with so many family matters in Russia, the burden of an AIDS-infected child usually falls on the mother. . . . Fathers, upon learning their children have AIDS, often leave their families or start drinking heavily." *Arizona Daily Star*, 24 Aug. 1993: A5.

34. Zoia Boguslavskaia, *Literaturnaia gazeta*, 5 Aug. 1987: 12. Anastasia Posadskaia, when asked in interview about the stresses in patterns of relationships in post-Soviet Russian society, admits that: "It is a bit difficult to answer that . . . because the subject doesn't lend itself easily to investigation, especially in our culture"; "Self-Portrait," 16.

35. Nina Yarina, "About the 'Almanac,' " in *Women and Russia: Feminist Writings from the Soviet Union*, ed. Tat'iana Mamonova (Boston: Beacon Press, 1984), 226.

36. I. Grekova, "A Summer in the City," in McLaughlin, *The Image of Women in Contemporary Soviet Fiction*, 32.

37. Barbara Heldt, "Daughters of the Russian Revolution," *The Women's Review of Books* 1, no. 10 (July 1984): 8.

38. In contrast, widespread expectations concerning men have to do with problem solving and mending parts of the whole with minimal disruption to and involvement of self. Ramona Asher invites feminist investigation of expectations of women by asking: "to what extent is an introspective, all-encompassing approach to problems women's . . . natural way — thus to be honored and preserved as their unique contribution? [and] . . . to what extent might this be a socially created, institutionalized gender pattern that confines women's energy and choices — thus to be examined, exposed, and perhaps modified?"; *Women with Alcoholic Husbands*, 199–200.

39. Alternative terminologies for this mode of discourse include "represented speech," "narrated speech," "erlebte Rede," "style indirect libre," and "free indirect discourse." In this mode, the viewpoint is limited and the voices of the author, narrator, and protagonist are often blurred.

40. Viktoria Tokareva, "Five Figures on a Pedestal," in *Soviet Women Writing: Fifteen Short Stories*, trans. Debra Irving, ed. Jacqueline Decter (New York: Abbeville Press, 1990), 159. Further references to this work will be included parenthetically in the text.

41. Codependency is a phenomenon by which those people around the drinker, that is, those that love him and/or whose well-being is linked with his, step in to protect him from the consequences of his irresponsible and often antisocial

behavior. Enabling wives act out of a sense of love and loyalty, out of shame (to preserve self-respect), and out of fear that she will have to share the consequences of the drinker's behavior. As Tony Crespi defines it: "the non-alcoholic begins to develop a repertoire of behaviors as an outgrowth of attempting to cope with alcoholism. In essence though, these behaviors make them as much a slave to the alcohol as the drinker, so the efforts at stability and comfort are actually ineffective." Tony Crespi, *Becoming An Adult Child of an Alcoholic* (Springfield: Charles C. Thomas, 1990), 8.

Some very important questioning of the "codependent" label has been recently voiced. Ramona Asher comments that "The designation of actions . . . as codependent means that women's experience is being judged in terms of "appropriate" male experience, which is based on standards of independence and separation, as Chodorow (1978), Gilligan (1982), and Rubin (1983) have established"; *Women with Alcoholic Husbands*, 198. She agrees with other critics of the codependent label that such behaviors would be more usefully thought of as essentially positive behaviors that have become extreme and unbalanced under certain conditions.

42. I. Grekova, *Ship of Widows*, trans. Cathy Porter (London: Virago Press, 1985), 75. Further references to this work will be included parenthetically in the text.

43. Galina Shcherbakova, "The Wall," in *Balancing Acts: Contemporary Stories by Russian Women*, trans. Helena Goscilo, ed. Helena Goscilo (Ann Arbor: Ardis, 1989), 91. Further references to this work will be included parenthetically in the text.

44. Liudmila Uvarova, "Be Still, Torments of Passion," in *Balancing Acts: Contemporary Stories by Russian Women*, trans. John Fred Beebe, ed., 180–81. Further references to this work will be included parenthetically in the text.

45. In Russia today, for a variety of interrelated social, economic, and political reasons, family has become associated with women, and fathers, having dissociated themselves from domestic and parenting responsibilities, are figuratively, and often literally, absent. Thus, support for women comes from other women and they rely on themselves and one another to solve daily problems.

46. Quoted by Attwood, *The New Soviet Man and Woman*, 195.

47. According to a 1981 report in a Russian sociological journal "only one in three men and one in five women marry a second time. This means that divorce results in an irrevocable loss in terms of the number of children born." Quoted by Attwood, *The New Soviet Man and Woman*, 200. Attwood goes on to present more Soviet views which hold that "women have gone beyond the achievement of equality and have created a new system of matriarchy under which men are the oppressed sex. As G. Naan puts it 'the battle against patriarchy has been transformed into a battle against the husband, against everything that he does or likes,' " 200.

48. Liudmila Petrushevskaia, "Our Crowd," in *Glasnost: An Anthology of Russian Literature under Gorbachev*, trans. Helena Goscilo, ed. Helena Goscilo and Byron Lindsey (Ann Arbor: Ardis, 1990), 24.

49. Barbara Heldt, "Motherhood in a Cold Climate: The Poetry and Career of Maria Shkapskaya," in Costlow, Sandler, and Vowles, *Sexuality and the Body in Russian Culture*, 238.
50. Heldt, "Motherhood in a Cold Climate," 243.
51. Georgii Viren, "Takaia liubov' " ("Such Love"), *Oktiabr'* 3 (1989): 303.
52. These terms are used and defined by Melissa T. Smith in one of the earliest critical discussions of Petrushevskaia's drama: "In Cinzano Veritas: The Plays of Luidmila Petrushevskaya," *Slavic and East European Arts* 1 (Winter–Spring 1985): 120.
53. Liudmila Petrushevskaia, "Ali-Baba," in *Po doroge boga Erosa* [Eros' Path] (Moscow: OLIMP, 1993), 8.
54. Larisa Vaneeva, "Parade of the Planets," in Decter, *Soviet Women Writing*, trans. Diane Nemec Ignashev, 331.
55. Goscilo, Introduction to "Skirted Issues," 14.
56. Helena Goscilo, "Coming a Long Way, Baby: A Quarter-Century of Russian Women's Fiction," *The Harriman Institute Forum* 1 (Sept. 1992): 3–4.

BIBLIOGRAPHY

Ardener, Edwin. "Belief and the Problem of Women." In *Perceiving Women*. Ed. Shirley Ardener. New York: Halstead Press, 1978. 1–17.

———. "The Problem Revisited." In *Perceiving Women*. Ed. Shirley Ardener. New York: Halstead Press, 1978. 19–27.

Asher, Ramona. *Women with Alcoholic Husbands: Ambivalence and the Trap of Codependency*. Chapel Hill: University of North Carolina Press, 1992.

Attwood, Lynne. *The New Soviet Man and Woman: Sex-Role Socialization in the USSR*. London: Macmillan, 1990.

Belov, Vasily. "Morning Meetings." In *The Image of Women in Contemporary Soviet Fiction*. Ed. Sigrid McLaughlin. New York: St. Martin's Press, 1989. 135–47.

Christian, David. *Living Water: Vodka and Russian Society on the Eve of Emancipation*. Oxford: Clarendon Press, 1990.

Crespi, Tony. *Becoming the Adult Child of an Alcoholic*. Springfield: Charles C. Thomas, 1990.

Gillespie, David. *Valentin Rasputin and Soviet Russian Village Prose*. London: Modern Humanities Research Association, 1986.

Goscilo, Helena. "Monsters Monomaniacal, Marital, and Medical: Tatiana Tolstaya's Regenerative Use of Gender Stereotypes." In *Sexuality and the Body in Russian Culture*. Ed. J. Costlow, S. Sandler, and J. Vowles. Stanford: Stanford University Press, 1993. 204–20.

———. "Coming and Long Way, Baby: A Quarter-Century of Russian Women's Fiction." *The Harriman Institute Forum* 1 (Sept. 1992): 1–17.

— — —, ed. "Skirted Issues: The Discreteness and Indiscretions of Russian Women's Prose." *Russian Studies in Literature*, 28, no. 2 (1992): 3–98.

Grekova, I. *Ship of Widows.* Trans. Cathy Porter. London: Virago Press, 1985.

— — —. "A Summer in the City." In *The Image of Women in Contemporary Soviet Fiction.* Ed. Sigrid McLaughlin. New York: St. Martin's Press, 1989. 2₽–48.

Heldt, Barbara. "Gynoglasnost: writing the feminine." In *Perestroika and the Soviet Woman.* Ed. Mary Buckley. Cambridge: Cambridge University Press, 1992. 160–75.

— — —. "Motherhood in a Cold Climate: The Poetry and Career of Maria Shkapskaya." In *Sexuality and the Body in Russian Culture.* Ed. J. Costlow, S. Sandler, and J. Vowles. Stanford: Stanford University Press, 1993. 235–54.

— — —. "Motherhood in a Cold Climate: The Poetry and Prose of Maria Shkapskaia." *Russian Review* 51 (April 1992): 160–71.

Heller, Michel. "Vasily Shukshin: In Search of Freedom." In *Snowball Berry Red and Other Stories.* Ed. Donald M. Fiene. Ann Arbor: Ardis, 1979. 213–33.

Mamonova, Tat'iana, ed. *Women and Russia: Feminist Writings from the Soviet Union.* Boston: Beacon Press: 1984.

Parthe, Kathleen. *Russian Village Prose: The Radiant Past.* Princeton: Princeton University Press, 1992.

Petrushevskaia, Liudmila. "Ali-Baba." In *Po doroge boga Erosa.* Moscow: OLIMP, 1993. 4–8.

— — —. "Our Crowd." In *Glasnost: An Anthology of Russian Literature under Gorbachev.* Ed. Helena Goscilo and Byron Lindsey. Ann Arbor: Ardis, 1990. 3–24.

Posadskaia, Anastasia. "Self-Portrait of a Russian Feminist." *New Left Review* 195 (Sept.–Oct. 1992): 3–19.

Segal, Boris. *The Drunken Society: Alcohol Abuse and Alcoholism in the Soviet Union. A Comparative Study.* New York: Hippocrene Books, 1990.

— — —. *Russian Drinking: Use and Abuse of Alcohol in Pre-Revolutionary Russia.* New Jersey: Rutgers Center of Alcohol Studies, 1987.

Shcherbakova, Galina. "The Wall." In *Balancing Acts: Contemporary Stories by Russian Women.* Ed. Helena Goscilo. Ann Arbor: Ardis, 1989. 88–121.

Shukshin, Vasily. " 'Oh, A Wife Saw Her Husband Off to Paris. . . .' " In *Snowball Berry Red and Other Stories.* Ed. Donald M. Fiene. Ann Arbor: Ardis, 1979. 97–104.

Smith, Melissa T. "In Cinzano Veritas: The Plays of Liudmila Petrushevskaya." *Slavic and East European Arts* 1 (Winter–Spring, 1985): 119–25.

Tokareva, Viktoria. "Five Figures on a Pedestal." In *Soviet Women Writing: Fifteen Short Stories.* Ed. Jacqueline Decter. New York: Abbeville Press, 1990. 153–201.

Treml, Vladimir. "Alcohol Abuse and the Quality of Life in the USSR." In *Soviet Politics in the 1980s.* Ed. Helmut Sonnenfeldt. London: Westview Press, 1985. 55–65.

Uvarova, Liudmila. "Be Still, Torments of Passion." In *Balancing Acts: Contemporary Stories by Russian Women.* Ed. Helena Goscilo. Ann Arbor: Ardis, 1989. 173–90.

Vaneeva, Larisa. "Parade of the Planets." In *Soviet Women Writing: Fifteen Short Stories*. Ed. Jacqueline Decter. New York: Abbeville Press, 1989. 317–32.

Zekulin, Nicholas. "Soviet Russian Women's Literature in the Early 1980s." In *Fruits of Her Plume: Essays on Contemporary Russian Women's Culture*. Ed. Helena Goscilo. Armonk: M. E. Sharpe, 1993. 33–58.

TWELVE

Gendering Cinema in
Postcommunist Hungary

Catherine Portuges

Where is that fragile line between different cultures, different religions, different
national or personal identities?

— Agnieszka Holland [1]

In the drive toward capitalism that has overtaken Hungary since the
collapse of communism, its consequences for the culture of cinema are
often overlooked in media discourses, with their relentless, and often
exclusive, focus on the vicissitudes of the transition to a market economy.
Yet it is in the realm of the visual arts — and, in particular, cinema — that
the evolution of subjectivity and political consciousness is perhaps most
dramatically inscribed. The annual review of film production held in
Budapest and known as "Film Week" offers an unparalleled opportunity
for assessing the impact of the post-1989 changes on the nation's consciousness. While dissident intellectuals and artists may no longer be
required to play their once vital role, a new generation of filmmakers is
emerging to foreground and contest issues in danger of being silenced
not by official censorship but by demands for commercial viability in the
"new Europe" of the 1990s. Based on several years of participation in
these Film Weeks since 1989, I offer here an exploration of recent trends
on the horizon of this postnational and dialectical culture of cinema
whose dialectics of contestation have long been its distinctive feature.

Paradoxically, in view of the region's acceptance — indeed, its passionate embrace — of postmodern capitalism, the gendered aspects of these

transformations have remained largely untheorized in scholarly milieux, and are still virtually taboo in the rhetorics of creative expression and interpretation.[2] Although recent theoretical and artistic works have begun to address questions of sexuality and gender, articulation of the particular experience of women, as well as that of ethnic and racial minorities, is constructed by many, particularly those of the generation born prior to 1956, as tantamount to a betrayal of a fragile new democracy, even, for that matter, a reactionary gesture harkening back to the days of what Milan Kundera, in *The Unbearable Lightness of Being*, has called "organized forgetting."

Suppressed under the aegis of Stalinist internationalism, these questions today invite renewed articulation. One response to Hungary's postcommunist transitional moment has been an embrace of profitability in the form of eroticized spectacles such as those of 1989–91 "transitional" films with titles such as *The Dames, Sexploitation,* and *Fast and Loose.* In these and other works by (primarily male) directors in which youthful (female) bodies are exhibitionistically fetishized, the ardently sought, yet highly elusive, free-market economy is both symptom and cause of the commodification of sexuality.

In contrast to many of their male colleagues, a number of women directors, of both "older" and "younger" generations, raise issues of class relations and gender, love and sexuality, deception and honesty in unsentimental and at times even ruthless fashion. These works have been particularly troubling for Hungarian audiences and critics discomfited by such uncompromising meditations on the double imperatives of national identity and gender inscription in post-Stalinist and postcommunist Eastern Europe. Concurrently, the film and television industries of the "unblocked" East have been undergoing a process of radical transformation scarcely less momentous than that of the political sphere, from the privatization of formerly state-owned studios, to the redefinition of the very meaning of national cinema itself. The Hungarian Motion Picture Foundation has replaced the socialist state enterprise, while a network of theaters has been created to protect a percentage of Hungarian screens from the onslaught of foreign — primarily American — distributors. Western cultural domination — perceived by many as U.S. monopoly — in the terrain of the moving image has emerged as a growing potential threat to these vulnerable visual economies, exemplified by the proliferation of Hollywood movies whose drawing power constitutes a far greater market share than that of any domestic product. This audiovisual assault is by no means limited to the former Eastern bloc: in France, long the strongest of European national film industries, the perception of an American "hostile takeover" has initiated aggressive legislative measures, backed by the European Parliament, to protect French-language cinema as a "national" industry.[3]

At the same time, cinema remains part of a larger cultural horizon, characterized by overlapping local, regional, national, and global institutions that grow increasingly deterritorialized.[4] The globalization of media consumption, in tandem with mass migrations on a greater scale than ever since World War II, have hence irrevocably altered the terms of local and national identity not long ago taken for granted in Eastern Europe and beyond.[5] The intensity of debate on this topic within its film industries indeed suggests the extent to which the language of cinema cuts to the very heart of national culture: for against these impressive odds, these filmmakers must contend with nothing less than a new media order in order to survive the postcommunist transition. As *Newsweek* has reported, "Some European Community members are terrified by the thought of a Europe without internal borders will allow millions of refugees to run wild."[6]

That Hungarian cinema in the 1990s appears to be managing,[7] albeit with great effort and uneven results at best, to produce a consistently substantial quota of feature and documentary films is remarkable indeed.[8] The active presence, visibility, and participation of younger (under 40) filmmakers in this phase of visual culture endows this struggle with a poignant energy, urgency, and sense of purpose.[9] Nonetheless, under the new decentralized system, a number of women directors report themselves to be at best underrepresented: the board of the Hungarian Motion Picture Foundation, for example – a panel whose responsibility it is to select film projects worthy of support each year – counts only a single female among its 73 members. While the terrain between individual authorship and the intersections of nationality and sexuality have come increasingly to occupy Western critical agenda, the status of women filmmakers who do not necessarily claim their own work to be specifically "feminist" or representative of a "women's cinema" deserves special consideration with regard to Eastern Europe. No longer constrained by the explicit claims of gender equality that constituted the socialist agenda, visual artists may be, in some sense, now better positioned to articulate gender-specific concerns. And, as in other small, former Eastern bloc nations undergoing similar processes of transformation toward diversified market economies and away from the centralization that, for decades, regulated the production of word and image, these filmmakers are investigating from new angles of vision Hungary's — and, for that matter, East-Central Europe's — resistance to the issue of difference, be it sexual, racial, ethnic, or generational.

To Western audiences generally unfamiliar with East-Central European culture, an obsession with interconnections between historical events and their cinematic representation often seems tenuous at best. In the late 1980s Poland's distinguished director, Andrzej Wajda, offered an eloquent (and, as it turns out, uncannily prophetic) lament for this marginalization of "minor cinemas":

Films made in Eastern Europe seem of little or no interest to people in the West. The audiences in western countries find them as antediluvian as the battle for workers' rights in England in the time of Marx. Thus our efforts here in Eastern Europe have nothing to show audiences in the West who look upon the world they live in as permanent. Those of our Eastern European film colleagues who have chosen emigration can — if they are young and talented and after they have spent years in the West — come up with some works of startling beauty . . . but they will not find audiences attuned to the same concerns that we in the Eastern bloc feel are vital. And that is a pity, for I am certain that those concerns are not ours alone but apply to the world at large, or will in the very near future.[10]

The films and videos produced by these directors are readable as a marker of the transgressive inscription of gender within Hungarian visual culture since 1989, when the end of state support for — and control of — the arts brought into being this transition in the structure and financing of Hungarian studios, as well as the end of centralized distribution, public relations, and marketing of its (post-)national cinema. In February 1994, for example, Hungary's Twenty-fifth Film Week — an annual review of film production[11] — held at the National Congress Center in Budapest, foregrounded a number of works by and about women directors, from beginning filmmakers to seasoned professionals, honoring them in categories that have traditionally been the province of their more established male colleagues, and continuing the trajectory begun in 1993 when prizes for best first feature and best director were awarded to women directors making their directorial debuts.

In a nation known for its masculinist tendencies as well as for its intellectual elegance, other renowned documentary and feature directors such as Lyvia Gyarmathy, Judith Elek, and Marta Meszaros are continuing to produce outstanding work undeniably (and, in some cases, uncharacteristically) inflected by gender. Arguably the most internationally celebrated of Hungary's (and Eastern Europe's) women directors, Meszaros's most recent film, *A Magzat* (*Foetus*, 1993; Budapest Film Studio/Magyar Televisio/Telewizja Polska production) was selected as Hungary's feature entry to the 1994 Berlin Film Festival, the largest and most prestigious European venue for Hungarian films, apart from the Cannes Film Festival.[12] Despite a rather contrived script, the film warrants attention because of its unrepentant foregrounding of gender and reproduction, subjects scarcely less controversial now than when the director first undertook them in her distinguished 1970s trilogy: *Orokbefogadas* (*Adoption*, 1975), *Kilenc Honap* (*Nine Months*, 1976), and *Ok Kette* (*The Two of Them*, 1977). Each of these films narrativizes maternity, parental loss, and female bonding, themes virtually absent from East European cinema of the period, as does her 1980 work, *The Heiresses*, whose audacious treatment of such subversive issues as infertility, class difference, and the solidarity of female friendship was met with nearly universal rejection upon release in Hungary.[13]

In *Foetus*, Meszaros recapitulates and refers to her earlier work by interrogating interconnections between the female body and the post-communist nation as a young, married mother of two (Anna), confronting Hungary's current preoccupation with an inflationary economy and unemployment, discovers that she is pregnant. Her husband has lost his job, leaving the couple at the mercy of Terez, a wealthy, married yet childless businesswoman who suggests that Anna serve as surrogate mother in exchange for a lucrative offer of support for her family and the construction of their unfinished new house. Despite intense emotional conflict between the women throughout this complicated scenario of deception and seclusion, the two women are transformed by a profound process of biological and psychic bonding, as in the end Terez returns the infant to the surrogate couple. The hostility that has long been Meszaros's lot in her native Hungary — in contrast to the favorable reception her work has received abroad — suggests the degree to which her insistence on gender and conflictual relationships strikes a resoundingly negative chord in both a primarily male critical establishment and the general public, as evidenced by the unalloyed disdain for the film manifested by the opening-night audience.[14]

Meszaros's frequent use of child-centered dream sequences and shots of a fetus suspended *in utero* regrettably undermine her focus on the symbiotic relationship between the two women, and in particular on Anna's emotional ambivalence during her isolated confinement in a countryside cottage. Reminiscent as well of shower sequences in the director's earlier films, including *Szabad Lelegzet* (*Riddance*, 1973),[15] is a scene in which, in a moment of physical and affective intimacy, the two women share a bathtub, their bodies framed in the director's signature mode of erotic yet uninvasive appreciation. Similar, too, to Meszaros's 1970s and 1980s work is the unadorned sexual and economic interdependency of her protagonists, a trope of Hungarian films under communism. Meszaros's insistence on portraying such complex and discomfiting issues that, in her view, transcend class, political ideology, and cultural difference is a courageous, even extraordinary gesture in the contemporary climate of Hungarian priorities.

Equally noteworthy is Ildiko Szabo's *Gyerekgyilkossagok* (*Child Murders*, 1993), winner of the top prize at the 1993 Hungarian Film Week and of the award for best feature by a young director at the Cannes Film Festival the same year. The title means "murders by children" as well as the killing of a child, suggesting at the same time the notion of "soul murder," the deadening of spirit by unfavorable early life circumstances. One of the few Hungarian films to be financed by a foreign producer, it is a strikingly composed, black-and-white portrait of a boy abandoned by his dissident mother and left to care for a bedridden, eccentric grandmother, herself once a famous primadonna and now a reclusive alcoholic in an impoverished area of Budapest. Zsolt, the 12-year-old boy, spends his time wandering hopelessly among secret places along the Danube banks, bathing and dressing his grandmother each morning. Into his isolated world comes Juli, a young, pregnant Gypsy living in an abandoned railway car; befriending her earns Zsolt rejection and abuse from other children; when Juli miscarries, the two throw the infant into the Danube, and the young Gypsy hangs herself. The director invites us ambiguously to ponder to what extent the children's violent actions are taken out of innate immorality or society's abandonment of another of its victims. Ildiko Szabo has crafted a precise and moving trajectory to these larger questions: scenes of Zsolt carefully bathing and singing to his grandmother, helping her put on her wig and makeup each morning, are portrayed with a kind of morbid fascination: "It's morning," reads a sign Zsolt leaves on the blackboard for her. "Everything is on the table." The bleakly affecting black-and-white photography contributes to the mood of the child's constrained, deprived inner world, tormented as he is on account of his thick eyeglasses by an immaculate neighbor girl in frilly white dresses, and who ultimately becomes the target of his most aggressive impulses. As in a number of recent films by women directors, the narrative is seen from the point of view of the child: although Szabo avoids psychologizing sentimentality, Zsolt's feelings are discernible in the expressionless demeanor he presents as a defensive gesture against a darkly hostile, uncaring world.[16] Szabo's cinematic language embodies the new directions by younger women directors in deterritorializing national identity and theorizing subjectivity otherwise than in the Soviet-inspired realism of earlier generations of filmmakers.

A number of women directors, in fact, have produced documentary and feature narratives under the triple sign of autobiography, exile, and marginality, contesting the contours of national cinema by collectively signaling a sense of slippage threatening to established understandings of national cinema. An earlier Hungarian Film Week (1990), for example, featured Judit Elek's *Tutajosok* (*Memoirs of a River*, 1990), the first post-1989 Hungarian feature to explicitly denounce Hungarian anti-Semitism and the first to be made from an explicitly Jewish viewpoint. The film takes as its subject the first serious outburst of anti-Semitism in Hungarian history — the Tiszaeszlar trial of 1883 (which had incidentally also formed the basis for *The Trial*, G. W. Pabst's "rehabilitation" film made in Austria in 1948). The director claims to have sought to make the film for over twenty years, in fact until the lifting of censorship in the postcommunist moment made it possible, to tell this long-suppressed story of the disappearance of a young Christian girl, the accusations of ritual murder, and the subsequent trial that anticipated the Dreyfus case and positioned liberals against anti-Semites.[17] As in the case of *Foetus*, the reception of Elek's film, also selected to open the festival that year, was polite on the surface but viciously negative in print and conversation; still, the film has since enjoyed a limited international afterlife in Jewish festivals and series, including the 1994 Jewish Museum/Film Society of Lincoln Center film symposium, "Artists, Activists and Ordinary People:

Jews in 20th Century Europe." Like other films from Hungary's distinguished cinematic tradition of historical allegory, *Memoirs of a River* draws unmistakable parallels between the Tiszaeszlar case and the Stalin show trials of the late 1940s and 1950s, and thus, in some sense, utilizes the dream reconstruction strategies deployed by other filmmakers, as I have noted. Elek interrogates the Tisza River to uncover its buried memories, as does the Soviet documentary filmmaker Alexander Rodnjanski in his film on the fate of the legendary Raoul Wallenberg, the Swedish diplomat who saved the lives of tens of thousands of Hungarian Jews, only to disappear into Stalin's prison camps.

Remarkable, too, during the 1994 Film Week was a concern with Hungarian Jewry and the Holocaust, a topic barely touched upon prior to 1989.[18] Perhaps the most lyrical example of this genre comes from Budapest-based filmmaker Peter Forgacs, who has refashioned home movies of the 1920s–1940s made by citizens of the Hungarian capital into *Privat Magyarorszag*, a diary of elegiac portraits of the city, a poetic ethnography that provides a riveting look at a culture about to vanish. Forgacs's *Notes of a Lady (Egy Urino notesza)*, Part Eight of his video diary, deploys the home movies of a beautiful Jewish baronness's life in Hungary in the 1930s and 1940s to signify and mourn the irrevocability of personal, familial, and historical loss. *Why Wasn't He There? (Senkifoldje)*, directed by Andras Jeles, long a contestatory force in contemporary Hungarian cinema,[19] foregrounds gender by using as its central text the diary of a 13-year-old provincial Hungarian Jewish girl to narrate the fate of Hungarian Jews, and their ultimate deportation to the death camp of Auschwitz. Despite inevitable comparisons with *The Diary of Anne Frank*, the film nonetheless represents, empathically yet lyrically and unsentimentally, the internal world of an adolescent girl whose age-appropriate struggle with her own subjectivity is destroyed, together with her family, by the relentless machine of Nazism.

No less important is the substantial work of documentary filmmakers, with more than 70 hours, most on video, to their credit in the past year alone, much of it addressing pressing social issues. Gamma Bak's *East, West, Home's Best* (1992) interrogates the wave of East European emigrants' return from exile from the point of view of her own father, pondering a return to Hungary after twenty years in Canada as a refugee of the 1956 uprising. Like many East European films of this period, it is about emigration, repatriation, identity, cultural belonging, a search for appropriate questions about East European life stories, fantasies, and dreams. Similarly, Judit Kothy's video documentary, *Isten Hozta Magyarorszagon* (*Welcome to Hungary*, 1992), shot in the fall of 1992 as thousands of refugees poured into Hungary from Romania, the former Yugoslavia, and elsewhere, inscribes their arrival by questioning Hungary's stance in accepting refugees, immigrants, businessmen, marriage partners, and students.

The theme of the exile is also taken up by Katalin Petenyi, directing with the well-known team of Barna Kabay and Imre Gyongyossy, *Holtak szabadsaga* (*Freedom of Death*), a narrative based on the true story of a deported couple's return to Lithuania with the coffin of their dead parents after 40 years in Siberia. The authors state: "Ours is the century of refugees, of exiles. Millions died in the camps of Hitler and Stalin: our film seeks to articulate the message of the displaced, the minorities, the down-trodden [people] of history." A continuation of their previous work on the homeless and the displaced, including *The Revolt of Job, Erdely* (1990), *Pusztai emberek* (*People of the Puszta*, 1980), and *50 Ev hallgatas* (*50 Years of Silence*, 1991), this film depicts the larger tragedy of a small nation, its past and present, its struggle for freedom and autonomy, through the fate of a particular Lithuanian family that might also be set in Latvia, the Crimea, or Kurdistan.

One of the most outstanding of Hungary's senior generation of women filmmakers, Livia Gyarmathy's recent films include the brilliant documentary *Recsk 1950–1958: Egy titkos munkatabor tortenete* (*Why Did the Peacock Scream?* 1988); *Hol zsarnoksag van* (Where There Is Tyranny, 1990) and *A csalas gyonyore* (*The Rapture of Delight*, 1991). The latter film is set in a contemporary Hungary undergoing drastic transformation, seen through the point of view of Julia, an electrical engineer in her thirties, who loses her job to restructuring and at the same time her husband Feri who begins an affair with the much younger daughter of his boss, an influential man in the new system. Feri is a casualty of his own honesty and integrity, one of those who opposed state socialism in his own way and who, as a result, went nowhere. Now he wants something for himself, even at the cost of his marriage. Eventually finding a job in a restaurant, Julia discovers herself in the midst of an entertainment mafia whose war degenerates into brutality. Rejecting her husband's pleas for reconciliation after he is himself rebuffed by his young lover, Julia begins a new life. In the tradition of Meszaros's films of the 1960s and 70s, Gyarmathy poses the question and the price of freedom in postcommunist Hungary. Her female character is reminiscent of the young women foregrounded by Istvan Szabo in his highly successful 1991 film *Edes Emma, Draga Bobe (Sweet Emma, Dear Bobe)*, a visually haunting, dramatically powerful treatment of former teachers of Russian teaching in a provincial town, that culminates in the suicide of a young girl. In each case, the director's unidealized portrayal of women's daily struggle against gender constrictions inescapably links the film to reminders of her country's failures, be they social (inadequate care for impoverished children), racial (a strong current of anti-Gypsy sentiment), or historical (Hungary's fascist moments and its treatment of political prisoners). A younger generation of women screenwriters, too,[20] are now engaged in directorial endeavors that interrogate their culture from the point of view of children, ethnic and racial and religious minorities, Gypsies, older people and others living on the edge of society. Sonia El Eini's two-part televideo, *Miert rikoltott a pava? (Why Did the Peacock Scream?* 1992) based on the works of the British psychiatrist and poet R. D. Laing, records the interstices of the incommunicable and unrepresentable through children's language, while Julia Szederkenyi's feature film, *Paramicha, vagy Glonci, az emlekezo (Paramicha, or Glonci the Rememberer*, 1993) chronicles the life of an aged Gypsy based on his written diary.[21]

The post-1956 generation,[22] no longer able to depend on support from a centralized economy organized to protect national film culture, compelled at once by the need to attract international audiences in an increasingly globalized film culture, are, as we have seen, at the same time concerned not to abandon the specifically national concerns of a native audience nonetheless all too eager to welcome nonnative cultural products.[23] One central aspect of these concerns is that of personal narrative autobiography, and biography, most often rendered in experimental avant-garde, or documentary form. Eszter Nordin's documentary video *Apam portreja 1–II (My Father's Portrait*, 1993), for example, offers he own diasporan biography and the border crossings that have come t typify filmmaking in Eastern Europe.

My father, Geza Partos, is a theatre director, and I a Television/film directc Unfortunately, due to circumstances, our paths had parted too early in my yout after our defection from Hungary, he finally settled in Israel, while I made r home in England. As a consequence, he could only follow my career from distance and I lost the opportunity to learn his "tools of the trade." For me, t' portrait film about my father is not merely a piece of theatre history — a record of his importance in Hungarian culture — but a personal quest for getting to know him and understanding him better.[24]

The "circumstances" to which the filmmaker refers are, of course, the persecution of Jews under Nazism; this film portrait, originally nine hours of uncut interviews, was made as a gift to her father, and, according to the director, transformed her perception of him from resentment of his profession to appreciation of his own generosity to the artistic world.[25]

A number of the most recent works by women directors take as their subject the condition of the poor and the aged. Marta Elbert's video documentary, *Folrajzolt almok* (*Dream Sketches*, 1993) is set in the Cserehat Mountains in Borsod-Abauj-Zemplen county, one of the most beautiful and most impoverished regions in the country. In a town composed of seven villages, unemployment has reached 80 percent, as fewer aging citizens receive unemployment benefits; at the end of 1993, according to the director, over half the adult population is living on social security provided by the central government and the municipality. *Oregseg* (*Old Age*, 1993) is Agnes Incze's tribute to those who address their final words to the next generation, interrogating the secret links between youth and old age, challenging the young to value the humanity of those whose bodies no longer conform to the desire of the soul: "Sometimes I forget and behave as if I were twenty, but the shocked, cold expressions around me are a painful reminder that the air is cooler around me, the world more morosely resistant. . . . I must give up this struggle between aging body and youthful soul against a well-armed, cunning enemy." On a more optimistic note, Julia Kovacs's *Odry Arpad muveszotthon* (*Arpad Odry House* [A Home for Old Actors], 1993) honors the 50-year history of this actors' home, a comfortable setting with a pleasant, intimate atmosphere for retired theatre and cinema actors who recall the glorious successes of their much-loved profession. That so many talented younger women directors choose to focus on the disadvantaged suggests not only an empathic cathexis toward those who suffer most, but the depth of suffering in the inequality of this postcommunist moment in which divisions between wealth and poverty are more pronounced than in decades, casting into even bolder relief the difficult life of Hungarian women as a strategy through which to interrogate a nation's painful transitions.

Filmmakers in Hungary flourished, indeed prospered, under conditions of internal constraint and, for that matter, deprivation; some have since expressed a sense of loss now that the struggle is over. Yet as the incongruities of the postcommunist moment emerge, new national and transnational narratives are required to address them, and women directors, together with their male colleagues, are rising to the occasion, less fettered than their more established counterparts by the hierarchies, rewards, and trade-offs of filmmaking under socialism. The reception of films and videos selected for and screened in national and international festivals, from Budapest to Cannes, from Toronto to New York, leaves little doubt that, despite the very real difficulties faced by cinemas from smaller, former Eastern bloc nations, often disparagingly referred to as "minor cinemas," a dynamic culture of cinema is emerging in the 1990s from which the West has much to learn. Passionate and even vehemently accusatory discussions, symposia, and press conferences have taken place during Budapest Film Week, an annual — and often contentious — retrospective of Hungarian national cinema (feature and documentary) produced during the preceding year: especially since 1989, filmmakers, journalists, critics, and other cultural workers have been debating the future of their visual culture, critiquing their own and their colleagues' practices, urgently seeking advice from visiting foreign participants.

In Budapest, as elsewhere in Eastern Europe, efforts to solicit Western partners are accelerating; at the 24th Film Week nearly a year ago, Zsolt Kezdi-Kovacs, director of Magyar Filmunio, introduced the festival by calling for a new attitude toward Hungarian cinema:

Making films is not an easy business nowadays (When has it been?) The general situation is also rather difficult (When was it easy?) It is a time to appreciate those who have the courage to make films today. Who knows what sort of audience, what sort of world these films are made for? What kind of public will see those films? Who are those people, who still want to look at their own lives, pleasures and pain, instead of a far-away universe tinted in rose and glamour? I think there must be such an audience. We filmmakers are a mirror to the world, and the mirror must be honest and true.[26]

This sense of loss and purposefulness is, to be sure, readable in a number of films produced since the changes. In the first flush of postcommunist openness, pornography of the hard- and soft-core variety was ubiquitous, from calendar pinups hung in shop windows and offices to a brisk trade in X-rated videos. Films produced in 1990, such as Gyorgy Szomjas' *Konnyu Ver (Fast and Loose)* and Peter Vajda's *Itt a Szabadsag (This Is Freedom)* bore unmistakable traces of Western mimesis in a profusion of seductive long-legged blondes hustling hard currency from Western customers, hip youth cavorting in postmodern urban settings, and Russian mafia controlling lucrative prostitution rings — the irresistible "junk food", the glamour (and depression) of the new, so different from the serious earnestness of the ancien régime. But there is something hypocritical, it seems to me, in what may be taken to be a Western censoriousness of the new frivolity, as if Eastern Europeans were somehow meant to enact the role of the West's nobler conscience, while foregoing its material excess. While one might well mourn the loss of the exalted status of cinema in the 1970s and 1980s, and, for that matter, literature, the proliferation of documentaries, videos, and feature films seeking to recover history and national memory was a necessary developmental stage in the process. For under state socialism, visual esthetics were based on the reality of censorship, in which coded narratives inscribed their oppositionality through the use of strikingly creative visual and allegorical language.

Yet despite these discursive inscriptions of regret for a time of paradoxically greater security — a perception of the "good old days" of the enemy that was known — important and vivid films are being produced throughout the region both by established and younger filmmakers, some willing to risk danger and even death to document this momentous era. Under pressure from nationalist and interethnic tensions, a number of filmmakers are confronting the challenges of "wild east" postcommunism by foregrounding formerly taboo subjects, and thereby serving to focus public attention on such repressed, secret, or otherwise uncomfortable topics as the existence of Stalinist labor camps; the persecution of ethnic minorities, Gypsies, and Jews; the persistence of alcohol abuse and suicide; homelessness and the suffering of individuals and families dispersed and dislocated in the wake of war, conflict, political and economic upheaval.

Finally, as the nations of the former Eastern bloc struggle with threatening expressions of national, ethnic, and religious identity, these subjects are emerging in contemporary documentary and feature films, experimental and avant-garde video, and in the critical and theoretical discourse produced by print media devoted to culture and the arts. They speak of a legacy of ideological and internal exile — that is, isolation, alienation, deprivation of means of production and communication, and exclusion from public life; of the disenfranchisement and psychic denigration of Stalinism; of the human trauma that has also given rise to ethical, political, and artistic resistance. But they speak equally persuasively of strong national and historical traditions, of literary and artistic accomplishment, and of a new generation psychologically and intellectually prepared to make the next move. Most importantly, they attest to the centrality of women filmmakers' role as intellectuals, as critics of existing systems, and as savvy entrepreneurs already making movies that give voice to the fears, anxieties, and desires of their compatriots, to the suffering and triumph of national selves as well as of an emergent transnational identity. Meanwhile, their persistence of vision, indeed their unflagging commitment to the need for cinema today, are more than worthy of sustained support, encouragement, and recognition.

NOTES

1. Agnieszka Holland, as quoted in *the San Francisco Chronicle*, 5 July 1991, in the context of the controversy over her 1991 film *Europa, Europa* when the Commission of German Film Functionaries declined to nominate any German film for an Academy Foreign Film Award in October of 1991. Thanks to Susan Linville, Department of English, University of Colorado at Denver, for this information from her unpublished manuscript *"Europa, Europa:* A Test Case for German National Cinema."
2. See, for example, Slavenka Drakulic, *How We Survived Communism and Even Laughed* (London: Vintage, 1993); Nanette Funk and Magda Mueller, *Gender Politics and Post-Communism: Reflections from Eastern Europe and the Former Soviet Union* (New York: Routledge, 1993); and Emily Hicks, *Border Writing: The Multidimensional Text* (Minneapolis: University of Minnesota Press, 1991).
3. It is worth noting that conflict within the audiovisual sphere in fact threatened to stall negotiations on the General Agreement on Tariffs and Trade talks in summer 1993, and did, in fact, result in exculsion of audiovisual products from the agreement.
4. Thanks to Miriam Hansen for sharing with me her manuscript "Early Cinema, Late Cinema: Permutations of the Public Sphere," forthcoming in *Screen* (1993), to which I am indebted for the connection between cinema as public sphere and post-1989 transformations. The erasure of the national becomes a trope of postcolonia, postcommunist discourse in transnational economies, as witnessed by the ubiquity of such relatively new (yet rapidly institutionalized) transnational corporate networks such as CNN.
5. Among the proliferating treatments of this topic see, for instance: Hamid Naficy, "Transnational Film Genre and its Phobic Spaces," mss. shared with me during Naficy's appointment at Rice University's Center for Cultural

Studies (1992); Arjun Appadurai, "Disjuncture and Difference in the Global Cultural Economy," *Public Culture* 2 (Spring 1990): 1–24; Frederic Jameson, *The Geopolitical Aesthetic: Cinema and Space in the World System* (Bloomington: Indiana University Press, 1992); Catherine Portuges, "Border Crossings: Recent Trends in East and Central European Cinema," *Slavic Review* 51, no. 3: 531–35; and John Corner and Sylvia Harvey, eds., *Enterprise and Heritage: Crosscurrents of National Culture* (London: Routledge, 1991), 21–44.

6. *Newsweek*, 9 December 1991, 36.

7. The qualification is intentional, out of respect to my Hungarian filmmaker colleagues whose view, based as it must be on the material realities of the projects in which they are engaged, is considerably more pessimistic than mine.

8. The shift has entailed profound transformations in the structure of media, from a new law under deliberation by the Hungarian Parliament, to the creation of Fuggetlen gondolkozot (Federation of Independent Thinkers), a group of 400 artists, intellectuals, and writers co-founded by writer Miklos Vamos and documentary filmmaker Pal Schiffer (personal conversation with Pal Schiffer, Budapest, 2/15/94). An Independent Producers' Association, including 13 production companies, has been formed to assist film directors from small studios to gain access to opportunities to compete with larger companies. The much-debated "media law" is intended to create closer links between television and cinema.

9. For other useful essays on gender issues in postcommunist Eastern Europe, see Eva Hoffman, *Exit into History: A Journey through the New Eastern Europe* (New York: Viking, 1993); Slavenka Drakulic, *The Balkan Express: Fragments from the Other Side of War* (New York: Harper, 1993); and Helena Goscilo, ed., *Balancing Acts: Contemporary Stories by Russian Women* (Bloomington: Indiana University Press, 1989).

10. Andrzej Wajda, *Double Vision: My Life in Film* (New York: Holt, 1989).

11. In the autumn of 1965, the first Film Week was held in the southern Hungarian city of Pecs, from which it eventually moved to Budapest. In 1986, the Hungarian Feature Film Week became the Hungarian Film Week, including all genres — 35mm feature, documentary, experimental, animation, and avant-garde film and video. The same year, the Hungarian Federation of Film Societies was constituted, providing a consistent venue for younger audiences to screen and debate films throughout the country. Over a 30-year period, about 600 films were made, one-third of all the Hungarian films ever made. (Hungarian Film Union publication, under the auspices of Ministry of Education and Culture and the Hungarian Motion Picture Foundation), Budapest, 1994.

12. Meszaros continues to make new films despite conflicts with the at times capricious decisions of a "curatorium" of filmmakers and producers who now decide the fate of filmmakers' projects in Hungary, and the perilous process of adjustment to a new production system that demands entrepreneurial skills from a generation of directors unaccustomed to privatization.

13. See my article "Lovers and Workers: Screening the Body in Post-Communist Hungarian Cinema," in *Nationalisms and Sexualities*, ed. A. Parker, M. Russo, D. Sommer, and P. Yaeger (New York: Routledge, 1992), 285–95.

14. With regard to the *ressentiment* of one's East-Central European countrymen in the face of celebrity abroad, the Czech writer Ivan Klima states: "Our critics don't like people who are too well known abroad." This interview concerned the lack of interest evinced in Prague toward Klima's latest work, *Waiting for Dark, Waiting for Light*, following the publication of his *Judge on Trial*, the story of a communist judge who compromised his way through life, and the mentality of the apparatchiks who ran the Czech dictatorship (*New York Times*, 22 February 1994, C15). I am reminded as well of the German director Alexander Kluge's famous line: "I love to go to the movies: the only thing that bothers me is the image on the screen."

15. The title refers to Meszaros's own life situation at the time of her divorce from the celebrated director Miklos Jancso, when she became more fully autonomous as a film director. The film's narrative concerns a textile mill weaver's denial of her working-class origins in order to be accepted by her lover, a university student. See Catherine Portuges, *Screen Memories: The Hungarian Cinema of Marta Meszaros* (Bloomington: Indiana University Press, 1993).

16. *Child Murders*, written and directed by Ildiko Szabo, in Hungarian; director of photography: Tamas Sas; edited by Panny Kornis; music by Janos Masik; produced by Istvan Kardos, Pal Erdoss, Gerd Haag, Istvan Darday, and Marton Ledniczky; production companies, Hetfoi Muhely and Studio Alapitvany (78 minutes). When I interviewed in director in Toronto in September 1993, she insisted upon the difficulty of making a film with such "depressing" and controversial material. As an example of the countereffects of postcommunist privatization in visual media, the director herself was responsible for preparing publicity and press documentation for screenings abroad.

17. The dreamlike inscription of history, memory, and experience in Jewish Eastern Europe has in fact become an important part of 1990s Hungarian and, for that matter, East European cinema: some 800,000 Jews survived the war in Eastern Europe, or returned afterwards, not including the millions who lived in Stalin's Soviet Union. Under the communist regimes, the story of the Jews was largely the story of their absence, for Jews had all but vanished from the Soviet screen even before World War II, despite the presence of millions of Jewish citizens. There were few, if any, Jewish characters in films produced after the war by Hungary and Romania, the other two nations with the largest surviving Jewish minorities; in Poland, once home to three million Jews, Jewish characters occasionally played supporting roles in movies of wartime suffering. With Eastern Europe's largest and most assimilated Jewish population, outside of Russia, Hungary produced a few films with discreetly Jewish characters before the mid-1980s; even then, Imre Gyongyossy and Barna Kabay's *The Revolt of Job* (1983), the first Hungarian film to focus on the wartime deportation of the Jews (followed in 1984 by Gyula Gazdag's

312   CATHERINE PORTUGES

Package Tour, 1988), was only shown to foreign critics after the filmmakers themselves arranged a special screening. Most characteristic of the early 1980s was *Daniel Takes a Train*, directed by Pal Sandor who, as a child, had lived through the liquidation of the Budapest ghetto.

18. The national elections in May 1994 put in power, by a significant margin, a Socialist government, composed of several former Communists, to replace the Christian rightist Hungarian Democratic Forum which eventually expelled playwright and Parliament member Istvan Csurka for anti-Semitic public statements.

19. Jeles is perhaps best known for his 1979 feature, *Kis Valentino*, a daring film about juvenile delinquency, and his *Dream Brigade*, a film of the early 1980s about the plight of Hungarian workers, considered sufficiently bold to warrant shelving for a number of years.

20. Fekete served as scriptwriter on a number of films directed by Gyorgy Szomjas, himself a respected and popular filmmaker internationally whose *Roncsfilm* (*Junkfilm*, 1993) earned two prizes at the 1993 Hungarian Film Week.

21. Another first film, *Haknibrigad (Making of the Tournee)* by Erika Ozsda, is based on the staging of a script entitled *The Tour*, written by filmmaker Geza Beremenyi. Ozsda follows the crew as they stage the eight actors in their chosen roles, observing the intimate composition of a theatrical piece, from rehearsals and performance to the downtime between sets, from the relationships among crew members to the minutiae of stagecraft. Actors are interviewed and express themselves with subtlety and honesty, contributing their talents to this experimental documentary financed under the aegis of Fekete Doboz, Hungary's video arts company for young filmmakers.

22. Since the changes, younger directors graduating from the Film Academy have increasingly been unable to complete a first feature before the age of 40.

23. The privatization of production and studio structure, the forging of production links between film and television, the drafting of new media laws and protective legislation for minority human rights, in tandem with the "communications superhighway" of mass-media news management, are rapidly altering the conceptualization and representation of identities and nationalities. These are, it seems to me, among the most pressing of subjects for those engaged in theorizing the new esthetics and visual practices of what was relatively recently known as the "other Europe," as recent international debate on protective legislation for European-language films attests.

24. Personal communication with the director, Budapest, February 10, 1994, following the premiere of her video.

25. Nordin adds: "Theatre is a narcissistic profession. . . . I admire and forgive him for not being a good parent; he gave me the confidence to be a director, perhaps the most important thing for me as a woman in a tough profession in which I might otherwise have been unable to survive. Once you sort out these emotional issues, you can apply what you have learned to professional life. . . . I am grateful to the BBC for training as an assistant director, learned on the

job, the British way. Hungary is, in contrast, very difficult for a woman, and it's every man for himself" (personal communication, Budapest, 2/10/94).

26. It is worth mentioning that Hungary's nominee for the 1994 Academy Awards was film director Robert Koltai's *Sose Halunk Meg (We'll Never Die)*. Koltai both directs and stars in this autobiographical story of Gyuszi bacsi (Uncle Joe), a lovable traveling salesman who frequents the racetrack, charms women of all ages, and manages to survive without worrying too much about money, all the while teaching his naive nephew the ways of the world. A low-budget, lighthearted farce, it has outsold many American productions at the Hungarian box office, making the rounds of festivals and international openings.

Contributors

ELLEN E. BERRY directs the Woman's Studies Program at Bowling Green State University. She is author of *Curved Thought and Textual Wandering: Gertrude Stein's Postmodernism* and coeditor with Anesa Miller-Pogacar *of Re-Entering the Sign: Articulating New Russian Culture* (forthcoming, 1995). She is currently writing a book with Mikhail Epstein on cultural production and difference in a postmodern moment.

MIKHAIL EPSTEIN teaches in the Russian Studies Department at Emory University. He is author of numerous works on contemporary Russian culture, literature, and philosophy, most recently *After the Future* (University of Massachusetts Press, 1994).

MASHA GESSEN, born and reared in Moscow and educated in the United States, is currently a journalist based in Moscow. The author and editor of several books, most recently *Confessions from the End of the World: Short Fiction by Contemporary Russian Women,* she has also published in various Russian- and English-language periodicals, including *Lingua Franca* and *Out/Look.*

HELENA GOSCILO is Chairwoman of the Department of Slavic Languages, Literatures, and Cultures at the University of Pittsburgh. She is the author of several books, including *Balancing Acts, GLASNOST: An Anthology of Literature Under Gorbachev,* and *Skirted Issues: The Discreteness and Indiscretions of Russian Women's Prose,* as well as the editor of a collection of essays devoted to contemporary Russian women's culture, *Fruits of Her Plume.*

315

EWA HAUSER, an associate of the Susan B. Anthony Center for Women's Studies, teaches the anthropology of Eastern Europe at the University of Rochester.

BETH HOLMGREN is Associate Professor of Slavic Languages and Literature at University of North Carolina, Chapel Hill. With Helena Goscilo, she is currently completing an anthology on women in Russian culture forthcoming from Indiana University Press.

KEVIN MOSS is Assistant Professor of Russian Studies at Middlebury College. He has written on Ol'ga Freidenberg, Mikhail Bulgakov, Aesopian language, and film. His current research interests include Evgenii Kharitonov's prose and the short fiction of East European gay writers.

HARRIET MURAV is Associate Professor in the Department of German and Russian at the University of California, Davis, and author of *Holy Foolishness: Dostoevsky's Novels and the Poetics of Cultura Critique.* Her current research includes a study of the interaction between law and literature in Russian culture.

VIDA PENEZIC, who is originally from Belgrade, Yugoslavia, is Assistant Professor in the Department of Popular Culture at Bowling Green State University. Her research interests include global and transcultural flows in popular culture and media; transcultural contacts of women; and the intersection of culture and mind.

TERESA POLOWY teaches Russian literature and language in the Department of Russian and Slavic Languages at the University of Arizona. She is currently working on a book-length study entitled *Alcoholism in Russia: Writing and Gender from the Sixties to the Present.*

CATHERINE PORTUGES is Professor of Comparative Literature and Director of the Film Studies Program at the University of Massachusetts, Amherst. She is the author of *Screen Memories: The Hungarian Cinema of Marta Meszaros.*

KAREN REMMLER, Assistant Professor of German, teaches in the German Department and Women's Studies Program at Mount Holyoke

College. She is coeditor with Sander Gilman of a forthcoming anthology on the reemergence of Jewish culture in unified Germany and is finishing a book on the structure of remembrance in the work of Ingeborg Bachmann.

KATRIN SIEG is a Lecturer in the Literature Department at the University of California, San Diego. She is the author of *Exiles, Eccentrics, Activists: Women in Contemporary German Theatre* (1994), as well as articles in the areas of German theatre, women's performance practices, and feminist criticism.

Guidelines for Prospective Contributors

Genders welcomes essays on art, literature, media, photography, film, and social theory. We are especially interested in essays that address theoretical issues relating sexuality and gender to social, political, racial, economic, or stylistic concerns.

All essays that are considered for publication are sent to board members for review. Your name is not included on the manuscript in this process. A decision on the essay is usually reached in about four months. Essays are grouped for publication only after the manuscript has been accepted.

We require that we have first right to any manuscript that we consider and that we have first publication of any manuscript that we accept. We will not consider any manuscript that is already under consideration with another publication or that has already been published.

The recommended length for essays is twenty-five pages of double-spaced text. Essays must be printed in letter-quality type. Quotations in languages other than English must be accompanied by translations. Photocopies of illustrations are sufficient for initial review, but authors should be prepared to supply originals upon request.

Place the title of the essay and your name, address, and telephone number on a separate sheet at the front of the essay. You are welcome to include relevant information about yourself or the essay in a letter to the editor, but please be advised that institutional affiliation does not affect editorial policy. Since the majority of the manuscripts that we receive are photocopies, we do not routinely return submissions. However, if you would like your copy returned, please enclose a self-addressed, stamped envelope.

To submit an essay for consideration, send *three* legible copies to:

319

Thomas Foster
Genders
Department of English
Ballantine Hall 442
Indiana University
Bloomington, IN 46405